Praise for *The Successful Business Plan: Secrets & Strategies*

"User-friendly and exhaustive...highly recommended. Abrams' book works because she tirelessly researched the subject. Most how-to books on entrepreneurship aren't worth a dime; among the thousands of small business titles, Abrams' [is an] exception."

— *Forbes Magazine*

"There are plenty of decent business-plan guides out there, but Abrams' was a cut above the others I saw. *The Successful Business Plan* won points with me because it was thorough and well organized, with handy worksheets and good quotes. Also, Abrams does a better job than most at explaining the business plan as a planning tool rather than a formulaic exercise. Well done."

— *Inc. Magazine*

"Abrams' book offers a complete approach to creating your plan. Surrounding her explanatory material with commentary from top CEOs, venture capitalists, and business owners, Abrams helps you see your idea through the eyes of potential investors. Her book and your idea deserve each other."

— *Home Office Computing Magazine*

"This book stands head and shoulders above all other business plan books, and is the perfect choice for the beginner and the experienced business professional. Rhonda Abrams turns writing a professional, effective business plan into a journey of discovery about your business."

— *BizCountry*

"If you'd like something that goes beyond the mere construction of your plan and is more fun to use, try *The Successful Business Plan: Secrets and Strategies*, by Rhonda Abrams...this book can take the pain out of the process."

— "Small Business School," PBS television show

"I would not use any other book for my course on Business Development. *The Successful Business Plan* is the best I've ever seen, read, or used in a classroom environment."

— Prof. David Gotaskie,
Community College of Allegheny County, Pittsburgh, PA

"It is my number one recommendation to SBDC clients looking for resources on the subject. I have always liked the layout, order of presentation, sidebar notes and real-world perspective on the planning process, components of the plan, etc."

— David Gay,
Small Business Development Center, College of DuPage

"In my opinion, your book is the definitive guide for successful business plans. I particularly appreciate and recommend the use of the Flow-Through Financial worksheets. Each is a great device to illustrate the connection between the qualitative and quantitative elements of a plan."

— Gene Elliott,
Business Consultant, New Mexico

"I've been using and promoting *The Successful Business Plan* since 1993, and it's great! I've taught business plan writing in several local SBDCs, as well as nationally, through the Neighborhood Reinvestment Training Institute (D.C.). My course is designed and delivered around your book."

— Ransom S. Stafford,
Business Consultant, Twin Cities, MN

"In December 1991, I came upon the book, *The Successful Business Plan: Secrets & Strategies.* It is the closest to what I know works in the real world, at least in high-tech industries."

— Barb Tomlin,
e-Business Strategy Consultant and President/CEO,
Westward Connections, Inc.

"One of the best books on business planning. The overall quality of this book is excellent, but three things make it stand out: First, it contains worksheets that walk you through the information gathering process. Fill them out, and even the financials—always the hardest part of a plan—will fall right into place. Second, it has a sample plan that reads like a real business plan, written by a real person for a real business. You can use much of the wording in your own plan. Third, it has tips from successful managers, leaders, and business owners, large and small. I was especially fascinated reading the tips from ex-49'er head coach Bill Walsh. You can't go wrong following his advice on planning and organizing!"

— Economic Chamber of Macedonia

"This is an excellent book and highly recommended. Includes easy worksheets for budgeting and forecasting, tips on finding money from bankers and investors and secrets from business owners and CEOs of major companies."

— Bizbound.com

"Thanks to Abrams, I discovered highly lucrative, related fields to the business I was originally intending to start. By adding some simple enhancements to my original vision, I will probably double my income. Had I not done the research this book recommends, I never would have known. The best 'proof of the pudding' was when I took a draft of my business plan into a meeting with an accountant. She was highly impressed, and instantly grasped the basics about my business based on this tight, well-focused, statistically sound presentation."

— Reader from Alexandria, VA on Amazon.com

"I chose *The Successful Business Plan* because of its ease of use, its clarity and its good examples. I have used the book for a number of years now…"

— Jean Morris, The Culinary Institute of America

"It has a clearly defined, comprehensive approach."

— Zane Swanson, Emporia State University, KS

"It combines, in a very clear way, both aspects of business planning and effective writing of business plans. The book is very well written. The forms are very useful."

— Eyal Yaniv, Bar Ilan University, Israel

"Your book has been both an inspirational read as well as a comprehensive guide for starting my business. Being relatively inexperienced with entrepreneurship, your book has not only given me the ability to create a solid roadmap for planning, but has also provided an encouraging and easy way to cope with the enormous amount of information and organization needed. I particularly enjoy the various quotes from business professionals who have had experience in business planning. They give precious insight and different viewpoints that I would not have seen. Thank you for writing this book!"

— Simon Lee, entrepreneur

Other Recognition for *The Successful Business Plan*

- Ranked one of the Two Best Books for small business by *Forbes*.
- Ranked one of the Six Best Books for start-ups by *Inc.*
- Ranked on of the 20 Essential Books for Entrepreneurs by *Home Office Computing*
- Main Selection, BusinessWeek Book Club
- Main Selection, Executive Book Club
- Used in colleges, universities, and business schools nationwide, including Stanford Business School, Haas School of Business, UC Berkeley; Northwestern University; California Polytechnic; Temple University; Texas A & M; University of Massachusetts, Amherst; Southern Oregon University; Arizona State; University of Washington; and dozens of others.

To my clients, who have shared with me their enthusiasm for the entrepreneurial spirit and have shown me that business can be a career for people of integrity, intelligence, and honor; and to the memory of my parents, who would have been proud.

The
Successful
Business
Plan SECRETS & STRATEGIES

Rhonda Abrams

foreword by legendary venture capitalist Eugene Kleiner

Fourth Edition

the**Planning**shop
Palo Alto, California

The Successful Business Plan: Secrets and Strategies™
© 1991, 1993, 2000, 2003 by Rhonda Abrams

Published by The Planning Shop™
Earlier editions published by Running 'R' Media and The Oasis Press/PSI Research

Services for our readers:

Colleges, business schools, corporate purchasing:

The Planning Shop™ offers special discounts and supplemental materials for universities, business schools, and corporate training. Contact: bizplan@planningshop.com or call 650-289-9120.

Free Business Tips and Information:

To be added to our mailing list for updates & special offers on future editions and to receive Rhonda's free newsletter and business tips, register as one of "Rhonda's Regulars" at www.RhondaOnline.com or write us.

Contact us:

Email: bizplan@PlanningShop.com
Write: The Planning Shop™
555 Bryant Street, #180
Palo Alto, CA 94301
Phone: 650-289-9120
Fax: 650-289-9125

The Planning Shop™ is a division of Rhonda, Inc., a California corporation.
Visit us at www.PlanningShop.com.

First Edition Editors: Virginia Grosso and Matthew Abergel
Third Edition Editor: Erin Wait

Fourth Edition:
Copy Editor: Deborah Kaye
Cover Designer: Arthur Wait

ISBN: 0-9669635-6-3

Printed in Canada

10 9 8 7 6 5 4

About Rhonda Abrams

Rhonda Abrams writes the nation's most widely-read small business column, distributed by Gannett News Service to over 100 newspapers throughout the country. In her column, Rhonda focuses on the concerns and challenges of entrepreneurs, offering common-sense advice based on solid business experience and real-life examples. Rhonda also writes a regular column for *The Costco Connection.*

Rhonda is the author of *The Successful Business Organizer* — a "take-with-you-everywhere" checklist and organizer for those in the process of setting up their new business. She is also the author of *Wear Clean Underwear: Business Wisdom from Mom,* which was a selection of The Book-of-the-Month Club.

Rhonda not only writes about business — she lives it! As the founder of three successful companies, Rhonda's experience gives her an extraordinary depth of experience and a real-life understanding of the challenges facing entrepreneurs. In 1986, Rhonda founded a management consulting practice working with clients ranging from one-person start-ups to Fortune 500 companies. In 1995, she was an internet pioneer, founding a web-content company for small business, which she later sold. And in 1999, Rhonda started a publishing company — now called The Planning Shop — focusing exclusively on topics of business planning, entrepreneurship, and new business development.

A popular public speaker and lecturer, Rhonda is regularly invited to address leading industry and trade associations, business schools, and corporate conventions and events. She conducts training workshops on business planning as well as delivering keynote speeches. She was educated at Harvard University and UCLA, where she was named Outstanding Senior. Rhonda lives in Palo Alto, California.

Rhonda's website is www.RhondaOnline.com and the company's website is www.PlanningShop.com.

About the Contributors

Eugene Kleiner

Founding Partner, Kleiner Perkins Caufield & Byers

Eugene Kleiner is a legend — in venture capital and in Silicon Valley. Mr. Kleiner was one of the country's first venture capitalists: in 1972, he founded what would become the nation's premiere venture capital firm, Kleiner Perkins Caufield & Byers. KPCB has funded some of the world's most innovative companies, including Compaq Computer, Genentech, Sun Microsystems, AOL, and Amazon. Mr. Kleiner is one of the so-called "Traitorous Eight" — the eight founding members of Fairchild Semiconductor — who are considered to be the "fathers" of Silicon Valley. Mr. Kleiner was an early investor in companies such as Intel, Tandem Computer, and Genentech. Mr. Kleiner is a trustee of the Polytechnic University of New York.

Andrew Anker

Partner, August Capital

As a Partner at August Capital — one of the nation's most respected venture capital firms — Andrew Anker focuses on investing in new media, e-commerce and other Internet-related companies. A veteran of two start-ups, Mr. Anker was the co-founder and Chief Executive Officer of Wired Digital, Inc., a pioneering Internet news and media organization which launched the first advertising supported web site (www.hotwired.com) in

October 1994. Mr. Anker led Wired Digital from its founding through 1998 and built it into one of the 20 largest networks of web sites. Prior to that, Mr. Anker was a Principal with the investment banking firm, Sterling Payot Company.

Michael Damer

Former Spokesperson, Community Affairs
New United Motor Manufacturing, Incorporated

New United Motor Manufacturing, Incorporated (NUMMI) is a joint venture between Toyota Motor Corporation and General Motors, designed to bring the benefits of the extremely efficient and cost-effective Toyota production system to the production of cars in the United States. Although located in Fremont, California, NUMMI's manufacturing plant is run entirely according to Japanese manufacturing principals and with Japanese management techniques. NUMMI began producing automobiles in 1984, and manufactures both Chevrolet and Toyota cars and light trucks. Mr. Damer served in NUMMI's Community Affairs Department.

Nancy Glaser

Management Consultant, The Glaser Group

Nancy Glaser is founder and President of The Glaser Group, a consulting firm specializing in early-stage business strategies and turn-arounds for troubled companies. Her focus is in specialty retailing, consumer-based, and service businesses. Previously, Ms. Glaser was a Partner at the venture capital firm, U.S. Venture Partners. Some of the companies she invested in and help direct include Gymboree, Fresh Choice and PetsMart. Prior in her career, Ms. Glaser helped take The Gap from a 35-store chain to 350 stores in less than five years, and served with Macy's and Lord & Taylor. Ms. Glaser was active in international venture capital, both in Poland and as a founder of the Apparel Innovation Center in St. Petersburg, Russia.

Mark Gorenberg

Partner, Hummer Winblad Venture Partners

Mark Gorenberg had the rare distinction of being a judge in three of the country's leading university business plan competitions: at the Massachusetts Institute of Technology (MIT), Stanford University, and the Haas School of Business at the University of California, Berkeley. As a Partner at Hummer Winblad Venture Partners, one of the best-known venture capital firms in the country, Mr. Gorenberg invests in cutting-edge technology companies and serves on the boards of both startup and public companies. Mr. Gorenberg has over 20 years experience in software development, including serving as a Senior Manager at Sun Microsystems, and over a decade experience as a venture capitalist. He is also a member of the Corporation Development Committee of the Massachusetts Institute of Technology.

Charles Huggins

President, See's Candies

Founded in 1921, See's Candies is one of the nation's oldest and best known makers of fine candies. Charles Huggins has been with See's for more than forty years and has served as President since 1972, overseeing much of the company's expansion. He has guided the company through its development from a regional confectionery into a multi-national model of manufacturing and retail operations. While limited in its geographic distribution, See's has earned a worldwide reputation as producing some of the finest and most desired chocolates anywhere.

George B. James

Former Senior Vice President and Chief Financial Officer
Levi Strauss & Company

As Chief Financial Officer, George James was responsible for all planning, risk management, accounting, tax and treasury affairs for this renowned manufacturer of jeans and sportswear. Levi Strauss & Company is the world's largest apparel company. Mr. James previously served as Executive Vice President and Group President of Crown Zellerbach Corporation, a leading paper, container, and distribution company and as a Vice President at Pepsico, Inc.

Martha Johnson

Restaurateur

In 1977, after a decade as a successful management consultant, Martha Johnson changed careers and followed her love of cooking into the food business. After writing a thorough business plan, she and partner Susan Snider opened their first restaurant with an investment of $10,000. Six years later, she sold the restaurant for $175,000. In 1985, the two partners opened a European coffee bar/café in San Francisco, California and later launched a restaurant serving regional American cuisine. Ms. Johnson's restaurants received substantial critical acclaim and have been featured in national publications such as *Food and Wine*.

William Leban, Ph.D.

Director of Business and Management Programs, DeVry University

In his role as Director of Business and Management Programs, William Leban oversees the bachelors programs in business and masters programs in management at Devry University. The University delivers its programs at campuses, centers and online to meet the needs of a diverse and geographically dispersed student population. Dr. Leban received his Ph.D. from Benedictine University in Organization Development. He is a registered professional engineer and a certified project management professional.

Larry Leigon

Founder, Ariel Vineyards

Ariel Vineyards was founded in 1985 to produce and market premium de-alcoholized wines. In its first four years of operation, Ariel grew to be larger than 95% of all the wineries in the United States. Larry Leigon was one of the four founding principals of Ariel and served as its first President, with primary responsibility for all marketing and distribution strategies – a unique challenge since Ariel was creating a new product category. Mr. Leigon was also a founding member of The Wine Trust, a wine marketing and sales company. Previously, he was Vice President of Clos du Bois Vineyards.

Robert M. Mahoney

Former Executive Director of Corporate Banking, Bank of Boston

In this leadership position, Robert Mahoney was responsible for commercial lending services throughout the New England states for the Bank of Boston, a bank that earned the reputation as one of the nation's most receptive of entrepreneurial companies. During his two decades with the bank, Mr. Mahoney served as President of Massachusetts Banking and Vice President for corporate banking in the United Kingdom.

Deborah Mullis

Owner, D.A.M.E.'S Foods

For twelve years, Deborah Mullis helped shape and launch products for some of the world's largest companies as Vice President/Associate Creative Director at Lintas, an advertising agency. Her love of food and her understanding of marketing led her to create her own line of food products, D.A.M.E.'S Foods. After successfully launching D.A.M.E.'S Nutsy Noodle Sauce and Nutsy Noodles in San Francisco, Ms. Mullis returned to her home state of Florida.

F. Gibson "Gib" Myers, Jr.

Venture Capitalist, The Mayfield Fund

Gib Myers is well known as a General Partner (Emeritus) of the prestigious Mayfield Fund, a venture capital firm with over $1.5 billion of capital under management. Mr. Myers joined Mayfield in 1970 and has participated in virtually all of the firm's portfolio company investments, including 3Com Corporation. He has nurtured companies in diverse areas of technology through every phase of growth, from start-up to maturity. In 1997 Mr. Myers and Mayfield Fund created the Entrepreneurs' Foundation, dedicated to bringing the entrepreneurial spirit and commitment to societal and community activities. The Entrepreneurs' Foundation is a nonprofit organization that assists entrepreneurs and young companies in developing a community involvement plan and in participating in unique philanthropic giving programs.

Andre S. Tatibouet

President, Aston Hotels and Resorts

At the age of 19, Andre S. Tatibouet developed his first hotel and has been a force in the hospitality industry ever since. Aston is the largest condominium resort and hotel operator in Hawaii and one of the largest in the nation. The rapidly growing chain also includes properties in California and Mexico. Mr. Tatibouet was named one of the top five entrepreneurs in the hotel industry and is active in numerous philanthropic and civic organizations.

Bill Walsh

Former Coach and President, San Francisco 49ers

When Bill Walsh was hired as head coach of the San Francisco 49ers football franchise in 1979, the team was hardly taken seriously. But within three years, under his innovative management, the 49ers had won a Super Bowl. He went on to win two additional world championships and was named "Coach of the Eighties." His management style was marked by intelligent, strategic planning of every detail and contingency. Formerly a commentator on NBC Television, he is a frequent speaker to business audiences.

Ann Winblad

Partner, Hummer Winblad Venture Partners

In high technology circles, Ann Winblad is a well-known software entrepreneur and venture capitalist. In 1976, she co-founded Open Systems with a $500 investment and sold the company in 1983 for $15.1 million. Prior to starting her venture capital firm with partner John Hummer, she served as a consultant to clients such as IBM, Microsoft, Apple, Price Waterhouse, and numerous start-up companies. Hummer Winblad has invested in companies such as Central Point Software, Powersoft, and Liquid Audio.

Acknowledgements

I would like to thank the many people who offered assistance and support during the course of the original preparation of this book, and also to thank those who have been instrumental in helping to create this new edition. In particular, I wish to acknowledge the help of these individuals:

Matthew Abergel, my editor and dear friend, who relentlessly pursued every "to be" verb; who greatly enhanced the quality of this book; and who understands the tyranny of working with words and provided many amusing diversions from them;

Eugene Kleiner, for his years of friendship and for serving as my personal business tutor; who first showed me what a good business plan should look like, and who continually shares with me his unequalled insight into the entrepreneurial process;

The expert "tipsters" who generously shared their expertise with me. They were, without exception, gracious, forthcoming, and insightful;

Andrew Anker and Mark Gorenberg, who served on the Advisory Board of my previous business, and who provide me not only with excellent counsel but enduring friendship;

Erin Wait, editor of the third edition, who oversaw every step of the production and who is a constant example of professionalism, thoroughness, and great ideas;

Deborah Kaye, my assistant, who keeps everything together and makes everything possible;

Arthur Wait, who managed to produce outstanding graphic design (including book covers and CD-ROMs) on short notice and under great pressure;

Charles Orr, for allowing me to adapt the basics of his company, Productivity Point International, into the fictional company ComputerEase and Pamela Richards, owner of Computer Ease of San Rafael, California, for allowing me to borrow the name for the fictional company featured in this book;

Jennifer Arthur, Scott Belser, Marilyn Burns, Kate Ecker, Edgar Holton, Edward Pollock, Andy Schneit, and Lori Silver, for their professional advice on the specifics of accounting, marketing, financing, and law; and for their friendship;

Jay Leshner for helping create the fictional town of Vespucci, Indiana;

Rhoda Goldman and Raquel Newman for arranging introductions to two of my contributors (tipsters);

Authors Donna Levin Bernick and David Chanoff for their advice about writing and publishing, and Elaine Petrocelli, owner of Book Passage in Corte Madera, California, for her insight into the book industry;

Mark, Randy, Charlie, Karen Cross, and the staff and sales representatives at Publisher's Group West for their support and commitment to this book;

Cathy Dobbs Goldstein, my attorney and dear friend, who not only provided wise counsel and served as a continuing source of information but understood when I had to cancel plans to stay at the computer;

My sisters and brothers: Janice, Arnie, Mary, Karen, and Scott, for their support, encouragement, and indulgence over the years;

And finally, thanks to my dog Teddy, who not only introduced me to my first business plan client on a walk in Golden Gate Park years ago, but who every day while I was writing energetically and persistently reminded me to go outside and take a break.

Table of Contents

Section III   Putting the Plan to Work

Section IV   Special Considerations

Section V   Reference

Sample Plan

Worksheets, Examples, and Charts in this Book

Worksheets, Examples, and Charts in this Book (continued)

Foreword

By Eugene Kleiner
Founding Partner, Kleiner, Perkins, Caufield & Byers

In today's environment, a business plan is an entrepreneur's most crucial business document. No company can expect to articulate its goals or to secure financing without a well-conceived and well-presented business plan. Without a convincing business plan, no one will seriously consider your business idea.

This wasn't always the case. The first business plan I ever wrote as an entrepreneur was not a business plan at all; it was just a letter. Eight of us from Shockley Laboratories for various reasons wanted to start a semiconductor company on our own, and we needed the money to make it possible. We drafted a letter, perhaps four or five pages long, describing what we proposed to do and sent that letter along with our resumes to an investment banker.

Fortunately for us, that letter found its way to the desk of a young business school graduate named Arthur Rock who felt that we might have promise. As a result, we were able to get our funding, and Fairchild Semiconductor was born. From Fairchild, the eight of us branched out and went on to form or fund such companies as Intel, Tandem Computer, and many other leading Silicon Valley firms.

Today, our letter might never be completely read. Investors now are far more structured and expect a far higher level of expertise and preparation from the entrepreneurs they choose to fund. When examining a proposal, they want to see much more than just a good idea and a bright young man or woman; they want to see a business plan showing that the concept has been rigorously assessed and that the entrepreneur has carefully thought through the issues for steps necessary to take the idea and fashion it into a successful company.

At Kleiner, Perkins, Caufield, & Byers, the venture capital firm I co-founded in 1972, we had a diligent system of evaluating business plans. A plan had to stand up to the most exacting scrutiny and toughest standards. Most plans, of course, never made it past the initial screening phases. Only the most interesting and well-conceived plans warranted the allocation of resources necessary for a more thorough examination. From that group, we narrowed our selection down even further, spending a great deal of time investigating each plan's merits. Finally, before deciding to invest in a company, part of the staff would serve as "devil's advocate," suggesting all the pitfalls. Only the plans that made it through that process were considered for final funding.

In this book, Rhonda Abrams has given you the tools you need to create a successful business plan. Working with Rhonda over the years, I've developed a strong appreciation and respect for her grasp of the business planning process. We have had many sessions evaluating what it takes to make a successful company, and I've seen her take what I've shared with her about long-term and strategic planning and expand upon that knowledge, bringing to bear her own experience with clients and her intelligent, practical approach to the entrepreneurial process.

Foreword to the Fourth Edition

"This is a great time to start a business."

In 2000, those words began the foreword to the Third Edition of *The Successful Business Plan: Secrets & Strategies.* The economy was booming; the Internet had spawned thousands of new enterprises; money for new ventures was flowing freely. Companies could get funded with the flimsiest of business plans.

A lot has changed since then. Customers are more cautious about expenditures. Investors are more realistic about their investments, giving far greater scrutiny to new ventures. The demands on entrepreneurs are higher, and the questions posed to them are tougher. Now, more than ever, you have to have a strong, compelling business plan.

But that should not deter you. Because it is STILL a great time to start or grow a business. And this book will help you create your business plan — a successful business plan.

Opportunities for enterprising entrepreneurs abound. Indeed, many of the best-known companies today were founded during times of economic uncertainty. The reason? Changing economic conditions create openings for new companies in old markets: established   companies weaken or fail, and customers search for new, more cost-effective ways to fulfill their needs.

xxvi *The Successful Business Plan: Secrets and Strategies*

Moreover, new technologies have opened up many new possibilities and reduced costs in old industries. The Internet continues to make it easier to do business across the world — or across town.

Since professional investors receive thousands of business plans a year, one of the goals of this book is to make certain your business plan gets read, and read favorably. That's the reason it is called The Successful Business Plan. The word successful, in one sense, is meant to describe the plan. I want to help your plan be a success in terms of doing what you need a plan to do – typically, raise money. But I have another objective: to help you build, grow, and expand a healthy company. This book is not just about developing a successful plan; it's designed to help you create a successful business.

New in the Fourth Edition

Since *The Successful Business Plan: Secrets & Strategies* was first published in 1991, it's become the nation's best-selling, most-acclaimed business plan guide, used by corporations, business schools, start-ups. Hundreds of thousands of people have used this book to write their business plans and grow their businesses.

One of the reasons for this book's success is that we continue to enhance and update it, adding and revising content and advice to enable you to effectively respond to ever-changing business and economic realities.

This newest edition – the Fourth Edition – of *The Successful Business Plan: Secrets & Strategies* has been thoroughly updated, responding to changes in the economy, technology, business practices, and financing. Some of the new features include:

- **Expanded and updated information and resources:** Since the last edition of this book, there has been a vast improvement in the quality and quantity of information available when doing business and market research. We've added resources that help you take advantage of the numerous resources on the Internet — with particular focus on those providing free or low-cost information. You'll be able to more quickly find the information you need.

- **Expanded and updated information for running an Internet-based businesses:** Reflecting the new realities of doing business on the Internet, the chapter on eBusiness has been updated and revamped to help you develop a business that can more successfully compete on the Internet today.

- **New chapter on business strategies for weak or strong economic conditions:** Economic conditions have changed dramatically since the last edition, so we have added a new chapter providing insight on how to consider economic conditions as part of your business planning process. Since conditions in your particular industry or geographic area may differ from national economic trends, we've included information for both strong or weak economic conditions.

And, in response to a flood of requests from our readers over the years, we are particularly excited about the newest addition to *The Successful Business Plan:*

- **Excel Templates:** We've created optional Excel templates that coordinate with many of the most important financial worksheets and spreadsheets in this book, enabling you to build your plan digitally, making revisions and changes easy. These templates are designed to work with this book and reflect the forms enclosed. You'll find the templates available to download for a modest fee from our new website, The Planning Shop, www.planningshop.com.

Finally, if you notice the new imprint on this book — The Planning Shop — you'll see that we've changed the name of our company to better reflect our focus. As the publisher of the leading business plan book in the U.S., we have decided to intensify our activities and expand our products that assist entrepreneurs in successfully developing their business plans. We here at The Planning Shop will continually be developing new books and other tools to help you achieve business success. So keep our website address handy, www.planningshop.com, as you start and grow your business.

I know that few things are as exciting as starting and running a company. It's challenging, rewarding, and occasionally frightening. We're here to help you successfully reach your goals and make your business a reality.

Rhonda Abrams
Palo Alto, California

How to Use this Book

The Successful Business Plan: Secrets & Strategies serves as an interactive tool for the action-oriented, busy entrepreneur. It helps you develop a comprehensive, effective business plan in a thoughtful, yet time-efficient manner.

As you work through this guide, you will find a number of features to make your business planning process easier, faster, and more complete. By the time you have finished this book you should have a compelling business plan.

Tips from Experts

Throughout this book you'll find tips from successful entrepreneurs, venture capitalists, and other business leaders. In these quotes, the experts share their secrets and strategies about business plans, and what makes a business work, that they have garnered through their real-life experiences. You will find their words a source of guidance, advice, and inspiration. (For more complete profiles of these experts, see "About the Contributors.")

How this Guide is Organized

This book is divided in four main sections to lead you step-by-step through the process of developing, preparing, and presenting your business plan.

Starting the Process

Section I, "Starting the Process," shows how to organize your planning activities, clarify your business concept, and gather the data you need. It helps you understand what makes a business successful so that you can keep those factors in mind while developing or expanding your business.

Business Plan Components

Section II, "Business Plan Components," clarifies the standard sections comprising a business plan and provides you with detailed information on each. You do not need to work through this section in any particular order; however, you will most likely find it helpful to identify your Target Market (Chapter 7) and Competition (Chapter 8) and Strategic Position (Chapter 9) before describing your Marketing Strategy (Chapter 10).

Putting the Plan to Work

Section III, "Putting the Plan to Work," gives you insight into the practical details that will make your plan more compelling to future readers, particularly funding sources. The chapter "Looking for Money" outlines the different kinds and sources of financing for your business and helps you organize and conduct your search for financing. If you are looking for money for your business, you will find this section particularly beneficial.

Special Considerations

Section IV, "Special Considerations" includes chapters affecting the business planning process in certain circumstances. The chapter "Using Your Plan for Classes & Competitions" helps you organize a group business planning process and gives insights into how competition judges and business school professors view business plans. The chapter "Considerations for Internet, e-Businesses" guides you through the unique business concerns of an online business. Other chapters in this section provide advice for existing and large corporations and give specialized information for retail, manufacturing, and service businesses.

Reference Information

Additional information is provided near the end of the book to help you find the resources you need, answer questions you may still have, and direct you to other sources of guidance during your business planning process. You will also find a glossary of commonly used business terms.

Worksheets and Forms

Four kinds of worksheets and forms, described below, are used throughout this guide.

General Worksheets

Use these worksheets to do your internal planning and gather and coordinate the information you will use to complete your plan. The information on these worksheets will not necessarily be included in the plan itself.

Plan Preparation Forms

These forms help you outline the information you will include in your completed business plan document. To complete these forms, synthesize the information you have recorded on the general worksheets. If you already know the basics of your business and need an extremely quick planning guide, go straight to the Plan Preparation Forms in each chapter.

Flow-Through Financials

Recognizable by the dollar-sign logo in the top right-hand corner, the Flow-Through Financials are a quick,

$ ➤ $$ ➤ $$$

efficient way to organize your financial and budgetary information. Once you complete these worksheets, you will have the basis of almost all the formal financial reports to be submitted with your plan. A directory explaining how to use the data from each Flow-Through Financial form is found in Chapter 16.

Standard Financial Forms

This book contains all the standard financial forms to be submitted along with your plan. These include Income Statements, Balance Sheets, and Cash-Flow Projections.

Electronic Financial Worksheets

An Excel-based Financial Worksheets package is available for purchase as a supplement to this book. The worksheets are identical to the financial worksheets found in the book and embrace the Flow-Through Financials methodology used here. In addition, the electronic worksheets perform all calculations for you, generate charts, and allow you to "tweak" your numbers to obtain the most accurate financial picture. Once you are satisfied with your numbers, you can print out all the financial forms necessary to include with your business plan. To purchase the Electronic Worksheets, visit www.planningshop.com.

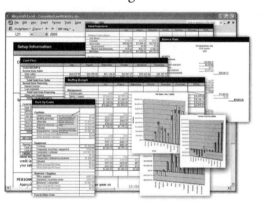

Sample Plan

At the conclusion of each chapter of Section II is an example of how the information conveyed in that chapter would translate into an actual completed plan. The Sample Plan (based on a fictional company) illustrates how you can incorporate the information provided in the text into your own plan, and helps you understand the concepts discussed. Space limitations require the Sample Plan to be in an abbreviated form; your own plan may be longer.

Introduction

If you don't know where you are going
how will you know when you are lost?

Why Are You Developing a Business Plan?

Quite possibly, you are developing a business plan because someone else wants you to do so. Perhaps the bank is requiring a business plan before granting you a loan. Or an investor or venture capitalist needs one to decide whether to finance your business. Maybe your attorney or accountant said you must have one, or your company president requires a strategic plan for your new division.

Reasons enough. But entrepreneurs are self-motivated people, used to setting their own goals and determining their own tasks. They undertake endeavors not merely to please others, but because they understand the importance of an activity in reaching their overall objectives.

Creating a business plan only as a response to an external request makes the process seem like a burden instead of an opportunity.

What a Business Plan – and this Book – Can Do for You

As you start developing your business plan, keep in mind that the greatest beneficiary of this project is not your banker, investor, or accountant — it's you. A complete, thoughtful business plan is perhaps the best tool you can have to help you reach your own long-term goals.

Whether your business is large or small, a startup or long established, developing a business plan enables you to:

"With the first edition of your plan, you shouldn't even think about getting money. Use the planning process to decide if the business is really as good as you think it is. Ask yourself if you really want to spend five years of your life doing this. Remember, that's about 10% of your active working life, so seriously examine whether the enterprise could really be worthwhile to you."

Eugene Kleiner
Venture Capitalist

> "The intensity in football incorporates, in one season, what a corporation must have over five years or so. You deal with people under stress; performance is measured by the bottom line; success is what the group accomplishes. To succeed, you must set goals, define roles, recognize excellence, acknowledge failure, recover from disappointment, and stay abreast of the competition. You must always be evolving systematically, improving the mechanisms for developing progress, and bring along younger players."
>
> **Bill Walsh**
> **Former Coach and**
> **President, S.F. 49ers**

- Make the crucial business decisions that focus your activities and maximize your resources.
- Understand the financial aspects of your business, including cash flow and break-even requirements.
- Gather crucial industry and marketing information.
- Anticipate and avoid obstacles your business is likely to encounter.
- Set specific goals and measurements to assess progress over time.
- Expand in new and increasingly profitable directions.
- Be more persuasive to funding sources.

Remember that when you start or expand a business, more than your money and time are at stake; you risk your dreams as well. A good business plan helps you realize your dreams.

Insiders' Secrets

Wouldn't it be nice to have an opportunity to learn directly from those who deal with business plans professionally? Bankers, chief executive officers, and venture capitalists all review business plans frequently and know what goes into a strong and compelling plan.

To enable you to gain the benefit of these experts' knowledge, some of the most successful and well-respected business leaders were interviewed for this book. Their views on every aspect of business plans were sought, and they shared their insider views and advice.

They were asked for their secrets — how to create a business plan that stands out from the pack; and for their strategies — how to develop a business that is successful and profitable over time. You can now put these secrets and strategies to work for yourself.

What They'll Tell You

This book addresses your real-life concerns; it is far more than just a textbook description of what a business plan should be. You will learn from a venture capitalist whose firm funded companies such as Ross Stores and Avia Shoes what must go into a retail operation to make it a likely candidate for venture capital. The president of See's Candies tells how his company manages to keep costs down and quality up through constant inventory control.

Champion manager Bill Walsh shares his advice on how to deal with competition. And owners of smaller businesses let you know the steps they took to get their companies started. This is practical information that will make a difference in the quality of your business plan and the success of your business.

A Roadmap to Success

A business plan is essentially a map to your targeted destination. Ideally, it gets you from your starting point to your goal: from your basic business concept to a healthy, successful business. It gives you a clear idea of the obstacles that lie ahead, and points out alternate routes.

Many people view the business planning process as a chore; in fact, it is an opportunity. While creating your business plan, you have the chance to 1) Learn about your industry and market; 2) Gain control over your business; and 3) Obtain a competitive edge.

Learning Your Industry and Market

One of the major benefits you'll receive from developing a business plan is getting to know your industry and market thoroughly. Even a small amount of information in this area can make a difference.

For example, one new entrepreneur, in the course of developing a business plan for his print and frame shop, learned that his target customers, middle-class women in the age range of 28 to 45, preferred Impressionist paintings and the colors blue and mauve. As a result, he chose a well-known Impressionist work as his company logo, and he always keeps a blue or mauve print in his window. This entrepreneur learned about his market and acted on what he learned. Business is booming.

Getting Control of Your Business

The business plan process also helps you, as the person most responsible for the growth of your company, gain more control over both the short-term and long-term progress of your business.

While developing your business plan, you'll increase your understanding of the many forces that have an impact on your company's success, which in turn will give you a stronger sense of control. A business plan provides mechanisms to enhance your management in these areas:

- **Marketing.** By developing a marketing plan based on a well-defined target market and evaluation of your industry and competition.
- **Operations.** By evaluating and establishing the procedures, labor deployment, and work flow necessary to run your business from day to day.
- **Finances.** By realistically projecting cash flow, income and expense, break-even points, and by creating channels of information to keep you fully informed of your financial picture.
- **Long-Term Development.** By setting specific goals and objectives; identifying milestones; devising an exit plan, if appropriate; and determining how your company will be positioned to respond to both internal and external changes.

Obtaining a Competitive Edge

By evaluating and refining your business concept through the planning process, you will be far more effective when you attempt to convey your message to your target market. Your message will be clearer, and customers will be better able to distinguish your company from the competition. Evaluating your competition and your company's strengths and weaknesses provides you with a better sense of how to position your

"Strategic planning is part of the ongoing management job. The plan itself is only a snapshot; planning should be going on all the time. And it's not enough to just have planning at the top; each division should have the resources to do its own planning."

George James
Former Sr. V.P. & CFO
Levi Strauss & Co.

"It's easy to sit in an office and think up a brilliant strategy, but you have to be able to execute it. The deciding factor of a plan is really whether it's able to be executed. We kept looking for what we could do, rather than what we wanted to do."

Larry Leigon
Founder, Ariel Vineyards

company in relation to competitors. Focus and consistency give you a competitive edge.

Why Preliminary Plans Don't Do the Job

It may be tempting to consider developing only a preliminary plan or "concept paper" to circulate to potential funding sources before making the effort to develop a complete business plan. The presumption is that through this abbreviated process, you can determine whether funders are likely to support your business concept and, if not, you can save the time it takes to create a full-fledged business plan.

This is not a good idea. Preliminary plans are not a realistic way to determine whether your business can succeed in securing financing, and they can hurt your subsequent efforts to obtain funding.

Sending a preliminary plan (which by its very nature is incomplete and raises unanswered questions) may leave the impression that you are not a careful planner and your business concept is flawed. It will most likely reduce your chances of having a subsequent complete plan examined fairly, if at all. The funder will just remember, "Oh yes, I looked at that. It had a lot of problems." Remember, you have only one chance to make a good first impression.

Moreover, the process of sending a plan, even a preliminary one, and receiving an answer takes a great deal of time; you may wait weeks, or even months, for a funder to respond. You may have to use valuable contacts to get your plan into the hands of the right investor, so you should ensure he or she will see you and your business in the best possible light.

A Good Business Plan Can Take You to the Top

A good business plan for a sound business concept helps you achieve your business goals. It saves you money and time by focusing your business activities, giving you more control over your finances, marketing, and daily operations, and helps you raise the capital you need.

Virtually no other endeavor propels you as far forward in your enterprise as building your business plan. The process is challenging, creative, and rewarding. It may even be fun!

Section I

Starting the Process

Chapter 1:
The Successful Business

Chapter 2:
Getting Your Plan Started

Chapter 3:
Making Your Plan Compelling

The Successful Business

It is not enough merely to survive;
the goal is to succeed.

Factors of a Successful Business

The ultimate purpose of developing a business plan is to have a success-ful business. In the long run, it is fruitless to write a business plan that can raise the funds you seek if your enterprise is so poorly conceived it is bound to fail. So, as you create your plan, be certain to address the long-term needs of your business and devise strategies that enhance both the overall performance of your company and your personal satis-faction.

The following factors, discussed in detail in this chapter, contribute most to business success and should guide your planning process:

- The Business Concept
- Understanding the Market
- Industry Health and Trends
- Consistent Business Focus and Clear Strategic Position
- Capable Management
- Ability to Attract, Motivate, and Retain Employees
- Financial Control
- Anticipating and Adapting to Change
- Company's Values and Integrity

"Even if you have all the money you need, you still need a business plan. A plan shows how you'll run your business. Without a plan, you don't know where you're going, and you can't measure your progress. Sometimes, after writing a business plan, you may change your approach, or even decide not to go into a certain business at this time."

Eugene Kleiner
Venture Capitalist

The Business Concept

Meeting needs is the basis of all business. You can devise a wonderful new machine, but if it doesn't address some real and important need or desire, people won't buy it, and your business will fail. Even Thomas Edison recognized this fact when he said, "Anything that won't sell, I don't want to invent."

Typically, entrepreneurs get their original business inspiration from one of four sources: 1) previous work experience; 2) education or training; 3) hobbies, talents, or other personal interests; or 4) recognition of an unanswered need or market opportunity. Occasionally, the impetus comes from the business experience of a relative or friend.

As you refine your business concept, keep in mind that successful businesses incorporate at least one of these elements:

- **Something New.** This could be a new product, service, feature, or technology.
- **Something Better.** This could be an improvement on an existing product or service encompassing more features, lower price, greater reliability, faster speed, or increased convenience.
- **An Underserved or New Market.** This is a market for which there is greater demand than competitors can currently satisfy, an unserved location, or a small part of an overall market — a niche market — that hasn't yet been dominated by other competitors. Sometimes, markets become underserved when large companies abandon or neglect smaller portions of their current customer base.
- **New Delivery System or Distribution Channel.** New technologies, particularly the Internet, allow companies to reach customers more efficiently. This has opened up many new opportunities for businesses to provide products or services less expensively, to a wider geographic area, or with far greater choice.
- **Increased Integration.** This occurs when a product is both manufactured and sold by the same company, or when a company offers more services or products in one location.

Your business should incorporate at least one of these factors — more than one if possible. Ideally, you can bring a new or better product or service to an identifiable but underserved market, perhaps using a more efficient distribution channel. Evaluate the ways your business concept addresses the elements described above. Your concept should be strong in at least one area. If not, you should ask yourself how your company will be truly competitive. The Basic Business Concept worksheet on page 3 helps you evaluate the strengths and weaknesses of your basic business idea.

Understanding the Market

It is not enough to have a great idea or new invention as the basis of your business; you must also have a market that is sufficiently large, accessible, and responsive. If your market isn't large enough, you can't reach it efficiently, or it isn't ready for you, your business will fail, no matter how

"In judging a business concept, by far the easiest and first place to start is, 'Do I want to use this myself?' If I'm not sold that I would want to use it — if I can't look at my partners and say, 'I know this fills a need because I know no one else does this; I would use it myself' — it's not going to go anywhere."

Andrew Anker
Venture Capitalist

"When starting on a new project, we always keep the negatives in mind. We don't try to sell ourselves."

Charles Huggins
President, See's Candies

Basic Business Concept

Using this worksheet as a guide, outline your business concept as you presently conceive it.

Is yours a retail, service, manufacturing, distribution, or Internet business? _____

_____

What industry does it belong to? _____

_____

What products or services do you sell? _____

_____

Who do you see as your potential customers? _____

_____

Describe your basic overall marketing and sales strategy: _____

_____

_____

Which companies and types of companies do you consider to be your competition? _____

_____

_____

List your competitive advantages, if any, in each area listed below.

New Products/Services: _____

_____

_____

Improved Features/Services and Added Value: _____

_____

_____

New or Underserved Markets Reached: _____

_____

_____

New/Improved Delivery or Distribution Method: _____

_____

_____

Methods of Increased Integration: _____

_____

_____

good your business concept. Consider the automatic teller machine (ATM) now seen on virtually every street corner. It was invented more than 10 years before it became popular, but the company that initially marketed the ATM was unsuccessful — people weren't yet willing to trust their banking to machines.

First, evaluate whether market demand is adequate to support your company. For instance, if you are opening a flower shop in a neighborhood where none currently exists, what indications are there that the neighborhood residents are interested in buying flowers? Do they currently purchase flowers at a nearby supermarket? Does national data on the demographics of flower purchasers coincide with neighborhood demographics? Perhaps you should conduct a survey of the neighborhood's residents, asking about their flower-buying habits and preferences.

Next, if you are creating a new product or service, what indications are there that the market will be receptive to you? Market readiness is one of the most difficult and most unpredictable aspects to measure. That is why companies spend substantial amounts of money on market research before launching a new product.

You may not have the funds to undertake extensive market research, but even a small amount of analysis can help you gauge the receptivity of a particular market to your idea. Methods of conducting market research and evaluation in a practical, economical fashion are discussed in Chapter 2. When gathering information for your business plan, spend considerable time learning about your market. The more you understand the various factors that affect your market, the more likely you are to succeed.

Industry Health and Trends

Your business does not operate in a vacuum; generally, your company is subject to the same conditions that affect your overall industry. If consumer spending declines nationally, there's a good chance your retail business — whether a neighborhood boutique or an online shopping mall — will also experience poor sales.

As you develop your plan, you need to respond to the industry-wide factors affecting your own company's performance. While it is certainly possible to make money in an industry that is experiencing hard times, you can only do so if you make a conscious effort to position your company appropriately. For example, if you are in the construction business and the number of new-home starts is down, you may want to target the remodeling market or the commercial real estate market rather than the new-home construction market.

Investors and lenders are particularly sensitive to issues of industry health. It is much harder to raise money to start or expand businesses in troubled industries. Even though opportunities exist in such fields, investors and bankers are concerned about the increased risks an enterprise faces in an unhealthy industry. Conversely, if your business is in a healthy and expanding industry, investors are likely to be more receptive.

"The main thing is to keep going back and talking to the people who actually use what you're making. See if what you're making is truly helpful to your customers."

Larry Leigon
Founder, Ariel Vineyards

"The planning process starts from the ground level. It begins with the sales force, estimating sales by product line. Then we develop a manufacturing and marketing plan to achieve those sales. The corporate office defines certain assumptions about the economic conditions, but a division is free to challenge those assumptions if they can make a case. The plan is vital, and bonuses are based on how performance meets or exceeds the plan."

George James
Former Sr. V.P. & CFO
Levi Strauss & Co.

What direction is your industry going? It is important to look at the major trends that will influence industry health in the future as well as examining its current condition. Is the industry consolidating as big companies merge into huge businesses? What is happening with pricing pressures, consumer demand, availability of parts and supplies, global competition? Several worksheets included in Chapter 6 help you identify and anticipate trends in your industry.

If you are seeking outside funds, your business plan must reassure investors or bankers that you understand the industry factors affecting your company's health and that you have taken those factors into consideration when developing your business strategy.

Clear Strategic Position and Consistent Business Focus

A crucial factor for a successful business is the development of a clear strategic position that differentiates you from your competition — and then maintaining focus on that position. All too often businesses fail because management loses sight of the central character of the enterprise.

Defining a clear strategic position enables you to capture a particular place in the market and distinguish yourself from your competitors. Different companies may sell a similar product, but each may have a very different sense of what its business is really all about.

For example, suppose four companies are making jeans. Company A defines itself as selling work clothes; Company B sees itself as a sportswear manufacturer; and Company C defines itself as being in the business of selling youth and sex appeal. But Company D has never clarified its mission — it just sells jeans.

These different positions affect the way each company markets itself, how it designs its jeans, what subsequent products it produces, even the employees it hires. The first three companies may all succeed and rarely be in competition with one another. But Company D, which misses the big picture, is almost certain to fail over time as it flounders in its attempts to compete with all of the other, more focused companies.

A second aspect of positioning your company and maintaining focus is the development of a company style or corporate culture. By creating a consistent style that permeates every aspect of your enterprise, from the design of your stationery to personnel policies, you give your customers and employees a sense of trust in your company.

Imagine two different restaurants on the same street, both with basically the same business mission: providing good, fast food, priced at only a few dollars a meal.

The first restaurant is a national burger chain. Its style is characterized by consistency, cleanliness, and impersonal friendliness. A strong corporate image is important, which is reinforced through the restaurant's decor, the food's packaging, and the employees' uniforms. The meals are prepared by standardized routines, and every customer is given the same greeting.

"What tips me off that a business will be successful is that they have a narrow focus of what they want to do, and they plan a sufficient amount of effort and money to do it. Focus is essential; there can be the possibility of the business branching out later, but the first phase of a company should be quite narrowly defined."

Eugene Kleiner
Venture Capitalist

The second restaurant is a diner. Management characterizes its corporate culture as that of a friendly neighbor. To help make sure that employees know customers' names and food preferences, management aims to retain employees for many years. A bulletin board features notices of local events. This restaurant's target market is the neighborhood regulars who know they will feel at home there.

With a strong company style, each restaurant clearly distinguishes itself from its competitors and gives its target customers a clear understanding of what to expect. Every business needs to consider its style as it relates to the company's overall mission, and then infuse that style into virtually all its undertakings.

To help clarify your company's position and focus as part of the business plan process, you should define a Statement of Mission. This Mission Statement should guide your company's short-term activities and long-term strategy, position your marketing, and influence your internal policies. A Mission Statement worksheet is in Chapter 5.

Capable Management

Perhaps more than any other factor, competent management stands out as the most important ingredient in business success. The people in key positions are crucial in determining the health and viability of your business. Moreover, because of the importance of capable management to business success, many investors and venture capital firms place the single greatest emphasis on this factor when evaluating business plans and deciding on loans or investments. They'll review the management section of a business plan with special scrutiny. Your business plan must inspire confidence in the capabilities of your management, and you should put your management team together carefully

Before submitting your business plan to investors, conduct your own analysis of your management team. Evaluate each individual (and yourself) to see if he or she fits the profile of a successful manager. Some of the traits shared by successful managers are:

- **Experience.** They have a long work history in their company's industry and/or they have a solid management background that translates well to the specifics of any business in which they become involved.

- **Realism.** They understand the many needs and challenges of their business and honestly assess their own limitations. They recognize the need for careful planning and hard work.

- **Flexibility.** They know things go wrong or change over time, and they are able to adapt without losing focus.

- **Ability to Work Well with People.** They are leaders and motivators with the patience necessary to deal with a variety of people. They may be demanding, but they are fair.

In developing your business plan, determine whether key members of your management team possess these characteristics. If not, perhaps you can increase training, add staff, or take other measures to enhance your management's effectiveness. For instance, if you have little or no experience in your chosen field, perhaps you should first take a job with an existing company in that field before opening your own business.

In addition to evaluating the traits of each individual, look at the overall balance of your management team. Do you have people who are capable and experienced in the various aspects of your business — marketing, operations, technology, finance, etc.? Are some managers better at dealing with internal issues and others at handling external relations? Or do the talents and traits of your managers duplicate each other?

Ability to Attract, Motivate, and Retain Employees

A company is only as good as its people. The ability to find, attract, and keep outstanding employees and managers is crucial to a company's long-term viability and competitiveness.

Demographic trends indicate a tight labor market in the United States well through the early part of the 21st century. Companies will have a difficult time competing for the relatively limited number of outstanding job applicants. Your company's reputation for treating employees well directly enhances both the number and the quality of job applicants and your company's ability to retain employees once hired.

Employee morale also has a significant impact on a company's productivity, the quality of its products or services, and its ability to provide outstanding customer service. Unhappy employees are less motivated to do excellent work. Satisfied employees are far more likely to want to see their company succeed, and they can dramatically alter a company's bottom-line.

Examine your management style and policies as part of your overall business planning process. Develop management practices that treat employees fairly, offer opportunities for advancement, afford reasonable job security, and provide fair pay and benefits.

Financial Control

Key to any business is how it handles money. Not fully anticipating start-up costs can immediately place impossible pressures on a new business. Poor cash-flow management can bring down even a seemingly thriving business. One of "Rhonda's Rules" is "Things take longer and cost more than anticipated." Build financial cushions in your plan to allow for unanticipated expenses and delays.

As you develop your business plan, make sure you have the information to understand your financial picture on an ongoing basis. What does it take to open your doors each month? Where is your real profit center? How much expansion do you need to maintain growth? What are the hidden costs of marketing your company? What are the consequences of your credit policies?

Build in mechanisms to keep you continually informed as your business develops. It is easier to establish good financial procedures right from the

"We don't just want to make secure loans; we want to make good loans. A good loan is a loan with a high probability of being repaid from the primary source, such as the business, without interrupting the lifestyle of the borrower. Collateral makes a loan 'safe,' not necessarily good. It's not fair to make a loan if the collateral is good if the business plan is shaky. We're not interested in getting people's homes; we're interested in successful businesses."

Robert Mahoney
Corporate Banker

start than to wait until you face a financial crisis. How frequently will you do your billing? What kind of credit policies will your business follow? How will you keep informed on inventory?

Make certain you receive detailed financial statements at least monthly and that you understand them thoroughly. Examine financial reports for any deviations from your plan or any indications of impending cash-flow problems.

Controlling and understanding your finances makes decisions easier. And you'll sleep better at night.

Anticipating Change and Adaptability

Change is inevitable, and the rate of change gets ever faster. In today's world, your company needs to anticipate and respond to change quickly and train its employees to be adaptable. Companies that are nimble and able to quickly evaluate and respond to changing conditions are most likely to be successful.

In planning for change, keep in mind the kinds of conditions that will affect your business' future. They include:

- **Technological Changes.** It's impossible to predict the exact technological developments that will affect your industry, but you can be sure that you will be faced with such changes. Even if you are making old-fashioned chocolate chip cookies, advancements in oven design, food storage, or inventory control software will place competitive pressures on your business. Competitors' technological advances may cause significant downward pricing pressures on you.

- **Sociological Changes.** Evaluate demographic and lifestyle trends in light of their potential influence on your business. In the cookie business, for example, consumer interest in natural foods or the number of school age children in the population may influence the number and kind of cookies you sell. What sociological factors have the greatest impact on your company? Keep your eye on trends that represent true change; be careful not to build a business on passing fads.

- **Competitive Changes.** New businesses start every day. How hard is it for a new competitor to enter the market, and what are the barriers to entry? The Internet has made it possible for companies all over the world to compete against each other, increasing the number and type of competitors you may face.

When developing your business plan, consider how your company deals with these outside changes. Also anticipate major internal changes, such as growth, the arrival or departure of key personnel, and new products or services.

No business is static. Planning a company responsive to change will make the inevitable changes easier. See Chapter 6, Industry Analysis and Trends, for more on anticipating change.

"We follow new developments in taste preferences, nutrition concerns, and interests in new products. We're always working to develop our line. But we have one basic philosophy: We won't bring a new product out until it's as good as or better than what we're presently making and we can be proud of it. The most important aspect of maintaining the See's mystique is insuring quality. After that, it is staying consistent with our image while developing new products to respond to market trends."

Charles Huggins
President, See's Candies

A Company's Values and Integrity

Every company must make money. You can't stay in business unless you eventually earn a profit. However, studies of business success over time have shown that companies that emphasize goals in addition to making money succeed better and survive longer than companies whose sole motivation is monetary.

As you develop your business plan, keep in mind those values you wish to have characterize the company you are creating or expanding. These values can be aimed externally — at achieving some business, social, or environmental goal — or they can be aimed internally — at achieving a certain type of workplace or quality of product or service — or both.

Articulating your company's values to employees, suppliers, and even your customers can strengthen their commitment to your business. Values-driven companies often have greater success in attracting and retaining good employees, and they can usually better weather short-term financial setbacks because employees and management share a commitment to goals in addition to financial rewards.

A company is likewise strengthened by maintaining integrity in all aspects of its dealings — with employees, customers, suppliers, and the community. Certainly, you will face situations where it appears that you will be at a disadvantage if you are more honest than your competitors or more fair than other employers. However, the long-term benefits of earning and keeping a reputation for integrity outweigh the perceived immediate disadvantages. A clear policy of honesty and fairness makes decision-making in difficult situations easier, inspires customer and employee loyalty, and helps avoid costly lawsuits and regulatory fines. It's also the right thing to do.

What Motivates You?
Personal Satisfaction: The Four C's

For smaller enterprises, sole proprietorships, or businesses in which one or two key members of management have primary control, issues of personal satisfaction can be a central element in determining long-term success. Some businesses fail, and others flounder, because their founders, owners, or key managers are uncertain what they really want to achieve or because they did not structure the company and their responsibilities in ways that satisfy their personal needs and ambitions.

It is useful to evaluate and consider your personal goals when deciding upon the nature of your business development. For most entrepreneurs, these goals can be summed up by the Four C's: Control, Challenge, Creativity, and Cash.

Control

How much control you need to exercise on a day-to-day basis influences how large your company can be. If you prefer to be involved in every business decision or are uncomfortable delegating or sharing authority, your business should be designed to stay small. Likewise, if you need a great

"Each year we select a 'theme' for the year and a slogan suggested by team members. Once a year, we hold an annual meeting of the entire company, all team members. At this meeting, the president and senior managers articulate the goals and objectives for the year. The entire plant is shut down while we hold this meeting. We have seven areas in which we define each year's goals and objectives: 1) quality; 2) cost reduction; 3) human resources; 4) corporate citizenship; 5) communication; 6) quantity; and 7) material management.

Michael Damer
New United Motor
Manufacturing Inc.

deal of control over your time (because of family or personal demands), a smaller business without rapid expansion is more appropriate.

In a large company, you will have less immediate control over many decisions, and others will share in decision-making. Structure management reporting systems to ensure that as the company grows, you continue to have sufficient information about and direction over developments to give you personal satisfaction. If you are seeking outside funding, understand the nature of control your funders will have and be certain you are comfortable with these arrangements.

Challenge

If you are starting or expanding a business, you are likely to be a problem-solver and risk-taker, enjoying the task of figuring out solutions to problems or devising new undertakings.

It is important to recognize the extent of your need for new challenges and develop positive means to meet this need, especially once your company is established and the initial challenge of starting a company is met. Otherwise, you may find yourself continually starting new projects that divert attention from your company's overall goals. As you plan your company, establish personal goals that not only provide you with sufficient stimulation, but also advance the growth of your business.

Creativity

Entrepreneurs want to leave their mark. Their companies are not only a means of making a living, but a way of creating something that bears their stamp. That's why many businesses carry the founder's name.

Creativity comes in many forms. For some, it is the creativity involved with designing or making a new "thing" — a fashion designer creating a line of clothes, a software developer writing a new program, a real estate developer building a new building. For others, it may be the creativity of coming up with a new business process. Creativity also comes into play in finding new ways to make sales, handle customers, or reward employees.

If you have a high need for creativity, make certain you remain involved in the creative process as your company develops. You'll want to shape your business so it is not just an instrument for earning an income but also a mechanism for maintaining creative stimulation and making a larger contribution to society. But don't overpersonalize your company, especially if it is large. Allow room for others, particularly partners and key personnel, to share in the creative process.

Cash

Understand how your personal financial goals have an impact on your business plan. For instance, if you need substantial current income, you may need investors so you have sufficient cash to carry you through the lean start-up time. This means you will share ownership interest with others, and the business must be devised for substantial profit potential to reward those investors appropriately.

"First and foremost you have to have passion. You've got to understand why you're in the business, you have to understand why you're going to be wildly successful, and you have to be able to sell it to people. It's very easy to write a business plan with lots of pretty charts and graphs and research quotes, and if you can't present it to coworkers, employees, investors, and ultimately to the customer, you're not going anywhere. You always have to have the passionate person who lives and breathes, eats and sleeps the idea.

Andrew Anker
Venture Capitalist

Likewise, if your aim is to build a very large company and accumulate substantial income or wealth quickly, you will need outside investors to finance such rapid development or expansion. Once again, this means giving up more control over your company.

If, on the other hand, your current income needs are less demanding or your overall financial goals more modest, you may be able to forego giving up a piece of your company to investors and instead expand your business more slowly through sales or through loans or credit lines. Keep in mind there is sometimes a trade-off between personal goals: wanting more cash often means having less control.

Examine your personal goals and those of key personnel using The Four C's Worksheet on page 12.

Chapter Summary

A successful business plan not only ensures you achieve your short-term objectives, but also helps secure the long-term viability of your business. When developing your plan, keep in mind the underlying factors affecting business success and personal satisfaction. Make sure your business concept is clear and focused and your market is well-defined. Understand the key trends in your industry and develop responsive, disciplined management procedures.

"Writing a business plan forces you into disciplined thinking if you do an intellectually honest job. An idea may sound great in your own mind, but when you put down the details and numbers, it may fall apart."

Eugene Kleiner
Venture Capitalist

The Four C's

Each founder or key employee in small or new companies should complete their own copy of this worksheet. Check the level of importance to you in each area.

	Extremely Important	Somewhat Important	Somewhat Unimportant	Not Important
Control				
Over own work responsibilities	☐	☐	☐	☐
Over own time, work hours, etc.	☐	☐	☐	☐
Over company decisions and directions	☐	☐	☐	☐
Over products/services	☐	☐	☐	☐
Over other employees	☐	☐	☐	☐
Over work environment	☐	☐	☐	☐
Over social/environmental impact of products/services	☐	☐	☐	☐
Over own future and business' future	☐	☐	☐	☐
Other: _____	☐	☐	☐	☐
Challenge				
Long-term problem solving	☐	☐	☐	☐
Critical problem solving (putting out fires)	☐	☐	☐	☐
Handling many issues at one time	☐	☐	☐	☐
Continually dealing with new issues	☐	☐	☐	☐
Perfecting solutions, products or services	☐	☐	☐	☐
Organizing diverse projects & keeping the group goal-focused	☐	☐	☐	☐
Other: _____	☐	☐	☐	☐
Creativity				
Determining the design or look of products/packaging	☐	☐	☐	☐
Creating new products or services	☐	☐	☐	☐
Devising new business procedures/policies	☐	☐	☐	☐
Identifying new company opportunities	☐	☐	☐	☐
Creating new business materials	☐	☐	☐	☐
Devising new ways of doing "old" things	☐	☐	☐	☐
Other: _____	☐	☐	☐	☐

Cash

List approximate dollar ranges for each of the following. Measure wealth as the value of stocks or company.

Income needed currently _____   Wealth desired in 2-5 years _____

Income desired within 12–24 months _____   Wealth desired in 6-10 years _____

Income desired in 2-5 years _____   Wealth desired 10+ years _____

## Chapter 2

Getting Your Plan Started

*You only find easy answers
by asking tough questions.*

The Business Plan Process

Once you determine a business plan is a necessary tool for your company, you may wonder, "Where do I start?" Because a plan requires detailed information on almost every aspect of your business, including industry, market, operations, and personnel, the process can seem overwhelming.

The business plan process entails five fundamental steps:

1. Laying out your basic business concept.
2. Gathering data on the feasibility and specifics of your concept.
3. Focusing and refining the concept based on the data you compile.
4. Outlining the specifics of your business.
5. Putting your plan in compelling form.

The first step is to lay out your basic business concept. In the previous chapter, you were provided a worksheet on which to delineate the various components of your business. With an existing operation, it may be tempting to skip over this step, but if you wish to develop strategies for future success, you must first examine the assumptions underlying your current efforts.

The focus of this chapter is on steps 2 and 3: gathering and interpreting the data you need. Solid information gives you a realistic picture of what happens in businesses similar to yours, as well as a better understanding

"You must have ongoing contingency plans to allow for miscalculations, disappointments, and bad luck. It's assumed that if you're a leader, you don't make mistakes. But it's not so; if you're decisive, you'll sometimes miscalculate, and sometimes just be unlucky. You need to openly discuss the possibility of mistakes, so people are prepared and aren't crestfallen when they occur. You need to rehearse your contingency plans."

Bill Walsh
Former Coach and President, S.F. 49ers

of your own company. You can then evaluate and refocus your concept in light of your newly acquired information; a worksheet provided at the end of this chapter will help you with this evaluation.

Once you have compiled sufficient information and re-evaluated your business concept, you can begin to actually write your plan. By following the chapters of this book and completing the Plan Preparation Forms, you can shape your plan into a compelling document.

Developing a business plan is much more a business project than a writing assignment. The process itself — not just the document produced — can positively affect the success of your business. During the everyday operation of your business, you seldom have time to think through the kinds of issues you'll examine while putting together your business plan; the planning process gives you a rare opportunity to enhance your knowledge of how your company, market, and industry work.

Gathering Information

Knowledge is power. With accurate information at your fingertips, you make better business decisions as well as a more persuasive presentation of your plan when meeting with a banker, potential investor, or divisional president. Savvy investors use a business plan not merely to learn about a new business concept but as a means to judge whether an entrepreneur has the knowledge and exercises the due diligence necessary to run a business. So take time to do your homework. Sufficient research prevents you from including inaccurate information in your plan — a mistake that can keep you from getting funded — and enables you to make informed decisions.

If you're new to an industry or to business management, allow yourself more time on your research efforts and start with general background information. Use the research project as an opportunity to educate yourself on the key issues of your industry, not merely as a way to find the specific details you need for your particular company.

To begin your information-gathering efforts, start by checking the resources listed later in this chapter and in the Resources chapters at the back of the book. First, seek general information about each of the areas you've identified in your Basic Business Concept worksheet from Chapter 1. As you progress, focus your research on more specific issues, compiling the details necessary to make operational and financial decisions. Chapters 4 through 17 outline the data you need to complete each section of your business plan, and in some cases include suggestions of possible sources of such information.

How Much Information Is Enough?

With the Internet, it is relatively easy to get a great deal of information; it is likewise easy to feel overwhelmed with so much of it. Conversely, you will also feel frustrated because some critical data is proprietary and unavailable. The difficult challenge is determining what information is important and how much information is enough to put in your plan, especially if you are seeking funding.

Don't try to be exhaustive in your research efforts; it's not necessary or possible. You are merely looking for information that will answer the key questions about your business. At the same time, your research must be thorough enough to give you, and those reading your plan, confidence that the answers are accurate and from reliable sources.

For example, if you are manufacturing dolls, you might identify your target market as girls between the ages of four and ten. One of the questions you need to address in your plan is, "How large is the market?" For this, you may have to consult only one source, the U.S. Census Bureau, to find a reliable answer. However, other questions that arise, such as, "What are the trends in doll-buying habits?" may require consulting three or four industry sources or undertaking your own market research to compile information you can trust.

"In our planning, we try to get away from just arithmetic projections, and try to get to the underlying issues. Planning is more than just a numbers game."

George James
Former Sr. V.P. & CFO
Levi Strauss & Co.

Start Your Research by Asking Questions

Start your research by making a general statement that is the basis of your business (or a portion of your business). For example, if you are planning to open a dry cleaning establishment, the statement might be, "There is a substantial need for a new dry cleaner to serve the Laurelwood neighborhood."

Next, make a list of questions that logically follow from and challenge that statement. Here are some questions you might then ask:

- How many dry cleaners now serve the neighborhood?
- How profitable are the current dry cleaners in the neighborhood?
- Are residents generally satisfied with the current dry cleaners?
- Is there more business than current dry cleaners can handle?
- What are the trends in the dry cleaning industry nationally?
- What are the demographic trends in Laurelwood?
- How do Laurelwood demographics relate to national dry cleaning trends and statistics?

As another example, your statement might be: "There is a profitable way to provide psychological counseling via the Internet." The questions following from and challenging that statement could include:

- What companies are already providing such a service?
- What is the size of the market for psychological counseling now?
- What indications are there that consumers would be willing to get counseling on the Internet?
- What portion of the existing psychological counseling market is it reasonable to expect would transfer to online counseling?
- How many consumers who do not currently get counseling could reasonably be expected to be attracted to online counseling?
- What are the key technology issues necessary to conduct such counseling, securely, on the Internet?
- What laws or regulations would affect the ability to offer such services?

After formulating your list of questions, look for answers. You will find some of your answers by searching government and trade associations' websites on the Internet. Others you'll find by consulting reference material through a library or business development center or by contacting industry associations or hiring paid research services. To get some answers, you will have to conduct your own market research by talking to potential customers, other business owners, or observing foot traffic at similar or nearby establishments.

As you start the business plan process, use the Research Questions worksheet on the next page to record the general questions you have at this point and the issues you will investigate. Look not only for specific current details but also for trends and patterns.

How much information you gather will be, to a large extent, a result of your resources, both of time and money. If you are working on a business plan for a one-person business while holding down a full-time job, you don't need to compile the same amount of information appropriate for a large corporation with a market research budget and staff.

Staying on Top of Your Material

During the course of your planning process, you will accumulate a great deal of information and many documents. Set up a way to organize the material you gather, such as your notes, ideas, and contact information, right as you begin.

Make individual files, either on your computer or in paper files, of the different topic areas corresponding to the chapters of this book. Add information to the files as you go along. Otherwise, you may find yourself unable to locate specific details you need when you are actually preparing your written document. As you gather data, write down the source and date of information; otherwise you may later find yourself with data and no way to verify or attribute it.

The planning process also enables you to meet many people who can be very helpful to you later, when you run your business. It is likely that you will interview potential customers, suppliers, competitors, strategic partners, as well as other industry sources. Keep a file of all these contacts as you do your research, so you easily know how to reach them.

Sources of Information

If this is your first time conducting business research, you may be surprised at just how much information exists. Mountains of statistics and bookshelves of studies are available concerning virtually every endeavor and activity of American life. Without difficulty, you can find data revealing the average purchase in a fast-food restaurant, how many personal computers were sold last year, and the likely number of new housing units that will be built in your community in the coming year.

You can locate most of the general information you require from government sources, business publications, and trade associations. To find more

Research Questions

List the questions you will examine in each area of your business, using the categories below as guidelines.

Industry / Sector: _____

_____

_____

_____

Products/Services: _____

_____

_____

_____

Target Market: _____

_____

_____

_____

Competition: _____

_____

_____

_____

Marketing & Sales Strategy: _____

_____

_____

_____

Operations/Technology: _____

_____

_____

_____

Long-Term Considerations: _____

_____

_____

_____

_____

_____

specific information relative to your particular business or industry, you may have to undertake some market research. In a limited number of cases, either when you lack the time to do the research yourself, or are involved in a new industry or one in which data is mostly proprietary, you may have to utilize paid sources of information.

Sources of general information are listed in this chapter and in the Resources chapters at the end of the book. Sources of more particular information relating to costs, equipment, or other specific areas of your business are listed in the appropriate chapters of this book.

Keep in mind that contact information, particularly website addresses, change frequently.

The Internet

The best, easiest, and least expensive place to start your research is the Internet. Governments have made most data they collect public and accessible on the Internet. Many trade or industry studies or publications are available online, free or relatively inexpensively. Research services are also available to instantly check articles, statistics, surveys, etc.

The Internet also makes it easy to quickly get good basic information about your competitors, potential customers, suppliers, and strategic partners. Begin by thoroughly going through their own websites. You can find additional information about them by checking their names in an Internet search engine.

Newspapers and periodicals also often archive back issues on their websites with useful information. There may be a small charge to retrieve some of these articles.

Government Sources and Statistics

As a taxpayer, you've already paid for your government to collect vast quantities of information, so you'll be able to get more data free from government sources than from private research services or other sources. This is true not only for the United States as a whole, but for most state and some local governments, and many other countries as well.

Most of the information collected by the U.S. government, as well as most states, is available on the Internet. As you begin your research, you may find it helpful to know your NAICS code. This may make finding specific information relating to your type of business easier.

NAICS Codes
www.census.gov/epcd/www/naics.html

NAICS is the abbreviation for North American Industry Classification System. It replaces the older Standard Industrial Classification (SIC) codes. Each industry — and subsector of each industry — is assigned a specific NAICS number.

Research Sources

U.S. Government	U.S. Census Bureau	Small Business Administration
	U.S. Department of Commerce & U.S. Department of Labor	Securities and Exchange Commission (Edgar database)
	Internal Revenue Service	
	Other government departments appropriate to your industry	
State Government	Sales Tax	Planning Departments
	Franchise Business Tax	New Business Licenses
	City and County Governments	
Quasi-Governmental Sources	Regional Planning Associations	
Industry & General Business	Trade Associations	Corporate Annual Reports
	Trade Publications	Thomas Register
Community Services	Chambers of Commerce	Merchants Associations
	Banks	Real Estate Agents
	Universities	Yellow Pages
	Newspaper and Online Libraries	
	Entrepreneurs' Associations	
Computer Databases	Business and Trade Information	
	Individualized Research Services	
Market Research Sources	Customers	
	Suppliers	
	Distributors	
	Independent Sales Representatives	
	Managers of Related Businesses	
	Loan officers/Factors/Venture Capitalists	
	Competitors	
Paid Services	Industry-Related Research firms	
	Survey/Polling Firms	
	Market Research Consultants	
Internal Data	For existing businesses	

U.S. Census Bureau
www.census.gov

The U.S. Census Bureau, part of the Department of Commerce, is the government agency with the primary responsibility for collecting and disseminating in-depth data on all aspects of American life. You may be aware that the Census gathers data on the American people: population, income, housing patterns, levels of education, and so on. But it also accumulates an enormous amount of data on the economic activity of the United States, right down to the number, type, and average sales of businesses, by particular business type, zipcode by zipcode.

Because Census Bureau data covers such a huge number of people and businesses, and because it is so detailed, Census Bureau data is considered among the most reliable information you can use. Those reading your business plan (for example, potential investors or bankers) will generally consider Census Bureau data reliable and conservative.

The Census Bureau has done an excellent job of making that vast resource of data easily available on the Internet. And remember – all that data is **free.**

Economic Census
www.census.gov (click on "Economic Census")

If you are looking for information about specific industries or types of businesses, from the Census Bureau's home page, click on "Economic Census." From there, choose the link to the latest results (left-hand column) or the years that you are interested in. A full Economic Census of the United States is conducted every five years; the last one covered the year 2002.

By exploring the tables, you can find data on the number of businesses by industries in any zipcode, county, metropolitan area, or state in the U.S. You'll also be able to find a vast amount of other information, such as distribution of business expenses and receipts by industry, data on women-owned and minority-owned businesses, product shipments. Be certain to drill down from many pages by clicking on the "More Data" or arrows for much greater detail in any report you select.

County Business Patterns
www.census.gov/epcd/cbp/view/cbpview.html

The Census Bureau produces annual reports on the number of business establishments -- detailed by industry, business size, and payroll – throughout the United States and Puerto Rico. This data is available on the national, state, county, metropolitan area, and zipcode levels. County Business Patterns are very useful in evaluating how well-served or underserved specific geographic areas are by particular business types.

Other ways to access Census data on the Internet include:

CenStats

http://censtats.census.gov

This site provides access to databases including Census Tract Street Locator, County Business Patterns, Zip Business Patterns, International Trade Data, and more.

American FactFinder

http://factfinder.census.gov

This has an easy-to-use pull-down interactive menu that allows you to find a range of demographic information about the American people – down to city or census tract level.

Quickfacts

http://quickfacts.census.gov

Quickfacts offers easy access to frequently-requested demographic data at national, state, or local level.

Current Industrial Reports

www.census.gov/cir/www/index.html

The U.S. Census Bureau publishes more than 100 *Current Industrial Reports,* providing very detailed data on tens of thousands of manufactured products – everything from baby clothes to consumer electronics to airplane engines. This information accounts for more than 40% of all goods manufactured in the United States. CIRs provide information on production, shipping, inventories, consumption and the number of firms manufacturing each product. The data is reported on a monthly, quarterly, and annual basis.

For other websites with federal U.S. statistics, visit these useful sites:

FedStats – Gateway to U.S. Government Federal Statistics

www.fedstats.gov

This main gateway to national statistics has links to statistics compiled by over 100 government agencies as well as government statistical agencies. It is a very good entry-point to all U.S. statistics.

Edgar Database – U.S. Securities and Exchange Commission

www.sec.gov

You can find annual, quarterly, and other financial reports required from publicly-traded companies by selecting the "Edgar" filings. You need the name of the corporation, not the brand name of the product, to find reports. For information about *USA Today,* for instance, enter the parent company, "Gannett Company."

Internal Revenue Service

www.irs.gov/taxstats/

Tax statistics are generally harder to maneuver than Census Bureau statistics. However, if you have a specific income or tax-related statistic you are seeking, this might be a source of that data.

Individual U.S. State and Local Sources

Each U.S. state, as well as many individual counties and cities, collect and maintain information that can be useful to you in planning your business. For instance, state sales tax receipts may be a good indicator of the health of your local economy and local planning department information regarding building permits can indicate where population growth is occurring.

Use a search engine to locate your state and local government websites.

State Data Centers
www.census.gov/sdc/www/

The U.S. Census Department maintains links to individual U.S. states data/statistics programs. This will help you locate state-wide economic statistics.

BusinessLaw.gov
www.BusinessLaw.gov

Operated by the U.S. Small Business Administration, this is a portal to government – federal and state-by-state – legal and regulatory information. Keep in mind this is a site for legal information, not statistics.

Statistics for Canada

The Canadian government not only collects extensive data about Canadian businesses and population, but it provides a number of sites to make accessing and using that information relatively easy.

Statistics Canada
www.statcan.ca

This is the primary entry point for statistical information about all aspects of Canada, including demographics and economic conditions.

Statistics Canada — Business Data
http://commerce.statcan.ca/english/commerce/

This is an excellent place to start to gather information about specific target markets and performance of industries.

BusinessGateway
www.businessgateway.ca

This site provides a single access point to all the Canadian government services and information to start, run and grow a business in Canada.

Strategis — Canada's Business and Consumer Site
www.strategis.gc.ca

This well-organized site makes the resources and data of the Canadian government department, Industry Canada, readily available.

Bank of Montreal – Economic Research
www.bmo.com/economic/

"To begin, I started by talking to people. I went to stores to see what products were already out there. I went to the Fancy Food Show and looked around for products similar to mine. I called the city Health Department to get names of commercial kitchens, so I could talk to people who made food products locally. From these kitchens, I got a lot of information about what I would need, as well as leads for production facilities."

Deborah Mullis
Entrepreneur

The Bank of Montreal is a good non-governmental source of Canadian and North American economic statistics, including economic outlooks.

International Statistics

The Internet has made it much easier to gather data globally. Most developed, and many developing, countries have substantial statistical information available on the Internet, and international economic organizations also make data available.

U.S. Census Bureau List of Foreign Statistical Websites

www.census.gov/main/www/stat_int.html

The U.S. Census Bureau maintains links to locate statistical sites of countries throughout the world.

The World Bank

www.worldbank.org

This international organization compiles data world-wide. It offers free data by topic or country, links to online databases, as well as publishing its own economic reports.

Export.gov — Country and Industry Market Research

www.export.gov/cntryind.html

A rich resource of information, designed primarily for American countries engaged in international trade, Export.gov provides substantial, in-depth information about markets and industries throughout the world.

State Department Country Background Notes

www.state.gov/r/pa/ei/bgn/

The U.S. State Department prepares background papers on virtually every country in the world. These background papers include statistics and overviews of each country's economy as well as useful links.

International Data Base

www.census.gov/ipc/www/idbnew.html

The International Data Base (IDB) contains statistical tables of demographic, and socio-economic data for 227 countries and areas of the world.

Non-Governmental Free Online Resources

In addition to the sources listed below, be certain to use search engines such as Google, www.google.com, and online directories, such as Yahoo, www.yahoo.com, to find information from many sources about the topics you're interested in. Other good sources are listed below.

Louisiana State University

www.lib.lsu.edu

LSU maintains a very well-organized index to research and data available on the web, including government sources and subject-specific search engines.

"To come up with projections of customer turnover and sales, we went around to restaurants in the neighborhood and similar restaurants in the surrounding communities. We counted the customers at different times throughout the day and timed them to see how frequently tables turned over. Then we knocked those numbers way down for our own conservative projections."

Martha Johnson
Restauranteur

National Association of Manufacturers
www.nam.org

This large industry association provides substantial information to manufacturing companies, as well as collecting data about manufacturing. Click on the "About Manufacturing" link to find data and economic analysis and reports on manufacturing topics.

Society for Human Resource Management
www.shrm.org

The leading organization for human resource executives, this site has some good information on personnel issues available to non-members (and a lot more information for members). However, it also has some excellent links to general business resources on the Internet.

Thomas Register
www.thomasregister.com

The Thomas Register is the ultimate resource for locating suppliers and vendors. They not only list suppliers by product category, but many suppliers have detailed product/part/equipment lists, some with prices.

You can also find information about industries, trends, and companies from publications, which may charge a fee for archived stories. A few to try include:

Wall Street Journal
www.wsj.com

Business Week
www.businessweek.com

Red Herring
www.redherring.com

The Economist
www.economist.com

Forbes
www.forbes.com

Fee-based Online Resources

Some of the websites listed below offer some information free, but for more in-depth information, you will have to pay a fee.

LexisNexis
www.lexisnexis.com

This service provides a wealth of information and should be the first place you start when you are ready to pay for information. It is indispensable to researchers and includes comprehensive company, country, financial, demographic, market research, and industry reports. LexisNexis offers access to hundreds of databases, thousands of worldwide publications, public and legislative records, data on companies and executives and more. Payment for access to the LexisNexis database is available on a per article, per day, per week, or subscription basis.

Hoover's Online
www.hoovers.com

From Hoover's, you can get free, basic information on individual companies, particularly public companies, as well as more detailed information for a fee. Look at Hoover's Publications for more information relating to your industry. Hoover's also has links to other sources of specific information on companies, mostly fee-based.

Dun & Bradstreet
www.dnb.com

D&B maintains credit reports and financial information on tens of thousands of companies. You can purchase a report about a competitor, customer, or supplier. You can also buy targeted marketing lists and industry reports.

For statistics and trends in technology-related industries, the following three websites are sources for fee-based research reports and data:

Forrester
www.forrester.com

Gartner Group
www.gartner.com

Jupiter Research
www.jupiterresearch.com

Offline Research Resources

While you may want to start your research online, you may find that some data is not available or is too expensive on the Internet. A number of "real-world" sources may provide additional information.

Libraries

Many public and university libraries subscribe to an array of paid online research services and/or purchase expensive statistical research publications. Visiting a library may give you access to this fee-based data for free. Choose the largest library convenient to you; the larger the library, the more likely it is to subscribe to these services or purchase these publications. You might want to make an appointment with a reference librarian at a nearby university. Many universities gather their own statistical data about regional economic performance.

Ask the librarian if they have access to any of the paid online services listed above, such as LexisNexis.

Some other services to ask about include:

Predicasts F&S Forecasts and Predicasts PROMT (Predicasts Overview of Markets and Technology)
Predicasts PROMT provides summaries and full text of articles from trade and industry publications. It is especially useful for finding detailed information on specific companies, industries, products and brands.

> *"You need to have numbers. If I ask you a question, you better know the answer. If you say you're going to sell shoes to people with very wide feet, you better know the number of people with very wide feet."*
>
> ***Andrew Anker***
> ***Venture Capitalist***

Predicasts F&S Forecasts provides an index to articles, full text of brief articles and excerpts from nearly 1,000 journals, newspapers, research studies, etc., covering all manufacturing and service industries and a wide range of business-related subjects.

InfoTrac

Many libraries subscribe to an online database service called InfoTrac (published by Gale Group), which allows you to search for magazine and journal articles, as well as have access to substantial proprietary information.

Standard & Poor's Industry Surveys

While designed for investors, this can be a source of insight about your overall industry and major competitors. It provides overviews of industry trends and reports revenues of more than 1,000 companies.

Wilson Business Full-Text

This provides full-text access to articles from more than 350 business publications, and in-depth abstracting of articles from more than 600 publications. If your library has access to the Wilson Business database, it may be a less expensive way to get archived articles from publications such as *The Wall Street Journal* than from other sources.

Gale's Business and Company Resource Center
www.galegroup.com/BusinessRC/

SBDCs and Other Support Organizations

Small Business Development Centers (SBDCs) and subcenters are located in many American communities and are an excellent source of information and assistance. In addition to maintaining a library of reference materials, SBDC staff can usually direct you to sources appropriate to your planning process. They may be able to help you in identifying local resources for your particular business, and they often conduct workshops on business topics and skills. Many SBDC centers are located at community colleges or universities.

SBDC Directory Online
www.sba.gov/starting/sbdclocations.html

This is where you can find an online listing of all SBDC centers.

Many communities have other private or quasi-governmental entrepreneurial support organizations and centers. These may be run by minority enterprise organizations, women's entrepreneur groups, regional industry associations or your local chamber of commerce. To find such organizations, check the business section of your local newspaper, ask at the SBDC or your local economic development office, and ask other entrepreneurs.

Chamber of Commerce Locator
www.uschamber.com/chambers/chamber_dir.asp

Trade and Industry Associations

There are over 35,000 trade and industry associations in the United States alone. These associations are frequently the best source of current data relating to specific industries. Many of them conduct surveys, track market trends of their industry, and publish research papers relating to industry topics. There is almost certainly at least one association serving your company's industry.

Industry trade shows (conventions, exhibits, etc.) are an outstanding source of information and market research. In a brief time, in one location, you can identify potential competitors, customers, and suppliers. Seminars held concurrently with trade shows can help you learn about the key trends and issues in your industry. Most industries have at least one major trade show per year. Contact your industry association(s) to find out when shows are being held, and how you can get accredited to attend. Some industries hold regional or local trade shows as well as national conventions.

To find your industry association, in addition to using an online search engine (www.google.com) and directory (www.yahoo.com), you might also want to check:

American Society of Association Executives
www.asaenet.org

This national association of directors of trade, industry, and professional associations also provides a "Gateway" on their site which can help you locate associations related to your business.

Gale's Encyclopedia of Associations

This publication lists over 135,000 membership organizations worldwide. You may be able to find it at a good library.

Internet Public Library – Associations on the Net
www.ipl.org/div/aon/

The Internet Public Library is a valuable resource maintained by the University of Michigan. In addition to this directory of associations, you can find a variety of other useful business information by searching elsewhere on this well-organized site.

TSNN.com
www.tsnn.com

A database listing more than 15,000 trade shows worldwide.

Paid Research Services

In some cases, you will want to use a private research firm as a source of data. Private firms gather information (sometimes from confidential sources), provide more detailed competitor-sales estimates, and undertake market research projects. These firms are all relatively expensive, so you should use them only when your time is very limited, when undertaking an unusually large or expensive enterprise, or when the information you are seeking is hard to find, proprietary, or has never been compiled.

Check with your industry trade associations for research firms that are particularly knowledgeable about your industry. Each firm provides different services, and costs vary dramatically. Sometimes these firms have reports or surveys they prepared for private corporate clients which, after a few months, they are able to sell to the general public. The reports may be a good source of information and a relative bargain.

Historical Performance of Your Company

If yours is an ongoing business (not newly established), you also need to gather historical data about your own company. In particular, you should examine your past internal financial records. Here is some of the financial information you may need to locate:

- Past sales records, broken down by product line, time period, store, region, or salesperson;
- Past trends in costs of sales;
- Overhead expense patterns;
- Profit margins on product lines; or
- Variations from budget projections.

If you cannot gather this information easily, change your reporting system so that in the future you will be able to have the data you need for adequate planning.

If you have created business plans or set goals or objectives in the past, you should also track how well your business has performed in terms of meeting your objectives. Have you consistently under-performed or exceeded your goals? Have you reached key milestones within the time period originally projected? A Milestones Achieved to Date worksheet is included in Chapter 15.

How to Conduct Your Own Market Research

Some of the most important information you need will not be available from any published source, particularly information that is quite specific to your market or new product. To obtain this data, you will have to undertake your own research. For most businesses, even very large businesses, this research needn't be expensive or prohibitively time-consuming.

Personal Observation Is an Easy Method

One fundamental way to gather information — and also one of the easiest — is through personal observation. Watching what goes on in other businesses or the way people shop gives you insight into factors affecting your own business. You can observe auto and foot-traffic patterns near a selected location, how customers behave when shopping in businesses similar to

"We taste-tested our product in all the places we wanted to sell it eventually: hotels, restaurants. We wanted to see what our potential consumers wanted and spent an enormous amount of time talking to them. We tested at supermarkets, parties, polo matches. We watched how people reacted physically as well as what they told us. We changed the product a dozen times in the first couple years in response to consumers. You have to be willing to make radical changes."

Larry Leigon
Founder, Ariel Vineyards

yours or for similar products, and how competitors market or merchandise their products or services. Personal observation is a vital tool in your planning process and applicable for almost every business, large or small.

Informational Interviews Can Be Structured or Informal

The second principal method of market research is informational interviewing. Since the amount of information you can garner from personal observation is limited and colored by your own perceptions, you should talk with as many people as possible who can provide you with information relating to your business.

Some of these interviews may be highly structured. For instance, you might make personal appointments with those you want to interview and have a prepared list of questions. In other cases, such as when you go into a competitor's store and chat with a salesperson, your questions will appear to be more casual.

Surveys Help You Spot Trends

If you decide you need information from a large number of people, you may want to conduct a survey, either by phone, by mail, on the Internet, or in person. Surveys are a good way to spot trends and are particularly useful in assessing customer needs and desires. You can conduct in-person surveys by going to an appropriate location and interviewing subjects on the spot. Develop a questionnaire of the most important concerns to ascertain from interview sources. Don't make your survey too long or people will refuse to participate. Mail surveys have a notoriously low response rate, so if you conduct one, it is a good idea to include some kind of incentive, such as discounts or free gifts to encourage people to respond.

Focus Groups Offer Candid Opinions

A popular form of market research is the focus group, a small group of people brought together to discuss a product, business concern, or service in great detail. For example, a few joggers might be brought in to examine and evaluate a new pair of running shoes. Focus group participants are often paid a small fee.

Market research firms conduct focus groups for businesses, bringing together the participants and leading the group discussion in a room with a one-way mirror, so that the businessperson involved can observe. However, if you do not have the funds to hire a market research firm, you might still consider assembling a focus group of your own, perhaps a group of potential consumers. Try, however, to find focus group participants you do not know personally.

Accessible Sources for Market Research

Here are some sources to consider for your market research:

- Potential customers, both end-users and buyers or distributors, if you are in a wholesale business;

"Vendors are a good source of information and even professional advice. We had a lot of help on kitchen design from our vendors."

Martha Johnson
Restauranteur

"The competitive analysis is hugely critical. We're going to find out if you're hiding competitors. We have good networks. If we find out about something you didn't tell us about, it gives us the impression you don't know your market."

Andrew Anker
Venture Capitalist

- Potential suppliers;
- Businesses related geographically or by product line;
- Similar businesses serving different cities and others in your industry;
- Banks, real estate agents, universities, local or regional chambers of commerce, merchant groups, or others observing the local economy;
- Your competitors; or
- Entrepreneurs' groups.

Suppliers, distributors, and independent sales representatives can give you a great deal of information about industry trends and what your competition is doing without violating confidentiality. Because they are in touch with the market, they know which products and services are in demand.

Learn from Other Businesses

Those in related businesses often know about conditions affecting your company. For example, if you are considering locating a retail store in a mall, managers of other mall shops can give you a realistic idea of foot traffic, slow periods, and shopper demographics.

"If you're truly creating something new, it doesn't show up in trends."

Larry Leigon
Founder, Ariel Vineyards

Try talking to people who are in the same industry or business as yours in a different city; they are an excellent source of information. If you are starting an onsite computer repair company in San Antonio, Texas, for instance, you might arrange to meet with a similar company in Houston. Since you will not be competing with Houston businesses, they may be very helpful in providing information not only on marketing but on operations and financial considerations.

In addition, large banks and universities frequently maintain information about the health of the local economy and particular industries. They are a good and reasonably reliable source of future-growth forecasts. Don't overlook real estate agents. They often have more up-to-date information about neighborhood trends than any other source.

Talk to Your Competition

Sometimes you can even talk to your competitors. In many industries and professions, and in instances where there is more work than the market can handle, your competitors may be willing to talk with you directly. In other cases, you need to use less direct ways of approaching them.

However, be careful not to use illegal or unethical methods of dealing with your competitors; not only is it wrong, but you'd be surprised at how such activities can come back to haunt you. Today's competitor may one day be a source of referrals, a strategic partner, or possibly in a merger or acquisition, the owner of your company.

Getting Help

Many people realistically feel they need assistance in researching, developing, and then preparing their business plan. You may also. Fortunately, there are many places to turn.

You may want to begin with one of the many sources of assistance available free or at little charge. In many communities, you might want to start with a Small Business Development Center (see above). There is also assistance offered by the Service Corps of Retired Executives (SCORE), minority or women's economic development centers, or local economic development agencies. Many universities offer extension or evening courses to assist entrepreneurs.

One of the best sources of assistance may be local organizations of entrepreneurs or industry support groups. Many entrepreneurs' groups hold business planning seminars or offer "Special Interest Groups" (SIGs) in particular industry or topic areas.

You may also want to turn to a paid consultant to offer more personal, in-depth assistance. Consultants are available in business planning, graphic design and desktop publishing, research services, writing and editing, accounting, and many other fields.

Evaluating the Data You've Collected

Once you start compiling information, you might feel you have more facts than you know what to do with. Here are a few tips to keep in mind about the information you gather:

- Use the most recent data you can find; printed information is often at least two years old and a lot can change in two years.
- Translate data into units rather than dollars whenever possible. Due to inflation, dollars may not give you consistent information from year to year.
- Give the most reliable source the most credence. Generally, the larger the group sampled for information, or the more respected the organization that conducted the research, the more trustworthy the numbers you collect.
- Integrate data from one source to another in order to draw conclusions. However, make sure the information is from the same time period and is consistent; small variations can lead to vastly inaccurate results.
- Use the most conservative figures. Naturally, you'll be tempted to paint the brightest picture possible, but such information often leads to bad business decisions.

"When you're done with your plan, put it aside for a week and then look at it again."

Andrew Anker
Venture Capitalist

Bringing Your Business Concept into Focus

Once you complete your initial research efforts, but before you lay out the specific components of your plan, re-examine your business concept. In light of the information you now have, check to see if your idea, as originally conceived, needs to be modified or refocused.

The business planning process is a learning process; it is appropriate for you to adapt your business in response to your increased knowledge.

Now is the time to ask yourself some hard questions, such as:

- Can the business be viable?
- Does a real market exist?
- Is there too much competition already?
- How does the financial picture look?

The worksheet, Evaluating Your Business Concept, on the next two pages helps you answer these and other crucial questions. Be sure to complete it after finishing your initial research.

Chapter Summary

The business planning process offers you an outstanding opportunity to better understand your business, market, and industry. Keep in mind that this process is a business activity, not a writing assignment.

Steps in the process include laying out your concept, gathering information, assessing that information and, finally, refocusing your business idea. A thorough planning process gives you ammunition to use when looking for money to fund your business, and an honest examination of your business concept increases your chances of success.

Evaluating Your Business Concept

Come back to this worksheet after conducting your initial research to further refine your focus and determine whether your business idea is viable. In answering the questions, be honest and be tough.

Your Business Industry

How economically healthy is your business industry or sector? _____

_____

Explain how your industry/sector is sensitive to economic fluctuations. _____

_____

Yes No
- ☐ ☐ Are the forecasts for your industry or sector positive?
- ☐ ☐ Is the industry or market changing rapidly?

Your Product / Service

Yes No
- ☐ ☐ Is your product or service unique?
- ☐ ☐ Can it be developed in a reasonable period of time?
- ☐ ☐ Are the costs of development prohibitive?
- ☐ ☐ Are necessary supply and support systems established?

Your Market

Yes No
- ☐ ☐ Is your market clearly identifiable?
- ☐ ☐ Is your market large enough to support your business?
- ☐ ☐ Is your market too large, and the costs to reach it prohibitive?
- ☐ ☐ Is your market growing?
- ☐ ☐ Are there indicators that your market is ready for your product or service?
- ☐ ☐ Is your product/service too new for customers?
- ☐ ☐ Do customers have strong loyalty to existing companies?
- ☐ ☐ Is it costly for customers to convert to your product or service?
- ☐ ☐ Does your product/service integrate easily with existing products or services?
- ☐ ☐ Are there demographic or sociological factors likely to affect the market?

Your Competition

How formidable is your competition? _____

Yes No
- ☐ ☐ Do one or two competitors dominate the market?
- ☐ ☐ Is market share widely distributed, making it easier to get a foothold?
- ☐ ☐ Is there a competitor with "deep pockets" who can drive you out?

Evaluating Your Business Concept (continued)

What barriers to market entry will your future competitors face? _____

_____

Your Suppliers / Distributors

How close are you to sources of supplies? _____

How reliable are your suppliers and distributors? _____

Yes No

☐ ☐ Are you dependent on one or two suppliers or distributors?

☐ ☐ Are your suppliers/distributors well-established and dependable?

Your Operations Concerns

Yes No

☐ ☐ Does your business entail unusually difficult operational problems? If so, describe them.

_____

☐ ☐ Will personnel be hard to find, retain, or train?

☐ ☐ Is manufacturing particularly complex?

☐ ☐ Must you make substantial initial capital expenditures?

☐ ☐ Will you need to maintain large, expensive inventories?

☐ ☐ Does new technology exist that will help you reduce costs?

☐ ☐ Do the principals have the expertise necessary?

☐ ☐ Will ongoing training be required?

☐ ☐ Will it be costly to retain additional experts?

☐ ☐ Are there rapid technological changes that will affect costs and competitiveness?

Your Insurance Concerns

Yes No

☐ ☐ Are you able to secure the necessary insurance?

☐ ☐ Is there a significant liability issue?

☐ ☐ Will you have to carry heavy insurance premiums?

Your Financial Concerns

Describe any financial problems you anticipate: _____

_____

Yes No

☐ ☐ Is overhead unusually high, thus putting extra pressure on cash flow?

☐ ☐ Will credit be hard to establish?

☐ ☐ Are profit margins narrow, making the business vulnerable?

☐ ☐ Will you have to carry a large amount of debt?

Making Your Plan Compelling

People don't read.

Five Crucial Minutes

Time is valuable for businessmen and businesswomen. Rarely can they give any one matter the attention it deserves. This is especially true of bankers, venture capitalists, and other investors who are inundated with business plans and proposals; a typical venture capitalist can expect to see more than 1,000 business plans a year.

Although you may spend five months preparing your plan, the cold, hard fact is that an investor or lender can dismiss it in less than five minutes. If you don't make a positive impression in those critical first five minutes, your plan will be rejected. Only if it passes that first cursory look will your plan be examined in greater detail.

The most important aspects of your plan must jump out at even the most casual reader. Even if your plan is intended for internal company use only, it will be more effective if it is presented in a compelling, vivid form. Highlighting specific facts, goals, and conclusions makes your plan easier to review, more effective as a working document, and increases your chances of making a positive impact.

As you start your business plan process, keep in mind the kind of information, statistics, and graphics your readers expect to see and that will enable your plan to make a greater impact. When it comes time to put your plan into final form, you will then have this information handy.

"The first thing I read are the first two paragraphs of the executive summary. They've got to get that right. If they can't describe it in two paragraphs — if I can't be dragged in — there's no way the next five million people can be dragged in. It doesn't take more than a minute to decide whether a business is interesting."

Andrew Anker
Venture Capitalist

How Your Business Plan Is Read

When evaluating a business plan, experienced business plan readers generally spend the first five minutes reviewing it in this order: first, the Executive Summary; second, the Financials; third, the Management section; and next, the Exit Plan and/or Terms of the Deal, if applicable.

The Most-Asked Questions

Funding sources primarily look for answers to these questions concerned with the heart of the plan:

- Is the business idea solid?
- Is there a sufficient market for the product or service?
- Are the financial projections healthy, realistic, and in line with the investor's or lender's funding patterns?
- Is key management described in the plan experienced and capable?
- Does the plan clearly describe how the investors or lenders will get their money back?

Within the first five minutes of reading your business plan, readers must perceive that the answers to all these questions are favorable.

Increasing the Reader's Interest

Three sections — the Executive Summary, the Financials, and the Management description — must spark enough interest and inspire sufficient confidence to make the reader decide it is worthwhile to spend additional time reading other sections of your plan. You may have done a bang-up job of describing how your company will operate, but it is unlikely the Operations section will even be read if your Executive Summary and Financials aren't enticing to the reader.

Some venture capitalists and investors have specific areas of interest, or are known for giving certain aspects of a plan more weight than others. If you know this information, highlight those areas that are consistent with the particular investor's funding patterns when sending out your plan; do this in the Executive Summary and in your cover letter.

For instance, if you know a venture capital firm is especially interested in new technology, emphasize any patents you have secured and the aspects of your company that represent ground-breaking technological developments. Or, if a member of your management team (or one of the Board of Directors) is known and respected by a particular investor, you may want to discuss management near the beginning of your Executive Summary.

You can tailor the order of the Executive Summary, even the entire plan, for individual recipients. More information about how to research your intended funding sources and how to prepare your plan to be sent out is discussed in Chapters 18 and 19.

Getting Your Facts Right

The worst mistake you can make in a business plan is to make a mistake. If the reader of your plan knows a statement you have made is not true, you have lost credibility, even if you were just mistaken, not trying to mislead. Make certain your facts are correct.

Your facts must not only be correct, but must also be attributable to a reputable source. As you do your research and prepare your plan, keep track of the sources of your information. You may want to indicate the source of your data in your plan, but even if you do not include the source in your written plan, you need to be able to quickly tell a reader or potential funder where you found your information.

Length of the Plan

How long should the perfect business plan be? No magic number exists, but here are some guidelines:

- Limit the plan itself (not including the Financials and appendices) to 15 to 35 pages; 20 pages are enough for nearly any business.
- Only a plan for a complicated business or product should be more than 30 pages (not including the appendices). If you need 40 pages or more, your plan had better be intended for a very motivated, sophisticated reader, or for use solely as an internal document.
- If you have an uncomplicated small business, you may not need 15 pages, but anything fewer than 10 pages will seem somewhat unsubstantial to the reader.
- Limit appendices to no more than the length of your plan. While they are a good way to present additional information, appendices should not be so long as to make the entire document appear burdensome.
- Make sure your business plan fits easily and comfortably into a briefcase; you don't want your plan to be the one left behind when an investor goes on a business trip. After all, it will receive uninterrupted attention if reviewed on a plane.

These guidelines apply to most business plans. But if you are confident that your business requires a different configuration, go ahead!

What Period of Time Should Your Plan Cover?

Most plans should project three to five years into the future, or until you have reached your anticipated exit strategy, whichever is earlier. However, you need only include monthly financials for the first year or two, depending on development time. For the second and third years, quarterly financials are usually adequate; annual projections suffice for the fourth and fifth years.

Similar time guidelines apply to how much detail you should include when describing your business operations. Quite thorough information should be provided for the first year or two; for subsequent years, a more general Operations description is acceptable.

"As an entrepreneur, you've got to have more skepticism than I will have. You've got to question the numbers. Some one is going to question those numbers; if you haven't you're going to look foolish."

Andrew Anker
Venture Capitalist

"I don't like a plan that's too long. To avoid that, put detailed plans in the appendices so that people can refer to them only if they want to. A well-written plan should be no more than 25 pages, 100 pages total or less with appendices. If an investor is interested, they'll ask for more details."

Eugene Kleiner
Venture Capitalist

Plans for existing businesses and in-house corporate use should include historical performance information for the past five years, or the duration of your business, if less than five years. If your business is longstanding, you may want to examine trends over the life of the business, or the last 10 years; this gives you insight into cyclical patterns and helps you anticipate events that are likely to recur.

Use Language to Convey Success

The language you use in your plan can give the impression you are thoughtful, knowledgeable, and prudent, or, conversely, it can make you seem naive and inexperienced. Your fundamental goal is to convey realistic optimism and businesslike enthusiasm about your prospects.

Use a straightforward, even understated, tone. Let the information you convey, rather than your language, inescapably lead to the conclusion that your business will succeed. Avoid formal, stilted language. Instead be natural, as if you were speaking to the reader in person; however, avoid slang and don't be "chatty." Always be professional.

Listed below are some other pointers to keep in mind when writing your business plan.

Be Careful with Superlatives

Readers are naturally skeptical of over-reaching self-promotion. Avoid using words such as "best," "terrific," "wonderful," or even "unmatched." They reduce credibility. Rather, use factual descriptions and specific information to make positive impressions.

Instead of saying, "Our widget will be the best on the market, clearly superior to all others," say, "Our widget will not only handle all the functions of existing widgets, but will also add features x, y, and z, and sell for $3 less than our closest competitor's widget. No competitor of ours offers these features at any price."

When trying to get additional financing for your restaurant, don't tell the reader that the food and atmosphere are "terrific." Instead provide specific information that proves you are doing something right: "Due to the restaurant's popularity, there is an average 45-minute wait for a table on Friday and Saturday nights, and a wait of 15 to 30 minutes on other evenings."

The only exception to this rule is when you use superlatives as part of your goal in a Statement of Mission. Then it is appropriate to state, "We intend to make a dog food unmatched in quality by any national brand." Even then, however, it is important to include the specifics of what you mean by such a goal.

Use Positive Comments from Third-Party Sources

Everyone expects you to think your product or service is outstanding; thus, your own glowing comments about your company are meaningless in your plan. Instead, as you do your research, look for statements by outside sources to give readers confidence in your business.

For instance, a reader of your plan is likely to tune out when encountering a comment such as: "Adeena's fashions are equal to those by top designers," or "Our restaurant serves the best food in the city." However, the same comment, when made by an authority, becomes quite powerful: "*Women's Wear Daily* states that Adeena's fashions are equal to those of the top designers," or "The newspaper's annual survey rated our restaurant among the top 10 in its price category."

You don't even have to quote a well-known authority; anyone with credible, related experience will do, as this example shows: "The breeder of the winner of last year's Tri-County Dog Show tested our dog food and concluded, 'This will be the best dog food on the market, superior to any national brand.'"

Use Business Terms

Although it is certainly not necessary to be a business school graduate to develop a business plan, you should know and use appropriate basic business terms. You don't want to be discredited or misunderstood by using words improperly. If business is new to you, familiarize yourself with the Business Terms Glossary at the back of this book.

Become familiar also with the terms of your specific industry and use those words when appropriate in your plan. If you don't know these already, you should be able to pick many of them up while doing background work for the Industry Analysis section of your plan. However, do not fill your plan with a lot of technical jargon in the hope of sounding impressive; there is a good chance that someone unfamiliar with your industry will be reading it, especially if you are seeking outside funding.

Certain terms and trends are more popular at one time than another. You may find it helpful to include these "buzzwords" in your plan. As you do your research, keep track of the terms and practices that are currently 'hot' with investors or industry leaders. Look to see what they are talking and reading about. Even if you do not include these buzzwords in your plan, you may be asked about them in a meeting with potential funders.

Points of Style

In addition to using the most beneficial and appropriate language in your plan, you should pay attention to the elements of style discussed below.

Use Numbers for Impact

People tend to put great faith in numbers, and using numbers to support your plan can add significant credibility. If the figures come from a reputable source, they have even more power.

One particularly good technique for making your plan stronger is to state, "Our _____ is supported by...," followed by specific figures relating to demographics, growth of market, information from other businesses, or market research. For example: "Our foot-traffic projections are supported by figures that show neighboring stores average 22 customers an

"The business plan had 15 pages of text. We also included an opening budget, cash-flow projections, a summary of return on investment, a furnishings and equipment list, a map of the area, and a site analysis based on Planning Department information on new and renovated housing in the vicinity. In the business plan for our next restaurant, we also included publicity the current restaurant had received."

Martha Johnson
Restauranteur

hour on weekdays and 43 customers an hour on Saturdays," or, "Our choice of the young adult market is supported by U.S. Bureau of Census figures projecting a growth of 32% in that age category over the next five years."

It is vital to bring data from your Financials into the text of your plan to indicate specifically why you will be able to achieve certain goals. For instance, state: "Our new production method will reduce each unit cost by 43% (currently projected savings: $1.57 per unit), thus allowing us to offer additional features at a competitive price while still maintaining our profit margin." Do not expect the reader to pick out these kinds of specifics just from looking at your Financials; the information must be incorporated into the text.

Use Bullet Points

Bullets are symbols that precede information offset from the text (such as the small boxes before the three sentences below). Bullets:

- Draw attention to specific information.
- Make long material more inviting to read.
- Eliminate the need to write whole sentences.

Bullet points are an excellent way to convey information, and they make writing your plan somewhat easier. Because they are read faster than text and quickly get the reader's attention, use bullet points only with information you particularly want the reader to notice.

Be careful not to clutter a plan with too many bullets; use them selectively. Bullets seem to work better with short items than with long ones. Also, each list of bulleted items must be presented in a consistent manner, such as starting with a verb or being a complete sentence. Keep in mind that lists can be as few as one item or as many as ten, but a long list weakens effectiveness.

Your bulleted items also become excellent candidates for slides in a computer/slide presentation, such as a Powerpoint presentation, that you may later put together for meetings with potential investors, department heads, or other readers of your plan.

Know How and When to Be Redundant

Writing a business plan gives you the rarely granted right to repeat yourself. People do not read a plan from start to finish; they turn first to the sections that most interest them and then skip around. For this reason, it may be beneficial to refer in one section to conclusions you have reached in another.

For instance, when addressing the issue of staff training in your Operations section, you can refer to the importance of high-quality service to your target market, and underscore the wisdom of choosing this market by restating information provided earlier in your plan: "Surveys indicate high-quality service is demanded by our target market — women ages 35

"Style shows thoroughness. Use lots of white space, so I can make notes in the margins. Use a binder that keeps the document together, preferably one that keeps the plan open to the page I'm on. Use bullet points. Use a block style rather than indented paragraphs. Don't misspell my name, and don't address me as 'Mr.' Imagine that you have to hand your plan to a customer. So if you don't know how to make a document look good, get some help."

Ann Winblad
Venture Capitalist

to 49 — who, as shown in the market analysis, spend the most per capita on our product."

Two cautions about repetition, however: 1) only repeat information that is important and impressive; and 2) don't repeat information within the same section.

Using Visuals in Your Plan

In the case of your business plan, a picture may be worth more than a thousand words. A thousand words, after all, most likely will not be read, but a picture will definitely be looked at. Graphs, charts, and illustrations also are visually appealing; they catch the reader's attention, forcefully explain concepts, and break up the monotony of the text.

As you do your research and prepare your plan, look for items that can have a strong impact if presented in a more visual form, such as positive statistics on the growth or size of market. You may also want to include some of these in any computer/slide presentation you later put together.

Photographs and Illustrations

Photographs can be extremely effective, especially if your company is producing a product that is unusual or difficult to understand. You can include pictures of your location, specialized equipment, or packaging but not of yourself or individual members of your management team. Photographs should be placed in the appendix only.

Illustrations help present information about products or marketing materials still in development. While generally placed in the appendix, a small illustration can be inserted directly into the text. If an illustration is not of good quality, don't use it; a business plan is not the place for exhibiting amateur art.

Graphs and Charts

Graphs and charts are excellent tools for communicating important or impressive information, and you should find ways of including graphs or charts in your plan. Place charts, particularly of half-page size or less, in the text rather than in the appendix; this will engage the reader with your plan, and many readers pay minimal attention to the appendix.

A number of inexpensive computer software programs are available for generating graphs and charts (the Excel-based Financial Worksheet package available as a supplement to this book will automatically generate professional charts based on your financial projections. Visit www.planning-shop.com). Do not draw charts and graphs by hand. The four examples on the next page help you identify various types of charts and judge when each would most appropriately be used in your business plan.

For even more impact, produce and reproduce some or all of your charts and graphs in color.

> "The physical appearance of a plan (layout, binder, etc.) isn't significant in making the investment decision. But it sets your mind in a certain frame if it is well done. And it is certainly a negative if it's done wrong or poorly."
>
> **Eugene Kleiner**
> **Venture Capitalist**

> "Quantity is not a virtue in a plan. Quantity of thought is important in an entrepreneur. But in some cases, there's an inverse correlation between the size of the plan and the quality of the plan."
>
> **Andrew Anker**
> **Venture Capitalist**

Examples of Charts to Use in Your Business Plan

Here are some different types of charts you can use to help convey specific information.

Bar charts work especially well when making comparisons:

Line charts are useful when demonstrating trends or drawing comparisons:

Pie charts are ideal for showing the specific breakdowns of products sold, markets, etc:

Flow charts illustrate development patterns and organization of authority.

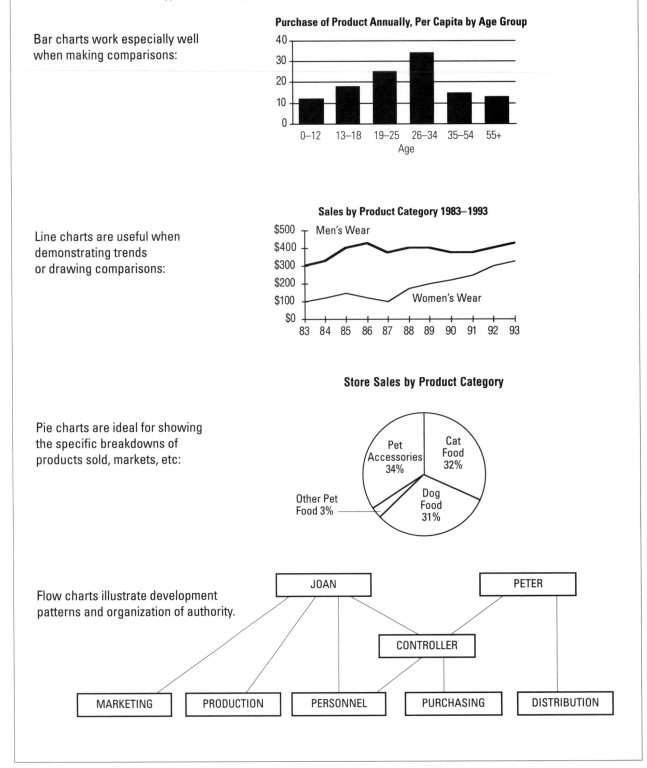

Chapter Summary

When researching and preparing your plan, look for information and statistics that will enable you to make the most positive impression on a reader in less than five minutes. Find items that will be visually interesting and attractive; use bullet points, charts, and other devices to bring attention to your most impressive information. Use numbers to support your conclusions. Keep your language believable, and use supportive comments from credible and authoritative sources. In every case, be accurate and do not make mistakes of fact.

Section II

Business Plan Components

## Chapter 4

The Executive Summary

If they don't get it at first, they won't get it at all.

The Executive Summary Is Crucial

Without a doubt, the single most important portion of your business plan is the Executive Summary. Only a clear, concise, and compelling condensation of your business right up front will persuade readers to wade through the rest of your plan. No matter how beneficial your product, how lucrative your market, or how innovative your manufacturing techniques, it is your Executive Summary alone that persuades a reader to spend the time to find out about your product, market, and techniques.

Write Your Summary Last

Because of this, it is imperative that you prepare the Executive Summary last. Although it appears first in your completed document, the Summary reflects the results of all your planning and should be crafted only after careful consideration of all other aspects of your business.

The Executive Summary is so important, in fact, that some venture capitalists prefer to receive just a Summary and Financials before reviewing an entire plan. If you want to send out only a "concept paper" to gauge investor interest before submitting a complete business plan, the Executive Summary should serve as that document. As important as the financial considerations are to investors and bankers, it is the Executive Summary that first convinces them that yours is a well-conceived and potentially successful business strategy.

"A good Executive Summary gives me a sense of why this is an interesting venture. I look for a very clear statement of their long-term mission, an overview of the people, the technology, and the fit to market. Answer these questions: 'What is it? Who's going to build it? Why will anyone buy it?' To paraphrase the movie Field of Dreams, we want to know, 'If we fund it, will they (buyers) come?'"

Ann Winblad
Venture Capitalist

Even if your business plan is for internal use only, the Executive Summary is still crucial. The Summary is the place where you bring all your thoughts and planning together, where you make a whole out of the disparate parts of your business, and where you "sum up" all that you propose. So, if you have not yet completed the other sections of your plan, proceed to the next chapter and return to the Executive Summary when you have finished the rest of your plan.

What to Convey in Your Executive Summary

The Executive Summary gives the reader a chance to understand the basic concept and highlights of your business quickly, and to decide whether to commit more time to reading the entire plan. Therefore, your goal in the Executive Summary is to motivate and entice the reader.

To do so, you want to convey your own sense of optimism about your business. This does not mean using "hype"; it simply means using a positive, confident tone and demonstrating that you are well-positioned to exploit a compelling market opportunity.

In a short space, you must let the reader know that:

- Your basic business concept makes sense.
- Your business itself has been thoroughly planned.
- The management is capable.
- A clear-cut market exists.
- Your business incorporates significant competitive advantages.
- Your financial projections are realistic.
- Investors or lenders have an excellent chance to make money.

If someone reading your Executive Summary concludes that all the elements above exist in your business, that person will almost certainly commit to reading the rest of your business plan.

Targeting the Summary

Ask yourself: "Who will be reading my business plan?" You can improve your chances for a positive reception if you know the answer to that question before you prepare your Executive Summary. Since the Summary is what the reader reads first (and perhaps is the only portion read at all), try to find out what "buttons" to push. Is the bank mostly interested in managers who have had previous business successes? Is the venture capital firm particularly interested in patentable new technology? Does the division president like to see new markets for existing products?

Do a little homework on your potential recipients (see Chapters 18 and 19, Preparing, Presenting & Sending Out Your Plan, and Looking for Money) and then organize your Executive Summary so the issues most important to each recipient are given precedence.

"In a business plan, I want to know the answers to these questions: 'What are they going to sell, to whom, and how?' In other words, what is the marketing aspect of the business? What sales force, advertising, and other marketing techniques are they going to use? And secondly, what are the costs? I want to know manufacturing or sourcing costs. How reliable and stable are these costs? At what costs will they sell their products or services? I want to see believable costs and believable pricing."

Robert Mahoney
Corporate Banker

Be careful, however, not to tailor the Executive Summary for just one person at a bank or venture capital firm; your plan is likely to end up in the hands of someone else. Target your Summary to address institutional concerns rather than individual preferences.

The Two Types of Executive Summary

Depending on the nature of your business and the capability of the writer, you can approach the Executive Summary in one of two ways: the synopsis Summary or the narrative Summary.

The Synopsis Summary

A synopsis Summary is the more straightforward of the two: It simply relates, in abbreviated fashion, the conclusions of each section of the completed business plan. Its advantage is that it is relatively easy to prepare and less dependent on a talented writer. The only disadvantage is that the tone of a "synopsis" Summary tends to be rather dry.

The synopsis-style Executive Summary covers all aspects of your business plan and treats each of them relatively equally, although briefly. In addition, it tells the reader what you are asking for in the way of financing — which you also state in your cover letter.

The Narrative Summary

The narrative Summary is more like telling the reader a story; it can convey greater drama and excitement in presenting your business. However, it takes a capable writer to prepare a narrative Summary that communicates the necessary information, engenders enthusiasm, and yet does not cross over the line into hyperbole.

A narrative Executive Summary is useful for businesses that break new ground, either with a new product, new market, or new operational techniques that require considerable explanation. It is also more appropriate for businesses that have one dominant element — such as holding an important patent or the participation of a well-known entrepreneur — that can be highlighted. Finally, the narrative Executive Summary works well for companies with interesting or impressive backgrounds or histories.

A narrative-style Executive Summary has fewer sections than the synopsis Summary. Greater emphasis is placed on the business' concept and distinctive features, and less attention is given to operational details.

With a narrative Summary, you want to get the reader excited about your company; you do this by taking the one or two most impressive features of your company and giving the reader an understanding of how those features will lead to business success.

A narrative Summary may do more "scene-setting" — recounting the sociological or technological changes that have led to the development of your company's products or services — than a synopsis Summary. It may be more personal, telling how the founders' relevant experiences motivated them to start the company.

"You need a business plan so you have a Bible of what you're going to do in your business, a clear statement of your company's mission. The important thing in a business plan is to tell the truth. If there's a problem, we (the venture capitalists) are going to learn it anyway, so it's better if you don't try to hide it."

Ann Winblad
Venture Capitalist

You may place the topics of a narrative Summary in any order that best showcases your company. The topics do not have to be covered equally; the business concept may be described in three paragraphs and the management team in only one or two sentences. Printing topic headings is not necessary, although you may do so if you wish.

You may likewise place the topics of a synopsis Summary in the most advantageous order. Most businesses are well served by a synopsis Summary, especially if the business concept is easily understood and the marketing and operations relatively standard. A synopsis is a very businesslike approach, and experienced business plan readers are comfortable reviewing such straightforward Executive Summaries.

Writing the Summary

Clear, strong writing pays off in the Executive Summary more than in any other section of your business plan. A dynamic, logical writing style can make the difference between a plan being considered or being discarded.

If you are unsure about your own writing ability, consider hiring a professional writer for the Summary or asking help from a friend or family member who is a good writer. Writing style is less important in a synopsis than in the narrative approach to an Executive Summary, and if your writing ability is limited, use the synopsis form for your Summary.

Length and Design of the Summary

The great advantage to the reader of the Executive Summary is that it is short. A busy funder must be able to read your Summary in less than five minutes. Thus, an Executive Summary should be no more than two to three pages in length. A one-page Summary is perfectly acceptable.

Refer to Chapter 18, "Preparing, Presenting & Sending Out Your Plan," for tips on page layout. Remember to use white space to make the page less intimidating. Bullet points can also be used effectively in the Summary. Since you are limited to so few pages, it may seem frustrating to have to give up space for visual considerations, but these techniques make your plan more inviting to the reader.

Use the Plan Preparation Forms on the next few pages to develop your Executive Summary; there is one for the synopsis type of Summary and one for the narrative type. A Sample Plan of each kind of Executive Summary is also provided.

Chapter Summary

Your Executive Summary is the single most important part of your business plan; it must motivate the reader to consider your plan as a whole. Target your Summary for particular readers and use the style of Summary, either synopsis or narrative, best suited for your business and writing ability. Prepare your Executive Summary last, only after your entire plan is completed.

Synopsis Executive Summary Plan Preparation Form

Take highlights from each section of your completed plan and address the areas listed below. Remember to be brief and clear. Cover each topic in no more than one to three sentences. Describe only the most important and impressive features of your business. After the first two topics, Company Description and Statement of Mission, place the remaining sections in any order that gives the best impression of your business to your target reader. For the reader's quick comprehension, print topic headings at the beginning of each paragraph (see the Sample Plan at the end of this chapter). If you'd like a Summary that seems less like a list, omit the headings. Feel free to combine related topics, such as "Target Market" and "Marketing Strategy," to create a more fluid document.

Company Description: List the company name, type of business, location, and legal status, e.g., corporation, sole proprietorship, partnership. _____

_____

_____

Statement of Mission: Write the concise statement of company purpose you developed in Chapter 5, Company Description. _____

_____

_____

Stage of Development: State whether your company is a startup or continuing business, when it was founded, how far along the product or service is in its creation, and if you've already made sales or started shipping.

_____

_____

_____

Products and Services: List the products or services your company sells or plans to sell; this can be generic for a company with many products, e.g., women's sportswear, or specific for a company with just a few.

_____

_____

_____

Target Market(s): List the markets you intend to reach and why you chose them; indicate the results of any market analysis or market research. _____

_____

_____

Marketing and Sales Strategy: Briefly describe how you intend to reach your target market(s), and the advertising, direct mail, trade shows, and other methods you will use to secure sales. _____

_____

_____

Synopsis Executive Summary Plan Preparation Form (continued)

Competitors and Market Distribution: Indicate the nature of your competition and how the market is currently divided. _____

_____

_____

Competitive Advantages and Distinctions: Show why your company will be able to compete successfully; list any important distinctions, such as patents, major contracts, or letters-of-intent. _____

_____

_____

_____

Management: Briefly describe the histories and capabilities of your management team, particularly those of company founders. _____

_____

_____

_____

Operations: Outline your key operational features, such as locations, crucial distributors or suppliers, cost-saving production techniques, etc. _____

_____

_____

Financials: Indicate your company's expected revenues and profits for years one through three. _____

_____

_____

_____

Long-Term Goals: Describe the expected status, e.g., sales, number of employees, number of locations, market share of your company five years from now. _____

_____

_____

Funds Sought and Exit Strategy: Indicate how much money you are seeking, how many investors you plan to have, how the funds raised will be used, and how investors or lenders will get their money out. _____

_____

_____

Use this information as the basis of your plan's synopsis Executive Summary.

Narrative Executive Summary Plan Preparation Form

This form provides you an opportunity to outline the Executive Summary portion of your business plan if you choose to write a narrative type of Summary.

The Company: Describe how your company is organized, its stage of development, stage of product creation, legal status, location, and company mission. _____

_____

_____

_____

_____

_____

_____

The Concept: Explain the background of your company, how the product came about, how the market opportunity was recognized, the products and services. _____

_____

_____

_____

_____

_____

_____

Market Opportunity: Describe your target market, market trends that exist, why there was a need for the company, the results of market research, the competition, and market openings. _____

_____

_____

_____

_____

_____

_____

Competitive Advantages and Distinctions: Indicate why your company can compete successfully; list important distinctions such as patents, major contracts, and letters-of-intent; specify barriers-to-entry for new competitors.

_____

_____

_____

_____

_____

Narrative Executive Summary Plan Preparation Form (continued)

Management Team: Describe the background and capabilities of your key managers, and relate past successful business experiences. _____

_____

_____

_____

_____

_____

_____

_____

_____

Milestones: List the milestones by which you will measure success and at what date you expect to reach them; these might include specific revenue or profit levels, the percentage of market share reached, shipments of first product, and the number of employees or locations. _____

_____

_____

_____

_____

_____

_____

_____

_____

_____

Financials: Specify the amount of funds sought, the number of likely investors, the use of funds secured, and how investors or lenders will get their money back — through an exit plan (acquisition, public offering, merger) or security (collateral) for a loan. _____

_____

_____

_____

_____

_____

_____

_____

Use this information as the basis of your plan's narrative Executive Summary.

SAMPLE PLAN: Synopsis Executive Summary

Executive Summary

The Company

ComputerEase, Incorporated, is an Indiana-based company providing computer software training services to corporations in the greater Vespucci, Indiana, area. Technology-related business services are among the fastest growing and healthiest areas of the economy, and ComputerEase intends to capitalize on the opportunities in that area. The company's stock is currently held by President Scott E. Connors and Vice President Susan Alexander.

States legal status, location, stock ownership, and industry opportunity.

The Company's Mission

ComputerEase views its mission as increasing the corporate community's productivity by helping them realize the maximum benefit from their personnel and computers through software training. ComputerEase is dedicated to building long-term relationships with customers through quality training and support, and to being known as the premiere software training company in the greater Vespucci area. The goal is steady expansion, becoming profitable by the third year of operations.

Provides a sense of how the company views itself and its long-term goals.

Products and Services

The company provides software training seminars targeted to the corporate market. Classes are conducted either at the customer's place of business or at ComputerEase's training center. Additionally, weekend classes are offered to the general public. Training is offered for all leading software programs or ComputerEase will devise custom programs at corporate customers' requests.

Marketing and Sales Strategy

ComputerEase differentiates itself in the market by aiming to satisfy not only students in the training classes, but the actual customers: the corporate clients. The company does this by emphasizing training that increases productivity and by providing comprehensive ongoing service and followup to the corporate customer. Sales are secured predominantly through face-to-face solicitation.

The Competition

No market leaders have yet emerged in the corporate software training field, and competition is diverse and uneven, creating substantial market opportunities. ComputerEase maintains the following advantages over existing competition: ongoing local support to clients, a strong marketing emphasis on increasing customers' productivity, a coordinated marketing program, professional image, authorization from software publishers, qualified management, consistent quality of training, and the availability of the ComputerEase training center.

Shows market opportunity.

Target Market

ComputerEase operates in the greater Vespucci area, targeting large and medium-sized businesses with high computer use. Vespucci is the 16th largest

SAMPLE PLAN: Synopsis Executive Summary (continued)

city in the United States, with a diverse and healthy economy. Reliable sources estimate that more than 10,000 companies and institutions with more than 50 employees are located in the area.

Management

Emphasizes past business ownership and directly related experience.

President and Founder Scott E. Connors brings significant technology-related management experience to his position and previously co-owned his own computer retail outlet. Immediately before starting ComputerEase, Mr. Connors served as Regional Vice-President for Chanoff's Computer Emporium, a large computer hardware retail chain. Earlier, he was a sales representative for IBM. Vice President Susan Alexander brings direct experience in marketing to, and contacts with, the target market from her prior position as Assistant Marketing Director for AlwaysHere Health Care Plan and sales experience as Sales Representative for SpeakUp Dictation Equipment.

Operations

On August 1, 2003, ComputerEase opened its first corporate training center with 10 personal computer stations. The company offers corporate training sessions at this center as well as at the customer's place of business. It plans to open a second training center by January 1, 2004. ComputerEase utilizes the excess capacity of the training center by offering Saturday classes to the noncorporate community. All training equipment is leased, and training materials are produced by the "just-in-time" method to reduce costs.

Stage of Development

ComputerEase began operations in January 2003, and opened its first Software training center classroom in August 2003.

Financials

Tells investors there is no return on capital for at least three years.

The financial strategy of ComputerEase emphasizes reinvestment of income for growth during the first few years of operation, with the company reaching profitability by year three. Annual revenue projections for the current year are $233,000; for 2004, $493,875; and for 2005, $818,615.

Funds Sought and Utilization

Uses specific numbers and uses for funds.

The company is currently seeking $80,000 in investment financing. These funds will be used for expansion activities, including the opening of an additional training center, hiring of new staff, and increasing marketing activities. Long-term plans call for the company to either develop a franchise operation or expand to become a regional chain, adding at least one training location annually.

SAMPLE PLAN: Narrative Executive Summary

Executive Summary

The Concept

Technology-related business services are among the fastest growing industries in the United States. The explosion of the use of computers in virtually every business setting has provided unprecedented opportunities to companies providing support and services for computer equipment. Because the field is relatively new, market leaders have not yet emerged, and customer loyalty has not yet been established. This enables a well-conceived and well-executed company to secure a leading position in the field.

Provides a sense of the health and opportunities of industry.

Background

Scott E. Connors, President and Founder of ComputerEase, Incorporated, recognized this opportunity when, as Regional Vice President for Chanoff's Computer Emporium, he conducted a study of the potential market for corporate software training in the Indiana, Ohio, and Illinois areas. As a result of this study, he realized that a professionally managed software training company could quickly become the region's market leader.

Gives history of motivation for business.

The Company

ComputerEase is positioned to become the premiere provider of corporate software training targeted to the corporate market. The company began operation in January 2003, and was quickly able to secure corporate clients with software training programs offered at the customer's location.

Tells developmental stage, products and services, long-term goals, legal status, and ownership.

The client base expanded when ComputerEase opened its first Training Center in August 2003, with 10 personal computer stations, allowing corporations to send their employees off-site for computer instruction. ComputerEase offers software training for all leading software programs, as well as custom programs at corporate customers' request. Additionally, the company offers Saturday classes to the general public.

ComputerEase is incorporated in the state of Indiana and stock is currently held by Mr. Connors and Vice President Susan Alexander.

The Market

The company targeted large corporations in the greater Vespucci, Indiana, area as the base of its initial operations. As the 16th largest city in the United States, Vespucci offers a diverse and healthy economy. More than 10,000 companies employ more than 50 employees.

Competitive Position

Currently corporate software training programs are offered in the Vespucci area by small, local, underfunded, and generally poorly managed companies

SAMPLE PLAN: Narrative Executive Summary (continued)

and through national programs providing no local support or sales. Market research indicates an extremely high level of dissatisfaction with current providers among current customers of software training. ComputerEase's coordinated marketing program to the corporate community, professional image, outstanding training, emphasis on training for business productivity, and its ongoing customer support sets the company apart from its competition.

Management Team

Emphasizes previous business ownership and related experience.

The current management of President Scott E. Connors and Vice President of Marketing Susan Alexander gives ComputerEase an excellent team with which to begin operations. Mr. Connors brings extensive technology-related management and sales experience from his years with Chanoff's Computer Emporium and IBM. Connors successfully managed his own business as a co-owner of Chanoff's downtown Vespucci retail store. He sold his interest in that store to finance the founding of ComputerEase.

In her position as Assistant Marketing Director for AlwaysHere Health Plan, Ms. Alexander gained significant experience in sales and marketing to ComputerEase's target market: corporate human resource directors. Her personal connections with this target audience are extensive, giving ComputerEase immediate access to the potentially most lucrative clients.

The Future

Provides investors with a sense of growth opportunities.

Long-term development calls for the company to progress in one of two directions. One, the company may become a franchise operation, selling franchise licenses, materials, and training for independent operations under the ComputerEase name. Two, ComputerEase may expand its own company-owned and -operated training centers throughout the Midwest region, becoming the dominant regional software training provider.

Financials

The company projects rapid growth, with sales revenues of $233,000 in 2003, $493,875 in 2004, and $818,615 in 2005. It emphasizes the reinvestment of income for expansion rather than profit taking, funding growth internally rather than through additional investment beyond that currently sought.

Funds Sought

Gives specific numbers and uses of funds.

The company anticipates only one round of financing (unless franchising is later undertaken) with $80,000 being sought from one investor. These funds will be utilized to add a new training center, hire staff, and expand marketing activities.

## Chapter 5

Company Description

*The reason most businesses fail is because
they don't understand the business they are in.*

Conveying the Basics of Your Business

Before you can discuss the more complex aspects of your business and the
meatier sections of your business plan, such as marketing strategy or new
technology, you must first inform the reader of the basic details of your
business. The object of this section is to convey information such as your
legal status, ownership, products or services, company mission and milestones achieved to date.

The Company Description may be relatively simple to complete, especially if you have been in business for some time. However, the simplicity
may be deceptive, particularly if yours is a new company. Many of these
basic issues require a lot of thought and planning. For instance, you may
find yourself spending a great deal of time trying to choose a business
name or deciding on which legal form your company should take.

If yours is a start-up company, you may feel you don't have the information to complete each category. As an example, you may not yet have
rented an office or legally incorporated. In that case, write down what you
intend to do. You might include information about your current situation
as well. Thus, you might say, "Rocket Science Technology will be headquartered in Austin, Texas with a manufacturing facility in Luckenbach,
Texas. Currently, the company's address is 1234 Bruce Springsteen Street,
San Antonio, TX 78216.

The most challenging aspect of the Company Description section is likely to be developing a "Mission Statement," which concisely describes the goals, objectives, and underlying principles of your company. A Mission Statement enables you and readers of your business plan to get a better picture of where you intend to go with your business, and it helps you more clearly articulate exactly what business you are in.

The following topics should be addressed in the Company Description section of your business plan.

Company Name

In many cases, the name of your company or corporation is not the same as the name(s) you use when doing business with the public. You may actually have a number of different "names" associated with your business, including:

- Your own name
- The legal corporate or company name
- A "dba" ("doing business as")
- Brand name(s)
- Model name(s)
- Subsidiary company name(s)
- Domain name(s)

The number and types of names you need depends on the kind of business you are in, how you interact with the public, whether you are incorporated, what kinds and how many products/services you have, and your own personal taste.

For instance, a company might list its legal name as AAA, Incorporated, doing business as Arnie's Diner, operating the subsidiary business, Rosie's Catering Service, selling products under the trade name "Arnie's Atomic," and operating the website www.arniesatomic.com.

If yours is a new business, and you have not yet chosen a name, consider one that meets your current needs but also gives you flexibility over the years. If you plan a company where most customers will do business with you because they know of you or your reputation, you may have no better name than your own. Many consultants, service providers, designers, etc., use just their own name. You can also combine your name with words that describe what you do, such as Erin's Editing Services.

However, using your own name or a business name that is very narrowly descriptive may limit your ability to grow, change focus, or sell the company in the future. Al's Airplane Repair is more confining than Take-off Aviation Services, or even Take-Off Transportation Services.

Having the legal rights to a memorable website or "domain" name may be a competitive business advantage, and if you have been able to secure the rights to such a name, you may want to highlight this fact in your business

"(Our mission is) To continually provide our members with quality goods and services at the lowest possible prices. In order to achieve our mission we will conduct our business with the following five responsibilities in mind: obey the law, take care of our members, take care of our employees, respect our vendors, reward our shareholders."

Mission Statement of Costco

plan. However, the mere fact of having the rights to a catchy domain name is not a business in and of itself.

In your business plan, include the legal name of your company and any brand or trade names, dba's, subsidiary company, and domain names.

Company's Objectives/Statement of Mission

Many, if not most, successful large companies describe the main goal of their internal planning process as articulating and clarifying their "philosophy" or "mission." The best, most effective, Mission Statements are not mere empty words, but principles and objectives that guide all other aspects and activities of the business.

You should be able to sum up the basic objectives and philosophy of your company in just a few sentences. One statement should encapsulate the nature of your business, your business principles, your financial goals, your "corporate culture," and how you expect to have your company viewed in the marketplace.

A Statement of Mission provides focus for your company and should be the defining concept of your business for at least the next few years. It should be the result of a meaningful examination of the foundations of your company, and virtually every word should be important.

A finished Mission Statement might be: "AAA, Inc., is a spunky, imaginative food products and service company aimed at offering high-quality, moderately priced, occasionally unusual foods using only natural ingredients. We view ourselves as partners with our customers, our employees, our community, and our environment, and we take personal responsibility in our actions towards each. We aim to become a regionally recognized brand name, capitalizing on the sustained interest in Southwestern and Mexican food. Our goal is moderate growth, annual profitability, and maintaining our sense of humor."

The Statement of Mission worksheet on pages 62–63 helps you outline your company's objectives.

Legal Issues

In forming a business, there are many critical legal issues for you to address. One of the first is which type of legal entity to choose for your company. Businesses often start as a sole proprietorship or a partnership. This has the advantage of being easy, since there may be no papers to file with the state. Being incorporated, on the other hand, provides you and your investors with much greater protection from personal liability. Most investors (and some lenders) are usually more comfortable dealing with an incorporated entity.

If you choose to incorporate, you will still have many decisions. What form of corporation will you choose? In what state will you incorporate? How many shares in your corporation will be issued, and to whom? Legal

"We ask each division to define its own Mission, as well as having an overall corporate Mission Statement. The statement is only a few paragraphs and is descriptive of what we're trying to accomplish. It's reviewed each year, but we discourage minor changes in the mission statement. The corporate mission statement hasn't been changed for five or six years now."

George James
Former Sr. V.P. & CFO
Levi Strauss & Co.

"Kaizen is the cornerstone of the company. This is a philosophy of continuous pursuit of improvement. We believe small, continuous improvements create greater value than anticipating major leaps. We can never stand still. We have a program of employee suggestions and rewards. We receive over 10,000 suggestions per year. The challenge to managers is to get a higher percentage of employees making workable suggestions. In Toyota's plants in Japan, on average, every employee submits a suggestion per month."

Michael Damer
New United Motor
Manufacturing Inc.

Statement of Mission

Describe your company's philosophy in terms of the areas listed below.

Range/Nature of Products/Services Offered:

One-on-one to group personal training

Quality: Top of the line

Price: $60's for 1 hour & $40's for ½ Hour

Varies for group training

Service: Top of the line

Customer service is top priority

Overall Relationship to Customer:

Close relationships

Management Style/Relationship to Employees:

Hands off

Give them a role, train them to let them do it

Nature of Work Environment:

Fun, relaxed, comfortable, intimate, clean

Relationship to Rest of Industry:

More upscale & value/emotion driven

More concentrated on giving what people want then just
what they need

Incorporation of New Technology/Other New Developments:

Growth/Profitability Goals: Grow to $20k/month then open next location.
2nd location w/in 1 year of opening

$3-5k profits/month/location @ $40k revenue

Relationship to Community/Environment/Other Social Goals:

The community expert

Other Personal/Management Goals:

concerns and agreements will have a profound impact on the future of your company.

In addition to the legal form of your business, there are many other legal considerations and issues to address in your business plan. Have you entered into licensing or distribution agreements? Have you secured trademarks, patents, copyrights or other legal instruments that may protect your proprietary business assets?

Here is an example of how to handle the legal description of a business: "AAA, Inc., is incorporated in the state of California, licensed to do business in Jackson County, California. The three shareholders — Arnie Matthews, Brendan Muir, and Aaron Joshua — each own 33 1/3% of the total shares in the company. The company has secured U.S. trademarks to the name "Arnie's Atomic Foods," which is used on its food product line, and to the Triple A Shooting Star logo. AAA, Inc. has entered into a three-year, exclusive distribution agreement with BBB Distributors, the largest distributors of Mexican and Southwestern foods in the Southwest."

The worksheet, Legal Issues is included on pages 65–66 to help you identify key legal concerns.

Products and Services

This part of your business plan can be relatively short, or it can be an entire section of its own. If your products or services are particularly technical, complicated, innovative, or proprietary, you will want to spend considerable time describing them. This is especially true if you are seeking funding for a new product or service and potential funders are likely to be motivated by the specifics.

In this part of your plan, clearly identify and describe the nature of the products or services you provide. Be fairly specific, but if you have a large line of products or services, you do not need to list each one, as long as you indicate the general categories. Also indicate future products or services planned by your company and when you expect to introduce them.

If you are developing an innovative product or service, particularly a technology product, you must walk a fine line in describing its details. While you must provide sufficient detail both to give a clear idea of what your product does and to inspire confidence that it actually achieves its intended purpose, you do not want to disclose sensitive information. Even if a reader of your business plan has signed a Non-Disclosure Agreement (see Chapter 18), be extremely cautious of putting highly proprietary or technical details in your written document. These can be disclosed at a later stage of discussions.

Once again using the fictional AAA, Inc., the 'Products/Services' section might read: "Arnie's Diner is a full-service restaurant specializing in Mexican and Southwestern cuisine. Rosie's Catering Services provides catering for both business and personal occasions. The Arnie's Atomic food line currently consists of seven shelf-stable chili and salsa products.

Legal Issues

Legal Form

What is the legal form of your company currently?

☐ Sole proprietorship   ☐ Limited Liability Company

☐ Partnership   ☐ No legal entity/status

☐ Subchapter S Corporation   ☐ Other, describe: _____

☐ C Corporation   _____

What is the intended legal form if different from above?

☐ Sole proprietorship   ☐ Limited Liability Company

☐ Partnership   ☐ Other, describe: _____

☐ Subchapter S Corporation   _____

☐ C Corporation   _____

Ownership

If a sole proprietor or partnership, list the owners: _____

_____

_____

If incorporated, how many shares of stock have been issued? _____

_____

_____

Who owns the stock and in what amounts? _____

_____

_____

In which state(s), province(s), country(s), etc. are you legally incorporated or registered to do business, list dates and specifics: _____

_____

_____

_____

Have you secured written agreements between/with:

☐ Principals, partners   ☐ Key employees/management

☐ Suppliers   ☐ Customers

☐ Investors   ☐ Strategic Partners

continued on next page

Legal Issues (continued)

List which of the following you have secured, include dates and specifics:

Trademarks: _____

_____

Copyrights: _____

_____

Patents: _____

_____

Domain names: _____

_____

List investments to date, including dates and terms: _____

_____

_____

_____

List loans or any other debts, including dates and terms: _____

_____

_____

_____

List property leases, purchase agreements, etc, including dates and terms: _____

_____

_____

_____

List equipment leases, purchase agreements, etc., including dates and terms: _____

_____

_____

_____

List any distribution or licensing agreements, including dates and terms: _____

_____

_____

_____

List other strategic partnerships, arrangements, etc., including dates and terms: _____

_____

_____

_____

We anticipate releasing a line of four packaged Southwestern spice mixtures in the next six months. In the second year of this plan, we anticipate introducing a line of tortilla chips."

Management/Leadership

Next, include the name of the chairperson of the board of directors, president, and/or chief executive officer. If there are other key members of management, especially those that might be known to potential investors, list their names here. Also, if you have a board of directors, advisory board, or other governing entity, indicate how many people serve on that body and how frequently it meets. If the membership of these bodies is particularly impressive, include their names; otherwise, it is not necessary to do so.

Business Location

List the location of your company's headquarters, main place of business (if different), and any branch locations. If you have more than one or two branches, you can list just the total number (although you might want to include a complete list in your plan's appendix). If you have not yet secured a location but intend to do so, indicate the general whereabouts of your intended operation. Also, it is very important to describe the geographical area your company serves.

For instance, state: "The corporate offices of AAA, Inc., are located at 123 Amelia Earhart Drive, Jackson, California. Arnie's Diner is located at 456 Lincoln Street in Jackson. Rosie's Catering Services operates from the diner and serves the entire Jackson County area. Arnie's Atomic food products will be produced at a plant to be leased in Jackson and will be sold in five Southwestern states."

Development Stage and Milestones Achieved to Date

Someone reading your business plan should be able to get a clear sense of how far along your company is in its development, and what progress you have made in building the company.

Even start-up companies often have a record of accomplishments. You may have already developed technology, raised seed funding, lined up strategic partnerships, or secured indications of interest from key customers. Showing the progress you've achieved to date inspires confidence in your ability to develop your company further and indicates the level of commitment you have made to your business. You will want to clearly indicate any positive milestones you've achieved.

Begin by stating when the company was founded. Next, indicate your phase of development: a seed company (with a business concept but without a product or service finalized); a startup (in early stages of operation); expansion (adding new products, services, or branches); retrenchment (consolidating or repositioning product lines); or established (maintaining market share and product positioning).

"Some potential milestones a business plan could indicate include product completion, product testing, first customer shipment, unit volume goals, company infrastructure developments, core agreements reached, and second product shipping."

Ann Winblad
Venture Capitalist

Indicate how far along your plans have progressed. Has the product been developed or tested? Have orders been placed or the product shipped? Are leases signed or suppliers secured? What have been the past milestones and successes of current operations? If you earlier set specific goals with target dates, indicate if you met those objectives.

A "Milestones Achieved" worksheet is included in Chapter 15, and you may wish to take highlights from that worksheet to include in your Company Description section of your business plan.

Using the above example of AAA, Inc., this section might read: "Arnie's Diner opened in 1999, and the company began packaging food products used in the restaurant in 2001. These were initially sold in grocery stores on a local basis. In January 2002, the company set an annual sales goal of $60,000 for the 'Arnie's Atomic' line of packaged food and exceeded that goal, achieving $103,000 in gross sales in 2002. In 2003, sales of packaged food products rose to $237,000. A leading distributor has been secured to sell 'Arnie's Atomic' products to grocery and specialty stores in five Southwestern states. The first orders have been received, placed, and renewed, and the company now plans to expand its production facilities to accommodate increased sales and develop new products."

Financial Status

You also want to give a brief idea of the status of your company in financial and personnel terms. For example, readers will want to know how you have been funded to date and any major financial obligations. You should also indicate any loans or investments you have received and on what terms. If you are seeking funding, briefly indicate how much money you seek and for what purpose. You will expand on your financial obligations and use of funds sought in the Financials section of your plan.

Thus, this section might read: "AAA, Inc., has maintained overall profitability through slow, careful expansion of its component companies. Total gross revenue for the previous year was approximately $1,247,000. Rosie's Catering is presently the most profitable, last year showing a profit of $128,000 on sales of $525,000; Arnie's Diner showed a profit of $81,000 on sales of $485,000; Arnie's Atomic Foods projects a current year loss of $77,000 on sales of $237,000. Currently the total work force is five full-time employees and seven part-time employees. We are now seeking to expand the production facilities, add employees, and increase our sales and marketing efforts. To do so, we are seeking an additional $500,000 in capital."

Chapter Summary

Your plan's Company Description communicates the basic details of your business in a brief form. From the Company Description section, a reader gets a clear idea of what your company is about, its legal status, how far along you have developed, and what you plan to do. The Statement of Mission shows that you understand the focus of your company and can articulate your objectives concisely.

Company Description Plan Preparation Form

List facts about your business according to the categories below.

Names

Legal/Corporate Name: _____

Doing Business As: _____

Brand/Trade/Domain Names: _____

_____

Subsidiary Companies: _____

Legal Form

Legal Form of Business: _____

State Incorporated (if incorporated): _____

County in Which Business is Licensed: _____

Owner(s) of Company or Major Shareholders: _____

Management/Leadership

Chairperson of the Board: _____

President: _____

Chief Executive Officer: _____

Other Key Management Members: _____

_____

_____

Governing/Advisory Bodies: _____

_____

Number of Members: _____

Location

Company Headquarters: _____

Place of Business: _____

Branches: _____

Geographic Area Served: _____

Developmental Stage

When Company was Founded: _____

continued on next page

Company Description Plan Preparation Form (continued)

Stage of Formation or Immediate Goals: _____

_____

When Product or Service was Introduced: _____

Progress of Current Plans and Milestones Reached: _____

_____

Other Developmental Indicators: _____

_____

Financial Status

Last year's Total Sales: _____

Last year's Pretax Profit: _____

Sales and Profitability by Division or Product Line: _____

_____

Current Number of Employees: _____

Amount of Funds Sought: _____

Basic Use of Funds Sought: _____

Previous Funding and Major Financial Obligations: _____

_____

Products and Services

General Product/Service Description: _____

_____

Number and Type of Lines: _____

_____

Number of Products or Services in Each Line: _____

_____

Patents and Licenses

Patents Held/Pending: _____

Trademarks Held/Pending: _____

Licenses Held/Pending: _____

Copyrights Held/Pending: _____

Use this information as the basis of your plan's Company Description section.

SAMPLE PLAN: Company Description

Company Description

ComputerEase, Incorporated is an Indiana-based company providing computer software training services to businesses in the greater Vespucci, Indiana, area. Corporate headquarters and the software training center are located at 987 South Main Street, Vespucci, Indiana.

Tells company basics: incorporation, location, services.

The Company's Mission

Our goal is to increase the customers' business productivity by helping them realize the maximum benefit from their personnel and computers. We do this by offering training programs of consistently high quality with an unequalled staff, and backing our programs with ongoing support. We are a service company, dedicated to long-term relationships with our customers. We aim to be known as the premiere software training company in the greater Vespucci area. Our development goals are for steady expansion, with profitability by the third year.

States how the company intends to distinguish itself to customers.

Services

The company offers software training seminars for all leading business software programs, as well as devises custom training programs. These classes are targeted to the corporate market, and training is conducted at the customer's place of business or at the training center. Saturday classes are offered at the training center for the general public.

Prior to opening the training center, the company was limited in the services it could offer potential clients. The most lucrative business, continuing corporate contracts, was severely restricted, and no public seminars could be offered. Nevertheless, in the first nine months of operation, the company conducted 21 on-site training programs and three Saturday public training programs, and secured continuing training contracts with three of the primary target corporate customers. This produced revenues of $85,500 through August 2003.

Shows how the company has grown and established revenues.

The company projects deficits for the first two years of operation, with income reinvested for expansion. We anticipate that the company will be profitable by the third year. In these three years, our goal is to become the premiere software training company in the greater Vespucci area. Trends in training, however, are toward nationally-known and online providers, so the company anticipates either joining or starting a national franchise and/or offering online training by year three.

Provides specific financial development data.

The company owns the trademark to the name ComputerEase, under which it does business, and to the slogan "We Speak Your Language."

Development to Date

Founded in January 2003 by Scott E. Connors, ComputerEase began operation by providing software training at customers' sites. In August 2003, the company opened its first software training center, at its present location. In March 2003, Susan Alexander became Vice President for Marketing. Ms. Alexander immediately began an extensive marketing program, targeting 200 large companies in the Vespucci area.

Legal Status and Ownership

Gives clear picture of current ownership and equity available.

ComputerEase is incorporated under the laws of the state of Indiana. Ten thousand shares in the company have been issued: 6,000 are owned by President and CEO Scott E. Connors; 1,000 are owned by Vice President of Marketing, Susan Alexander; and 3,000 shares are retained by the company for future distribution.

Funding of the company to date has come from the personal savings of Mr. Connors, a $15,000 loan from Connors' family members, and from the income generated by sales. The company is now seeking $80,000 from outside investors. These funds will be used to add a classroom, hire payroll trainers and additional staff, and expand marketing activities.

## Chapter 6

Industry Analysis & Trends

A company must know both how it is
like, and how it is unlike, other businesses.

Your Business and Industry

No company operates in a vacuum. Every business is part of a larger, overall industry; the forces that affect your industry as a whole will inevitably affect your business as well. Evaluating your industry increases your own knowledge of the factors that contribute to your company's success and shows potential investors that you understand external business conditions.

An industry consists of all companies supplying a similar product or service, other businesses closely related to that product or service, and supply and distribution systems supporting such companies. For example, the apparel industry comprises companies making finished clothing, including the fabric and notion suppliers, independent sales representatives and clothing marts, trade publications, and retail outlets.

In this chapter, you are given the tools to examine your industry. Most of the forms are for your internal planning use, and once you complete them, you will have the information necessary to prepare your Industry Analysis. In your plan, you want to focus on:

- A description of your industry;
- Trends in your industry; and
- Strategic opportunities that exist in your industry.

Naturally, you will need to do some research to get this information. For guidance in your research endeavors, see Chapter 2.

> "Doing an industry analysis reinforced our initial business premise. The analysis showed restaurants with limited menus, such as the one we planned, were the most rapidly growing segment of the industry. Looking at industry surveys, we saw the trends in eating at that time were towards smaller portions and less formal dining, particularly among the demographic group we intended to serve. So we knew we were on target."
>
> **Martha Johnson**
> **Restauranteur**

If you have been in your industry for a long time, and both you and the probable readers of your business plan are well aware of industry conditions, you may not need to spend much time on this section.

Your Economic Sector

Your economic sector is the broad category into which your industry or business falls; the four general sectors are 1) service; 2) manufacturing, 3) retail; and 4) distribution. Your business may belong to more than one sector; for example, you could both manufacture products for resale by others and sell them yourself at the retail level.

Economic sectors experience trends, and it's useful to note your sector's patterns. Because an economic sector is large and diverse, your business can vary dramatically from overall sector performance and trends. It is unnecessary to do a detailed analysis of your sector, but you should understand its past performance and growth projections. Study articles in business publications, and then fill in the worksheet below.

Past and Future Growth of Your Business Sector		
Business Sector	**Past Growth** (Low, Med., High)	**Future Growth** (Low, Med., High)
1. _____	_____	_____
2. _____	_____	_____
3. _____	_____	_____

Your Industry

Your business may intersect two or more industries. For instance, you may produce electronic devices utilized in new and used automobiles. Thus, you are part of three industries: electronics, new automobiles, and the automobile after-market. (The used car industry has many different issues than the new car industry.) If your business falls in more than one industry, research each of the applicable industries, giving particular weight to issues most relevant to your business. Below list the industry or industries in which your company operates.

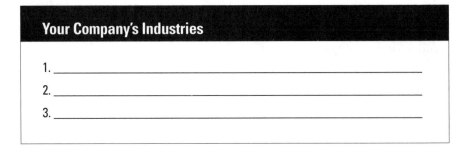

Your Company's Industries
1. _____
2. _____
3. _____

Size and Growth Rate of Your Industry

Pay particular attention to the rate at which your industry is expanding; this gives you insight into the opportunities available for your business. How does the growth rate for your industry compare with the growth of the gross domestic product (GDP), which measures the national economy? This comparison will give you an idea of the current health of your industry.

For example, if your industry is growing at 2% a year, and the GDP at 5% a year, your industry is losing ground, and opportunities will be few. However, if your industry is growing at 15% a year, while the GDP is at 5%, you are in an industry with far greater potential.

If information for your overall industry is difficult to find, you may be able to estimate its approximate size and growth by evaluating the largest companies in your field. Get copies of their annual reports or analyses from stock brokerages and read articles about them in trade and business publications.

After obtaining these basic facts about your industry, fill in the worksheet below, indicating the industry's past and projected future growth. Of course, your own company's development may differ greatly from industry averages — statistics may show that on a national scale, fewer people are dining out, yet your restaurant could be booming.

If your business plan's figures are far out of line with industry averages, you need to explain in your plan how you account for the variation.

"Look at annual reports of companies engaged in similar businesses and see what they're doing in the way of financials. Your numbers, of course, won't be the same, but the ratios should be similar. If your plan shows you doing much better than these big companies (in areas like profit margins), you won't be believable.

Eugene Kleiner
Venture Capitalist

Past and Future Growth of Your Industry					
Factor	**2 Years Ago**	**Past Year**	**This Year**	**Next Year**	**Next 5 Yrs (Avg.)**
Total Revenue					
Total Units Sold/Volume					
Total Employment					
Industry Growth Rate					
GDP Growth Rate					
Rate Compared to GDP (+ or %)					

Maturity Characteristics of Your Industry and Associated Opportunities / Risks

Growth Rate: _____

Opportunities/Risks: _____

Competition: _____

Opportunities/Risks: _____

Market Leaders/Standards: _____

Opportunities/Risks: _____

Marketing Goals: _____

Opportunities/Risks: _____

Market Share Strategy: _____

Opportunities/Risks: _____

Product Range: _____

Opportunities/Risks: _____

Customer Loyalty: _____

Opportunities/Risks: _____

"The big wineries aren't willing to spend the time and money on something that looks too small. They want to see a large number of cases sold before they move in. So we figured we had a healthy niche for a while. But as the market gets bigger, we have to either sell out to one of the big guys or we have to bring in additional financing in return for equity."

Larry Leigon
Founder, Ariel Vineyards

Industry Maturity

Industries don't remain static; they may change dramatically over time. Generally, the life cycle of an industry comprises four phases 1) new; 2) expanding; 3) stable; and 4) declining. The last phase, decline, is not inevitable; many long-standing, stable industries show no sign of decline.

Industries have distinct attributes in different stages of maturity. Even industries that seem closely related are quite dissimilar based on development stage. For instance, the soft drink industry is relatively stable, and a few major companies dominate the field. Little room exists for newcomers, and it would be extremely expensive to try to compete. On the other hand, bottled water is a developing industry with lots of competition and variation.

The Industry Maturity Chart on page 77 describes characteristics of industries in the four different stages. Examine the chart and the descriptions of the growth stages, then list the maturity characteristics of your industry and the opportunities and risks they represent on the worksheet above.

Sensitivity to Economic Cycles

Some industries are heavily dependent on strong economies, either nationally or internationally, and it is crucial to understand how vulnerable your industry is to economic conditions.

Industry Maturity Chart

Characteristic	Development Stage			
	New	**Expanding**	**Stable**	**Declining**
Growth Rate	Very High	Very High	Plateau	Minimal/None
Competition	Increasing	Shake-Out	Entrenched	Decreasing
Market Leaders/ Standards	None	In Flux/Emerging	Fixed	Contracting
Marketing Goals	Exposure and Credibility	Differentiate from Competition	Industry Leadership	Survive
Market Share Strategy	Gain Foothold	Build Market Share	Maintain Share	Cannibalize Weakened Competitors
Product Range	Limited	Expanding	Wide	Reduced
Customer Loyalty	None	Hardening	Strong	Weakening

The four stages of an industry's life cycle are described below.

New industries provide excellent entrepreneurial opportunities. Smaller companies are well-suited to respond to rapid changes, and larger companies have not yet recognized the field's potential. The market, however, is limited because customers are not yet comfortable with the product or service.

Expanding industries enjoy rapidly growing markets as customers begin to recognize the need for the product or service. Competition is brisk as well-funded companies begin to enter the field. All companies are vulnerable, even those that looked strong when the industry was new.

Stable industries have arrived at a plateau with markets leveled off at a reasonably high level. The rate of growth is slow, and customers maintain strong brand loyalty. It is relatively difficult to enter these industries.

Declining industries result from technological, demographic, and sociological changes, and from overwhelming foreign competition. Corporations leave the field or go bankrupt, and the few major companies fight to survive by stealing remaining customers from weakened competitors.

Construction, large consumer items (autos, furniture), and tourism all prosper when the economy is healthy. Industries dependent on new business formation or business expansion, such as office and technical equipment, also perform far better in good times.

Industries such as discount department stores and used-car dealerships are counter-cyclical, doing relatively better in poor economies than in strong ones. And some industries, such as personal care products and low-cost entertainment, are fairly immune to economic cycles.

If your business is located in a smaller community that is heavily dependent on one industry or one major employer, take into account the effect of the economy on that industry or company and thus, your own business.

Considering the economic conditions or cycles that affect your business helps you anticipate and plan for growth in good times and belt-tightening in difficult times. On the worksheet below, describe the effect, if any, of each of the listed factors on your industry.

Effects of Economic Conditions on Your Industry and Business

High Business Expansion/Formation: _____

Low Business Expansion/Formation: _____

High Unemployment/Low Unemployment: _____

Low Interest Rate: _____

High Interest Rates: _____

Low Inflation: _____

High Inflation: _____

Strong Dollar/Weak Dollar: _____

High/Low New Home Construction: _____

Seasonality

For many industries, certain times of the year produce higher revenues than others. For example, toy companies are dependent on Christmas sales, while summer is the big season for bathing suit manufacturers.

Many industries fluctuate based on holidays. Most retail businesses and consumer products are affected by the Christmas season, which may account for one-third to one-half of all sales. Non-essential products and services may actually suffer during the Christmas season, as consumers reduce nongift expenses. Halloween is now the second largest holiday in the U.S. in terms of retail sales.

Spring is an important season for any wedding-associated industry. Tourism-related businesses usually depend heavily on the summer. Construction-related industries may experience slow-downs in winter months, especially in colder climates. When preparing your financial forms, particularly cash-flow projections, it is imperative that you understand and account for the seasonal factors that have an impact on your income and expenses. Your product may be sold in December, but you may have to pay for raw materials in June.

On the worksheet below, describe the impact, if any, that the various seasons or holidays have on the economic health of your industry.

"Forty-seven to forty-eight percent of our volume occurs around Christmas. We keep historical records of our sales volume and timing, so we know what the sales pattern is likely to be, both in the stores and when mail order and quantity orders will be placed. If Christmas is on a Tuesday this year, we go back and look at the last time it fell on a Tuesday, to see sales volume by day of the week, so we'll know what to expect the Friday before Christmas. We put together a 'game plan,' a complete schedule, so we can keep fresh product churning."

Charles Huggins
President, See's Candies

How Seasonal Factors Affect Your Industry

Christmas/Holiday: _____

_____

_____

Summer: _____

_____

_____

Winter: _____

_____

_____

Other: _____

_____

_____

Technological Change

Technological advances affect every industry. Technology changes the way products are made and sold, how information and communication is managed, and how costs are reduced. The Internet has dramatically affected many aspects of even the most traditional industries, including sales and distribution channels, customer service, and relationships with suppliers.

It is, of course, impossible to imagine all the technological developments that may affect your industry in the next five years. But it is useful to take note of the trends of the last five or ten years. If yours is an industry in which technology changes rapidly, assume that you will need to be positioned to respond to change, and indicate in your business plan your strategy to do so and the financing required. Some technological developments in your industry provide you with strategic opportunities that you want to emphasize when writing your plan.

On the checklist below, indicate the rate of technological change each area of your industry has experienced over the last five years.

Technological Change in Your Industry Over the Last Five Years

Product / Service Features	High	Moderate	Low	None
Manufacturing/Production	☐	☐	☐	☐
Billing/Administration	☐	☐	☐	☐
Information Management	☐	☐	☐	☐
Inventory Control	☐	☐	☐	☐
Delivery Time/Method	☐	☐	☐	☐
Marketing/Communication	☐	☐	☐	☐
Sales Channels	☐	☐	☐	☐
Customer Service	☐	☐	☐	☐
Other: _____	☐	☐	☐	☐
_____	☐	☐	☐	☐

Regulation/Certification

Certain industries are particularly affected by the actions of governmental authorities. While all businesses are influenced by regulation to some degree, regulation, licensing, and certification can dictate in large part how certain industries conduct business. Take time to think about how, if at all, your business and industry are influenced by governmental regulations.

Consider the actions of governmental entities at all levels — national, state, county, municipal, or special regional bodies — when analyzing the regulatory trends in your industry. Some regulatory measures actually create strategic opportunities. In the environmental field, for instance, increased governmental regulation over pollution has led to whole new industries dealing with waste management and energy conservation.

You may also find your business is subject to certification, either by a governmental body or an industry association. You may be required to take state tests to qualify to conduct your business. If your company benefits from regulatory actions, in your plan emphasize how you intend to capitalize on these opportunities.

Indicate your industry's sensitivity to regulation and certification on the checklist below.

How Sensitive Is Your Industry to Government Regulation?

Area of Sensitivity	High	Moderate	Low	None
Environment	☐	☐	☐	☐
Health and Safety	☐	☐	☐	☐
International Trade	☐	☐	☐	☐
Performance Standards	☐	☐	☐	☐
Licensing/Certification	☐	☐	☐	☐
Fair Trade/Deregulation	☐	☐	☐	☐
Product Claims	☐	☐	☐	☐
Other: _____	☐	☐	☐	☐
_____	☐	☐	☐	☐
_____	☐	☐	☐	☐
_____	☐	☐	☐	☐

Supply and Distribution Channels

The supply and distribution channels in your industry can be crucial in determining your company's success. In some industries it is notoriously difficult to gain access to distribution, and in others there are few reliable sources of supply. In industries with a large number of suppliers and distributors, costs remain lower and entry is relatively easy.

Be cautious when entering industries with extremely limited supply or distribution systems. Imagine, for instance, that you are considering starting a new magazine. While the lines of supply present little or no problem (many sources of paper, printing plants, writers), distribution may be problematic. One or two companies may control all magazine newsstand distribution in your area, making costs extremely high, if they are willing to carry your magazine at all.

In some industries or businesses, the company itself can control its supply or distribution channels. The Internet has also made it technically possible for a company to distribute directly to its customers; without intermediaries, however, this may not necessarily be the most advantageous business choice.

"We started with the technology; we didn't really know what we were going to make. We could have used our process to produce low-alcohol wine, nonalcoholic wine, bottled water, or a soft drink. In taste tests, we got a very high response to the soft drink, but it would have been beyond our resources to get distribution for a soft drink. We had contacts and experience in distribution in the wine industry, and an excellent response to our nonalcoholic wine, so we went with the plan we could execute. I would hate to start a product in a distribution system I didn't know."

Larry Leigon
Founder, Ariel Vineyards

Below, indicate the relative numbers of supply and distribution channels in your industry.

Supply and Distribution Channels in Your Industry				
Number of Channels	**High**	**Medium**	**Low**	**Self-Control**
Supply	☐	☐	☐	☐
Distribution	☐	☐	☐	☐

Financial Characteristics

No area of your Industry Analysis is more important than an evaluation of the financial patterns characterizing your industry, especially if you are new to the field. Knowing the standards of such aspects as markups, commissions, and returns on sales will substantially help your own budgeting process.

Much of this information may seem difficult to locate if you are just entering the industry. Perhaps the best way to get this information is to interview those already in the industry, especially those who are not your direct competitors. Just make certain the information is industry-specific; knowing the retail markup on apparel won't tell you the markup on food, consumer electronics, or fashion accessories.

The Financial Patterns worksheet on page 83 helps you keep crucial financial specifics handy when preparing budgets. Established businesses should complete this worksheet with actual company data.

Preparing the Industry Analysis for Your Business Plan

Once you have analyzed your industry for your internal planning purposes, coordinate that information and incorporate the highlights in the Plan Preparation Form on page 84. This form, when completed, will contain the information that will serve as the basis for the Industry Analysis segment of your business plan.

Chapter Summary

Evaluating the standards, trends, and characteristics of your industry helps you ensure your own company's success and assists you in planning your budgets. Although each company is unique, no business completely escapes the realities and constraints of the industry in which it operates. Anticipating changes in your industry can help you position your company for future developments. You need to understand the larger environment before you can successfully differentiate your own business.

"This is a capital-intensive industry; inventories are expensive to maintain. You get a low asset turnover because your inventory has to sit around in barrels for a long time. Profit margins are not good. You must determine what are the key ratios in the business, even if the formal financials don't follow for six months. Stay on top of the payables and receivables turnover, the gross profit margin, the inventory turnover ratio."

Larry Leigon
Founder, Ariel Vineyards

Financial Patterns   *$* ➤ *$$* ➤ *$$$*

Fill in this worksheet with figures representative of the financial standards in your industry.

Normal Retail Markup of Goods: _____
_____
_____
_____

Normal Distributor Markup of Goods: _____
_____
_____
_____

Typical Sales Commission Percentage: _____
_____
_____
_____

Standard Credit Terms: _____
_____
_____
_____

Days of Inventory Maintained: _____
_____
_____
_____

Average Percentage of Return on Sales: _____
_____
_____
_____

Other Financial Patterns of Note: _____
_____
_____

Percentage of Merchandise Price due to

Cost of Labor: _____   Fixed Costs: _____

Cost of Materials: _____   Shipping: _____

Energy: _____   Other: _____

Industry Analysis Plan Preparation Form

Using this form as a guide, summarize the main points you wish to convey in your Industry Analysis.

Industry Description: _____

_____

_____

_____

_____

_____

_____

_____

_____

_____

_____

Industry Trends: _____

_____

_____

_____

_____

_____

_____

_____

_____

_____

_____

_____

Strategic Opportunities: _____

_____

_____

_____

_____

_____

_____

_____

_____

_____

Use this information as the basis of your plan's Industry Analysis.

SAMPLE PLAN: Industry Analysis and Trends

Industry Analysis

ComputerEase is well-positioned to take advantage of the significant opportunities presented by the rapidly expanding industry of computer-related business services.

Computer-Related Services on the Rise

Service industries represent the fastest growing sector of the national economy, and computer-related business services reflect that continued growth. These services as a whole grew in excess of 125% over the five years from 1998–2002, compared to an overall GDP of approximately 29.5% during that period.

Cites statistics, showing real knowledge of industry.

Newly Developing Industry

Computer software training is a relatively new industry, an outgrowth of the phenomenal expansion of computer use. The industry is still in a state of flux, with no market leaders, nationally known providers, or widely recognized accreditation programs. Individual software manufacturers do offer certification as trainers for their products, but this certification is yet to be standardized, and such certification is not always a key issue for consumers.

Shows market opportunity.

Open Competitive Environment

Currently, the level of service is broadly uneven, and providers enter and leave the field rapidly. Some training is marketed through direct mail by national companies generally offering one- or two-day sessions by traveling trainers. These companies do not maintain an ongoing local profile or relationship with customers. Other software training is offered by individual consultants. Generally, these are not presented or marketed in any continuing, professional manner. They are not perceived in the marketplace as "businesses," and quality and pricing are widely uneven.

Barriers to Entry

The costs of purchasing current computer equipment and continually updating expensive training materials (software is revised approximately every six months) makes it difficult for undercapitalized companies to enter or stay in the software training field. Moreover, software providers are becoming more selective about which companies they will allow to serve as "authorized training companies." These relationships are crucial to the training company in terms of receiving advanced copies of software updates, purchasing training copies of software below cost, and co-sponsoring product introduction events.

Indicates limits to new competition.

Long-Term Opportunities

Thus, the long-term outlook for the industry is to develop regionally or nationally known companies, as is currently the case with other business services, such as accounting or employment services. These companies will be able to develop revenues and market share sufficient to sustain the high overhead. National franchises or affiliations will make it possible to share training materials and other resources.

ComputerEase Can Develop Strong Position in Region

The current lack of industry leaders represents an exceptional opportunity for ComputerEase to develop a dominant presence in the software training field in the greater Vespucci area. The company will then be well-situated to take advantage of national affiliations, either with franchisors, national associations, or software providers.

## Chapter 7

Target Market

*It's easier to get a piece of an existing market
than it is to create a new one.*

Know Your Customers

Essential to business success is a thorough understanding of your customers. After all, if you don't know who your customers are, how will you be able to assess whether you are meeting their needs? Since success depends on your being able to meet customers' needs and desires, you must know who your customers are, what they want, how they behave, and what they can afford.

Is Your Company Market Driven?

Moreover, if you are using your business plan to secure financing, defining the nature and size of your market is critical. Many investors look for companies aimed at substantial-sized markets and that are market driven. In other words, they seek to fund companies whose orientation is shaped by the demands and trends of the marketplace rather than the inherent characteristics of a particular product or service.

Being attuned to your market may lead you to make changes in your advertising, packaging, location, sales structure, even the features and character of the product or service itself. In the long run, a market analysis will save you money. When deciding which marketing vehicles to use (advertising, trade shows, etc.), you can then choose approaches based on whether they reach your specific target market.

A market analysis differs from a marketing plan. An analysis enables you to identify and understand your customers; a marketing plan tells how

"You have to be market driven. Who will buy it? What do they feel about it? Do they think it's a luxury or commodity? Do they need a big bottle or a small bottle? Particularly with a brand new product, you have to understand your market."

Larry Leigon
Founder, Ariel Vineyards

you are going to reach your customers. Laying out a marketing plan is covered in Chapter 10.

If you do not sell your product or service directly to the end-user but rather to retail outlets, distributors, or manufacturers, you have two markets, and you should define the characteristics of both of them — the ultimate consumer and the intermediary who is your actual customer. These target markets may have very different habits and concerns, and you need to understand both of them, as they each affect your sales. For instance, you may sell software you develop to a computer manufacturer who then includes it with the computers they sell to consumers. The computer manufacturer's biggest concern may be cost; the consumer's may be ease-of-use.

To gather information for this chapter, use the methods discussed in Chapter 2.

Defining Your Target Market

You may be tempted to describe your market in the broadest possible terms, choosing to include all those who might potentially use your product or service. Doing so gives you the comforting sense that you have a huge market to exploit. Unfortunately, this gives you little genuine information on which to base your business decisions. You could end up defining the market for furniture as everyone who lives indoors, hardly helpful if you're trying to come up with a marketing plan for your furniture store.

Instead you need to identify the particular market segments you wish to reach. These segments describe distinct, meaningful components of the overall market and give you a set of specific characteristics by which to identify your target market.

Let's say you are considering opening a discount dry cleaning establishment. You plan your service to be less expensive and faster, but, as a result, it may also be of slightly less quality than the dry cleaner now serving the area.

Thus, you might define your target market in these terms: "Employed women in white-collar jobs, price and time sensitive, commute by car, ages 25 to 50, household incomes of $20,000–$50,000 per year, children living at home, reside in the Laurelwood neighborhood." You then need to determine whether the neighborhood has enough consumers who fit this profile to support your business.

To be a useful planning tool, the definition of your target market must meet these criteria:

- **Definable.** It should have specific characteristics identifying what the potential customers have in common.
- **Meaningful.** The characteristics must meaningfully relate to the decision to purchase.
- **Sizable.** It must be large enough to profitably sustain your business.

> "Be willing to look at different market segments instead of just the obvious or largest market to secure some degree of market penetration. Take, for instance, the credit-card electronic key for hotels. Even though these keys represented substantial savings, established hotels at first were reluctant to make the change-over from traditional locks. Instead, new hotels were the first to put in this type of lock, and existing hotels followed later, once the benefits were well-known."
>
> **Eugene Kleiner**
> **Venture Capitalist**

- **Reachable**. Both the definition and size must lead to affordable and effective ways to market to your potential customers.

Once you have defined your market, you should then assess its size and trends, evaluate your competitors for that particular market, and probe the market for strategic opportunities.

Demographic Description

Begin describing your market by the most basic, objective aspects of the customer base. These details are the specific and observable traits that define your target market.

Demographic information is particularly useful when devising your marketing plan. Many marketing vehicles, such as publications, mailing lists, radio, and TV, accumulate this kind of data about the market they reach. Thus, you are better able to judge whether such vehicles are appropriate for your company.

Remember, you want to define those characteristics of your target market that meaningfully relate to the interest, need, and ability of the customer to purchase your product or service.

In the previous definition of the target market for the Laurelwood dry cleaner, for instance, the definition "white-collar jobs" directly relates to the need for regular dry cleaning; "women" relates to the fact that most dry cleaning nationally is purchased by women; "commute by car" is important because the location is not near public transportation; and "$20,000–$50,000" relates to the customer's ability to pay for dry cleaning while being less likely to afford the more expensive cleaners.

On the Demographic Description worksheet on the next page, describe the demographic details of your target market, whether you are marketing to consumers or businesses.

Geographic Description

Next, define the primary geographic area(s) you intend to serve. This definition should be as concrete as possible, indicating whether your business serves a particular neighborhood, city, state, region, nation, or portion of the international market.

Also, look at the density of the area — whether urban, suburban, or rural, and, if customers will be coming to your place of business, indicate whether the location is in a mall, strip center, business district, or industrial area, or will be a stand-alone facility. Some businesses define their geographic market by climate, serving only cold-weather or hot-weather locations.

If you are making your product or service available on the Internet, you may be tempted to view the entire world as your geographic target market. However, even on the Internet, there are limitations to which geographic areas are your primary target markets. These limits may be due to issues of fulfillment (e.g., shipping goods) or language, and there are certainly limits of realistic market demand from different areas.

> *"Customers can be categorized in several ways, by income level or by lifestyle issues. The income levels can fall into one or more of the following categories: luxury, upscale, upper moderate, moderate, and budget. Lifestyle issues are more subjective. The target customer is less dependent on income level and more on her attitude about how she spends her disposable income."*
>
> **Nancy Glaser**
> **Business Strategies**
> **Consultant**

> *"It's very difficult to create a new market, even if there's a need. Developing a new market takes years, even if you're 100% right about the need and the product. The best market to look for is a market that already exists, that is already being served, but being served in a marginal fashion."*
>
> **Eugene Kleiner**
> **Venture Capitalist**

Demographic Description

Consumer

Age Range: _____

_____

_____

Income Range: _____

_____

_____

Sex: _____

_____

_____

Occupation: _____

_____

_____

Marital Status: _____

_____

_____

Family Size: _____

_____

_____

Ethnic Group: _____

_____

_____

Level of Education: _____

_____

_____

Home Ownership: _____

_____

_____

Other: _____

_____

_____

_____

Business

Industries: _____

_____

_____

Sector: _____

_____

_____

Years in Business: _____

_____

_____

Company Revenues: _____

_____

_____

Number of Employees: _____

_____

_____

Number of Branches: _____

_____

_____

Square Footage: _____

_____

_____

Company Ownership: _____

_____

_____

Other: _____

_____

_____

_____

On the worksheet below, describe the geographic details of your target customers, whether consumers or businesses.

Geographic Description

Area Served (city, region, nation, etc.): _____

_____

_____

Density (urban, rural, suburban, etc.): _____

_____

_____

Nature of Location (mall, strip center, business district, etc.): _____

_____

_____

Climate Conditions: _____

_____

_____

"The decision to locate in Napa was a marketing decision. We could have made our product anywhere, but Napa is associated with premium wines. We wanted Napa on the label."

**Larry Leigon,
Founder, Ariel Vineyards**

Lifestyle/Business-Style Description

In the Target Market section of your plan, convey a sense of the concerns and interests of your customers. How do they spend their time? What issues are they facing in their lives or businesses? With whom do they associate? How do they relate to their employees and community?

Your natural instincts and experience with customers gives you some sense of what your customers are interested in. It's logical, for instance, to assume that receptive targets for your expensive specialty food product are fairly likely to subscribe to *Gourmet* or other food magazines and might belong to local food and wine organizations. Or, if the market for your business service is law firms, you would naturally assume they belong to the local Bar Association.

A little research can help you identify other aspects of your target market's lifestyle or business style. Observe customers in places where they shop or live. What other products or services do they buy? What kinds of cars do they drive? What kinds of clothes do they wear?

Review the publications you think target customers subscribe to. What other companies are advertising? What are the articles about? Survey your customers, either in person, by mail, or on the phone, and ask them about some of their activities.

What kind of people or businesses need or want your product or service? Do they go to the movies, watch TV, or rent videos? Do they entertain at home? If so, for whom? What other kinds of products or services would be used in the same setting with yours?

Develop a mental picture of your customer's entire week. Be creative, but logical and realistic. You want to relate to your customer as a whole, which makes you more responsive to their needs and gives you ideas for marketing vehicles and approaches. The worksheet on the opposite page helps you achieve this.

Pyschographic Description

In addition to the observable, objective characteristics of your market, less tangible but equally important psychological factors also influence your targeted customer's purchasing decisions. These are aspects of self-image: how customers see, or want to see, themselves. Some of these are fairly self-conscious attributes, for example, a homemaker priding himself or herself on being a smart shopper. Some are less conscious, perhaps being status-seeking or gadget-happy. Marketing experts segment consumers into different psychographic and lifestyle groups. Some of these segments become well-known, for instance, the term "early adopters" is widely used for those consumers who are eager to be among the first to try new technologies.

Business customers as well as consumers can be described in psychographic terms. Some companies view themselves as being on the cutting edge of technology, others as fiscally responsible, and others as socially responsible. These distinctions can help you determine marketing efforts and positioning of your product or service.

On the checklist below, check off the psychographic traits that characterize your target customer.

> "I had a strong sense of my target market from the beginning. I clearly defined the user profile: 30 years and up, $35,000-plus income, urban, sophisticated palate, leisure travel, exposure to foreign foods, subscribe to a food magazine, busy. Then I looked at retail outlets that I thought served that profile end-user. My customer is really the retail outlet, and I had to focus on them as well. There's a tendency to look only at the end-user and neglect your real customer. But ultimately, to serve the retailer, you have to make a product that sells."
>
> ***Deborah Mullis***
> ***Entrepreneur***

Psychographic Description

Consumer	Business
☐ Technically Adept	☐ Technically Advanced
☐ Status Seeking	☐ Industry Leader
☐ Trend-Setting	☐ Innovative
☐ Conservative/Responsible	☐ Conservative/Responsible
☐ Socially Responsible	☐ Socially Responsible
☐ Environmentally Conscious	☐ Environmentally Conscious
☐ Smart Shopper	☐ Smart Business Operator
☐ Family-Oriented	☐ Fiscally Prudent
☐ Fun-Seeking	☐ Good Manager of Employees
☐ Good Housekeeper	☐ Influenced by Leading Companies
☐ Other: _____	☐ Other: _____

Lifestyle / Business-Style Description

Consumer

Family Stage: _____

_____

_____

Vacation Choices: _____

_____

_____

Television Shows Watched: _____

_____

_____

Favorite Websites: _____

_____

_____

Hobbies / Sports / Other Forms of Entertainment: ____

_____

_____

Publication Subscriptions: _____

_____

_____

Organizations/Affiliations: _____

_____

_____

Political Affiliation: _____

_____

_____

Type of Car Owned: _____

_____

_____

Other: _____

_____

_____

_____

Business

Business Stage: _____

_____

_____

Employee Relations: _____

_____

_____

Trade Association Memberships: _____

_____

_____

Business Products & Services Used: _____

_____

_____

Workforce Type: _____

_____

_____

Publication Subscriptions: _____

_____

_____

Community Activities: _____

_____

_____

Management Style: _____

_____

_____

Other: _____

_____

_____

_____

Purchasing Patterns Description

In planning, it's particularly important to understand the buying patterns of your customers. For instance, if Fortune 500 companies are your target market, you must recognize that these large companies have slow decision-making processes and, due to their size, resist change even when presented with compelling facts. You must keep these realistic constraints in mind when forecasting your sales to this market.

Complete the worksheet below to describe the likely purchasing patterns of your target customers, whether consumers or businesses.

Purchasing Patterns Description

Reason / occasion for first purchase: _____

Number of times they'll purchase: _____

Interval between purchases: _____

Amount of product / service purchased: _____

Motivation for continued use: _____

How long to make decision to purchase: _____

Where customer first learned about product / service: _____

Place where customer purchases product / service: _____

Where customer uses product: _____

How customer uses product: _____

Method of payment: _____

Special needs: _____

Other: _____

_____

Buying Sensitivities Description

What factors are most important to your customer when deciding to buy? Of course, all customers would say that they want the highest quality, best service, and greatest convenience, at the lowest price. But in reality, customers know they have to make tradeoffs: paying a little more for extra features, driving farther to get a lower price. What aspects are your customers least willing to give up? What are the areas of their greatest sensitivity?

The checklist on the next page helps you indicate how sensitive your customers (consumers or businesses) are to various factors.

Market Size and Trends

Once you have defined the characteristics of your target market, you must then assess the size of this market and evaluate the trends likely to influence both market size and customer behavior in the near future.

Buying Sensitivity Description

	High	Medium	Low	Not at All
Price	☐	☐	☐	☐
Quality	☐	☐	☐	☐
Brand Name	☐	☐	☐	☐
Product Features	☐	☐	☐	☐
Salesperson	☐	☐	☐	☐
Sales/Special Offers	☐	☐	☐	☐
Advertising	☐	☐	☐	☐
Packaging	☐	☐	☐	☐
Convenience of Use	☐	☐	☐	☐
Convenience of Purchase	☐	☐	☐	☐
Location	☐	☐	☐	☐
Store Decor/Environment	☐	☐	☐	☐
Customer Service	☐	☐	☐	☐
Return Policy	☐	☐	☐	☐
Credit Availability	☐	☐	☐	☐
Maintenance Program	☐	☐	☐	☐
Warranty	☐	☐	☐	☐
Nature of Existing Customers	☐	☐	☐	☐
Other: _____	☐	☐	☐	☐

"We want to understand what our customers are buying and how they are buying our product. We analyze our sales by distribution channel, by customer type. We see how many of our goods are sold off-price. It's not enough to just know how many sales you have; you also need to know what kind of sales you are making."

George James
Former Sr. V.P. & CFO
Levi Strauss & Co.

Size

You want to make sure your customer base is large enough to sustain your business and, if seeking funding, to convince potential investors that your company can grow to a size that will make their investment profitable.

Surprisingly, you generally don't want your target market to be either too small or too large. Markets that are too small are obviously in trouble from the start, as you won't have enough customers. (The exception: niche markets may be quite small, serving a limited number of customers with a very specific need, but can still be lucrative and able to support a well-defined business if the product or service meets a very specific need and is aggressively priced.) Very large markets, however, invite numerous well-financed competitors, and require extremely expensive marketing campaigns. (The exception: if you are developing a very large, well-financed business.)

For some businesses, particularly smaller retail operations, determining whether your market is sufficiently sizable will be mostly a matter of intuition and observation. You needn't do a scientific study. But if you are unsure about your market, or need to convince investors, you must gather data to support your plan.

When assessing the size of the market, you will find demographic and geographic information easiest to locate. Much of this data is available from U.S. Census Bureau reports, local governmental agencies, real estate brokerages, chambers of commerce, and business directories.

Information about other characteristics of your market can be gleaned from existing market research studies about the general population or from trade associations. For more information on how to research market size, refer to Chapter 2.

Trends

Equally important as estimating the size of your current market is evaluating the trends that may affect the market in the coming years. Doing so will give you a sense of your company's continuing viability, the strategic opportunities the market presents, and how the company must plan to respond to changing behavior of customers.

Preparing for change is not so much a matter of predicting the future as analyzing the recent past. Much of your analysis can be based on observable changes in demographics and customer behavior. For instance, let's say your product is designed to appeal to retired individuals in the American Southwest. You can analyze increased population figures for that age group in particular states and membership trends in organizations such as the American Association of Retired People (AARP). This will provide you with a sense of how the market size is changing. Studies of new hobbies, disposable income growth, and altered buying habits for the age group will give you indicators of the issues and opportunities facing your company in the near future.

Use the worksheet below to describe your market size and the trends likely to affect customer behavior in the next few years.

> *"We use our suppliers to give us information about buying habits. Suppliers usually have national information. They know what's selling."*
>
> **Charles Huggins**
> **President, See's Candies**

Market Size and Trends

What is the current approximate size of your target market? _____

What is the rate of growth of the target market? _____

What changes are occurring in the makeup of the market? _____

What changes are affecting ability to afford the product/service? _____

What changes are affecting the need for the product/service? _____

How are customers changing the use of the product/service? _____

What changes in social values and concerns are affecting the product/service? _____

Preparing the Target Market Section of Your Plan

Based on what you have learned by analyzing your potential market, you are now ready to prepare the Target Market section of your written business plan.

Using the Plan Preparation Form on the next page as a guide, focus primarily on these three areas:

- Description
- Trends
- Strategic Opportunities

This section of your plan particularly lends itself to the use of bullet points, which makes writing easier.

Chapter Summary

A concise description and thorough understanding of your target market will give you focus when developing your product or service, designing your marketing plan, and forecasting sales and expenses. Potential investors want reassurance that your market is sizable and that you comprehend the opportunities and limitations of the market. You need to make certain your target market is definable and reachable.

"Before they'll fund a company, a venture capitalist will always do due diligence; test out the market, call potential customers."

Mark Gorenberg
Venture Capitalist

Target Market Plan Preparation Form

Outline the Target Market portion of your plan on this form. More detailed descriptions of your market and results of market research can be included in your plan's Appendix.

Market Description: _____

_____

_____

_____

_____

_____

_____

_____

_____

_____

Market Size and Trends: _____

_____

_____

_____

_____

_____

_____

_____

_____

_____

_____

Strategic Opportunities: _____

_____

_____

_____

_____

_____

_____

_____

_____

_____

_____

_____

Use this information as the basis of your plan's Target Market section.

SAMPLE PLAN: Target Market

Target Market

Market Description

ComputerEase operates in the greater Vespucci, Indiana, area, targeting those large- and medium-sized businesses with high computer use. The geographic area includes the incorporated cities of:

- Vespucci
- Abergel Peak
- Newman City

and the suburban communities (with business centers) of:

- Karen's Springs
- Gaspar
- Lake Arthur

Indicates specific geographic market.

Market Size and Trends

Vespucci, with its surrounding communities, is a large and economically healthy area. The city of Vespucci has a population of approximately 675,000, according to 2002 census figures, making it the 16th largest city in the U.S. The Vespucci Metropolitan Statistical Area (MSA) has an overall population approaching 1,500,000.

The business climate has been consistently strong due to its diverse economic base. The Vespucci MSA includes three county seats and is the home to numerous government offices. Also located in the greater Vespucci area are:

Relates health and diversity of target market.

- An international airport.
- The regional processing centers for three national insurance companies.
- The data processing center for the state's highway patrol.
- A state university and six other colleges and universities.
- A major medical center.

The economic base has been expanding, and recently a national research institute with 280 employees announced its intention to relocate to Vespucci. A survey for the local newspaper, *The Vespucci Explorer,* showed that 43% of larger companies intended to add employees in the next 24 months.

The breakdown of employment by industry is approximately:

- 25% retail and wholesale sales
- 25% government

SAMPLE PLAN: Target Market (continued)

- 25% manufacturing
- 25% education, health, and services.

Target Customers

Clearly identifies characteristics of target customers.

The businesses ComputerEase targets for its services have these characteristics:
Business attributes:

- Over 50 employees
- High computer use (data processing and retrieval, financials)
- Relatively high employee turnover; expanding number of employees

Industries:

- Government
- Insurance
- Financial/Banking
- Accounting
- Colleges and Universities
- Engineering
- Hospitals and Other Medical Facilities
- Airlines

The Vespucci Chamber of Commerce estimates that of the more than 10,000 companies and institutions with more than 50 employees in the area, at least 2,500 are in the industries listed above.

Indicates self-image and sensitivities of potential customer.

Management personnel in these industries generally view themselves as responsible and professional. They prefer to deal with service companies that present a stable, conservative image. They are generally more sensitive to quality than price, and can be considerably influenced by the fact that similar companies already use the service provider.

Market Readiness

Shows real market exists

ComputerEase's Vice President for Marketing conducted a market research survey with a selection of targeted companies. This survey indicated the particular patterns of these companies in relation to computer training need:

- 97% indicated a need for employees trained in computer use.
- 83% indicated some need for company-provided computer training.
- 67% indicated a need for occasional or specialized training.
- 41% indicated a need for continuing training programs.

The survey also revealed that such companies currently spend funds on computer training. Specific data indicates:

- 42% of these companies have a "training" amount allotted in their current year's budget.

- 18% specifically have "computer or software training" budgeted for the current year.

- 34% have purchased software training services in the last year.

- 66% indicated they would purchase more training than at present if better-quality, more reliable training were available.

Fully 74% of those using computer training said they were either highly unsatisfied or somewhat unsatisfied with their current training arrangements. This level of dissatisfaction is substantially higher than the satisfaction level with other business services (27% average dissatisfaction level with services such as accounting and legal).

Strategic Opportunities

Computer training services in these companies are overwhelmingly purchased, recommended, or approved by the Human Resources/Personnel Director (83%), providing a clear target for marketing efforts.

Clearly, there is a real need for ComputerEase's services in the Vespucci area, an expanding and healthy market, a highly dissatisfied market, and an identifiable way to reach the market. This provides a substantial opportunity for ComputerEase to fill a void in the provision of software training services.

"Where do I get reliable data about my industry? Do I have a meaningful, reachable target market? How can I get the low-down on my competition?"

Get the Research Numbers You Need—Fast.

IDEAL FOR BUSINESS PLAN RESEARCH!
Easy step-by-step approach

From the author of the top-selling
The Successful Business Plan: Secrets & Strategies

Successful Business Research
WHERE DO I GET THE NUMBERS?
Rhonda Abrams

◆ *Answer in-depth questions about your business, using reliable government and private sources*
◆ *Up-to-date hot links to research sources*
◆ *Learn to interpret the data you find*
◆ *Find accurate data quickly and in an organized fashion*

◆ *Perform a detailed Industry Analysis including economic sector analysis, industry and product data and trends*
◆ *Identify your Target Market, including detailed demographics and purchasing patterns, geographic data, psychographics*

◆ *Get the dirt on your Competition, including market share distributions, data on individual competitors, and competition in local markets*

Successful Business Research: Where do I get the numbers?
by Rhonda Abrams with Veronica Adams
Available as a PDF download

Seeking outside financing for your business? Then expect to be quizzed about your industry, target market, and competition.

You've got to have well-researched, verifiable numbers to support your business plan—whether or not you're seeking funding. But the process of finding that data has been painful (and expensive) until now.

Key Features:

- Interactive, step-by-step, guide to finding key data about your industry, market, and competition
- Totally interactive—with up-to-date hot links to the leading research sources
- Shows you in "cookbook" fashion how to grab the data you need quickly and interpret it
- Dramatically reduces the time spent on research and improves the quality of results
- Can save you hundreds, even thousands, of dollars in research expenses

Download yours today at our lowest price: www.PlanningShop.com/research

## Chapter 8

The Competition

It is not enough just to build a better mousetrap;
you have to build a better mousetrap company.

Know What You're Up Against

Famed baseball player Satchel Paige used to say, "Don't look back; someone may be gaining on you." But in business it is imperative to see who's gaining on you. It is far better to know what you're up against than to be surprised when your sales suddenly disappear to an unexpected competitor.

Every business has competition. Those currently operating a company are all too aware of the many competitors for a customer's dollar. But many people new to business — excited about their concept and motivated by a perceived opening in the market — tend to underestimate the actual extent of competition and fail to properly assess the impact of that competition on their business.

One of the very worst statements you can make in a business plan is, "We have no competition." A knowledgeable investor will immediately disregard a plan with such a statement because it indicates that either: 1) you have not fully examined the realities of your business; or 2) there is no market for your concept.

You can see this by looking at the example of the photocopier. When the first one was invented, no competition existed from other makers of photocopiers, of course. But competition still came from many sources, including suppliers of carbon paper and mimeograph machines. And if the copier worked and the market was receptive, future competition could realistically be projected. If no competition truly existed at the time

"Don't allow yourself to be awed by an opponent, or, on the other hand, to have contempt for them. Don't allow the extremes of your emotions to dictate your assessment of the competition. Never over-react to a great deal of success or failure, either your own or the competition's."

Bill Walsh
Former Coach and
President, S.F. 49ers

it was invented — if people weren't duplicating documents by some means — it would have meant no market for photocopiers existed.

Honestly evaluating your competition will help you better understand your own product or service and give investors a reassuring sense of your company's strengths. It enables you to know how best to distinguish your company in the customer's eyes, and it points to opportunities in the market.

Learn from your competition. The basic concept of competition is responsiveness to customers, and watching your competitors can help you understand what customers want.

As you begin your competitive assessment, keep in mind that you need to evaluate only those competitors aiming for the same target market. If you own a fine French restaurant in midtown Manhattan, you don't have to include the McDonald's next door in your competitive evaluation: you're not aiming for the same customer at the same time. On the other hand, if you are thinking of opening the first sports memorabilia shop in Alaska, you have to look far afield, at any such retail stores in Seattle or Vancouver, mail-order dealers from all over the country, and Internet dealers from all over the world, as that is where your potential customers shop now.

When preparing the competitive analysis portion of your business plan, focus on identifying:

- Who your major competitors are;
- On what basis you compete;
- How you compare;
- Potential future competitors; and
- Barriers to entry for new competitors.

Competitive Position

It is tempting to want to judge your competition solely on the basis of whether your product or service is better than theirs. If you have invented a clearly superior widget, it is comforting to imagine that widget customers will naturally buy your product instead of the competitors' and the money will roll in.

Unfortunately, many other factors will determine your success in comparison to other manufacturers of widgets. Perhaps their brand name is already well-known. Perhaps their widgets are much cheaper. Perhaps their distribution system makes it easier for them to get placement in stores. Or maybe customers just like the color of your competitors' packages better.

The objective features of your product or service may be a relatively small part of the competitive picture. In fact, all the components of customer preference, including price, service, and location, are only half of the competitive analysis.

The other half of the equation is examining the internal strength of your competitors' companies. In the long run, companies with significant financial resources, highly motivated or creative personnel, and other operational assets will prove to be tough, enduring competition.

Thoroughly Evaluate Your Competition

Two Competitive Analysis worksheets in this chapter help you evaluate your competitive position both in terms of customer preference and internal operational strengths.

The worksheets enable you to give greater or lesser importance to each competitive factor, depending on the significance of those particular aspects. To complete each worksheet, give each factor listed a maximum possible number of points, ranging from 1 to 10, with 1 being least important to your overall target market and 10 being the most important. Place the maximum number for each factor in the Maximum Points column.

For instance, on the Competitive Analysis: Customer Perception Factors worksheet, let's say your target market is extremely price sensitive but willing to travel a long way to get a bargain. The purchase price factor might be given a maximum of 10 points and the location factor a maximum of 2.

Once you have finished numbering the factors for your company and competitors, you will see how this weighting system gives you a better picture of the actual strength of your competitors as opposed to your own.

Keep in mind that you can also allot negative numbers. If, for example, your target market is interested only in items perceived as luxuries, having too low a price may be a liability. If your market is particularly socially conscious, the fact that your competitor conducts tests on animals may be a negative for the social image factor in their evaluation, giving you a competitive edge.

In your analyses, look at both specific competitors — particular companies you compete against — and at the overall type of competition. In the example of the Alaskan sports memorabilia store, for instance, the Competitive Analysis might have four competitors listed: each of the two specific retail stores in Seattle and Vancouver, mail-order dealers and Internet dealers as categories.

If desired, you can include these completed worksheets in the Appendix of your plan, as well as use them for internal planning purposes.

Customer Perception Factors

When doing your analysis, consider these customer perception factors:

- **Product/Service Features.** Specific inherent attributes of the product or service itself; if key features are particularly important, list separately.
- **Indirect/Peripheral Costs.** Costs other than the actual purchase price, such as installation or additional equipment required.

> *"It's always easier to have an enemy. "We try harder" is a very good business plan. They're the old guys, we're the new guys. Our job is to beat them — that's a very clear message. You can raid the best people from your competitors, you can look at their business plan and see how they developed and you can follow the good parts and throw out the bad parts. It's straightforward."*
>
> **Andrew Anker**
> **Venture Capitalist**

Competitive Analysis: Customer Perception Factors

Following the directions on page 105, allocate points for each of the factors listed below for both your company and your competitors.

Factor	Maximum Points (1-10)	Your Company	Competitor:	Competitor:	Competitor:	Competitor:
Product / Service Features						
Purchase Price						
Indirect / Peripheral Costs						
Quality						
Durability/ Maintenance						
Image / Style / Design						
Perceived Value						
Brand Recognition						
Customer Relationships						
Location						
Delivery Time						
Convenience of Use						
Credit Policies						
Customer Service						
Social Consciousness						
Other:						
Other:						
Total Points						
Comments:						

Competitive Analysis: Internal Operational Factors

Following the directions on page 105, allocate points for each of the factors listed below for both your company and your competitors.

Factor	Maximum Points (1-10)	Your Company	Competitor:	Competitor:	Competitor:	Competitor:
Financial Resources						
Marketing Budget/Program						
Technological Competence						
Access to Distribution						
Access to Suppliers						
Economies of Scale						
Operational Efficiencies						
Sales Structure/Competence						
Product Line Breadth						
Strategic Partnerships						
Company Morale/Personnel						
Certification/Regulation						
Patents/Trademarks						
Ability to Innovate:						
Other:						
Other:						
Other:						
Total Points						
Comments:						

- **Quality.** Inherent merit of the product or service at the time it is provided.
- **Durability/Maintenance.** Quality of the product/service over time; ease of maintenance and service.
- **Image/Style/Perceived Value.** Added values derived from design features, attractive packaging or presentation, and other intangibles.
- **Customer Relationships.** Established customer base and customer loyalty; relationships of sales personnel to customers.
- **Social Consciousness.** Perception of the company, product, or service relative to issues such as environment, civic involvement, etc.

Internal Operational Factors

Some internal operational factors that increase competitiveness include:

- **Financial Resources.** Ability of the company to withstand financial setbacks, and to fund product development and improvements.
- **Marketing Program/Budget.** Amount and effectiveness of advertising and other promotional activities.
- **Economies of Scale.** Ability to reduce per-unit costs due to large volume.
- **Operational Efficiencies.** Production or delivery methods that reduce costs and time.
- **Product Line Breadth.** Ability to increase revenues by selling related products; ability for customers to purchase needed items from one provider.
- **Strategic Partnerships.** Relationships with other companies for purposes of development, promotion, or add-on sales.
- **Company Morale/Personnel.** Motivation, commitment, and productivity of the employees.

Other Factors Affecting Your Ability to Compete

First Mover Advantage

In new industries or new market segments, the first company to gain a reasonable foothold in the market can often leverage being early into a significant competitive advantage. Having a market to oneself for even a brief period may enable a company to define the product, set standards, establish key strategic partnerships, capture customer attention, or in other ways gain dominance. This rush to market, however, does not guarantee success, and many industries have instances of early market leaders being overtaken by later-stage competitors.

Installed User Base

If a sizable portion of the market currently uses a product that performs a similar function or is incompatible with your new product or service, customers may resist the cost and inconvenience of making the transition. This is particularly true for products involving technology or electronics. Often even superior products have a difficult time getting a foothold in such markets. One of the most cited examples is the familiar "QWERTY" keyboard. Keys on early typewriters were arranged to intentionally slow down typing to prevent the mechanical keys from sticking. Although later keyboards improved on this arrangement, typists were already comfortable with the "QWERTY" keyboard, and it remains to this day.

The Internet

The Internet substantially lowers barriers to entry in many industries, and in some cases, allows competitors to operate at very narrow profit margins. The Internet also arms customers with substantially more purchase information, sometimes even wholesale prices. Companies that previously may have been able to compete effectively in a particular geographic area may now face worldwide competition.

Inertia

Customers don't do what they should do; they do what they have to or want to do. In almost every case, customers have the option not to buy at all. It's not enough for you to know the customer needs your product or service, the customer must truly believe they need or want to buy from you.

Market Share Distribution

Some competitors are more important than others, due entirely to the fact that they command a large percentage of the market sales. Although these companies may not necessarily provide the best product or service at the best price, they nevertheless represent a crucial component in evaluating your competitive position.

Companies that generate a significant portion of all sales to the target market must be carefully considered because they:

- Generally define the standard features of the product or service;
- Substantially influence the perception of the product or service by customers; and
- Usually devote considerable resources to maintaining their market share.

Take time to understand the companies that dominate the market, if only to better distinguish yourself from them. Of course, if your company is fortunate enough to control a major share of the market, then you gain the advantage of defining the product or service in the marketplace; you are the proverbial "800-pound gorilla." Even so, you cannot be complacent but must plan on committing the resources necessary to preserve or expand your share.

How Will You Obtain Sufficient Market Share?

If yours is a new business, it is generally easier and less expensive to enter a market with many diverse competitors than one dominated by a few major players. If you are preparing a business plan for financing purposes, you will have to demonstrate to potential funding sources through your

"When it comes to competition for a technology-based company, in the early stages, I'm more worried about the small operator than the large company. With the large well-known companies, you generally know what they're working on. Also, they have large overhead. But the small competitor can come in and compete against you head on, especially if the technology is low enough to allow easy entry to the market."

Eugene Kleiner
Venture Capitalist

Market Share Distribution

List below the current market leaders and the approximate percentage of the market each one commands.

Competitor	% of Total Revenues	% of Total Units Sold	Trend of Market Share (increasing or decreasing?)
1.			
2.			
3.			
4.			
5.			

Which competitor(s), if any, have historically been the market leader(s)? _____

_____

Which competitors have increased market share substantially in the last three years? _____

_____

Is overall competition increasing, stable, or decreasing? _____

Briefly describe the most important characteristics of the market leader(s):

Competitor #1: _____

Competitor #2: _____

Competitor #3: _____

Divide the pie charts below to indicate market distribution. (These charts can be included in your written plan for visual interest.)

Market Share By Revenues
(estimate)

Market Share By Volume
(estimate)

marketing plan how your company plans to gain and maintain a reasonable market share.

Complete the Market Share Distribution worksheet on page 110 to outline how sales are distributed among the competition, both by total sales revenues and by unit volume. (Some companies make fewer but higher-priced sales by targeting the most lucrative customers; others sell greater volume at lower per-unit prices.) Once again, look at competitors both by individual companies and by categories of competition, as they apply to your situation.

You will probably have to estimate the figures required by the worksheet, based on information gleaned from trade associations, annual reports, business publications, and independent industry research firms. Definitive information on sales is notoriously difficult to locate.

Future Competition

Finally, in your competitive analysis you have to do a little fortune-telling. You must make a few reasonable predictions of what the competition will look like in the future. New competitors enter markets all the time, and sometimes current competitors drop out. Don't take comfort in the fact that other companies have overlooked a particular product or service. Once you show you can be successful, someone will want to take a piece of that market from you. Who are your new competitors likely to be? How long will you have the field to yourself before other competitors jump in?

Forecasting the competitive situation over the next five years or so, based on logical conclusions from concrete evidence such as current product lines, gives you and potential investors a better sense of the long-term viability of your business.

One of the most important factors to examine is barriers to entry: those conditions that make it difficult or impossible for new competitors to enter the market. Every company can gain a sense of how best to prepare for future competition by examining the barriers to entry.

If your company's competitive position depends on new technology, new manufacturing techniques, or access to new markets, outlining the barriers to entry is essential. This will be one of the first areas judged by potential funding sources.

Barriers to Entry

Some common barriers to entry for new competition are:

- Patents, which provide a measure of protection for new products or processes.
- High start-up costs, which effectively protect against small competitors entering the field.
- Substantial expertise required, or manufacturing and engineering complexities, making it less likely for competitors to have the knowledge to compete.

"As a barrier to entry, it should take significant money and significant skill to enter the business. Patents, while desirable, are not sufficient to protect against new competition, although they help the entrepreneur in raising money because they show the product is unique. Service businesses have a harder time securing venture capital funds because competitors can enter the field easily, and investors are wary. You need barriers to entry to protect your market."

Eugene Kleiner
Venture Capitalist

- Market saturation, which reduces the possibility of competitors gaining a meaningful foothold.

Few barriers to entry last very long, particularly in newer industries. Even patents do not provide nearly as much protection as is generally assumed. Thus, you need to realistically project the period of time by which new competitors will breach these barriers.

Complete the worksheet on page 113 indicating future competition and barriers to entry.

Preparing the Competition Segment of Your Plan

To prepare the Competition portion of your business plan document, synthesize the information from the worksheets in this chapter into a brief synopsis. In particular, you want to provide:

- Description of Competition
- Market Share Distribution
- Competitive Positions
- Barriers to Entry
- Strategic Opportunities

Use the Plan Preparation Form on page 114 to outline the Competition section of your business plan. Don't be afraid to use bullet-point lists and charts (see Chapter 3 for suggestions) in this section. Also, include pertinent information from market research, particularly customer surveys.

Chapter Summary

You have to understand your competition if you're going to be an effective competitor yourself. Develop a strong sense of your competitive position — your strengths and weaknesses in terms of customer perception and your internal company resources; this will be vital when preparing your marketing strategy. Always assume competition will get more intense, and be prepared for new competitors to enter the market.

"Quality means continuing to improve on your competitors."

Michael Damer
New United Motor
Manufacturing Inc.

Future Competition and Barriers to Entry

Potential future competitors include: _____

_____

_____

_____

_____

Current competitors likely to expand efforts: _____

_____

_____

_____

_____

Current competitors potentially leaving the field: _____

_____

_____

_____

_____

Indicate below how strong the following barriers to entry are and how much time (check the How Long Effective column) it will take before new competition overcomes each barrier.

Type of Barrier to Entry	Extent of Effectiveness Factor				How Long Effective
	High	Medium	Low	None	
Patents					
High Start-up Costs					
Substantial Expertise Required					
Engineering, Manufacturing Problems					
Lack of Suppliers or Distributors					
Restrictive Licensing, Regulation					
Market Saturation					
Trademarks					
Other:					

Competition Plan Preparation Form

Using this form as a guide, summarize the main points you wish to make in the Competition section of your business plan.

Description of Competition: _____

_____

_____

_____

_____

Market Share Distribution: _____

_____

_____

_____

_____

Competitive Positions: _____

_____

_____

_____

_____

Barriers to Entry: _____

_____

_____

_____

_____

Strategic Opportunities: _____

_____

_____

_____

_____

Use this information as the basis of your plan's Competition section.

SAMPLE PLAN: The Competition

The Competition

Competing with ComputerEase to supply software training services to the target market (businesses with substantial use of computers, more than 50 employees) are these categories of software training providers:

- Individual independent training consultants.
- Local software training companies.
- National training companies (periodic traveling workshops).
- Software developers.
- Community college classes.
- Trainers from within the targeted companies themselves.
- Online distance learning/training programs.

Lists categories of competitors

ComputerEase does not intend to compete with training provided by software developers. Such software is usually highly specialized and training is included in the cost of the software itself. Community college classes are generally not competitive in the marketplace; classes are held in the evenings for at least 10 weeks, conditions that do not meet business customers' needs.

Local Competitors

Eight local businesses and four individuals listed in the current Yellow Pages under the classification "Computer Software, Services" indicate they provide training. An unknown number of additional individual consultants provide such training but are not listed in the phone directory. Since the publication of the directory, two of the eight companies have ceased operation.

Only one local company has developed a substantial presence with the target market: JMT Training. JMT has operated for more than six years and is the single largest local software training company.

Indicates specific competitors

The individual independent consultants generally provide training for merely one or two software programs, and only one consultant, Seth Rose, has a meaningful client base for his highly regarded spreadsheet training programs.

Other Competition

Three major national software training companies periodically conduct workshops in hotels in the Vespucci area. Lesser known national companies also occasionally provide such services, generally targeting recent purchasers of particular software. Online training is relatively new, with little or no market acceptance.

SAMPLE PLAN: The Competition (continued)

In-house training taught by employees of the targeted companies varies widely in content, form, and quality. Very few companies have "trainers"; most training is provided on an ad hoc basis from supervisors and fellow workers. A conservative interpretation of ComputerEase survey results would indicate at least one-fifth of such training would be contracted out if satisfactory training could be obtained.

Market Share Distribution

In response to a ComputerEase survey, target companies currently conducting software training utilize providers as indicated by the pie chart below:

Current Total Market Share Distribution for Business Software Training in Vespucci, Indiana

Community College 2%

Software Developers 8%

Local Training Companies 14%

National Training Programs 14%

Individual Contractors 17%

In-house 45%

Advantages Over Competition

A chart outlining ComputerEase's competitive position is included in the Appendix. Generally, the advantages ComputerEase has in relation to its competitors are:

- Local, as opposed to national, provider.

- Ongoing support and repeat training at no or low cost, as opposed to those with no support services or added expense.

- Add-on "high productivity" training for customers to realize maximum potential from employees and computers; rarely offered by competitors.

- Coordinated, consistent marketing and sales programs.

- A professional, business-oriented image.

- Status as "Authorized Training Centers" for software publishers (two such relationships secured, six others to be approved within six to eighteen months) giving credibility, joint programs, and prerelease and steeply discounted software.

- Business-oriented, rather than computer-oriented, management.

- High-quality, professional trainers on staff, rather than contract workers.

- Availability of downtown training center with new computers.

- Consistent, highest-quality training.

Competitive Positions

This is how ComputerEase ranks the strength of its competitors:

1. JMT Training
2. Seth Rose, independent
3. In-house trainers
4. National training sessions/online training
5. Other local companies
6. Other independent contractors

JMT is positioned to be the strongest competitor, due to its current client base, and the personality and sales skills of its owner, Janice Tuffrey, and its potential to associate with national franchise training operations. However, JMT's current training staff and materials are of inconsistent quality, and current clients have expressed dissatisfaction with the lack of quality control. Moreover, JMT lacks skilled management of its financial affairs, resulting in insufficient capital for marketing and updating equipment. No other local companies have either the financial or personnel resources to adequately respond to a well-organized, sufficiently funded competitor.

Seth Rose has established a reputation as an effective trainer of spreadsheet programs and has a loyal client base. However, he has expressed a lack of interest in expanding his operation by hiring additional trainers, and he has reached full or near-full capacity. ComputerEase has begun negotiating a strategic partnership with Mr. Rose to sell additional training to his current customers. No other independent contractor has a substantial client base or adequate resources to respond to new competition.

National training companies market their services entirely through direct mail and have little or no ongoing contact with their customers. Their customer base is neither loyal nor particularly satisfied with the service.

Barriers to Entry

It is relatively difficult for new competitors to enter the field. Substantial start-up costs are involved with purchasing or leasing equipment, and high-quality trainers are difficult to find. Moreover, software providers are becoming increasingly selective about which companies they will allow to serve as

Ranks competitors and describes strengths and weaknesses

SAMPLE PLAN: The Competition (continued)

"Authorized Training Companies." These relationships are crucial in terms of receiving prerelease, below-cost copies of software, co-sponsoring product introduction events, and customer perception.

Considers potential future competition

However, the long-term outlook for the industry points to nationally franchised local training companies and online "distance learning." This represents the most substantial threat. Recognizing this evolution, ComputerEase plans to affiliate with the highest-quality national franchise or independent trainers association as soon as practical, and potentially add its own distance learning training.

Strategic Opportunities

The market for computer training services is highly dissatisfied at present as shown by a survey of human resource directors of target companies. Their level of satisfaction with current training arrangements is shown below:

Highly satisfied   8%

Somewhat satisfied   18%

Somewhat unsatisfied 43%

Highly unsatisfied   31%

This unusually high dissatisfaction level with current providers represents a unique opportunity for ComputerEase in a rapidly expanding market.

## Chapter 9

Strategic Position & Risk Assessment

Strategy is Destiny

In today's highly competitive and constantly changing business environment, it's no longer enough just to know HOW to run a business; you also have to know WHAT business you're really running. While you must, of course, attend to the basics of operating your business, you also have to see exactly where you stand in the marketplace, what makes you compelling to customers, and what advantages you have over the competition. You need a clearly-defined strategic position.

Defining a strategic position is as important for the proverbial "mom and pop" family business as for a high technology company. The old neighborhood hardware store now competes not merely with another hardware store down the street, but also with Home Depot and other "big box" home repair retailers. And the owners of that local hardware store can no longer fall back on the comforting belief that "we're more convenient" — not when they also compete with hardware suppliers that sell over the Internet and deliver directly to customers' doors.

Today's business reality is that customers have easy, convenient access to many of your competitors, some of whom may sell the same or similar products or services for lower prices. In this environment, you have to develop a distinct impetus for your customer to keep doing business with you.

A Strategic Position Defines What You Do

One of the great advantages of outlining a strategic position is it gives you a touchstone when making business decisions. Just as a well-written

"If there's one thing I've found as an entrepreneur, as an investor, is there are a lot of different ways to make money. You just have to know which one you're pursuing. The problem comes when you think you're in one market, but you're really in another."

Andrew Anker
Venture Capitalist

mission statement guides your company's values and long-term vision, a well-delineated strategic position influences almost every aspect of your business, such as the development of your products or services, marketing, operations, and choice of location.

You can differentiate your company from its competitors in many ways. You have probably started a company with a sense of vision or purpose. You may have felt a lack in the market or wanted to pursue a particular passion. The key is to find the strategy that best aligns your strengths and interests to real opportunities in the competitive environment. Your strategic position should be where you find the following coming together:

- Your strengths and interests
- Industry trends and developments
- Market changes and opportunities
- Competitive changes and opportunities
- Changes and opportunities brought through new technologies

If you're already in business, you may have already evolved a strategic position, whether or not you realized it. You may have innately understood that you needed to carve out a distinct identity for your business to separate you from the competition and to help focus your activities.

Take the example of a flower shop in a large city. Two partners opened their store in a middle-class neighborhood, beginning as just a "bucket shop" — a place where people picked up a dozen flowers on their way home from work or sent a birthday bouquet. Over time, however, their talents and interests led them to start designing floral decorations for high society events and weddings. While that market was being served by others, demand for high-end florists was growing in their city. Because of their talents, they were able to compete effectively for this business.

To reinforce their new position, the two partners changed their operations and marketing. To gain visibility with their target market, they donated floral arrangements to charity benefits, created new brochures, and worked with different, more exotic and expensive flowers. Eventually, only a small percent of their income and profits came from the local neighborhood. As a result, when the nearby supermarket began selling cut flowers (and later, when customers could order arrangements over the Internet), it had little impact on this florist's business.

Instead of pursuing the obvious business strategy — serving their neighborhood — they instead found an opening in the overall competitive market that fit their abilities. They found their strategic position.

A Strategic Position Also Defines What You Don't Do

Defining a strategic position is particularly important for new companies that must quickly distinguish themselves from the competition. Since your resources are always limited (especially in younger companies), having a clear strategic position assists you in figuring out how to allocate those resources.

As important as helping you determine what to do, a well-defined strategic position is a boon in helping you decide what NOT to do. This not only saves you a lot of time and money, but also makes you more confident of your business decisions, some of which may not be understood by others.

In the case of the florist, for instance, on any given day, a shopper might have walked into their store and not been able to find so much as a dozen roses or daisies. The partners stopped advertising in the Yellow Pages. When their lease was up, they moved to a less-convenient, second-story location, which could hardly be seen from the street.

These all seem like foolish moves if you think of this florist as a typical retail flower shop, but they were all decisions consistent with the partners' strategy: to target the upscale event market. With minimal desire for walk-in traffic, location was less critical, and they had little need to keep flowers on hand. They had carefully chosen their position, which helped them understand what activities were of lower priority. They didn't try to be all things to all people.

Strategic Position Is More than Advertising

Don't be confused: a true strategic position is not the same as an advertising campaign or slogan. Advertising and marketing are means to achieving your strategic position — they help you create the image consistent with your position and get your message to potential customers. Defining a strategic position is about creating a meaningful place for yourself — a position — in the market.

How does Coke differentiate itself from Pepsi? Very little of the difference is based on the qualities of the products or the market segment they are targeting. The two companies may have incorporated some operational differences, but they differentiate themselves primarily on the basis of advertising — not strategic positioning. When Snapple came along, they created a totally different position for themselves in the market. Snapple didn't try to compete head-to-head with Coke and Pepsi; instead, they looked for a different segment of the soft drink market: the non-cola, non-carbonated soft drink.

If a luxury car company that has sold primarily to older consumers decides to market to younger drivers, it won't be enough to take the same kind of car they've been making and devise a clever advertising campaign. The product itself — in this case a car — has to be redesigned to fit the tastes of their target market. It may have to be smaller, sportier, faster, with more electronic gadgets. Not only will the marketing materials need to be geared toward a younger audience, but the salespeople will have to be trained to learn that the twenty-something kid in the rock band T-shirt may not be just killing time with a test drive but may actually be an Internet millionaire ready to buy.

What Kinds Of Strategic Positions Are There?

What makes a company different? Is it the nature of their products or services? The quality or cost? The geographic area or type of customers served? Perhaps the company has proprietary products customers can't find elsewhere.

There are many ways to distinguish yourself from your competitors, including:

- Customer Perception Factors
- Market Segment
- Market Share
- Operational/Technological Advantages
- Proprietary Products, Technology, Abilities, or Relationships
- Sales Channels

Each of these strategic approaches offers opportunities but also poses pitfalls. And they may be related: if you are positioning your company on the basis of low price, you'll also need operational efficiencies to reduce costs or else you won't be able to survive against competitors with higher profit margins.

Customer Perception Factors

This is the "better, faster, cheaper" approach based on how customers distinguish your company and its products and services from the competition. Some key customer perception factors include:

- Price
- Quality
- Features
- Customer service
- Societal impact (environmental, animal testing, etc.)
- Convenience

Concentrating on customer perception factors is the most typical method of attempting to differentiate yourself from the competition. They seem the simplest, most straight-forward way to compete. Surprisingly, they may be the most difficult to achieve and maintain. For instance, competing on the basis of price is often perilous. While it is easy — in the short run — to attract customers on the basis of low price, highly price-sensitive customers are the most fickle, quickly tempted away by the next company offering a lower price. Once you appear to be attracting a significant portion of the market, well-funded established competitors can lower prices (even if they have to take a loss) to compete temporarily until you are no longer able to sustain your losses.

Other perception factors may be harder to "prove" to the market. You may have to spend a lot of money on marketing and advertising to get

> *"You have to understand the consumer's need. What's their pain? Why do they need to change? Solve that pain, and then get that message out."*
>
> **Andrew Anker**
> **Venture Capitalist**

customers to realize that you offer additional features, more convenience or higher quality. Once you do, however, you may be able to build a loyal and committed customer base that appreciates the differences between you and your competition.

Market Segment

This strategy is based on targeting a specific portion of the total market. Some possible ways of segmenting the market are:

- Geographic location
- Age, income, interests, family size, etc. of consumer served (in business-to-consumer companies)
- Age, size, and/or industry of business served (in business-to-business companies)
- Customers' specialized need

Deciding to aim at a particular market segment or "niche" offers many competitive advantages, especially for newer and/or smaller companies. While you trade having a larger total market from which to attract customers, you can more easily (and often more inexpensively) gain visibility and credibility with a smaller, more focused market. Targeting a small market also gives you the opportunity to develop special expertise and experience, giving you an edge when competing head-to-head with others. For instance, a human resources consultant who specializes solely in serving hospitals will have a far easier time attracting additional hospitals as clients than a general human resources consultant.

The pitfalls in targeting a market segment are that the market size may not be big enough to sustain or grow your company, the target market may already be saturated with specialists, or, once you've proven that the target market is big enough and rich enough, larger companies will come in and compete with you.

Market Share

This strategy is based on establishing and commanding such a dominant portion of the total customer base that it becomes difficult for others to compete. The goal is to become the "800-pound gorilla" of a market.

It's almost impossible — and very expensive — to displace entrenched market leaders in established market segments. In the soft drink market, for instance, it's forbidding to try to compete against Coke and Pepsi. Even well-funded competitors (such as Virgin Cola) have difficulty gaining a few percentage points of market share. Newcomers in mature markets typically must pursue niche market strategies (such as Snapple).

But when factors allow new markets to open — as has happened with the Internet or with falling trade barriers that let foreign competitors enter a nation's market — tremendous opportunities become available. Then, there's a rush to capture customers' awareness — or "mind share" — hoping to translate that to market share. In such instances, entrepreneurs try to get their companies, products, or services established before the competition. In Internet and technology instances, there's typically a particular urgency to gain a "first mover advantage" (see below).

Operational and/or Technological Advantages

Another strategy is to gain significant competitive advantages through instituting better internal procedures, operations, or technology, giving you substantial benefits — such as higher profit margins — over the competition. Because these advantages are often unseen — directly — by customers, their significance is often unrealized. However, many companies have succeeded not by clever market strategies but by running their business better than the competition. For instance, See's Candies' inventory management system results in very fresh candy at its stores with minimal waste; this results in better tasting candy and higher profit margins.

Proprietary Products, Technology, Abilities, or Relationships

Another strategic position is to develop or secure exclusive assets that will be difficult or impossible for competitors to replicate. For manufacturing and technology companies, these may be patents, processes, or copyrights. For others, proprietary assets might include distribution agreements, licenses, strategic partnerships, even hiring certain employees with exceptional talents. The key to this being an effective strategy is that you have to identify those aspects of your business where proprietary assets make a real difference, and then you must secure those assets in such a way that your competitors can't easily replicate or circumvent them.

Sales Channels

In some instances, you may be able to differentiate your company by the manner in which you reach and sell to customers. For instance, some computer companies, such as Dell, distinguished themselves early on by selling directly to consumers rather than through retail computer outlets. Later, the Internet opened up the opportunity for many other companies to circumvent existing sales channels and sell directly to customers. But using different sales channels as a key strategy doesn't necessarily require a high tech approach — Tupperware uses house parties instead of retail outlets to compete against Rubbermaid.

First Mover Advantage?

"No one's ever done anything like this before." Many entrepreneurs believe their key strategic position is that they've developed a new concept — product, service, technology, Internet business — before anyone else. They recognize that there's a big advantage in being first; the fear of others beating them to market keeps many entrepreneurs working around the clock.

If you can get your company, product, service, or website established before the competition, you gain what is called the "first mover advantage." Being first potentially enables you to capture so many customers that it becomes difficult for a significant portion of the market (in technology terms, the "installed user base") to change.

"The fact that we were first meant that we had to fight the least to get attention. That gave us a period of five or six months of being one of the very few games in town, and that enabled us to build the customers' sense of habit that you need. By the time we had to market ourselves against the competition, we had built customers' habits."

Andrew Anker
Venture Capitalist

Being first to a market brings many advantages, including the ability to:

- Capture significant market share before competitors enter the market;
- Secure key strategic partners, making fewer opportunities available to later competitors;
- Attract outstanding employees and management;
- Capture media attention;
- Lock in financing sources, such as venture capitalists.

Going after a "first mover advantage" carries its own risks as well as rewards. In most businesses, there are few truly effective barriers-to-entry. Will you end up merely serving as the research-and-development arm of copy-cat companies? There's also the very real risk that if you're doing something truly new, the market (and financing sources) may not be ready for you. In fact, many second- or third-to-market companies benefit from avoiding the costs of educating the market, conducting extensive research and development, and hiring highly creative people.

If gaining the first-mover advantage is part of your key business strategy, ask yourself, "How defensible is this position? What will I need to make it defensible?" Remember, patents, copyrights, and other proprietary information only go so far. Can you develop strategic alliances or lock in customers, distributors, and financing sources to make it difficult for future competitors to take you on?

With a first mover strategy, there is also the risk of doing something fast but not well, allowing your inevitable competition to honestly tout itself as a much improved version. So continually work on improving your products, services, marketing, and operations. Look for ways to leverage being first into being best.

Branding

One increasingly important strategy that many companies pursue is intentionally trying to build a brand. By becoming a brand name, customers develop such a strong relationship with your company that it is difficult for others to compete.

There are, obviously, many advantages to being a brand name, but it is not easy to achieve. First, it is usually expensive. You must spend a great deal of money on marketing and advertising just to get your name well-known. And, although it seems like some brand names develop over night, especially with Internet businesses, building a brand is hard to achieve quickly.

Building a truly strong brand is more than just a matter of name recognition. A real brand gives customers trust in your products and services because you are consistent in quality, price, service, or convenience — over time. This doesn't mean you have to promise the highest quality or the lowest price — it just means being consistent, so the customer can depend on what they'll get from that brand. McDonald's doesn't have to

"It's all about brand — being in front of the customer. On the net or in media in general, everything is about brand and creating habits."

Andrew Anker
Venture Capitalist

promise gourmet food to be a reliable brand. McDonald's built its brand by giving customers the same experience, the same type and quality of food, the same cleanliness, at every one of their restaurants.

If your goal is to build a brand name, you have to look at those factors that you are able to offer and deliver to your customers consistently and repeatedly over time, making certain you put sufficient company resources into supporting those factors.

Risk

Every business involves risk. Only the most naive and inexperienced entrepreneurs believe their business "just can't fail." Use this section to sit down and think through the various risks facing your new endeavor.

This task might seem daunting. So why shake your enthusiasm? Because risk assessment helps you prepare for and prevent threats to your success. If, for instance, you identify a major risk as the possibility that a well-funded competitor will enter the market, you will want to take steps to quickly secure key customer contracts or line up significant funding yourself.

Evaluating your risks isn't meant to be an exercise in fear (although if you are intimidated by the risks involved than perhaps you are not yet ready to start your business). Many entrepreneurs think that if they describe the risks they're likely to encounter, they'll scare off potential investors. Quite the contrary is true. For all but the least sophisticated investors, an evaluation of risks shows them you're willing to take a cool, hard look at the situation facing you, and you understand the scope of the threats to your success. It reassures investors that, because you understand the risks involved, you're more likely to take steps to counter those threats.

What kinds of risk?

It's not just a matter of high risk or low risk. It's also what kinds of risk. Some risks are more tolerable or more important to different investors — and to you. A few of the key types of risk facing companies include:

- **Market Risk:** that the market will not respond to your products or services, either because there is no real market need or the market isn't yet ready. Market risks are very difficult to overcome.

- **Competitive Risk:** that the competitive situation will change dramatically, and new competitors will enter the market and/or established competitors will reposition their products or services to more effectively take you on. You should carefully think through how other competitors might respond to your entering the market and not assume that the competitive environment will remain the same.

- **Technology Risk:** that the technology or product design and engineering won't work or won't work as well as you envision. This may be critically important to your company's success, or it may be totally unimportant, depending on the nature of your company, its products/services, customers, etc. If your business faces substantial technology risks, what is your ability to quickly and effectively improve the technology?

- **Product Risk:** that the product won't materialize, won't be finished in time, or won't work as promised. This is very similar to the above, only with non-technology products or services.

- **Execution Risk:** that you won't be able to effectively manage the roll-out and growth of the company because management isn't sufficiently capable, the time allowed isn't adequate, operations aren't in place, etc. You should be able to demonstrate specific steps you are taking to reduce or eliminate such risks.

- **Capitalization Risk:** that you've badly underestimated costs or over-estimated income, and you will run out of money. The best way to avoid these risks is to budget realistically and get enough funding so you do not run out of money prematurely. Look for investors who have the ability and inclination to offer additional funds as your company progresses.

Use the Risk Evaluation worksheet on page 128 to assess the risks your business faces.

Balancing Risks & Opportunities

Once you've outlined your risks, you may feel overwhelmed. But while there are many risks, there are also substantial rewards — otherwise why are you bothering to start this endeavor?

A typical method to illustrate the balance between risks and opportunities is to develop a "SWOT" chart, delineating your company's strengths, weaknesses, opportunities, and threats (thus "S.W.O.T.") This is a good exercise for quickly sizing up your company's position.

Complete the "SWOT" grid on page 129. Be sure to include both internal and external, current and potential, factors.

Chapter Summary

In today's business environment, it is critical for every company to understand the ways it is meaningfully different from its competitors. Defining your strategic position enables you to more clearly and thoroughly answer the question, "What business are you in?" When you find excellent opportunities in the market that fit with your strengths and interests, you can carve out a strategic position to distinguish your company from others. There is no one "correct" strategy, and your strategic position will evolve over time. Honestly assessing your risks enables you to better reduce potential threats to your success. It also reassures potential investors that you have a clear-eyed view of what you're getting into.

Risk Evaluation

Specify the major risk(s) facing your company in each area, rate the approximate extent of that risk (high-, medium-, or low-risk), and note steps you can take, or have taken, to lessen that risk:

Type of Risk	Risk Probability/ Percentage	Steps to Reduce This Risk
Market Risk		
Competitive Risk		
Technology Risk		
Product Risk		
Execution Risk		
Capitalization Risk		

SWOT: Strengths / Weaknesses / Opportunities / Threats

In each appropriate box below, list your company's strengths or weaknesses, and the opportunities or threats facing it.

Strengths

Weaknesses

Opportunities

Threats

Strategic Position Plan Preparation Form

The information you provide on this form can be used as the basis for the Strategic Position & Risk Analysis section of your business plan.

Industry Trends: _____

_____

_____

_____

_____

_____

Target Market: _____

_____

_____

_____

_____

_____

Competitive Environment: _____

_____

_____

_____

_____

_____

Your Strengths Relative to the Competition: _____

_____

_____

_____

_____

_____

Risks: _____

_____

_____

_____

_____

Use this information as the basis of your plan's Strategic Position section.

Strategic Position & Risk Analysis

ComputerEase's objective is to be the premier software training company in the greater Vespucci area. To achieve that goal, we have developed a strategic position that emphasizes:

- In-person, hands-on training
- Customized training developed for customers' proprietary software or specific needs
- Training that emphasizes productivity as much as skills.

ComputerEase's Strategic Position is based on evaluating the following factors:

A. Industry Trends

B. Our Target Market

C. The Competitive Environment

D. Our Strengths

E. Risks

Industry Trends

The software training industry is trending toward development of regional or national providers rather than small training companies or individual consultants. Online, distance learning, is becoming a major, cost-effective delivery system for training programs, and the number and quality of such programs keeps increasing. Certification from national software developers continues to be a critical requirement for doing business.

Target Market

Our target is the corporate training market (rather than consumer). This market is strong and growing and is less price-sensitive than the consumer market. They often develop customized software for their specific needs as well as using "off-the-shelf" products.

Competitive Environment

There is no other national or regional software training provider yet in the Vespucci area. This affords us the opportunity to build substantial relationships with our target market — corporations and government entities — before an effective competitor enters the area. However, there are already a few, extremely well-funded Internet-based training companies, and we anticipate substantial competitive pressure from them.

Our Strengths

We excel at in-person training, and select our instructors not only on their computer knowledge but their ability to translate complex technology issues

SAMPLE PLAN: Strategic Position & Risk Analysis (continued)

into understandable language, their patience, and their teaching effectiveness. Another of our strengths is our ability to quickly and effectively develop customized training programs, built around the customer's proprietary software, or to meet other specific customer needs.

Risks

One major potential threat is the growth in online, distance learning. Internet companies and national software training companies already offer such training programs for a number of leading software products at substantially lower fees than ComputerEase can offer. A related risk is that major software companies will fund, buy, or start their own online training programs, making it more difficult to compete with and get certified by such software companies. A third risk is the health of the economy: economic downturns lead to fewer new employees being hired, and thus trained, by our target market. Finally, a fourth potential risk, one that appears minor at this point, is that software developers will make software that is easier to use, thus reducing the need for training.

Strategic Position

Evaluating those factors has led us to conclude that our major threat is online training. While we intend to develop some distance learning programs ourselves, this is not the area of our greatest strength, and we will not be able to compete effectively against better-funded competitors in this arena.

Even in light of the substantial potential for online learning, we are confident there will be a continuing need for outstanding live, in-person training. A significant percentage of customers require or prefer an instructor present to answer questions and demonstrate techniques, often on a one-to-one basis. We are confident that many customers will find online training programs insufficient. Moreover, online companies are unable, or far less able, to develop training programs based on customers' proprietary software. Customers will instead need to have customized training programs developed to meet their particular needs. Further, we believe our target market will be willing to pay more to receive both customized and/or in-person training.

Devising our training programs to achieve increased productivity as well as to train basic software skills enables us to continue to offer valuable training programs to customers even if they reduce the number of their new hires. Productivity programs are less vulnerable to economic downturns.

To achieve this strategic position, we place particular emphasis on the skills, attitudes, and personalities of our instructors. We recognize that the quality of their instruction, their patience, and their effectiveness must be substantially superior to online teachers. We must also retain effective training program developers capable of devising customized programs.

## Chapter 10

Marketing Plan & Sales Strategy

*Tell them what they get,
not what you do.*

Reaching and Capturing Customers

You have to have customers to stay in business: it's the most basic business truth. That's why an effective marketing plan to communicate with, motivate, and secure customers is vital for your company's success. Since reaching customers costs money, and money is always limited, your marketing strategy must be carefully and thoughtfully designed. If you are developing a business plan to seek outside funding, remember many investors read the marketing plan portion closely. They want to know you have a realistic and price-conscious strategy to get your product or service into the hands of customers.

In your marketing plan you define:

- How you make customers aware of your product or service;
- What message you are trying to convey to customers about your product, service, or company;
- Specific methods you use to deliver and reinforce that message; and
- How you secure actual sales.

Note that marketing and sales, although closely related, are two different activities. Marketing is designed to increase customer awareness and deliver a message; sales is the direct action taken to solicit and procure customer orders. Thus, marketing includes activities such as advertising, creating brochures and collateral materials, and public relations; sales encompasses telemarketing, sales calls, and direct-mail solicitations.

"Some people think it's either win or lose. But every game is followed by another. An analogy in business is that every sales call will be followed by another. You're always preparing for the next one. So it's important to make each game as close as possible, do as well as you can on each call. Even in the process of losing, even if you don't make the sale, you're improving and refining your skills, and how well you perform when you lose is important in determining whether you will eventually win."

Bill Walsh
Former Coach and
President, S.F. 49ers

In devising and implementing your marketing strategy, you may wish to use the services of specialists such as marketing consultants, advertising agencies, and public relations advisors. While these professionals can increase the focus and effectiveness of your efforts, you must never relinquish the marketing program entirely to outsiders — it is far too crucial to the definition and success of your business.

This chapter provides the basic tools you need when outlining a marketing strategy to be included in a business plan document.

Your Company's Message

Anyone who's ever seen an ad for Calvin Klein jeans, with an attractive model seductively suggesting, "Nothing comes between me and my Calvins," quickly gets the message, and it has nothing to do with price or durability. This company is selling sex appeal by telling customers, "Wearing Calvin Klein jeans will make you more attractive."

Every business sends a message in its marketing. This message, based on the strategic position the company stakes out for itself, emphasizes particular attributes, such as "low-price leader" or "one-day service." Or perhaps the message exploits a market niche: "specialists in estate planning" or "software for architects." Maybe the message is less direct and aimed more at the customer's self-image: "the choice of a new generation" or "you deserve a break today."

The Four P's of Marketing

What messages do you give customers to motivate them to purchase your product or service? Traditional marketing experts emphasize the elements described below, known as "the Four P's," in influencing customers to buy.

1. **Product.** The tangible aspects of the product or service itself.
2. **Price.** The cost advantage.
3. **Place.** The location's convenience and decor.
4. **Promotion.** The amount and nature of the marketing activities.

These elements leave a lot out of the marketing picture, however, especially as customers have become more discriminating over the years and look for products or services not just to fill an immediate need but to enhance their overall sense of well-being.

Most marketing strategists agree that people buy benefits, not features. In other words, customers are more concerned about how a purchase will affect their lives than about how the company achieves those results. So your marketing message must tell customers what they get, such as security or an enhanced self-image, rather than just the detailed specifics of what your product or service does.

What Customers Want: The Five F's

"The Five F's," shown below, are a convenient way to sum up what customers want.

"Even in a small business, you've got to come up with a concept that's just a little bit different. Finding the concept is critical. We went for a European coffee bar atmosphere, with people standing at a bar for coffee and cappuccino; no one else was doing that at the time. We reinforced the concept by paying attention to details. Little things make a big difference. We have hooks under the bar for customers to hang hand-bags or hats; we have books as well as newspapers for customers to read. Using large European bowls, instead of cups, to serve our cafe lattes made us memorable, and now they are widely copied."

Martha Johnson
Restauranteur

1. **Functions.** How does the product or service meet their concrete needs?
2. **Finances.** How will the purchase affect their overall financial situation, not just the price of the product or service, but other savings and increased productivity?
3. **Freedom.** How convenient is it to purchase and use the product or service? How will they gain more time and less worry in other aspects of their lives?
4. **Feelings.** How does the product or service make customers feel about themselves, and how does it affect and relate to their self-image? Do they like and respect the salesperson and the company?
5. **Future.** How will they deal with the product or service and company over time? Will support and service be available? How will the product or service affect their lives in the coming years, and will they have an increased sense of security about the future?

Customers, of course, want to receive benefits in all these areas, and you should be aware of how your product or service fulfills the entire range of their needs. However, your primary message must concentrate on one or two of these benefits that most effectively motivate your customers and that stake out a competitive position for your company.

You communicate these benefits through every interaction you have with your customers, not just through your advertising. Naturally, your company slogan and any words you use in advertisements deliver an overt statement to the potential customer. Perhaps the name of the business itself is a direct message, for example, "One-Hour Photo" or "Cheap Tickets."

Power of the Indirect Message

Indirect messages can leave an even stronger impression with customers. If brochures are cleanly designed and sales representatives conservatively dressed, it conveys the impression that the company is professional and responsible. If the decor features trendy colors and rock music plays in the background, the implication is that the company is youthful and contemporary.

Sometimes, unfortunately, a company sends out mixed messages, for example, having nicely dressed salespeople but poorly printed sales material. How will you convey an image to your customer that reinforces your direct message? How will you add value to your product or service through design, packaging, and presentation?

The Five F's worksheet on page 136 helps you organize your answers to these questions; the information then can be incorporated into the Marketing section of your business plan. This worksheet helps you summarize how you reinforce your company's image and what you are trying to tell customers about your product or service. Use the information for internal planning as well as in your business plan.

"We're always looking for ways to maintain a positive image. For instance, when we decided we wanted to make sure we were exposing our product to health conscious people, we supplied our lollipops to runners after a footrace. At a convention of physicians, we had a table promoting the idea of nutritional balance. Our product can be part of a healthy lifestyle, and we want to reinforce that idea."

Charles Huggins
President, See's Candies

"Everything supports the vision. That's the key in retailing. Everything must reinforce the central concept you are trying to convey to your target market, including your product lines, the customer service you offer, architectural design, the hours you're open, even the type of bags you use."

Nancy Glaser
Business Strategies
Consultant

The Five F's

Keeping the Five F's in mind, describe the message you are trying to convey to customers about your product or service.

Functions: _____

_____

Finances: _____

_____

Freedom: _____

_____

Feelings: _____

_____

Future: _____

_____

Which of these messages is the most important in motivating your target market to purchase? _____

_____

How will you express this message to your customer in the areas listed below?

Business Name: _____

Slogan: _____

Key Words in Marketing Material: _____

_____

Product Design: _____

Logo: _____

Website Design: _____

_____

Other Graphic Images/Design: _____

_____

Packaging: _____

Decor: _____

Style of Clothing Worn by Employees: _____

Merchandising/Displays/Presentation Materials: _____

_____

Other: _____

_____

_____

Marketing Vehicles

Once you have clarified what you want to tell customers about your company, you must describe how you disseminate that information.

How do you reach potential customers? Do you advertise? If so, where? Do you send direct mail? If so, to what mailing lists? Do you participate in trade shows? If so, which ones and how frequently?

Since every marketing vehicle costs money, carefully plan how you intend to spend your marketing dollars. In devising your overall marketing program, be sure you look for:

- **Fit.** Your marketing vehicles must reach your actual target customer and be appropriate to your image.
- **Mix.** Use more than one method so customers get exposure to you from a number of sources.
- **Repetition.** It takes many exposures before a customer becomes aware of a message.
- **Affordability.**

Use the Marketing Vehicles worksheet on page 138 to document how you employ various marketing vehicles in your business.

Be Resourceful

Often the best marketing vehicles are not the most obvious or the most expensive. A large ad in a specialty publication may prove far more effective and less expensive than a small one in a general newspaper.

You may want to consult the *Standard Rate and Data Service* to find names and advertising rates of specialty and general publications. To find information on trade shows, look on the Internet for trade organizations in your industry, The website of the American Society of Association Executives is particularly helpful.

American Society of Association Executives Online
www.asaenet.org

You can also find an extensive listing of trade shows online at

TSNN.com
www.tsnn.com

Or refer to books, such as the *Trade Shows and Professional Exhibits Directory,* published by Gale Research; *Trade Show & Exhibit Schedule,* published by Successful Meetings Data Bank; or *Trade Show Week Data Book,* published by Trade Show Week. If you are marketing to businesses, identify potential customers for direct mail or telemarketing efforts through the *Thomas Register.*

Some of the marketing vehicles you may choose include:

Marketing Vehicles $ ➤ $$ ➤ $$$

Use this worksheet to outline your marketing schedule, listing each type of marketing vehicle, the frequency with which you use it, and what it costs you annually. This is the basis of your marketing budget and will be used in the Financials section of your business plan.

Vehicle	Specifics	Frequency	Cost per Year
Professional Assistance			
Marketing / PR Consultants			
Advertising Agencies			
Direct Mail Specialists			
Graphic Design / Web Design			
Brochures / Leaflets / Flyers			
Signs / Billboards			
Merchandising Displays			
Sampling / Premiums			
Media Advertising			
Print (newspaper, etc.)			
Television and Radio			
Online			
Other Media			
Phone Directories			
Advertising Specialties			
Direct Mail			
Website			
Development / Programming			
Maintenance and Hosting			
Trade Shows			
Fees and Setup			
Travel / Shipping			
Exhibits / Signs			
Public Relations Activities / Materials			
Informal Marketing / Networking			
Memberships / Meetings			
Entertainment			
Other			
Total			$

- **Brochures.** Leaflets, flyers, or other descriptive circulars; these are particularly useful for service businesses.
- **Company Website.** A very effective way to describe your products or services in depth and be available to customers everywhere at all hours.
- **Print Media.** Newspapers, magazines, and specialty publications.
- **Broadcast Media.** Radio can be targeted to specific markets; cable television can likewise target specific markets; network stations can be very expensive.
- **Online Advertising.** Paying for visibility on other websites; these can be banner ads, sponsorship of other sites, purchasing of 'words' in search engines, participating in online 'malls.'
- **Advertising Specialties.** Items imprinted with the company name given to customers, e.g., calendars, caps, desk sets, and gifts.
- **Direct Mail.** Flyers, catalogues, brochures, and coupons.
- **Email mailings.** Regular or infrequent mailings to email mail lists; these can be direct advertisements or online 'newsletters.'
- **Public Relations.** Free feature and news articles in the media and other publicity, usually secured by public relations specialists.
- **Sampling.** Distribution of free product samples, or coupons entitling recipients to free or discounted samples of your product or service.
- **Informal Marketing/Networking.** Activities such as joining organizations, public speaking, or attending conferences.

"Our marketing strategy included a large opening party for neighbors, bankers and insurance providers; limited advertising targeted only to neighborhood publications; menu distribution to all major institutions and employers in the area; and word-of-mouth to friends and local businesses."

Martha Johnson
Restauranteur

Marketing Tactics

In addition to direct marketing methods, you can employ a number of creative strategies to promote your company. These tactics often involve little or no extra cost and can be the source of substantial increased revenues. Complete the Marketing Tactics worksheet on page 140 to indicate marketing tactics you utilize to increase sales.

Various industries have particular marketing tactics, and enterprising entrepreneurs devise unique methods to reach customers. A few important strategies to consider in your marketing approach are described below.

Media Advertising

Advertising works. Customers expect to learn about products and services from ads in newspapers and magazines, on the radio or television, or from the Internet. Advertising gets your company's name and message to a large number of people with relatively little work on your part. But it costs money. Don't buy ads based merely on the number of people reached; make sure the ad is reaching the right people: your target market. A badly designed and written ad may be worse than no ad at all, so spend the time and money to develop a good one. Run ads repetitively; professionals estimate it takes nine exposures to an ad before someone even notices it.

Customer-Based Marketing

Often neglected, this is one of the most fruitful types of marketing. Two particularly effective approaches are to emphasize repeat sales by positioning your product or service to be consumed or replaced, and add-on sales, whereby you increase the total revenues per customer through the sale of extra products or services.

Another approach is point-of-purchase promotion: merchandising displays or other offers presented to customers at time of sale to encourage impulse purchases.

Strategic Partnerships

Identify a related company with which to associate for promotion, sales, or distribution. Ways in which you might use such a partnership include:

- **Cooperative Advertising.** This type of advertising occurs when two companies are mentioned in an advertisement and each company pays part of the costs. This is a frequent practice in many industries.
- **Licensing.** One company may grant permission to another to use its product, name, or trademark. For instance, instead of selling your computer software program directly, you might license it to another software publisher to incorporate in its program.

Marketing Tactics $ ➤ $$ ➤ $$$

Customer-Based Marketing: How do you increase sales to current customers? _____

_____

_____

Strategic Partnerships: What relationships do you have with other companies to help promote, sell, or distribute your product or service? _____

_____

_____

Special Offers / Promotions: What reduced-priced values do you offer to encourage sales? _____

_____

_____

Premiums: What gifts or prizes do you offer to build goodwill and sales? _____

_____

_____

Other Tactics: _____

_____

_____

- **Distribution Agreement.** This is an agreement whereby one company carries another's product line and distributes another company's products or services
- **Bundling.** This is a relationship between two companies where one company includes another company's product or services as part of a total package.

Special Offers/Promotions

Special offers and promotions enable you to increase sales revenue and build market share by offering customers special values. The tendency is to consider this primarily a retail tactic, but service companies and business-to-business marketing can also incorporate the practice.

Strategies include leader pricing — products or services on which you make little or no profit — to entice first-time customers and increase patronage, and introductory or limited time offers to build cash flow at critical points.

Premiums

The use of premiums in marketing includes encouraging sales and creating goodwill through gifts, sweepstakes, discounts, and other perceived added values. These "extras" can be packaged with products or services, such as free wine glasses with a two-bottle box of wine, given as gifts with a purchase, or offered as discounts, often in conjunction with other companies (such as travel discounts), for established customers. Many websites use sweepstakes with prizes to attract visitors to their sites.

Your Sales Structure

Directly related to your marketing strategy is your sales structure — how you achieve actual customer orders. In this section of your plan, describe the two main components of your sales system: the sales force and the sales process.

If your business plan document is being used for external funding requests, you don't need to go into great detail; it is enough to provide a general outline, giving a sense of your understanding of what is necessary to produce sales. For internal planning, however, you should flesh out these concepts more thoroughly.

The Heartbeat of Your Sales Force

At the center of your company's income-producing activities are those members of your staff with specific sales responsibilities. These are the people who come in direct contact with your potential customers and who most immediately determine whether your product or service is actually purchased. These key staff members are your sales team, and you must carefully plan how you make the best use of their skills and time.

What responsibilities do you give your sales team? What commissions and incentives do you provide? How do you train and supervise the people responsible for bringing in your revenues?

"We want our salespeople emotionally involved with the product. We let them know about new products and encourage employees to sample the product. We also provide periodic seminars and training programs. We offer opportunities for advancement, and we have bonus incentives based on the overall performance of all shops in a manager's area for all employees in that area."

Charles Huggins
President, See's Candies

"With public relations, you need to keep your best foot forward at all times. You should be scrupulously honest, as direct as possible; at the same time, you want to protect your long-term goals and the reputation and dignity of any individuals involved. It's important to maintain a certain public perception of your organization, so you can't go into all the details of each decision. The public has a hard time handling negatives. You must have standard, acceptable methods and forms of response to critical questions and inquiries."

Bill Walsh
Former Coach and
President, S.F. 49ers

Of course, every employee actually has a part in attracting and retaining customers: If the janitor does a poor job and the store looks dirty, customers may not want to buy from you. Thus, some companies incorporate some form of sales-related training for all personnel. But certain staff members (and nonemployees, as well) have particular responsibilities for securing sales, and these individuals are the center of your sales team.

Sales Activities

Sales activities can be conducted either on your business' premises or by calling on customers at their homes or places of business. And your sales force can consist of either inside or outside salespeople.

- **Inside Sales Personnel.** Employees who remain on the company's premises to secure sales; includes floor salespeople in retail stores, personnel who take phone orders, and telemarketing.

- **Outside Sales Personnel.** Salespeople who go to customers' locations to solicit orders; these can be company employees working on salary alone, salary plus commission, or straight commission; or they can be independent contractors — sales representatives and manufacturer's agents, either representing many product lines or handling one company's products exclusively, usually on a commission-only basis.

You can also hire independent telemarketing services to conduct your telephone sales from their place of business, using their employees.

Once you determine the nature of your sales team, delineate how you divide responsibilities among personnel, for example, assigning sales representatives by territories, product lines, or customer types.

Employee Compensation and Training

How do you pay your sales force? Some form of commission is common in most selling situations. What commission percentage do you provide? Do you give bonuses for reaching certain goals?

Do you use other incentives, such as awards, gifts, or vacations? Do district managers or other supervisors receive commissions on their staff's sales?

You also need to consider how you continue to train, motivate, and supervise your sales force. Selling is a difficult, often dispiriting, task, and salespeople need frequent encouragement and support. Who will be responsible for this? The Sales Force worksheet on page 144 helps you outline the structure of your sales team.

Sales Process

Finally, you need to identify the procedures you use in making sales calls and presentations, and the level of results you expect from your sales force. Although this information is not necessary to include in a business plan prepared for external financing purposes, the data on sales productivity is important in developing realistic sales forecasts.

How will actual sales be achieved? Some methods include:

"In seeking strategic partners, the first criterion is to find those groups that have a shared view of what we are trying to do. We have four criteria for choosing a strategic partner: 1) similar strong emphasis on marketing; 2) shared understanding of the target market; 3) agreement on the geographic area we're serving; and 4) ethical, quality people. We next try to find people who can give us better access to different types of media, and at better rates than we could secure. Often potential partners approach us, in other cases, our vice-president of sales contacts her counterpart in an organization we are interested in. Then we make sure that the partnership is as profitable for them as it is for us, or else they won't be coming back to us. This ensures their support for the endeavor and opens the door for future business partnerships."

Andre Tatibouet
President, Aston Hotels

- On-site sales
- Mail order sales
- Telephone sales
- Online sales
- Off-site sales (such as at the customer's place of business)
- Third-party sales

Some of the aspects you should consider in evaluating your sales process include:

- **Cold-Calling.** Contacting targeted customers before they have indicated any interest in purchasing your product or service; this can be done in person or on the phone.
- **Leads.** Developing or purchasing names of potential customers who have expressed at least some level of interest in your product or service.
- **Productivity.** The amount of time it takes to secure sales, and the level of sales realistically expected from each salesperson.
- **Order-Fulfillment.** Ensuring that orders are completed promptly and accurately, an essential completion of the sales process.
- **Goals.** Establishing specific, measurable objectives for each salesperson and the total sales force; realistically assessing the number of sales possible for each sales representative given the nature of his or her assigned territory/product line/customer base; setting sales quotas base; setting sales quotes based on these assessments.
- **Follow-up Efforts.** Ensuring that the sales representative maintains ongoing contact with the customer after the sale and seeks out repeat sales opportunities.

Use the Sales Process and Productivity worksheet on page 145 to outline the procedures and productivity levels you expect in your sales efforts.

Preparing the Marketing Section of Your Plan

You need to distill the highlights of your marketing and sales planning into a concise and compelling statement of how you reach customers and convince them to purchase from your company. The Marketing section of your business plan should include:

- The message you attempt to send customers; how you position your company in the market.
- The marketing methods and vehicles you use.
- The sales force and sales procedures you use.

The Monthly Marketing Budget and Monthly Sales Projections worksheets and Plan Preparation Form on the next several pages help you organize information for completion of your business plan's Marketing section.

"We book travel packages together (air transportation, hotel, etc.) with our strategic partners. We work in tandem with their salespeople. They may be making a heavy volume of sales calls, and they sell our hotel along with their product."

**Andre Tatibouet
President, Aston Hotels**

Sales Force

List below the type of sales force you use, and how many salespeople you have in each category.

Inside Sales Force: _____

Outside Sales Force (company–employee): _____

Outside Sales Representatives, Agents (nonemployee): _____

Telemarketing Services: _____

Other: _____
_____

How do you divide responsibilities, e.g., by product line, territory, customer type, etc.? _____
_____
_____

Do sales personnel have additional responsibilities as well as sales? _____
_____

What commissions do you pay sales personnel? _____
_____

Do commissions vary by product line or goals achieved? _____
_____

What other incentives or bonuses do you provide? _____
_____

For which expenses do you reimburse sales personnel, e.g., travel, entertainment? _____
_____
_____

What expenses must sales personnel pay for themselves? _____
_____
_____

Who supervises sales personnel? _____

Do they receive any commissions or bonuses based on performances of people they supervise? ☐ Yes ☐ No

Who trains sales personnel? _____

How often is training provided? _____

What kind of training is provided? _____

Which other employees are involved in generating sales? _____
_____

Sales Process and Productivity

On this worksheet outline the procedures and productivity levels you expect in your sales efforts.

Customer Identification

How do you identify potential customers? _____

Do you use "cold-calling"? _____

What prospect lists, if any, do you purchase? _____

What other methods do you use to determine customer interest? _____

Customer Contact

Who contacts potential customers? _____

How many times is a potential customer contacted before he or she is discarded from the list? _____

When are potential customers contacted? _____

How long does each contact take? _____

How frequently are current customers contacted for additional follow-on sales? _____

Who contacts current customers? _____

Sales Productivity

What are your sales goals? Delineate volume and revenues expected within a certain time frame. _____

_____

How many times, on average, must a potential customer be contacted before securing:

    An appointment? _____ A sale? _____

What percentage of potential customers agree to an appointment or demonstration? _____

What percentage of those agreeing to an appointment or demonstration subsequently purchase? _____

How many calls will each salesperson be expected to make, and in what time period? _____

Who handles phone, mail, or email orders? _____

Who ensures orders are filled promptly and properly? _____

Does this information get reported to the salesperson? ☐ Yes ☐ No

How? _____

Who checks credit? _____

Other Sales Procedures: _____

_____

_____

_____

_____

Refer to the previous worksheets in this chapter when completing your marketing budget estimates for the Monthly Marketing Budget worksheet. Some of this information will also be used in the Financials section of your business plan. To complete the Monthly Sales Projections worksheet, estimate income by each product line, then total the income from all product lines and transfer this information to the appropriate financial forms in Chapter 16.

Chapter Summary

Your marketing plan and sales strategy are at the heart of your company's business. To stay in business you have to reach customers and secure sales. That is why this section of your plan is likely to be closely reviewed by prospective investors. When studying your marketing plan, these investors want to see that you have a realistic, cost-effective approach to positioning your products or services in the market and to motivating customers to purchase.

In your sales strategy section, potential funders want to see that your sales methods are appropriate for your business and that your sales force is both large enough and trained well-enough to be able to secure the sales levels necessary to sustain your business.

Marketing and Sales Strategy Plan Preparation Form

Use the information recorded on this form to summarize the points you will cover in the marketing portion of your business plan.

Describe the message you are attempting to send customers: _____

_____

_____

_____

_____

_____

_____

Describe how you are positioning your company in the market: _____

_____

_____

_____

_____

_____

_____

_____

Describe the marketing methods and vehicles you use: _____

_____

_____

_____

_____

_____

_____

_____

Describe your sales force and procedures: _____

_____

_____

_____

_____

_____

_____

_____

Use this information as the basis of your plan's Marketing section.

Monthly Marketing Budget

	January	February	March	April	May
Professional Assistance					
Marketing / PR consultants					
Advertising agencies					
Direct mail specialists					
Graphic design / web design					
Brochures / Leaflets / Flyers					
Signs / Billboards					
Merchandising Displays					
Sampling / Premiums					
Media Advertising					
Print (newspaper, etc.)					
Television and radio					
Online					
Other media					
Phone Directories					
Advertising Specialties					
Direct Mail					
Website					
Development / programming					
Maintenance and hosting					
Trade Shows					
Fees and setup					
Travel / shipping					
Exhibits / signs					
Public Relations Activities / Materials					
Informal Marketing / Networking					
Memberships / meetings					
Entertainment					
Other:					
TOTAL					

NOTE: *A computerized version of this worksheet is available as part of The Planning Shop's* **Electronic Financial Worksheets** *package, available from www.PlanningShop.com.*

							$ ➤ $$ ➤ $$$
June	July	August	September	October	November	December	TOTAL

Monthly Sales Projections	January	February	March	April	May
Product Line #1					
Unit volume					
Unit price					
Gross sales					
(Commissions)					
(Returns and allowances)					
Net Sales					
Product Line #2					
Unit volume					
Unit price					
Gross sales					
(Commissions)					
(Returns and allowances)					
Net Sales					
Product Line #3					
Unit volume					
Unit price					
Gross Sales					
(Commissions)					
(Returns and allowances)					
Net Sales					
Product Line #4					
Unit volume					
Unit price					
Gross sales					
(Commissions)					
(Returns and allowances)					
Net Sales					
Totals for All Product Lines					
Total unit volume					
Total gross sales					
(Total commissions)					
(Total returns and allowances)					
Total Net Sales					

NOTE: *A computerized version of this worksheet is available as part of The Planning Shop's* **Electronic Financial Worksheets** *package, available from www.PlanningShop.com.*

							$ ➤ $$ ➤ $$$
June	July	August	September	October	November	December	TOTAL

SAMPLE PLAN: Marketing Plan

Marketing Plan

ComputerEase distinguishes itself from its competitors by better understanding the needs of its customers. Other computer software training companies in the Vespucci area market their services as if their customer were the individual student taking the class. ComputerEase, on the other hand, knows that the customer is actually the student's employer, the business that has contracted with ComputerEase.

ComputerEase Meets Customers' Needs

Employers have slightly different motivations than the students themselves. Although the companies, as well as the students, want high-quality, easy-to-understand training, the businesses also want:

- Increased overall productivity.

- One company to deal with for all computer training needs.

- Ongoing support for their employees.

- The convenience of not having to disrupt the workplace for computer training sessions.

These business customers want to deal with a training company with which they can have an ongoing relationship.

Describes the company's message.

ComputerEase incorporates reassurance and relationship in all its marketing efforts. The slogan "We speak your language" is designed to imply not only that the training will be comprehensible, but that ComputerEase is able to maintain ongoing communication with the business customer. Also, as a play on the word "computerese," the name is designed to be memorable, with the implication that the company makes dealing with computers easy.

ComputerEase Emphasizes Training

ComputerEase emphasizes high-productivity training. This is accomplished by selling training not only at the introductory, basic user-level, but additional, advanced training to substantially increase the benefits to the corporate client. This additional training expands the number of services ComputerEase can sell each customer, and increases the revenues produced from each sale.

Tells sales mechanism.

Since the average training contract is projected at approximately $5,000 per training session, and the goal is to target companies for regularly repeated sessions, most of the marketing will be done by face-to-face solicitation. An outside sales force, currently consisting of the company president and vice-president for marketing — both of whom have experience selling to the target market — will call on human resource directors to introduce the company and make sales presentations. Appointments are generally made by the vice-president for marketing, except in those cases where the president has existing relationships with potential customers.

Organization of Sales Team

All company personnel are considered members of the sales team. The registrar, who takes phone registrations, is trained in phone manners and order solicitation, and she is given incentive gifts for registering targeted numbers of students for "add-on" classes. Even the software trainers themselves participate in monthly sales training meetings. All employees receive financial bonuses if the company reaches overall sales goals.

Quality printed sales material has been prepared (see the Appendix) to support personal sales calls and for mailing in responses to phone requests (The Registrar is trained to attempt to set up personal sales presentations for larger businesses phoning in.) In year two, funds are budgeted to produce a computerized video presentation, to augment the printed material and enhance the sense of professionalism and computer expertise.

Indicates sales training for staff.

Direct Mail Program Key

Direct mail is key in the company's marketing. A schedule of ComputerEase's classes is sent out every two months to the target audience. (Currently 3,500 pieces are sent; the company purchases lists of human resource directors and subscribers to a leading computer magazine, both limited to names in the greater Vespucci area.) Once a year, a four-color brochure explaining ComputerEase's services is inserted in the schedule.

The company's advertising is aimed at supporting its other marketing and sales efforts rather than securing actual sales. Two main vehicles are used: a small ad in the Yellow Pages, and a half-page ad in each quarterly issue of the newsletter of the Vespucci Association of Human Resource Directors.

Gives specifics of marketing plan.

Cooperative Marketing Plans

A number of cooperative marketing activities are planned with software publishers. These include cooperative advertisements and sponsoring events to introduce business customers to new software. The goal of such efforts is to give ComputerEase added exposure to potential customers and increased stature through being associated with leading software publishers.

Two local computer hardware stores, and four computer hardware consultants, now refer customers to ComputerEase for training, and the company will continue to seek referral programs with other hardware suppliers.

The company is currently negotiating with Seth Rose, a well-regarded independent trainer, to conduct joint marketing activities, so that the company may benefit from his established client base.

SAMPLE PLAN: Marketing Plan (continued)

ComputerEase is also a member of the Vespucci Area Chamber of Commerce and will participate in the Chamber's annual trade show, which features providers of business services and products.

The company receives additional revenue from its Saturday training classes, which are aimed at individual students and businesses smaller than 50 employees. These classes are conducted primarily as a way to use the training center's excess capacity. These Saturday classes realize a lower profit margin than corporate training, and far less emphasis is placed on promoting these classes.

The marketing plan for these Saturday classes consists of printing additional copies of the ComputerEase schedule (presently 6,500 extra) and distributing them at local computer hardware and software retail stores, office supply stores, and college campuses. No paid advertising is done for these classes.

## Chapter 11

Operations

Ninety percent of success comes from
properly executing the fundamentals.

Describing How You Run Your Business

How are you actually going to run your business? The Operations section of your business plan is where you begin to explain the day-to-day functions of your company. This is where you translate your theories into practice.

Much of the information in this chapter appears mundane, for instance, how you keep track of inventory, or what equipment you need and when it must be replaced. These seem like the kind of details that take care of themselves. But there's a far greater chance that a business will fail because fundamentals aren't handled properly than because the basic business concept is faulty.

Examining your basic operation is particularly important for internal planning. A capable manager does not take any activity in the business process for granted. Each step is worthy of evaluation and improvement. A little bit of extra planning in operational areas can mean marked improvements in profit margin. Assessing and developing the underlying mechanisms of your business will certainly pay off.

To do a thorough job planning your internal operations, you may want to develop a separate operations or procedures manual. Such a manual should describe the specific details of the processes by which you produce, distribute, or maintain your products and services.

For the purpose of preparing a business plan, however, your operations section does not need to be thoroughly detailed. Be brief. Describing your operations too specifically in a business plan is not only unnecessary, it may be counterproductive, especially if you are seeking outside funding. Focusing on very small details may make it appear that you are not seeing the big picture in your business.

A section to help you plan your technology needs follows. However, if you are seeking financing, you do not need to include a separate Technology section in your written business plan unless yours is a technology-based business. You can instead incorporate key technology issues in your operations section.

What Your Operations Section Should Cover

This chapter describes most of the subjects commonly included in an Operations section of a business plan. In your own plan, you do not necessarily need to address each of these topics. Rather, limit your Operations section to those issues that:

- Are essential to the nature and success of your company;
- Provide you with a distinct competitive edge; and
- Overcome a frequent problem in businesses of your type.

Thus, if yours is a manufacturing business in which distribution is often a major difficulty, you may want to include one or two paragraphs clarifying your company's improved approach to distribution. However, if yours is a retail business, distribution may not be an issue at all, and you needn't discuss it.

Of course, if your business is an enterprise that develops or relies heavily on new technology, you need to explain those aspects fairly thoroughly. Likewise, if you are counting on a new manufacturing or merchandising method to significantly improve your competitive position, you must describe the mechanisms and importance of those techniques.

Many sources of information exist if you need to locate resources to prepare your Operations section. Commercial real estate agents can easily describe the advantages, disadvantages, and resources available in your location. Trade associations can assist in helping you find consultants for plant and manufacturing design and direct you to sources of equipment. The *Thomas Register,* available in most large libraries or online, is an invaluable source of suppliers, distributors, and equipment manufacturers.

Operations, naturally, have many financial implications. You should note these in the Flow-Through Financial worksheets in this chapter and transfer the numbers to your financial statements in Chapter 16. If yours is a new business, you should include the Start-Up Costs worksheet in your business plan. For both new and existing businesses, the Equipment Schedule worksheet, which you need for internal financial projections, can also be included in the Appendix of your business plan.

"The biggest part of becoming a winner is developing standards of performance. Know how you go about doing things; know your process. Constantly develop the application of your knowledge and skills. Having standards means many, many people function within a framework. That framework includes more than just how you do the job at hand. For instance, it might include punctuality and how people dress. Sometimes almost symbolic, ritualistic matters become important; on the 49ers, everyone's shirt had to be tucked in at all times. It reinforced the sense of professionalism and being part of a team."

Bill Walsh
Former Coach and
President, S.F. 49ers

Facilities

In real estate the old saying is that the three most important factors are location, location, location. In business, as well, location can prove the critical factor for success. For example, with retail operations, a bad location can mean you just don't attract enough customers to your store. Likewise, in manufacturing and distribution companies, a location lacking adequate access to transportation or suppliers may prevent you from manufacturing or distributing your product in a timely or cost-effective manner.

The physical aspects of the facilities themselves can be extremely important for a company's continued growth. Are your facilities large enough to accommodate expansion in the coming years? Are the necessary utilities available and energy efficient? Are you near an airport or rail terminal? Or, are you locked into an inadequate facility that reduces your overall production and distribution capacity?

Occasionally, the length and terms of a lease may be a particularly attractive (or problematic) aspect of a business. Having a long-term, low-rent lease in a desirable area may be, in and of itself, a significant business asset. A lease that needs to be renegotiated in the near future may spell trouble for your company, as you may be facing substantially increased rents. In a new lease, look to negotiate certain concessions, such as leasehold improvements or a few months' free rent (particularly while construction is occurring).

When evaluating your facilities, examine those aspects most important for your particular business. Do you need a prestigious address in a downtown office building for your law firm? Do you need to be close to key suppliers for your manufacturing plant? Do you need access to environmentally approved disposal sites for your chemical company?

In the Facilities worksheet on page 158, describe all the facilities in which your company operates, emphasizing any competitive and cost-saving advantages they may have. Specific points to mention are listed below.

Location

Include company headquarters, retail store(s), branch offices, additional plants, distribution centers, etc. Describe any mobile facilities. List square footage, and how the square footage is allocated (office space, retail, production, shipping, etc.). Describe access to parking and transportation; air, rail and surface shipping access, and loading docks, warehouse, and other necessary facilities.

Lease

What are the terms and length of the lease? Do you pay straight rent or rent plus a percentage of gross or net profits? Can you sublet? Did you receive concessions in the lease? What restrictions are in the lease (for instance, hours of operation or promotional activities that are often mandated in mall leases)?

"People have no idea you're there if they can't see you. Get a good location; it's money well-spent. As a start-up, it's hard to advertise; so, instead of a big advertising budget, spend the money on a better location. Find a good real estate broker with retail experience. Have them identify successful businesses serving your target customer and then locate near them. Capture their customers."

Nancy Glaser
Business Strategies
Consultant

Facilities   *$ ➤ $$ ➤ $$$*

Describe the attributes of your facilities.

Principal Location(s)

Location: _____

Square Footage: _____

Description of Use: _____

Parking/Transportation: _____

Shipping Access/Facilities: _____

Warehouse Facilities: _____

Other: _____

_____

Branch Offices/Additional Plants/Distribution Centers/Other Facilities

Number: _____

Locations: _____

Square Footage: _____

Description of Use: _____

Other Aspects: _____

_____

Lease(s)

Length of Lease: _____

Rent/Terms of Rent: _____   Other Terms: _____

Restrictions: _____

Concessions: _____

Improvements

Existing: _____

To be made: _____

Paid by landlord: _____   Paid by company: _____

Utilities/Maintenance

Average monthly utility costs? _____   How do costs vary seasonally? _____

How do costs vary due to production levels? _____   Are there energy-efficient methods in use? _____

Average maintenance costs? _____   Do any maintenance costs vary? _____

Other: _____

Improvements

What additions, such as walls, signage, or utility hook-ups, have been made to the property, or remain to be made? Who pays for such improvements — you or your landlord?

Utilities/Maintenance

Include the costs of gas, water, and electricity. Note seasonal or production level variation. List the cost of janitorial, trash-removal, and other ongoing facility maintenance expenses. Emphasize energy-efficient measures. Is the facility wired for high speed data transmission, ethernet connections, or otherwise fitted out for technology uses?

Key Factors

What aspects of your facilities are most likely to affect your company's success? Are you near your target market? Are you in a prestigious or convenient location? Does your lease have particularly favorable terms? Will you be able to grow in these facilities without moving?

Production

Every manufacturing business has a production process — the way it goes about fabricating a raw or component material and creating an item with greater usefulness or desirability. But even if yours is a service or retail business, you have a method of "producing" something of value for your customers, although you may not have given this process much thought.

Take time to evaluate and assess your production plan to see if you can enhance efficiencies, improve the quality of the finished "product," and, in the long run, increase your profit margin. Look at the various stages involved in creating your product or service: Can these stages be shortened? If so, you will be able to produce and sell more in less time.

Examine how you organize and deploy your work force. Do you use a team approach — with one group of workers responsible for a job from start to finish? Or, do you use a production-line approach, with a worker doing the same portion of each job and then passing it along to someone else? Do you have clear-cut lines of authority, or do workers often not know who is responsible for making decisions?

Increasingly, companies are utilizing variable labor in addition to permanent employees, as an integral part of their workforce. Variable labor — employees hired to perform a specific task for a specific period of time — is particularly useful for seasonal work or unusually large or special orders. Many companies even use variable labor, in the form of consultants, for professional positions. Utilizing variable labor gives you more control over ongoing expenses, since you can add these employees in good times but don't have them on the payroll when business is slow. Maintaining high quality in a variable labor force is frequently difficult, however, and employee motivation is often low.

"When scouting a new city, we put together a group of managers to visit the location. Then we visit every shopping mall, every department store, every confectionary store, and every bakery. We stand and watch people buy. We buy a cross-section of local candies and eat them; we want to determine the local taste. Then we drive around and look at residential patterns. We might even rent a helicopter to look at traffic patterns and count swimming pools."

Charles Huggins
President, See's Candies

Another way to increase flexibility in fixed costs is to subcontract — or 'outsource' — various aspects of production to other companies. These companies then have the responsibility for maintaining the workforce, facilities, and equipment necessary to produce their component piece. While the per piece cost to you includes a profit to these companies, and thus, your per piece cost is probably greater than if you had all the necessary means of production in-house, the advantages of not having your money tied up in overhead may be well worth the additional cost. Even service businesses can consider ways to subcontract portions of their contracts.

You should also pay particular attention to the issue of quality in your production process. Poor quality can be costly — it can not only cost you in the form of goods you have to discard as being faulty, but it can cost you customers. If you intend to sell your goods internationally, you will likely want to follow procedures to get your products or processes certified as meeting international quality standards, such as ISO 9000. These measures are set by The International Organization for Standardization and have been adopted by more than 90 countries worldwide. To find out more about such procedures, check the ISO website at www.iso.ch. Another useful website is ISO Easy at www.isoeasy.org.

Assessing Your Production Plan

Two worksheets on the next few pages help you evaluate your production process. The Production worksheet covers the major aspects other than equipment, which is handled on a separate form, the Equipment Schedule worksheet. You may wish to include the Equipment Schedule in the Appendix of your business plan. If yours is a manufacturing business, you might also wish to include a flow chart of your production process in the Appendix.

The aspects covered in the Production worksheet are:

- **Labor/Variable Labor.** What kinds of and how many employees do you require to produce your product or service? How do you utilize them? How are decisions reached in the workforce? Do you use variable labor, employ subcontractors or outsource portions of the production process?
- **Productivity.** Productivity measures how long and how many people it requires to produce your product or service. This can have a major impact on your profit margin.

  If you can produce more goods in less time, you increase the amount of profit earned from every dollar spent on salaries, equipment, and rent. What methods can you use to increase productivity without reducing quality?
- **Capacity.** Capacity is the measure of how much work your current facilities, labor force, and equipment can handle. If you have excess capacity, you have the ability to produce more than you are currently selling using your current work force, equipment, and plant.

  Excess capacity represents a waste of already paid-for earning potential. Can you find ways to use or reduce excess capacity? If you are operating

"We wanted to have neighborhood pricing and high quality. That meant we had to keep our food costs under control. To do so, we spent about six months testing different recipes, so we would know the exact cost of each item."

Martha Johnson
Restauranteur

at close to full capacity, what plans do you have for expansion, to handle growth?

- **Quality Control.** All the various measures you take to ensure that you maintain the same standards with each product or service come under the category of Quality Control.

  Such activities include regular inspection throughout the production process, occasional testing or sampling of randomly-selected goods, employee-involvement training and reward programs for quality assurance, and solicitation of customer comments.

- **Equipment and Furniture.** (List separately on the Equipment Schedule worksheet). Include manufacturing equipment, transportation vehicles, store fixtures and office equipment, and furniture. List any payment obligations or leases. Under "Status" describe the state of the equipment in terms of future use potential, technological development, and substantial maintenance required. Also indicate date to be replaced, if known.

Inventory Control

Many businesses overlook the vital contribution that careful inventory management makes to the profitability of a company. How much money you have tied up in supplies or finished product sitting in your warehouse makes a direct impact on your bottom line. Every box of raw material is not just taking up space; it's money sitting around, losing value.

Of course, if you don't have sufficient inventory, you occasionally can't make sales. Every business dreads the possibility of receiving lucrative orders it can't fill due to inadequate supplies. And sometimes you don't just lose sales; you lose a customer. This is the risk in maintaining too low an inventory.

The answer is to develop inventory management systems that substantially increase the flow of information from the sales point to the production and purchasing teams. Information can reduce the amount of guesswork that goes into maintaining inventory. Know how sales are going, even on a daily basis.

Suppliers can help. Work with them to see how to reduce the amount of time necessary to receive goods and to explore the potential of lowering the amount of minimum orders. Large businesses often have significant clout with suppliers, but even smaller companies should look for suppliers who are willing to increase flexibility in their orders and deliveries.

Methods of Inventory Management

One of the approaches to inventory management is "just-in-time" inventory control. This concept emphasizes keeping inventory stocked only to the levels needed to produce goods just in time for delivery, usually in response to orders in-hand. Such a system is highly dependent on adequate communication systems and good supplier relationships.

"To plan for change, you must build flexibility not only into the process, but into the workforce as well, because team members will be called on to do many jobs."

Michael Damer
New United Motor
Manufacturing Inc.

"We take inventory in each store daily. This information is sent to the main computer through the telephone, and this determines what will be manufactured. Very perishable items are made to order the day before delivery. We have two manufacturing plants, and stores receive two deliveries a week. So product is delivered to stores, even those in Hong Kong and Hawaii, no more than the third morning after production. It's fresh."

Charles Huggins
President, See's Candies

Production

Describe the key factors (other than equipment) involved in producing your product or service.

Processes

What are the stages of production? _____

_____

How does the product/work get transferred from one stage to another? _____

_____

How does the process utilize new technologies? _____

_____

What are the advantages of your production process? _____

_____

What are the drawbacks of your production process? _____

_____

What components are contracted for others to produce? _____

_____

What are the costs of these outside services/components? _____

_____

Briefly describe the subcontracting company(s): _____

_____

What other costs are directly associated with the production process? _____

_____

Labor

Total number of employees: ___ permanent: full-time: ___ part-time: ___ variable: full-time: ___ part-time: ___

When do you use variable labor? _____

How many shifts do you operate? ____ How long are the shifts? ____ What are the hours of operation? ____

What are the basic qualifications required of employees? _____

_____

How are employees organized: ☐ team approach? ☐ production line? ☐ other? _____

Who supervises employees? _____

_____

Other labor issues: _____

Other labor costs: _____

_____

$ ➤ $$ ➤ $$$

Productivity

For each product or service, list how many minutes, hours, days, weeks, and workers it takes to produce one unit.

_____

_____

_____

_____

How many units can each worker produce in a minute, hour, day, week? _____

What methods could reduce the amount of production time required without reducing quality? _____

_____

What other methods can you use to increase productivity? _____

_____

Capacity

How many units of goods or services can be produced in your current facility in a day ___ week ___ month ___?

How many units of goods or services can your workforce handle in a day, week, month? _____

At what percentage of capacity are you now operating in terms of workforce ___ equipment ___ facilities ___?

How is excess capacity currently utilized? _____

_____

What are other ways to use excess capacity? _____

_____

How can you provide for increased capacity, if needed for growth? _____

_____

Quality Control

Who is responsible for overall quality control issues? _____

What steps are taken to inspect finished goods or services? _____

_____

What intermediate steps are taken to ensure quality in the process? _____

_____

Are products and services tested for quality? _____

How are employees motivated to ensure quality? _____

How do you solicit customer comments? _____

What other steps are taken for quality control? _____

_____

Equipment Schedule

List your company's existing and anticipated equipment.

Currently Owned Equipment

Description (Name/Model #)	Status	Date Purchased	Cost	Payments

Equipment to Be Purchased

Description	Purchase Date	Cost	Terms	Payments

In devising your inventory control and communication procedures, you will want to devise a Management Information System (MIS). Usually such a system centers around the computerized maintenance and communication of information, such as order and stock levels, reorder dates, historical tracking of sales, and so forth. Computer professionals can help you select and adapt an MIS for your company.

You will also need to discuss how you want to value and record your inventory. Two commonly used methods are LIFO — last in, first out, or FIFO — first in, first out. These are basic methods of valuing your remaining stock, and they can have significantly disparate tax implications, so this decision should be reached in consultation with your accountant. Complete the worksheet on page 166 to assess your inventory control procedures.

Supply and Distribution

Almost every business has goods or materials coming in to the company and finished products or services going out. The companies you rely on to provide you with incoming goods, and the methods you use to sell and distribute your product are essential to the continuing well-being of your business.

Most businesses will experience difficulties with their suppliers or distributors at some point. So it can serve you well to explore the abilities, flexibility, and alternatives of your current suppliers and distributors.

Try not to be dependent on just one supplier or distributor; your financial future will be too vulnerable if they fail you. Work to develop excellent relationships with your suppliers and distributors; you want them to feel that you are in a partnership together so that they will try to do everything possible to meet your needs. Be responsive to their needs as well; work out payment plans and communication methods to reduce pressures on them.

Select Suppliers that Understand Your Needs

Usually, competitive supply sources exist, giving you a number of choices and enabling you to negotiate better prices. But don't make your decisions based on price alone, for you may find the price right but the delivery time and quality problematic. Select suppliers with whom you can communicate well; make certain they understand your specifications and can consistently meet your standards.

Reliable Distribution Is a Must

Reliable distribution often presents a far more difficult problem. If your product is distributed through a wholesaler or "middle-man," you need to carefully examine your choice of such distributor(s). Your selection of distributor(s) may be one of the single most important decisions you make, especially if they are responsible for most of your sales.

> *"To finance our growth rate, we opted to lease everything. The only thing we purchased was the equipment necessary for our patents. From an ultimate financial strategy, leasing was the only way we could grow the way we did. For us growth was the objective rather than net profit."*
>
> **Larry Leigon**
> **Founder, Ariel Vineyards**

Inventory Control

This worksheet helps you get a clear picture of your inventory control procedures.

Who is responsible for inventory control? _____

What is the minimum level of inventory necessary to be maintained at all time? _____

_____

_____

What is the minimum amount of time necessary to get materials from suppliers? _____

_____

_____

What is the minimum amount of time necessary to produce goods to order? _____

_____

_____

_____

What is the minimum amount of time necessary to ship goods? _____

_____

_____

_____

How is information about sales translated to the production and purchasing departments? _____

_____

_____

_____

What Management Information Systems does your company use? _____

_____

_____

_____

_____

What steps do you take to reduce theft of inventory? _____

_____

_____

_____

What other inventory control steps does you company take? _____

_____

_____

Once again, try not to put all your eggs in one basket. If you can ethically use more than one distributor, do so. Ask retailers or consumers about the reputation of distributors who sell to them so that you can be certain you are dealing with a reliable company and one that is well-regarded.

Complete the Supply and Distribution worksheet on page 168 to assess your sources of supply and distribution.

Order Fulfillment and Customer Service

Remember, your work is not finished when you produce a product or secure an order from a customer. You still need to make sure your customer receives the product he or she wanted, in good condition, and in a timely fashion. You need to know that you have satisfied your customer.

Surprisingly, many companies pay relatively little attention to order fulfillment and customer service since they do not seem like pressing concerns or sources of increased profit margin. However, order fulfillment is part of any current sale, and customer service is part of any future sale.

Customers are constantly demanding better and better service. They expect to get what they want, when they want it, and to be treated graciously and fairly in the process. Many companies are renowned for their customer service and have built entire marketing strategies around it.

Some companies assume they are doing just fine in the way of customer service because they don't receive many complaints. But you can't judge how well you are serving your customers just by the number of complaints you receive; the unhappy customer who doesn't complain is almost certainly a lost customer. At least a customer who tells you the problem gives you a chance to make it right.

So, it is your job to make certain customers have little reason for complaints. Training all employees — from the shipping clerk to the sales representative — in customer service can pay off for you in customer retention and referrals. Build sufficient flexibility into your policies so that you can easily handle unusual or difficult requests. Empower employees to make certain decisions on the spot (such as accepting returns) instead of requiring each customer request to be approved by a manager. Make it easy for your customers to let you know what they want by soliciting customer suggestions and feedback.

Examine your order fulfillment processes. Often, orders are not communicated clearly or quickly to the processing department, and valuable time is lost due to inadequate internal communication. Assess the methods by which you prepare goods for shipping and deliver goods to customers. If you hire outside companies to ship or deliver your product directly to the customer, make certain they can deliver on emergency or rush time schedules, or line up other shippers for such deliveries.

Look at the kinds of services you provide customers after sale. Good customer service emphasizes developing an on-going relationship with your

"One method of insuring quality-control is to put guest comment sheets in each room. The comment sheets are read, assessed, and charted. Every month, we do detailed assessments of cleanliness, friendliness, ground maintenance, telephone service, and so forth, for each managed property."

Andre Tatibouet
President, Aston Hotels

Supply and Distribution

$\$ \blacktriangleright \$\$ \blacktriangleright \$\$\$$

These questions help you evaluate your current supply and distribution needs.

Suppliers

Who is responsible for your purchasing decisions? _____

What are the key goods or materials necessary? _____

What are the average costs of these goods? _____

List your sources of key goods or materials: _____

_____

List any alternative sources of these supplies: _____

_____

Are any goods available from only one or two suppliers? ☐ Yes ☐ No

If so, how reliable or secure are these suppliers? _____

Can your suppliers provide you with "on demand" or short-notice goods? ☐ Yes ☐ No

If so, what additional costs do you incur? _____

Will your suppliers negotiate no- or low-minimum order contracts? ☐ Yes ☐ No

What kind of credit terms will your suppliers offer? _____

What are your average credit costs? _____

Which key factors determined your choice of suppliers? _____

Other supplier issues: _____

Distribution

How is your product or service distributed to the consumer? _____

_____

Is there a wholesaler or distributor between you and the consumer? ☐ Yes ☐ No

If so, how many such companies do you use? _____

What are the key qualifications and advantages of such companies? _____

_____

What are the drawbacks of such companies? _____

If you use only one or two distributors, how secure are these companies? _____

What is their reputation among consumers? _____

What kinds of payments or commissions do these distributors receive? _____

Describe any alternative distribution methods available: _____

_____

customers, so you need repair, service, warranty, and return policies that reassure customers that you continue to be interested in them even after you have their money.

Complete the worksheet on page 170 to evaluate your order fulfillment and customer service practices.

Research and Development

A business that stands still is one that is almost certainly going to fail. You must keep on top of new developments that are going to affect your business. Your target market is always changing: growing older, developing new tastes, using new products. Your competitors understand this, so you need to stay aware of what they are doing if you wish to increase your ability to compete effectively.

All Companies Need Ongoing Product Development

Some companies need relatively large research and development components because they deal with constantly evolving technology or rapidly changing consumer preferences. But even companies that sell old-fashioned products (chocolate chip cookies, for instance) need to be developing new products based on changing customer values and concerns (such as low-fat cookies).

Your research and development activities may range from running a complete department staffed with researchers experimenting with new products and new equipment, to merely subscribing to certain publications and attending conferences. Regardless of the extent of such activities, research and development must be a priority in any business.

Examine the ways you plan to stay aware of developments likely to change your company's products, services, and practices. Make certain that key employees are likewise involved in research and development activities.

Complete the Research and Development worksheet on page 171 to evaluate research and development in your company.

Financial Control

Amazingly, some businesses give relatively little attention to how they handle money. Businesses may have serious cash-flow problems just because they don't send out invoices in a timely manner. Or, they may incur substantial credit charges because they don't process their bills when due. Even very large companies are often guilty of inadequate financial control systems.

Set up procedures to ensure that your financial information is handled promptly and accurately. Invoices should be sent out quickly, and a system of regular followups should be established for delinquent accounts. Accounts payable records should be thorough and easily retrieved, and sent regularly to appropriate decision-makers within the company. Make

Order Fulfillment and Customer Service   *$ ➤ $$ ➤ $$$*

Describe your company's order fulfillment and customer service practices.

Who processes orders? _____

How are orders communicated from the salesperson to the order fulfillment department? _____

_____

How are online orders transmitted to the order fulfillment department? _____

_____

How are orders checked to be certain they are filled promptly and accurately? _____

_____

What percentage of orders are prepared incorrectly? _____

How are goods prepared for shipping? _____

_____

How do you ship products? _____

_____

What is the shipping cost of your average order? _____

Are your shippers able to ship on short or emergency notice?   ☐ Yes   ☐ No

If so, are extra expenses incurred?   ☐ Yes   ☐ No

Who pays these: ☐ you or   ☐ the customer?

What alternative methods exist to ship products? _____

_____

_____

What service programs do you offer? _____

What maintenance or repair programs do you offer? _____

_____

_____

What percentage of your orders require repairs? _____

What is the average cost of the repair to your company? _____

What is your return policy? _____

What is your average rate of returns? _____

What is the cost of the average return? _____

Do you have a complaint or customer service department?   ☐ Yes   ☐ No

How do you solicit the opinions of customers? _____

_____

Research and Development

This worksheet helps you assess your ongoing research and development efforts and costs.

Describe any new products currently in development: _____

_____

_____

_____

Describe any new services currently in development: _____

_____

_____

_____

Which staff members have research and development responsibilities? _____

_____

How are staff members used for research and development? _____

_____

What percentage of your staff's time is devoted to research and development? _____

Costs: _____

What equipment is needed for research and development? _____

_____

Costs: _____

What supplies are needed for research and development? _____

_____

Costs: _____

What publications are needed? _____

_____

Costs: _____

What conferences will your employees attend for research and development purposes? _____

_____

Costs: _____

List any other research and development activities your company is involved in: _____

_____

_____

Costs: _____

certain your accounting practices and data retrieval systems are such that you can receive ongoing information on sales and expenses. Don't depend on monthly reports.

One particularly difficult problem is how to make certain that employees do not have the opportunity to embezzle or pilfer. Work with your accountant to set up practices that ensure there are adequate safeguards against theft in your financial procedures. Bring in a computer consultant to design safeguards in your data processing programs as well.

Design your financial systems to be a source of regular information and constant feedback. Avoid cumbersome systems that bury your employees in paperwork; this increases your costs and reduces efficiency. Streamline the process as much as possible.

Complete the Financial Control worksheet on the next page to examine your financial control systems.

Contingency Planning

Bad things happen even to good companies. Sooner or later, your company will face an emergency. It could be a natural disaster — flood, fire, earthquake — or it could be something more mundane — a burglary, power interruption, slowdown from a supplier, product failure. As you develop your internal operational procedures, include contingency planning to help you anticipate and prepare for the unexpected. These contingency plans do not need to be included in any written plan for funding, but they may prove to be a substantial benefit to your company's future.

Develop procedures to safeguard your records and data in case of emergency. These procedures should include regular backup and storage of data offsite. Next, look at those things that are absolutely critical for your specific business and find ways to make certain they are protected or able to continue even in the event of an emergency. Devise a disaster plan to ensure the safety and well-being of employees and a method for you to communicate with employees during emergencies. Examine your business insurance. In addition to insurance to cover loss of physical equipment, records, and inventory, you can also get business interruption insurance to cover the costs of lost income and other costs incurred if an emergency closes your business.

Emergencies also come in the form of personal disasters — illnesses and accidents — so examine your procedures to get bills paid, checks deposited, and payroll out if key personnel are unavailable.

Other Operational Issues

A variety of other operational concerns will face your company, depending on the size and nature of your business. Some of these topics might include protecting the safety of your workers, protecting the environment, dealing with governmental regulations, or exporting goods. Other

Financial Control

This worksheet helps you evaluate your company's financial control methods.

Who is primarily responsible for designing financial control procedures in your company? _____

_____

Which other employees are involved in financial control processes? _____

_____

_____

Who is responsible for invoicing? _____

What is the average amount of time that elapses before an invoice is sent after an order? _____

How are delinquent accounts handled? _____

_____

_____

Who is responsible for handling your accounts payable? _____

What is your company's policy on paying outstanding bills? _____

☐ Pay when due

☐ Pay when received

☐ Pay on 30 days

☐ Other

Who makes decisions on variations in payment or billing procedures? _____

_____

What protections have been designed to reduce theft? _____

_____

_____

_____

What systems have been designed to produce ongoing reports of financial status? _____

_____

_____

_____

What other financial control systems have been devised? _____

_____

_____

_____

_____

Other Operational Issues   *$ ➤ $$ ➤ $$$*

The questions below elicit your company's concerns and plans involving other operational issues.

Safety and Health

What procedures do you take to protect the safety and health of your workforce? _____

_____

What safety programs do you have in place to encourage your workers to maintain safety precautions? _____

_____

Other safety issues: _____

_____

Insurance and Legal

What types of insurance do you need for your business? (include fire, accident/liability, malpractice, auto, etc.)

_____

_____

What amounts of coverage do you require to be adequately protected? _____

_____

What kinds of legal problems do you face in your business? _____

_____

Does your company need on-going legal advice and assistance? _____

Other insurance and legal issues: _____

_____

Regulations and Environmental

What licenses or permits are you required to have by law? _____

_____

What kinds of regulations cover your type of business? _____

_____

What kinds of environmental regulations affect your business? _____

_____

What precautions can your company take voluntarily to protect the environment? _____

_____

How can your company use products or processes that don't cause harm to animals? _____

_____

Other regulatory or environmental issues: _____

_____

Other operational issues: _____

resources for some of these topics are listed in the Resources chapters in the back of this book.

To briefly look at some of these concerns, complete the Other Operational Issues worksheet on the opposite page.

Preparing the Operations Section of Your Business Plan

In preparing the Operations section of your business plan, emphasize these aspects of your operations:

- Key characteristics
- Competitive advantages
- Cost and time efficiencies
- Problems addressed and overcome

The aim of this section is to show that you have a firm grasp on the operational necessities of carrying out your business, that you understand how those operations relate to your overall business success, and that you have taken steps to achieve maximum efficiency at the least cost. You do not want to give a step-by-step explanation of how your company functions or go into the specific details of your activities. Save that information for your internal procedures manual.

The Start-Up Costs worksheet on the following page can be used by new businesses to explain the initial investment necessary to begin their operations. The Plan Preparation form that follows lays out the basic areas you should cover in your written document.

Chapter Summary

While the Operations section of your written business plan should not be overly detailed, careful planning in this area brings you meaningful rewards. Analyzing the day-to-day operations of your business will pay off in the form of increased profits as you find ways to reduce costs and improve productivity. You can find ways to make your money work harder and go farther, at the same time improving the quality of the product or service you produce and enhancing the work environment for your employees.

Start-Up Costs $ ➤ $$ ➤ $$$

List the specific details of your start-up cash requirements. Remember, these are expenses you plan to incur before you launch your business. Post-launch expenditures should be entered in your Income Statement.

		Cost
Facilities	Land Purchase	
	Building Purchase	
	Initial Rent	
	Deposits (Security / Utilities / Etc.)	
	Improvements / Remodeling	
	Other:	
	Other:	
Equipment	Furniture	
	Production Machines / Equipment	
	Computers / Software	
	Cash Registers	
	Telephones / Telecommunications	
	Vehicles	
	Other:	
	Other:	
Materials /	Office Supplies	
Supplies	Stationery / Business Cards	
	Brochures / Pamphlets, Other Descriptive Material	
	Other:	
	Other:	
Fees and	Licenses / Permits	
Other Costs	Trade or Professional Memberships	
	Attorneys	
	Accountants	
	Insurance	
	Marketing / Management Consultants	
	Design / Technical Consultants	
	Advertising / Promotional Activities	
	Other:	
TOTAL		

NOTE: *A computerized version of this worksheet is available as part of The Planning Shop's* **Electronic Financial Worksheets** *package, available from www.PlanningShop.com.*

Operations Plan Preparation Form

On this form record specific information relating to your company's operational processes.

Key Aspects of Operations (possibilities include facilities, production process, equipment, labor force utilization):

_____
_____
_____
_____
_____
_____
_____

Cost and Time efficiencies: _____

_____
_____
_____
_____
_____
_____
_____
_____
_____
_____

Competitive Advantages: _____

_____
_____
_____
_____
_____
_____

Problems Addressed and Overcome: _____

_____
_____
_____
_____
_____
_____
_____
_____

Operations

Describes a key aspect of operations

At the core of ComputerEase's strategic concept is the corporate training center. These centers — classrooms equipped with computer stations — will be the location for conducting the largest percentage of the company's software training programs.

Operating these centers is vital, because most of ComputerEase's potential customers have limited, if any, extra computer facilities on their premises. Thus, ComputerEase can grow to an adequate level of income only if it has training facilities of its own to offer.

Corporate Training Centers

On August 1, 2003, ComputerEase opened its first corporate training center, at 987 South Main Street in Vespucci, along with its company's headquarters. This training center is equipped with 10 personal computer stations. Prior to the opening of the training center, ComputerEase was limited to conducting training programs at the client's place of business (referred to as on-site programs).

Cost and Time Effective Programs

Shows method of increasing profitability

These on-site programs produce lower profit margins than training center classes. Generally, fewer students attend each on-site training session; instructors spend additional time for travel and setup, and costs arise from transporting training materials. While ComputerEase charges higher fees per student in these on-site classes, the market will not bear prices that truly absorb the increased costs.

Moreover, the potential customer base for training center classes is substantially larger than that for on-site programs. Research shows a much larger number of businesses can afford to send a few employees to a class at the center, or even have a class developed for them at the center, than to incur the costs of an on-site program.

Thus, ComputerEase's strategic plan called for the opening of at least one classroom as quickly as possible.

ComputerEase will open a second training center in January 2004, dependent upon receiving the capital investment currently being sought. This addition will be either a second classroom at the present location, or a satellite classroom in the city of Abergel Peak (where many of ComputerEase's target corporate customers are located).

SAMPLE PLAN: Operations (continued)

Competitive Advantages

The training center also offers Saturday training classes primarily for individuals or operators of very small businesses. The fee per student for Saturday classes is less than half the average fee of the corporate classes. However, ComputerEase reduces costs for these classes by utilizing more concise training materials and by requiring students to pay fees in full at the time of registration. (Corporate clients, on the other hand, pay 50% at time of class, and 50% within 30 days; contract clients are billed monthly.) Thus, these Saturday classes provide a quick source of cash while using the excess capacity of the training center.

Indicates how excess capacity is utilized profitably

Management decided early on to lease rather than purchase the computer equipment necessary for the current training center. This not only significantly reduced the amount of initial capital outlay, which would have exceeded $50,000, but it also ensures that ComputerEase will always be able to provide its students with the latest computers.

Problems Addressed

With the type of corporate training offered by ComputerEase — high quality, premium price — a major cost arises from the printed training materials provided to each student. Not only are substantial costs incurred in developing and writing the training manuals for each software program (revised for each new edition; the average life span is only six months), but the actual production costs can be staggering (average cost is $45 per student, per class). ComputerEase has reduced the amount of waste (to virtually none) by printing manuals just one day before each class begins (enabled by the purchase and lease of high-speed copying, collating, and binding equipment).

Details way to minimize inventory and cost of goods

Nevertheless, ComputerEase must work to substantially reduce materials costs in the future. To share the costs of developing and producing such materials, national associations of software training companies are now forming. ComputerEase will join such an association, (or participate in creating one) as soon as practical (projected by July 2004).

ComputerEase emphasizes high-quality, productivity-oriented training. To help ensure quality, the company conducts interviews with each corporate client approximately one week after the training session to ascertain that the customer is satisfied. In the case of problems, the company offers free remedial training, preferably at the training center. To date, only two students have required remedial training.

In the future, ComputerEase, in conjunction with appropriate industry associations, intends to develop interactive computerized multi-media training programs. Such programs should substantially reduce materials costs.

Explains choice of location

The choice of location for the training center was key. It had to be within walking distance of a large number of Vespucci target customers (located in a five-block radius in the central downtown business district). It needed to be close to transportation and parking facilities and had to present a professional image. And, of course, rents had to be affordable. For this reason, South Main Street stood out as the best choice. It is downtown, immediately available to the prime office locations, but it offers significantly lower rents than offices on the north side of Main.

## Chapter 12

Technology Plan

"Computers are useless. They can only give you answers."
— *Pablo Picasso*

Every business needs technology. Even if your company makes old-fashioned chocolate chip cookies, you'll rely on technology to handle many, if not most, routine business operations, from maintaining financial records, to processing orders, to staying in contact with suppliers and customers. Because technology is so central to running a business today, you need to plan what technology you will use and how you will use it.

This section helps you outline your technology needs. If yours is a technology-intensive company, your technology needs may be far more complicated than indicated in this chapter.

Why A Technology Plan?

Sometimes even the simplest technology issues prove to be difficult and time-consuming. For example, options for today's telephone systems can be surprisingly confusing, even for relatively small companies. Few of us have the technical expertise to understand the wide-range of technology choices available to us. Often, we don't even know the right terms to use or questions to ask.

Many decisions you make about your technology, such as the choice of your database program, may be costly or cumbersome to change later. When outlining your technology plan, keep in mind how your company might grow or change; try to choose technology that is flexible enough to grow and change with you. As much as possible, choose technology that, while meeting your needs, is simpler rather than overly complex. All those

"I can sit at my desk as a venture capitalist and come up with 30 ideas; I have the money in the bank to play with – that's not the hard part; the hard part is figuring out all the mechanical issues of how you make a business. That's the part we really need to see."

Andrew Anker
Venture Capitalist

extra "features" may just make your technology, whether it be a software program or a telephone, harder to use.

You may benefit greatly by using the services of a technology consultant to help you figure out the best products and systems for your company. There are consultants who can help you design a total system — hardware, software, telecommunications, etc. — and there are also specialists in specific areas.

Some industries have vendors who produce specialized software or hardware to meet industry-specific demands. Your trade association can help you identify vendors of such industry-specific technology, and you can typically find many sources exhibiting at industry trade shows. Although these products may be more expensive than general "off-the-shelf" software, these products may better suit your company's specific needs, and they're less expensive than having software created specifically for you. Check, however, to see how compatible these industry-specific items are with common software or hardware; you'll probably want to be able to use some "off-the-shelf" products.

If you are just starting your business, you may not need to figure out each of these technology issues in detail, but you should have a realistic sense of costs as you put your financial statements together.

The Technology Budget worksheet and Technology Plan Preparation Form at the end of this chapter will help you assess your technology needs and costs.

Planning for Technology Businesses

If you are preparing a business plan for a company that is heavily dependent on technology, expect some potential funders, especially venture capitalists, to scrutinize your technology plan in fairly great detail. They will want to see both that you understand the nature and scope of your technology needs and that you have planned adequately for your hardware/software needs and your need for specialized personnel.

Of course, some companies are specifically in the business of developing or exploiting new technology, not just using technology to achieve other business goals. In these companies, technology is essentially the core business, and potential investors want detailed information about the nature of your technology. This description can be included as part of the section on "Products and Services" or it can be a separate section of your plan. It should describe the basic concept and features of your technology with a level of detail geared to the expertise of the potential reader.

Be careful, however, about how you provide the necessary data. You'll need to show the viability of your concept without revealing extremely sensitive company secrets (which should not be put in a written business plan). If, on the other hand, you are seeking conventional financing (e.g., bank loans) or investment from less knowledgeable sources, then the description of your new technology should be fairly general. If your plan is for internal use only, your technology section may be very detailed and include sensitive information about product development. In this case, be extremely cautious as to how the plan is distributed; you don't want it to fall into the wrong hands.

What Do You Use Technology For?

If you walk into a computer store and say, "I need a computer," the first question the salesperson will ask is, "What do you need it for?" Base your technology choices on your actual and projected business needs.

When you examine your business operations, look at which functions require or could benefit from technology. Common business needs that utilize technology include:

- Accounting, taxes, finances
- Order taking and tracking
- Order fulfillment/shipping
- Inventory management
- Database management, such as customer, product, supplier, or inventory
- Mailing lists
- Communication with customers
- Internal communication
- Presentations
- Desktop publishing/graphics
- Personnel/human resources management
- Production: design, cost-tracking, supply management
- Internet marketing/website/email
- Internet sales

Many of these functions are offered online by Application Service Providers (ASPs). ASPs enable you to access your data anywhere you have Internet access and to pay monthly for the service instead of purchasing costly software outright.

Choosing Technology

Key issues when choosing technology include:

- Functions
- Ease-of-use
- Cost
- Security
- Ability to be upgraded and expanded
- Integration with existing data, technology, systems, etc.

As a guideline, ask yourself the following questions:

- What features do you absolutely need? Make certain the technology can handle your most important functions. If you can't do the things you have to do, you'll waste your money.

"You have to work with and understand the existing infrastructure, the existing distribution channels, the existing brick and mortar manufacturers. Navigating those waters, understanding their issues and working both within and outside the system are very important things."

Andrew Anker
Venture Capitalist

- What features would be helpful, although they are not absolutely essential? In addition to meeting your essential needs, some technology products or features can save you time or money in the long term. Look for those solutions that can improve your business and review them in light of the extra cost and complexity they present.

- How often will you need to change or update computer software? The biggest problem with computers is not that they fail, but that as new software and peripheral devices are introduced, they don't work with older computers. Newer versions of software require more and more memory and faster processing speed. If you'll need to upgrade frequently, purchase hardware that is more liable to be able to handle such upgrades.

- Does your equipment have to be compatible with other equipment or lots of software? With a piece of stand-alone equipment, such as a copier, you have a lot more flexibility when making your selection, and it may not matter if you buy an unknown brand. If you have equipment that has to be integrated or connect with other equipment, such as a computer or some smaller telecommunications devices, look for well-known products. You'll want to avoid the hassles of trying to make an off-brand work with your other equipment. Software programs, for instance, usually come equipped with drivers to handle only the most popular brands of computers, printers, or scanners.

- With equipment that uses "consumables," such as ink cartridges for printers, find out if replacement supplies are readily available. Office and discount stores usually carry only the most well-known brands. Take into account the availability and costs of supplies before making your final selection.

- Do you do tasks like design, desktop publishing, presentations? If so, go for the latest equipment. Those types of software programs eat up lots of memory and processing speed.

- If you are operating internationally, what types of steps do you need to take to integrate different systems, etc. (e.g, paper size, electrical current, currency exchange/reporting). Make certain your technology can handle your international needs.

- How cool do you want to be? Some people and some companies want to be seen as on the cutting edge of technology.

Chapter Summary

Technology is a critical aspect of all businesses today, used in most areas of business operations and marketing. Because technology decisions can be confusing and costly, you may want to seek the help of outside experts to help you make your technology choices. Developing an overall technology plan gives you a framework to understand the scope of your technology needs and create a more realistic technology budget.

Technology Budget $ ➤ $$ ➤ $$$

Use this worksheet to specify the costs of your ongoing technology needs.

	Year 1	Year 2	Year 3	Year 4	Year 5
Software					
Accounting					
Customer relationship mgmt.					
Human resource mgmt.					
Inventory mgmt.					
Office suite					
Custom software					
Other:					
Other:					
Hardware					
Desktop computers					
Portable computers					
Servers					
Backup systems					
Printers					
Networking					
Peripherals					
Other:					
Other:					
Telecommunications					
Telephone system					
Mobile phones/pagers					
Fax machines					
Internet access					
Other:					
Other:					
Consulting Personnel					
Systems design / maintenance					
Tech support / help desk					
Other:					
Total					

NOTE: *A computerized version of this worksheet is available as part of The Planning Shop's* **Electronic Financial Worksheets** *package, available from www.PlanningShop.com.*

Technology Plan Preparation Form

Using this form as a guide, summarize the key technology concerns and technology needs of your business, which you can then include in your business plan, either in a separate Technology section, or in the Operations section.

Software Needs: _____

_____

_____

_____

_____

_____

_____

Hardware Needs: _____

_____

_____

_____

_____

_____

_____

Telecommunications Needs: _____

_____

_____

_____

_____

_____

_____

Personnel Needs (specify in-house or outsourced): _____

_____

_____

_____

_____

_____

Use this information as the basis of your plan's Technology section.

SAMPLE PLAN: Technology Plan

Technology

ComputerEase is in the technology business. As such, we must always stay on top of new developments and continually upgrade not only our equipment, but our skills.

The most critical component of our technology plan is making certain our instructors are fully capable of using new software and hardware in the most productive ways possible, so that they, in turn, can train our students and develop appropriate training materials. To that end, our instructors are given pre-release copies of software programs and receive pre-release training from major software manufacturers.

Key to ComputerEase's success are our training centers. One training center is already in operation, and we anticipate opening a second center by January 2004. This center will have 10-15 of the most up-to-date personal computers, 3-4 printers, overhead projection equipment and other audiovisual equipment. We lease our computers for the training centers rather than purchase them; this enables us to always offer students the latest equipment.

Our internal operations also depend on technology. In addition to the computers and information systems we use to conduct our ongoing business, we have also acquired a high speed printer/copier to enable us to produce training materials in-house less expensively. Our offices are equipped with high-speed Internet access and we have our own internal local area network (LAN).

ComputerEase currently has a website giving background information on the company and listing the schedule of training classes for the public. We intend to extend the capabilities of our Internet site, allowing students to register for classes online, and to provide password-protected areas for students of corporate training classes to receive additional assistance after their training sessions are complete. This will enable us to provide more continual support for our corporate clients.

ComputerEase intends to pursue investigating online, distance learning capabilities. National competitors currently offer such training (although it is still in its relative infancy), and we want to be prepared to be able to take on such competition. Additionally, we believe our online distance learning programs will enable us to expedite our geographic reach into other areas of the Midwest.

## Chapter 13

Management & Organization

No matter what you sell,
you're selling your people.

Your People Determine Your Success

People are the heart of every business. Overwhelmingly, the quality of the people determines the success of the business. Many investors base their investment choices almost entirely on the strength of the people involved in the enterprise. They know that the experience, skills, and personalities of the management team have a greater impact on the long-term fortunes of a company than the product or service provided.

For this reason, investors and lenders are likely to review the management portion of a business plan before they read many other sections. They read this section thoroughly, carefully scrutinizing the qualifications of the people behind a business. They look not only to see if the management team has the expertise necessary to run the business, but also if the internal structure makes maximum use of the talents of team members.

So, if you are preparing your business plan for financing purposes, you need to take particular care in crafting your Management section. Even if you are developing your business plan solely for internal use, an honest evaluation of your key employees' strengths and weaknesses will help you make the best use of your management team.

Most entrepreneurs give serious thought to choosing people for key positions. They may undertake extensive recruitment efforts, often using professional executive search firms, to find just the right person. But what do they do with that man or woman once on board?

"Part of planning is 'people planning.' We want our managers to tell us about their people resources. People issues make up one of the largest sections of our business plan. We want to know how people will be used, and how managers are training their people and preparing for succession."

George James
Former Sr. V.P. & CFO
Levi Strauss & Co.

All too often, no one gives careful consideration to creating clear lines of organizational responsibility and developing a management style that motivates employees. This is particularly true in newer companies. Even outstanding people will only do their best work in a system that encourages, recognizes, and rewards achievement. If you can create such an atmosphere, you can give yourself a true competitive edge.

Thus, in developing your Management plan, focus on two main areas: 1) the people who run your business; and 2) your management structure and style. Together, these two thrusts represent the core of your management system.

Your Management Team

Who are the people most important to your company's future? Who are the people determining the strategies you will pursue? Who makes final decisions? Which members of your management decide on the products or services you will sell and the prices you will charge? Who is in charge of your sales efforts?

In all but the smallest businesses, these tasks are assigned to or shared by many people. So when you evaluate your management team, include:

- Key Employees/Principals
- Board of Directors
- Advisory Committee
- Consultants and Other Specialists
- Key Management Personnel to Be Added

Key Employees/Principals

Usually, the most important person in a business is the founder or founders, especially if the company is a startup. In startups, the founders usually serve as the top managers and exercise day-to-day control over affairs. For this reason, the first person to evaluate in your management assessment is the founder, even if it is yourself.

Occasionally, either the founders themselves or major investors will bring in others to serve in top positions, such as president and chief executive officer. But if the founders remain active in the business in any way, either by serving on the Board of Directors, remaining as a company consultant, or taking a secondary management position, their skills and qualifications must be described in your plan. Other managers to evaluate in your business plan include:

- Top decision makers: president, chief executive officer, division presidents.
- Key production personnel: chief operating officer, plant manager, technical director.
- Key technology personnel: chief technology officer, MIS director, systems administrator.

> *"There are lots of companies to be created, lots of technologies to be built. There's an excess of money to fund those companies. The limiting asset is still people."*
>
> **Andrew Anker**
> **Venture Capitalist**

- Principal marketing staff: director of marketing, director of sales.
- Primary human resources staff: personnel director, training director.
- Head of research and development.

In looking at these key players, ask yourself:

- Do they possess the skills necessary for their specific jobs?
- Do they have a record of success?
- Have their business setbacks given them insights that will help them in their current roles?
- Do their personalities make them effective members of the team?
- If they have supervisory responsibility, are they able to direct and motivate employees effectively?
- Taken as a whole, does your team incorporate the full range of expertise and management skills you require?

If you are preparing your business plan solely to seek outside financing, you should limit the number of key employees discussed in this section to no more than five or six. Focus only on those who are most responsible for the company's long-term success.

Some companies are fortunate enough to have enlisted the services of "stars," individuals with particularly outstanding track records. If you have such a star associated with your company, be certain to highlight the role that he or she plays in your enterprise. You will want to feature them prominently in your Executive Summary as well. If key personnel have been associated with well-known, successful companies, be certain to indicate those associations as well. If you choose, you can include the resumes of key personnel in your plan's Appendix.

Complete the Key Employees Evaluation worksheet on the next two pages to outline the attributes of your top managers. Assess their:

- **Experience.** State the specific positions held and job responsibilities that directly relate to the current position. This is not a resume, so do not list every previous job, only those that indicate a skill or talent transferable to the job at hand.
- **Successes.** Describe noteworthy successes, particularly those that can be quantified. Include accomplishments that indicate the ability to plan, manage, overcome obstacles, and reach a goal.
- **Education.** Include education in the written plan only if the person is new to business or the education is directly related to or necessary for the task at hand.
- **Strengths.** Describe the individual's best attributes in a business setting, including traits such as the ability to motivate others, industry knowledge, and financial capabilities.
- **Areas Lacking Strength.** Describe the attributes the individual must enhance to become a more effective manager; such traits might include specific skills or knowledge, better communication techniques,

Key Employee Evaluation

Describe the attributes of your top managers.

President / CEO: _____

Experience: _____

_____

Successes: _____

Education: _____

Strengths: _____

Areas Lacking Strength: _____

Chief Operating Officer: _____

Experience: _____

_____

Successes: _____

Education: _____

Strengths: _____

Areas Lacking Strength: _____

Chief Financial Officer: _____

Experience: _____

_____

Successes: _____

Education: _____

Strengths: _____

Areas Lacking Strength: _____

Marketing / Sales Director: _____

Experience: _____

_____

Successes: _____

Education: _____

Strengths: _____

Areas Lacking Strength: _____

Production Manager: _____

Experience: _____

Successes: _____

Education: _____

Strengths: _____

Areas Lacking Strength: _____

Human Resources Director: _____

Experience: _____

Successes: _____

Education: _____

Strengths: _____

Areas Lacking Strength: _____

Chief Technology Officer / Technical Director: _____

Experience: _____

Successes: _____

Education: _____

Strengths: _____

Areas Lacking Strength: _____

Other Key Personnel: _____

Experience: _____

Successes: _____

Education: _____

Strengths: _____

Areas Lacking Strength: _____

Other Key Personnel: _____

Experience: _____

Successes: _____

Education: _____

Strengths: _____

Areas Lacking Strength: _____

or ability to handle additional tasks. While you might not include this in your written plan, this information can help you develop more successful leaders.

Management Compensation and Incentives

Next, you need to discuss the compensation and incentives you offer your key employees as a way of retaining and motivating them. Most incentives have monetary implications, and investors often want to know the financial stake top management has in the company.

Some of the incentives you can offer include:

- **Salary.** Amount of money paid annually to the manager, regardless of company or personal performance.
- **Bonuses.** Additional cash given, usually at the end of the year, based on company or personal performance.
- **Commissions.** Cash given based on a percentage of sales made; rarely given to top management.
- **Profit Sharing.** Cash distributed to all eligible employees, based on the company's annual profit.
- **Equity.** Stock in the company, which gives the employee a direct financial stake in the overall performance of the business.
- **Stock Options.** Ability to buy stock at a future date at a currently set price; if the worth of the company goes up, these options can be exercised, giving the employee a financial gain.

In the Compensation and Incentives worksheet on the next page, list the financial incentives given key employees.

Board of Directors

Businesses that are incorporated must have boards of directors. In very small corporations, the directors are usually just the principals running the company. The board then serves little more than a legal function.

In larger companies, however, the board often includes members outside of management. Most frequently, these board members are people who have invested large sums in the company. Venture capitalists often require board seats as a condition of their investment.

Obviously, investors serve on boards to protect their money; they want to exercise some control over the management and direction of the company. But management should not view these investor–directors only as "Big Brothers," watching their every move. They often bring valuable insight and judgment to the company and contribute to its overall viability and success.

In forming your board of directors, you might also want to include members who bring you specific business expertise, such as financial acumen or industry knowledge. Such directors typically receive compensation for their service on the board.

"Once you get beyond a credible salary, motivation is more a matter of pride, respect and acknowledgment. You want motivation derived from the satisfaction of playing the game well and the relationship with the other players."

Bill Walsh
Former Coach and
President, S.F. 49ers

"We reinforce our team concept by having only one cafeteria, one parking lot; there are no special eating or parking areas for senior management. We have no private offices; white collar managers often wear blue work shirts. Likewise, there is no time clock for our production workers. We have only two job classifications within our hourly workforce: production worker or skilled trade. No one receives a change in salary because of seniority; the only factor seniority affects is vacation time."

Michael Damer
New United Motor
Manufacturing Inc.

Compensation and Incentives
$* ➤ *$$* ➤ *$$$

Describe the compensation package for each of your key employees.

President/CEO

Salary: _____ Bonuses: _____

Other Incentives: _____ _____

Chief Operating Officer

Salary: _____ Bonuses: _____

Other Incentives: _____ _____

Chief Financial Officer

Salary: _____ Bonuses: _____

Other Incentives: _____ _____

Marketing/Sales Director

Salary: _____ Bonuses: _____

Other Incentives: _____ _____

Production Manager

Salary: _____ Bonuses: _____

Other Incentives: _____ _____

Human Resources Director

Salary: _____ Bonuses: _____

Other Incentives: _____ _____

Chief Technology Officer/Technical Director

Salary: _____ Bonuses: _____

Other Incentives: _____ _____

Other Key Personnel

Salary: _____ Bonuses: _____

Other Incentives: _____ _____

Other Key Personnel

Salary: _____ Bonuses: _____

Other Incentives: _____ _____

Remember, however, that the board of directors has legal responsibility and authority for the corporation. Thus, outsiders should be chosen very carefully.

Advisory Committee

You may identify a number of individuals whose ongoing judgment and advice you want for your company, but whom, for legal considerations, you don't want on your board of directors.

One way of using their services, other than hiring them, is to institute an informal advisory committee. Such a committee would have little or no legal responsibility but could still render great assistance in your company's development.

An advisory committee can also be helpful to a proprietorship or partnership that does not have a board of directors.

Complete the Board of Directors/Advisory Committee worksheet on the next page to describe the members of your board of directors and advisory committee, if applicable.

Consultants and Other Specialists

"Our management consultant was extremely helpful in developing an overall strategy and helping us understand financial implications. Our accounting firm was helpful in setting up internal controls and helping us to know what is going on."

Larry Leigon
Founder, Ariel Vineyards

Smaller businesses often think that consultants and specialists are only for large corporations. But hiring consultants can bring you the specific expertise of highly qualified individuals without the expense of a full-time employee. Both large and small businesses benefit from the services of outside consultants and specialists.

The use of consultants can also enhance the image you present in your business plan. Being represented by one of the leading law firms in town, or having your accounts prepared by one of the major accounting firms, adds credibility to your company.

Consultants with particular skills can help fill in the gaps in your management team. For instance, you might not yet be able to hire a full-time marketing director, but you could use the assistance of a marketing consultant.

Every business, no matter how small, should use an attorney and accountant, at least to set up the initial books and review contracts and leases. If you can't afford their services, you can't afford to go into business. It is a foolish economy to forego their advice for the sake of a few hundred dollars. Consultants and specialists you might use, other than attorneys and accountants, include:

- **Management Consultants.** To help you plan your business, develop strategies, solve particular problems, and improve management techniques.
- **Marketing Consultants.** To design ways to position your company in the market, oversee the creation of advertising and promotional materials, and structure your sales strategy.
- **Designers.** To add perceived value and improve your company's image through the talents of graphic design, product design, packaging design, website design, or interior design.

Board of Directors/Advisory Committee

List the members of your Board of Directors, their financial stake in the company, and their professional expertise:

_____
_____
_____
_____
_____
_____
_____
_____
_____
_____
_____

Describe how often the Board of Directors meets and its responsibilities: _____

_____
_____
_____
_____
_____
_____

If you have an Advisory Committee, state its functions and responsibilities and how often it meets: _____

_____
_____
_____
_____
_____

List the members of your Advisory Committee, their professional expertise, and their compensation, if any:

_____
_____
_____
_____
_____
_____
_____
_____

- **Industry Specialists.** Every industry has areas requiring special knowledge or specific technical skills, and "experts" offer consultation in these areas; examples might be kitchen design for restaurants, production line design for manufacturing companies, or merchandising specialists for retail stores.
- **Technology Specialists.** To help you identify your technology needs and solutions, set up your database, website, communications systems, etc.

Complete the Professional Services worksheet on the next page to describe the consultants and specialists utilized by your company.

Key Management Personnel to Be Added

Don't worry if your management team is not fully complete, especially if your company is a startup. Investors and bankers are accustomed to seeing plans for companies that have key positions vacant.

You must, however, indicate the positions you intend to add in the future and the qualifications of the individuals you will seek to fill the positions. This gives a more complete picture of your overall management team and indicates that you understand the gaps in your organization.

When thinking about what you are lacking, consider not only the specific functional responsibilities that have yet to be covered, but also how you can create a sense of "balance" in your total team.

If most of your current management has strong technical experience in your industry, but less in business management, business experience should be a primary requirement of your new managers.

Sometimes your top manager is a good "inside" person, able to run production, supervise employees, and manage accounts, yet you still need a strong "outside" person, able to secure sales, entertain clients, and conduct promotional activities.

Complete the Key Management Personnel to Be Added worksheet on page 200 to describe the key employees you intend to add to management.

Management Structure and Style

How will you actually run your company? How will decisions be made? What are the lines of authority? How do you want employees to feel about the company? What voice do employees have when company policies and goals are set?

A company's organization and management style act as powerful invisible forces shaping both the daily working atmosphere and the future of the company. But all too often managers, especially new managers, pay only cursory attention to the development of their structure and style. In looking at your company's structure, examine both the formal lines of authority that exist and the informal ways in which decisions are made and employees are treated.

"Building a sense of the 'team' must be planned and orchestrated. You must continually note that the team is all-important. The only bottom line, the only true satisfaction, is when the team does well. Team-building is an on-going process. In your training, use every conceivable example from other fields to bring home the importance of the concept of the team. Look to develop an atmosphere where players expect and demand a lot of each other, where they feel that individually they are an extension of their team-mates. This doesn't just happen, it must be planned."

Bill Walsh
Former Coach and
President, S.F. 49ers

Professional Services

$ ➤ $$ ➤ $$$

Profile your key consultants below.

Attorney

Firm name: _____

Lawyer's name: _____

Qualifications: _____

Ways used by the company: _____

Annual compensation: _____

Accountant

Firm name: _____

Accountant's name: _____

Qualifications: _____

Ways used by the company: _____

Annual compensation: _____

Management / Marketing Consultants

Firm name: _____

Consultant's name: _____

Qualifications: _____

Ways used by the company: _____

Annual compensation: _____

Industry Specialists

Firm name: _____

Specialist's name: _____

Qualifications: _____

Ways used by the company: _____

Annual compensation: _____

Others

Firm name: _____

Specialist's name: _____

Qualifications: _____

Ways used by the company: _____

Annual compensation: _____

NOTE: *A computerized financial version of this worksheet is available as part of The Planning Shop's* **Electronic Financial Worksheets** *package, available from www.PlanningShop.com.*

Key Management Personnel to Be Added

$ ➤ $$ ➤ $$$

Describe the factors concerning management personnel you intend to add to your staff.

Position: _____

Qualifications Sought: _____

_____

_____

Approximate Date to be Added: _____

Approximate Level of Compensation: _____

Other Incentives to be Offered: _____

Position: _____

Qualifications Sought: _____

_____

_____

Approximate Date to be Added: _____

Approximate Level of Compensation: _____

Other Incentives to be Offered: _____

Position: _____

Qualifications Sought: _____

_____

_____

Approximate Date to be Added: _____

Approximate Level of Compensation: _____

Other Incentives to be Offered: _____

Position: _____

Qualifications Sought: _____

_____

_____

Approximate Date to be Added: _____

Approximate Level of Compensation: _____

Other Incentives to be Offered: _____

Lines of Authority

When examining their organization, managers usually begin with the formal structure — the official lines of authority. They decide how employees will be supervised and how job functions will be allocated. While clear lines of authority are vital in large organizations, they are equally important in small companies. A frequent source of tension in partnerships is the failure to plainly delineate areas of responsibility and decision making.

Increasingly, companies use "horizontal" management structures rather than strict hierarchical, "top-down" lines of authority. In such organizations, employees have greater authority for decision-making in their own areas of responsibility. This enables those closest to the customer or to the production process to make decisions quickly and respond to change faster than in more centrally-controlled organizations.

Some questions to ask when examining your company's structure are:

- Should responsibilities be allocated by functional area, product line, or geographic divisions? For example, should all your marketing efforts be assigned to a marketing department, or should each division handle all aspects of a product or service, including marketing?
- Which employees will each manager supervise, and over what functions will each manager have responsibility?
- Will you use a production line or team approach in producing your product or service? Thus, will each worker be responsible for one particular task, or will a group be responsible for many tasks?

Perhaps the quickest and clearest way to communicate your management structure is through a graphic organizational flow chart. You can use two kinds of charts: one describing areas of responsibility, and the other outlining reporting or supervisory relationships. Examples of each are shown on page 202. You should also provide a short narrative description explaining the relationships shown on the charts. If you do not wish to use a chart in your business plan, you need not do so. Just expand the verbal narrative to encompass the same material.

Informal Relationships

Flow charts describe your formal organizational structure, but every business also has an informal structure which can have at least as much impact on the company. Although you should not discuss these informal relationships in a business plan prepared for outside funding, you should look at less formal relationships within your company when undertaking internal planning.

Questions to ask when evaluating your informal organization include:

- Which managers have the most impact on decisions?
- Which managers have ready access to the president or members of the Board of Directors?
- Do decisions at the top get effectively translated into action by others?

"Our management structure assumes people care about their jobs and want to belong to an organization that takes pride in what it makes. We demand more from our work force, but the trade-off for the worker is excellent pay and job security. We believe in developing employee potential through: mutual trust and respect; recognizing worth and dignity; developing individual performance; developing team performance; and improving the work environment."

Michael Damer
New United Motor Manufacturing Inc.

Examples of Flow Charts

Areas of Responsibility

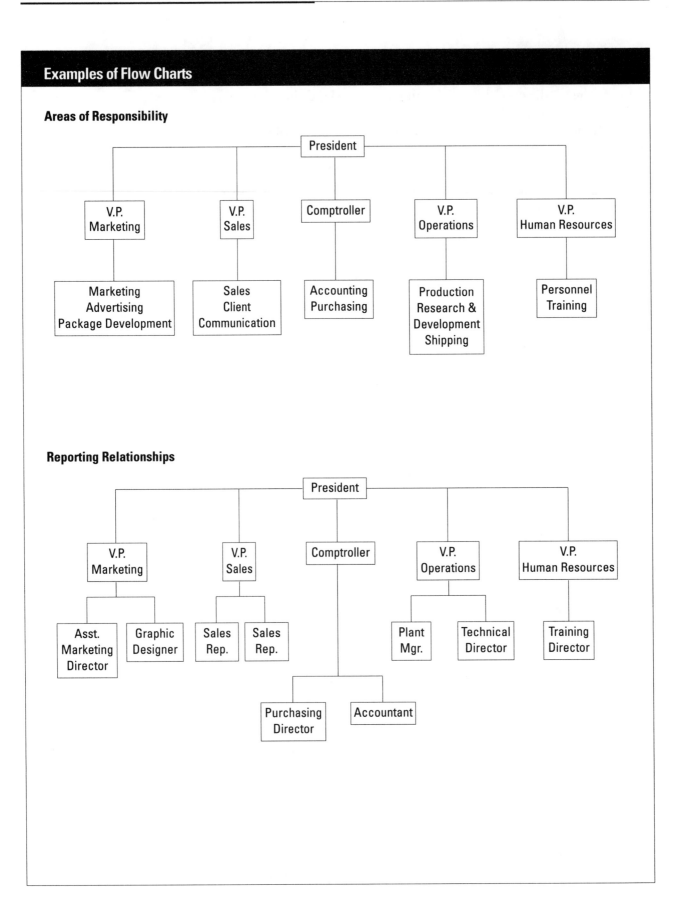

Reporting Relationships

- Which subordinates have substantial influence on their superiors?
- Which divisions or groups of employees have the greatest morale problems? Who do they report to?
- How do you communicate and share values throughout the company?
- How do you create an atmosphere of tolerance for differences and diversity?

Generally, you want to evaluate how authority is distributed and how decisions are made in reality, not just on paper.

Management Style

All managers have management styles, even if they've never thought about their approach to management. Most managers define their jobs in terms of the tasks to be done rather than the methods to be used. They see their role as making widgets, rather than motivating and aiding the widget makers. Their management styles are usually just extensions of their personal styles.

Managing people is far too important to be left to chance. Your employees are one of your most valuable resources. Just as you need to take care of other resources in your company, such as equipment and materials, you must make certain you are not wasting your human resources.

Developing your managers' capabilities in such skills as communication, leadership, motivation, team-building, etc., affects your company's productivity, employee retention, and customer loyalty.

Moreover, you want to develop an overall company management and communication style that is independent of the personalities of your key managers and that fits your corporate culture. As discussed in Chapter 1, your corporate culture should permeate every aspect of your business and should reflect how you want your employees and customers to see you.

For most companies, especially smaller companies, building a sense of teamwork is essential. Help your employees feel they are an important part of the organization and that their contribution matters. Communication is a vital ingredient in team building; if employees know what's going on in the company, they feel a part of the whole picture.

Regardless of your management style, remember that everyone, whether mailroom clerk or company president, wants to feel important. Recognize achievement, both privately and publicly. Reward initiative with both monetary and non-monetary awards. Acknowledge jobs well done. Solicit suggestions, and be responsive to concerns.

The five most important elements of your management style are:

1. Clear Policies
2. Communication
3. Employee Recognition
4. Employee's Ability to Affect Change
5. Fairness

"We rotate jobs among members every two to three hours for safety, fairness, avoiding strains, and reducing boredom. Members are encouraged to make decisions on their own. Team members design the way the jobs will be done. The theory is the people closest to the function can best design how to perform the task."

Michael Damer
New United Motor
Manufacturing Inc.

"The best management is management by walking around. Employees know the boss is accessible and a real person they can identify with, not an anonymous entity. It gives management a personal quality. I shake hands with every employee; everybody calls me by my first name, from the mail room clerk on up. I'm listed in the telephone book; any employee or any guest can call me. With 1,500 employees and over one million guests, this could be a problem if we didn't have an effective operation."

Andre Tatibouet
President, Aston Hotels

Complete the Management Style worksheet on page 205 to evaluate your company's management style.

Preparing Your Management Section

How you prepare the Management section of your business plan depends a great deal on whether it is being written for internal use only or whether it will be submitted to outside investors.

If your plan is for internal use, emphasize the management aspects centering on structure, style, and gaps in personnel. However, if you are preparing the plan for financing purposes, you should focus primarily on the relevant backgrounds of your management team members. These summaries should be brief and written in an objective style. Even if your vice president for marketing truly is "highly motivated, results-oriented, and exceptionally creative," those types of judgments appear naive when read in a business plan.

The upcoming Management Plan Preparation Form enables you to outline the Management section of your business plan.

Chapter Summary

People are the key to success for every business. It takes capable people, with appropriate experience and abilities, to develop both a management structure and style that make full use of the personnel and financial resources of the business and keeps the company focused on its mission. Thus, potential investors will thoroughly examine the backgrounds of the management team that will be running your company.

Management Style

Describe the nature and functions of your company's management.

How does your company's management style fit with your corporate culture? _____

_____

_____

_____

How do the personalities of your key employees complement or contrast with the company's management style?

_____

_____

How do you develop a sense of teamwork among your employees? _____

_____

_____

Do you have a clear set of company policies, covering items such as benefits, termination, and promotion?

_____

_____

_____

How do you ensure ongoing communication with your employees? Do you hold meetings, informal conferences, or print newsletters? _____

_____

_____

_____

How do you recognize and acknowledge employees' achievements? What financial rewards do you give? What nonmonetary recognition do you provide? _____

_____

_____

_____

How do you solicit and act on employee suggestions? How can employees affect the development of company products, services, or policies? _____

_____

_____

Are policies enforced evenly? Are rewards and acknowledgments given fairly? Does management play "favorites"? _____

_____

_____

Management Plan Preparation Form

List the key members of your management team, with a brief description of each person's relevant business background, responsibilities they have in your company, and the compensation they receive.

_____

_____

_____

_____

_____

_____

_____

_____

_____

_____

_____

_____

_____

Key Decision-Makers and Advisors for the Company: _____

_____

_____

_____

_____

_____

_____

_____

_____

_____

_____

Management Structure and Style: _____

_____

_____

_____

_____

*Use this information as the basis of your plan's **Management section**.*

SAMPLE PLAN: Management & Organization

Management

Key Employees

<u>Scott E. Connors, President.</u> Prior to founding ComputerEase in January 2003, Scott E. Connors was the Regional Vice President for Chanoff's Computer Emporium, a franchised computer hardware retail chain, with 23 stores in the Midwest. Connors began his association with Chanoff's Computer Emporium as manager of the downtown Vespucci store in 1995. In his first year, he increased sales by over 42%, and in his second year by 39%. Because of these sales, he was named "Manager of the Year" in 1997 for the Chanoff's chain. In March 1998, Connors purchased a half-interest in the ownership of the Vespucci store. In October 2002, he sold this interest.

Gives examples of achievements

Connors assumed the role of Regional Vice President of the Chanoff's chain in August 2000. In that position, he was responsible for the company's strategic development for Indiana, Ohio, and Illinois. His duties included approving franchise proposals, selecting locations, and providing direct assistance to store managers in marketing, operations, and administration. He remained in that position until October 2002, when he left to begin work on ComputerEase.

Shows relevant experience

As Chanoff's Regional Vice President, Connors conducted an evaluation of the potential of adding software retailing and training components to augment the chain's computer hardware sales. This evaluation led Connors to believe that a substantial need for corporate software training existed but could not be met by a hardware retailer. Instead, a stand-alone operation should be formed. This was the concept behind ComputerEase.

Connors' association with Chanoff's Computer Emporium, coupled with the five years he spent as a sales representative for IBM, has given him extensive experience in selling technological equipment and services to large corporations.

Connors owns 60% of the stock in ComputerEase and serves as Chairman and Treasurer of the Board of Directors.

Specifies ownership interest in company

<u>Susan Alexander, Vice President, Marketing.</u> In March 2003, Susan Alexander joined ComputerEase with primary responsibility for the company's marketing and sales activities.

Prior to joining ComputerEase, Alexander served as Assistant Marketing Director for AlwaysHere Health Plan. Her responsibilities in this position included direct sales to human resource directors, developing marketing materials and campaigns, and supervising sales personnel. She held that position from 2001 until coming to ComputerEase. Alexander's experience marketing to the human resources community gives her the ideal background for

Shows directly applicable experience

SAMPLE PLAN: Management & Organization (continued)

ComputerEase, which sells its services primarily through human resources and training directors.

In previous relevant positions, Alexander was a sales representative for SpeakUp Dictation Equipment, where she sold technological equipment to corporations, and copy editor for Catchem Advertising Agency.

Alexander owns 10% of the stock in ComputerEase.

Lists manage-
ment to be
added at a
later date

Vice President, Training (To Be Selected). In January 2004, ComputerEase will add a third key management position, Vice President for Training. The individual selected will have substantial experience in conducting a training organization, teaching others to train, and supervising a training staff. The future vice president will possess outstanding training skills and have experience with computer software programs, either in teaching or developing such programs. Ideally, he or she will have experience in developing training manuals or other training material.

Board of Directors

Scott Connors is the Chairman of the Board and Treasurer. The position of Vice Chairman has been reserved for an outside investor. The company's attorney, Cathy J.Dobbs, serves as Secretary.

Consultant

A.A. Arnold, Ph.D. Dr. A. A. Arnold, Professor of Instructional Media at Vespucci State University (VSU), serves the company as a consultant in the conception and development of training manuals. A specialist in the design of instructional materials, Dr. Arnold received his Ph.D. in Education with an emphasis on interactive computer-aided training. Currently, Dr. Arnold designs training programs for industry in addition to holding his position at VSU.

Advisory Committee

An informal Advisory Committee was formed in April 2003 to provide guidance to the officers and staff of ComputerEase. The committee meets quarterly, and members of the committee are available as resources to the company on an ongoing basis.

Advisory
Board reflects
business
leaders and
potential cus-
tomers.

Members of the committee are:

Virginia Gross, Director of Human Resources, RockSolid Insurance Company

John Caruso, Director of Training, Vespucci National Bank

Mark Richards, Marketing Director, SANE Software

Dr. A. A. Arnold, Professor of Instructional Media, Vespucci State University

Additional members are expected to be added by the end of 2004.

Management Structure

President Scott Connors is involved in the day-to-day operations of all aspects of the company. He directs the administrative and financial aspects of the company and works closely with the vice presidents to help guide and support activities over which they have specific responsibility. However, each vice president is given a wide degree of decision-making authority in his or her assigned areas.

Management responsibilities in ComputerEase are divided as shown on the flow chart below.

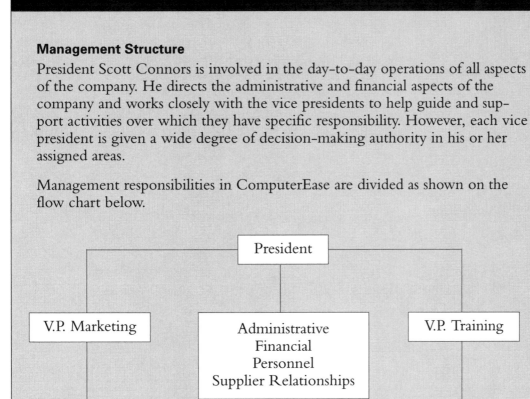

Because the company's emphasis is on building relationships with its customers and constantly improving quality, ComputerEase has instituted an incentive program in which all employees receive awards for providing outstanding customer service and making accepted suggestions for improvement.

## Chapter 14

Community Involvement & Social Responsibility

"At the point in life where your talents meet the needs of the world is where God wants you to be."
— *Albert Schweitzer*

As you start your business, you have many goals. You're focused on developing your business concept, getting funded, making money. What does social responsibility have to do with these?

Just as individuals have responsibilities to their communities, companies likewise have responsibilities and obligations to society at large. "Corporations" are unique entities with many rights and privileges. Society, through its laws, grants "corporations" special and favorable benefits, such as the limits on personal liability of a corporation's shareholders. Imagine, if you can, if every shareholder in a company had personal liability for that company's actions: there certainly wouldn't be much of a stock market. Every business, whether they realize it or not, relies on the continuing support of society.

Moreover, being socially responsible is part of the overall health of your company. First, it establishes your company's values and fosters your corporate culture. Businesses that act with integrity and honesty are more likely to have their employees act with integrity and honesty towards the company and their fellow workers. Being a good corporate citizen makes it less likely that your company will get in trouble with regulatory agencies, taxing authorities, or face law suits or fines.

Additionally, employees themselves get value from being part of an organization that is committed to enhancing the social good. Programs that allow employees to be involved in community causes as part of their

"Entrepreneurs are a great resource for community involvement; they can use the same kind of skills for building the community that they do for building a business."

Gib Myers
Venture Capitalist

company activities are viewed as a valuable benefit, much like other employee benefits. Prospective employees often look at a company's values and social commitment when comparing job offers. Being able to attract and retain the kind of people you want is critical to the success and growth of your business, so your social commitment helps the long-term value of your company.

Corporate social responsibility is:

- Good for business
- Good for the community
- Good for the economy

Being socially responsible is the right thing to do, and there's always strength in doing the right thing.

What's In It For You?

> *"Community involvement becomes an asset of the company."*
>
> **Gib Myers**
> **Venture Capitalist**

Your business derives a number of benefits by being committed to social responsibility and involved in community activities and causes. Among your company's direct benefits are:

- **Visibility:** gives your company increased visibility in the community and your industry; this can be particularly helpful to small, new companies, as community activities may be a very effective way to become known at less cost than other marketing methods.
- **Positive Corporate Image:** being seen as a good corporate citizen helps foster positive feelings about your company in the community and by potential customers, employees, and others.
- **Recruitment Tool:** aids your company's effectiveness in attracting employees; potential employees often choose to apply to those companies whose values and social commitment they respect.
- **Stronger Team:** having shared values and shared activities helps develop cohesiveness and commitment among all your employees and management.
- **More Satisfied Employees:** enhances the work experience of employees, not only by allowing them to be involved directly or indirectly in community/social affairs, but also by knowing they work for a company that acts with integrity in all its dealings; employees never have to lie for an employer.
- **Contacts with Other Companies:** by being active in community activities, you and your employees will meet and work with people from other companies, giving you valuable contacts with potential strategic partners, customers, and suppliers.

Being a Good "Corporate Citizen"

The most basic component of social responsibility is being a good "corporate citizen." Good corporate citizenship begins with a company's own internal practices and policies. It starts with corporate integrity.

Aspects of being a good corporate citizen include:

- Obeying the law, acting ethically, and being honest and responsible in all your dealings;

- Treating employees fairly and with respect; compensating employees fairly, and considering the well-being of employees as part of decision-making;

- Being honest and fair to your customers and suppliers, and in your advertising and marketing;

- Being cognizant of the impact your actions have on the environment; and

- Being involved in your community and concerned about the well-being of others.

Ethics

Most companies, especially large corporations now develop clear ethics guidelines and policies. Because employees are faced with many situations that have ethical implications, it is extremely useful to have a set of clear consistent policies that are firmly and fairly enforced throughout the company on matters such as accepting or giving bribes, the nature of gifts, gratuities, or special favors that will be given or accepted.

For a new or small company, an ethics policy doesn't have to be complex, but laying out clear guidelines on certain issues, such as expense reimbursement policies and adhering to all laws, can help avoid conflict or legal trouble.

Describe your ethics policy as part of the Social Responsibility Plan Preparation Form at the end of this chapter.

Social Responsibility Activities/Projects

"Social responsibility" can encompass or describe many of a company's activities and attitudes. Often it is used to describe companies with very active social or charitable programs. Some companies, including many new entrepreneurial ventures, are developing creative ways to act on their social commitment and contribute to their community. For example, the Internet company eBay, before their IPO (Initial Public Offering) of stock to the public, set aside a fair amount of company stock to establish a philanthropic foundation. As eBay's stock rose dramatically, the value of their foundation also rose.

Because more and more entrepreneurs are interested in and committed to issues of social responsibility, there are a number of new sources to assist companies in their social responsibility efforts. One source is the Entrepreneurs' Forum in Menlo Park, California, which helps companies harness their entrepreneurial creativity and spirit for the benefit of society.

There are many ways your company can be involved in social responsibility activities. The first, of course, is to be a good corporate citizen. Beyond that, many companies want to take a more active role in their communities, often donating time or money to various causes and organizations.

"Create a culture of community involvement. Start early. Start easy. Some of the kinds of things you can do include goodwill drives for clothing, food, toys, blood, etc.; volunteering in a local elementary school; working on a park clean up day or a Habitat for Humanity day."

Gib Myers
Venture Capitalist

> *"If the plan is well thought out and the social responsibility component is an added benefit, then it has the impact of making everybody feel good. But if the social good detracts from the competitiveness of the company, then it's not considered a positive. For instance, a company building software and arbitrarily deciding it wouldn't sell to the military, confining its market, would be considered a negative."*
>
> **Mark Gorenberg**
> **Venture Capitalist**

> *"It's a pretty tricky thing to put social responsibility in a business plan. As a venture capitalist looking at the plan, you still say, 'What does this mean for this team? Are they going to get carried away with this and not be as focused as I want them to be?' It depends on the strength of the team, and whether you have a really good team that knows what it's doing."*
>
> **Gib Myers**
> **Venture Capitalist**

You have many options for choosing how your company can incorporate social responsibility. One of the best ways to decide on your social responsibility activities is to involve employees themselves in choosing the projects and policies and to discuss how your company's values intersect with your programs.

While a company is young and/or small, you may want to limit your social activities to simple things: after all, you do have a company to build. You might only select one-time activities that could involve all members of your company as a team, such as participating in a walk for a community charity or volunteering one day to work on building a house for Habitat for Humanity. These can help promote team spirit, but the time commitment is clear and limited. You can also choose an ongoing project that is not too demanding; one new company gives one hour a week to help out at a local school. As your company grows, you may choose more ambitious projects.

The Social Responsibility Plan Preparation Form at the end of this chapter can assist you in outlining your company's social responsibility activities.

Should You Include a Social Responsibility Section in Your Plan?

What happens when you include social responsibility in a business plan that you are submitting to potential funders? How will potential investors view such interest and activities?

Some companies find being socially responsible can be a critical component of their business concept. They may develop a strategic position in the marketplace based on certain of their actions or policies, such as developing organic baby food, non-animal-tested cosmetics, or non-polluting electric cars. Other companies may plan key marketing campaigns around social issues, such as an Internet company drawing traffic to their site by giving a portion of each sale or donating an amount for each visitor to support certain social causes. In companies such as these, including social responsibility as part of your plan is definitely warranted, and in fact may be necessary to indicate how you will remain credible with your market.

But as important as it is for a business to think through issues of social responsibility, some potential investors may view such interest and activities as distractions. You want to be careful to demonstrate that your social responsibility plan enhances, rather than distracts, from the likelihood of your business success. Social responsibility goals often lead to higher profits — by reducing waste, being more innovative in personnel use, appealing to specific market segments, etc. — and then you might include that in your business plan. Otherwise, if your social responsibility activities do not obviously relate to your business activities, you may want to leave the Social Responsibility section out of the copy of the plan you submit to potential funding sources. But don't leave it out of the plan you use to run your company.

Chapter Summary

While a new business should not be overly focused on social issues to the extent that it takes attention away from more fundamental business concerns, being socially responsible brings many benefits to your company. It aids in building a corporate culture, attracting employees, and gaining visibility for the company. Every company should be a good corporate citizen, acting with integrity in all its dealings.

"I think a lot of people would like to do more for the community, but they're afraid to bring it up."

Gib Myers
Venture Capitalist

Social Responsibility Plan Preparation Form

Describe the attributes of your social responsibility plan in the space below.

Corporate Citizenship

Describe the ways you will insure your company:

Obeys the laws: _____

_____

Treats employees fairly/with respect: _____

_____

Deals honestly with customers, suppliers: _____

_____

Is honest in its advertising and marketing: _____

_____

Considers the impact of its actions on the community: _____

_____

Acts with integrity in all its dealings: _____

_____

Other: _____

Ethics

How will your company handle issues such as:

Gifts from or to suppliers/potential suppliers/vendors: _____

_____

Special favors, recreational outings, meals from or to suppliers/vendors, customers: _____

_____

Conflicts between laws in different countries where your company operates: _____

_____

Selecting suppliers based on their ethics: _____

_____

Insuring that subcontractors act ethically: _____

_____

Personal use of company property, e.g., company cars, phone, email: _____

_____

Expense Accounts: _____

_____

Social Responsibility Activities/Projects

What are your business goals?

☐ Visibility in community

☐ Visibility in industry

☐ Aid in recruiting employees

☐ Enhancing employee morale/employee involvement

☐ Developing contacts with other companies

☐ Other: _____

In what ways will you participate?

☐ Donate money from operating budget

☐ Donate a set percentage of profits/sales

☐ Allow employees to be active in projects on paid time

☐ Encourage employees to be active on a volunteer basis/after-hours.

☐ Donate company facilities for use by community groups

☐ Donate product overuns

☐ Participate as a company in community events

☐ Donate in kind products or services

☐ Formulate socially responsible operations practices (e.g. waste disposal management)

☐ Encourage company personnel/management to serve on agency boards

☐ Formulate socially responsible purchasing practices (e.g., environmental-friendly only products or type of vendor)

☐ Other: _____

What period of time are you willing to commit for? (e.g., day, week, year) _____

What types of concerns do you want to be involved with?

☐ Animal Welfare

☐ The Arts

☐ Children

☐ Community Enhancement & Improvement

☐ Economic empowerment

☐ Education

☐ Environment

☐ Gender Equality/Issues

☐ Health Issues

☐ Recreation/Athletics

☐ Safety

☐ Other: _____

Use this information as the basis of your plan's Community Involvement and Social Responsibility section.

SAMPLE PLAN: Community Involvement & Social Responsibility

Community Involvement & Social Responsibility

ComputerEase is committed to making a positive contribution to our community and to being a good corporate citizen in all our actions.

Recognizing our responsibilities, ComputerEase has adopted a number of operational policies and developed a community involvement program. This program and these policies reflect the reality that we are still a new, small company and our primary efforts are directed towards building and growing a healthy business.

Company Philosophy

Reflecting our desire to be a good corporate citizen, ComputerEase has adopted the following "Company Philosophy:"

- We will, as a company and as individuals, take responsibility for our actions;
- We will, as a company and as individuals, deal fairly and honestly with our customers, students, suppliers, the public, and each other;
- When making decisions, we will, as a company and as individuals, consider the impact of our decisions on others and on the environment;
- We will consistently try to give the highest level of performance to each customer and each student;
- We recognize that without profits our company can not survive, so we will make our best efforts to increase the profitability of our company within an ethical and honest framework;
- We will give back to our community and society and make a positive commitment to its health and well-being;
- We will respect our co-workers and recognize their needs as employees and as human beings;
- We will listen to each other.

Community Involvement

In developing our community involvement program, the staff of Computer-Ease first looked to identify those ways in which we could use our corporate strengths (given our limited time and financial resources) to make a meaningful contribution to our community. We recognized that our unique strength is our ability to teach computer programs in an understandable manner, along with our computer training center facility located in the heart of downtown Vespucci.

ComputerEase has entered into a partnership with the Downtown Vespucci Community Center to provide free computer training programs for inner city youth, low-income residents, and "welfare-to-work" program participants. These training programs are held once-a-month at ComputerEase's downtown computer training center on days or times when the Center would otherwise not be in use (Sundays/evenings, etc.). ComputerEase management and instructors have volunteered their time to conduct these sessions, and the company, in turn is contributing meals, transportation expenses for volunteer instructors and an imprinted T-shirt for all program participants. ComputerEase will also donate all its older computers to the Community Center.

In addition to the project with the Downtown Vespucci Community Center, ComputerEase staff determined they would like to do a one-day community project each year to make a contribution together. The staff chose to participate in the annual Vespucci Friends of the Trees Arbor Day Planting & Picnic. As a team, we will work with other members of the corporate and civic community to plant trees in public parks, boulevards and other locales.

Other Policies

As part of our commitment to being conscious of the effect of our actions on others, the company has adopted a number of environment-conscious policies, including using only recycled paper, recycling used computer supplies, providing a subsidy to employees who use public transportation, etc.

## Chapter 15

Development, Milestones, & Exit Plan

You can't reach a goal you haven't set.

Where Do You Want To Go?

If a business plan serves as a road map for your company, then to use it properly you need a sense of your ultimate destination. What do you want your business to look like in three, five, or seven years? You can't hope to just stumble across success; you have to figure out how to get there. One of the most important aspects of the business planning process, therefore, is the examination of your long-term goals.

Moreover, in the course of your planning process you will find it useful to establish markers — milestones — to keep you on track. By developing specific objectives, you have signposts to measure progress along the way.

Investors are greatly interested in this section of your business plan. When they invest capital in your company, they want to see what they are getting in return. They know how much money they can lose — the downside risk. But they also want to gauge what they might gain, how big the company might become — the upside reward. Lenders, on the other hand, are somewhat less interested in long-term growth than investors. They already know their upside potential; it's defined in the terms of the loan.

In this section you will spell out the specific ways whereby your company can be judged and the risks involved. You may find this prospect a bit unsettling, perhaps you even fear that it will scare off financing sources. Don't be intimidated. Sophisticated investors and lenders give greater credence to entrepreneurs who acknowledge risk and are willing to be

"Every business grows in phases. I want to see one respectable phase in which they can succeed before they go on to the second and third phases. They can have other things in mind, but I want them to finish the first thing to show what they can do."

Eugene Kleiner
Venture Capitalist

measured against clear-cut objectives. They understand that progress takes time and that risks are an inherent part of doing business.

In developing your company's long-term plans, you must evaluate your goals, milestones, risks, and exit plan, each of which are discussed in this chapter.

Goals

What do you want in the future, both for yourself and for your company? In founder-led and small companies, the personal goals of the entrepreneur(s) and the goals for the business should reasonably relate to one another. Otherwise, the inherent tensions will undermine the success of the business. There's no use envisioning running a $50 million dollar company, when what you really want is to take long vacations and be home every afternoon by 3:00 p.m. That's just not a realistic fit. (Refer to the worksheet "Four C's," in Chapter 1.)

You probably have a vision of what your company may be. The vision may not be well-formed, perhaps something like, "One day I'd like this company to be known for making the very best product of its type." Or the vision may be very specific, set by you or investors; it might be a goal such as "Sales of $10 million within five years."

The vision that you and the other decision-makers hold for your company shapes the nature of your day-to-day activities and should determine the priorities for the expenditure of your resources. You want to emphasize those actions that support your eventual aims. Grow towards your vision.

In assessing your business concept, consider which of the following visions you have for your company and yourself:

- **Steady Provider.** Maintain a stable level of profit; earn a good, reliable income while owning your own business.
- **Innovator.** Produce new and different products or services; change the way the market views the product or service; act on your creativity.
- **Quality Leader.** Produce the product or service everyone would buy if price were no object; develop a reputation for excellence; take pride in creating the best.
- **Market or Industry Leader.** Dominate the market in terms of sales and products; have a well-known name and run a large operation.
- **Niche Leader.** Carve out a narrow place in the market that your company dominates; do only one thing, but do it extremely well.
- **Exploiter.** Take advantage of the trends of the moment or copy the successes of others; take risks for quick rewards.

These goals are not necessarily mutually exclusive, and you can choose more than one, if they aren't contradictory. Or, perhaps you have another vision for your company. Use the Company Vision worksheet on the next page to focus your thoughts about the future.

"Lifestyle objectives are major issues. Wanting to be your own boss, wanting a degree of freedom you don't have as an employee, these were important goals for us."

Larry Leigon
Founder, Ariel Vineyards

Company Vision

Describe the vision you hold of your company for the next decade.

Overall Long-Term Development: _____

_____

_____

_____

Specific Goals	One Year	Five Years	Ten Years
Number of Employees	_____	_____	_____
Number of Locations	_____	_____	_____
Annual Sales	_____	_____	_____
Profits or Profit Margin	_____	_____	_____
Number of Products or Services	_____	_____	_____
Awards or Recognition Received	_____	_____	_____
	_____	_____	_____
	_____	_____	_____
Ownership Allocation	_____	_____	_____
	_____	_____	_____
Other: _____	_____	_____	_____
_____	_____	_____	_____
_____	_____	_____	_____

Business Strategies

One year: _____

_____

_____

_____

Five years: _____

_____

_____

_____

Ten years: _____

_____

_____

_____

Although these concepts are relatively intangible, they have tangible consequences. If you see your company as an innovator, you may have to sacrifice short-term profits for the ability to experiment. If you want a company that is a market leader, you must position your company to grow to a substantial size.

To give substance to your vision, express your goals in concrete terms. This process will help you understand and articulate your goals; it is meant for internal planning rather than for inclusion in a written business plan, especially one prepared for outside funding.

Strategies

You now must consider what business strategy will take your company from its present situation towards your long-term goals. Developing an overall strategy gives you the basis for deciding on the priorities for specific actions and expenditures of funds.

Among the business strategies you might undertake are:

- **Market Penetration.** Gain a foothold in the market as you introduce either the company or a new product or service and attempt to develop sufficient sales to sustain your initial development.
- **Promotion and Support.** Intensify the marketing and development of your current product or service lines to increase sales and gain market share.
- **Expansion.** Add products or services in existing lines, additional locations, production capacity, or distribution systems in an effort to increase sales.
- **Increase Focus.** Narrow the scope of activities of your company by eliminating some products or services and marshaling your resources on your remaining line(s) to increase profit margin.
- **Diversify.** Add new product or service lines (or buy other companies), thus broadening the nature of the company, in an effort to expand the overall size and sales of the company and making you less dependent on your current products or services for survival.
- **Refocus.** Modify the essential nature of the company in terms of market, products, or services to respond to changing conditions or substantial business reverses.

Consider the above strategies when assessing the long-term development of your company.

Priorities

To implement those strategies you must undertake specific actions. For instance, if your strategy is to promote and support, you will want to use any additional resources, either of money or time, on your marketing efforts. If, on the other hand, your strategy is to diversify, you want to accumulate resources to expend on the introduction of new product lines or the purchase of new companies.

"Turnoffs to me as a venture capitalist? Calling yourself a visionary; your work should speak for itself. A huge focus on my return on investment; I can figure out where I can make my return. I do want to know you care about financial returns, but you can't come across as so focused on an IPO that it seems you're not in this to build a business, you're in it to take it public."

Andrew Anker
Venture Capitalist

Priorities

Rate each area's priority for the expenditure of funds, in hierarchical order (1-2-3, with 1 being the highest priority). Describe the specific priorities or amounts in each area.

Priorities	Specifics	Rating
Add Employees	_____	____
Add New Lines	_____	____
Increase Marketing	_____	____
Add Locations	_____	____
Add Capacity	_____	____
Increase Salaries	_____	____
Increase Inventory	_____	____
Increase Profits	_____	____
Retire Debts	_____	____
Increase Reserve	_____	____
Acquire Other Companies	_____	____
Other: _____	_____	____

To clarify the significance of particular activities relative to your long-term goals, develop a set of priorities for the expenditure of your resources. A list of priorities is a critical tool for every business. Although this list does not need to be included in a business plan for outside financing sources, it would be wise to refer to it whenever making major business decisions.

On the Priorities worksheet on page 225, specify the relative importance of each activity when it comes to the expenditure of funds.

Milestones Achieved To Date

You may describe your company as a startup. Your potential investor may think of you as a startup. But many new companies already have histories, sometimes impressive histories, before they have a written business plan. You can inspire confidence in your company by indicating this past history in your plan. You also demonstrate your ability to set and meet goals.

Delineating the milestones you've achieved to date likewise shows the level of commitment you've made to your new business. A potential investor can get a sense of the financial and time expenditures that you've had to invest to reach the achievements to date.

The Worksheet "Milestones Achieved to Date" on the next page helps you record your accomplishments. A list of such Milestones can be included in the front of your written plan, directly after your Executive Summary, especially if your progress has been particularly impressive. If yours is an annual plan for an existing company, you can indicate the milestones achieved since your last plan.

Future Milestones

How will you and your investors know that you are making sufficient progress towards your goals? If your long-term goal is to reach sales of $3 million in year five, how much do you need in sales by year two and year three?

In the daily press of business, it can often seem that you're making no progress at all. At any given time, you'll have a stack of bills to pay, troublesome customers, and problems with your staff. So you need a reminder that you have, in fact, been going forward.

A milestone list allows you and your financing sources to see what you specifically plan to accomplish, and it sets out clearly delineated objectives. These objectives are part of your business plan and are included with the written document.

A milestone list focuses on the specific objectives you intend to achieve and the dates by which you expect to accomplish them. These must be defined in concrete terms and a number assigned to any measurable activity. Thus, omit goals expressed in ways such as: "developing a substantial customer base." Instead, specify: "reaching annual sales level of 50,000 units by the end of the third fiscal year."

"Long-term planning must be a part of everything you do. You must continually work to stay contemporary. Be inquisitive and open-minded. Don't make comments like, 'We've always done it this way,' or 'We've tried it before.' Look for reasons to respond to new ideas and evaluate how they can improve your performance."

Bill Walsh
Former Coach and
President, S.F. 49ers

"Our strategy is to build sales in the stores we're in before expanding into more stores and a wider area. This gives us the opportunity to develop our product line, and to show retailers good sales figures when presenting our products."

Deborah Mullis
Entrepreneur

Milestones Achieved to Date

State the specific objectives you have achieved and when you achieved each one.

Event	Specifics	Date Completed
Incorporation	_____	_____
Lease Signed	_____	_____
Key Employees Hired:	_____	_____
_____	_____	_____
_____	_____	_____
_____	_____	_____
_____	_____	_____
Initial Financing Secured	_____	_____
Product Design Completed	_____	_____
Market Testing Completed	_____	_____
Trademarks / Patents Secured	_____	_____
Strategic Partnerships Secured	_____	_____
First Product Shipped	_____	_____
Level of Sales Reached ($)	_____	_____
Level of Sales Reached (units)	_____	_____
Level of Employees Reached	_____	_____
Profit Level Reached	_____	_____
Second Product Line Developed	_____	_____
Second Product Line Tested	_____	_____
Second Product Line Shipped	_____	_____
Additional Financing Secured	_____	_____
Debts Retired	_____	_____
Additional Location Opened	_____	_____
Other: _____	_____	_____
_____	_____	_____
_____	_____	_____
_____	_____	_____
_____	_____	_____

Future Milestones

State your specific future objectives and when you plan to achieve each one.

Event	Specifics	Goal Date
Incorporation		
Lease Signed		
Key Employees Hired:		
Initial Financing Secured		
Product Design Completed		
Market Testing Completed		
Trademarks / Patents Secured		
Strategic Partnerships Secured		
First Product Shipped		
Level of Sales Reached ($)		
Level of Sales Reached (units)		
Level of Employees Reached		
Profit Level Reached		
Second Product Line Developed		
Second Product Line Tested		
Second Product Line Shipped		
Additional Financing Secured		
Debts Retired		
Additional Location Opened		
Other:		

A milestone list also shows how you intend to build your company, roll-out products, add new locations, secure strategic relationships, etc. This list creates a very detailed picture of your company's future, and gives readers of your plan a clear idea of the size and scope of the company you envision.

When assigning dates to your milestones, remember that everything takes longer than planned; problems always arise. One of the frustrations of all entrepreneurs, but especially new entrepreneurs, is realizing how long everything takes to get done. Progress comes slowly. So allow yourself plenty of time when you are establishing chronological goals.

Complete the Future Milestones worksheet on the opposite page to outline your objectives. This list should be included with your business plan, whether used for internal planning or raising funds.

Risk Evaluation

Investors make financing decisions based on an evaluation of the potential risks versus potential rewards. They will naturally consider what risks your company faces, whether or not you outline such risks in your plan. Showing that you have already assessed the potential risks in your business reassures investors that you are not just naively optimistic in your planning.

On the Risk Evaluation worksheet in Chapter 9, you assessed the nature of the risks facing your company in each area and described the steps you can take, or have already taken, to lessen that risk. Include this risk assessment either in the Strategic Positioning section or the Development and Milestones section of your plan.

Exit Plan

When banks or individuals lend you money, it's clear how they expect to get their money back and make a profit: you are to pay them out of income, with interest. They evaluate your business on the basis of whether they think there's enough profit in your operating budget to pay back the loan.

But how do investors get their money back? Since investors become owners of the company (through their stock holdings), their profit is earned in a different manner than banks and lenders. Some investors may be putting money in for the long-run, expecting to take an active part in the development and operation of the company and getting their reward through the distribution of profits.

Other investors however, especially venture capitalists, eventually plan to liquidate their investment — to convert their holdings to cash or easily traded stock. Ideally, these investors want to know at the outset how they will get a substantial profit out of their investment. They want to see your exit plan.

"A plan should tell us how, as funders, we will know you're making progress, that you're on the road to success. Spell out what challenges you face in getting to market, what specific accomplishments you must achieve to build your company. We want five or six milestones to measure as we go along. For us, these are 'risk-reduction points' — they let us know you're on the right track."

Ann Winblad
Venture Capitalist

Developing an Exit Plan

Considering your potential exit plan benefits you as well as investors. After all, you've devoted substantial time and money of your own to this company, and you should have an idea of the way in which you'll reap rewards. Annual income is the major motivation for many entrepreneurs, but ideally your company will have worth beyond its annual profits, and you should eventually benefit from that worth.

If there is more than one partner or principal in the business, having a clear exit strategy can reduce the friction that comes from having unspoken exit assumptions. One founder may dream of building a company worth millions with the aim of selling it in the next few years, while the other founder may hope to build a modest business to run for many years to come.

A number of options exist for exiting from a company, although venture capitalists may be interested in only two or three of them. Generally, sophisticated investors look for companies that can go public (sell stock that will be traded to the general public on stock exchanges or "over the counter") or that are candidates for acquisition by larger companies. Investors like these exit strategies because they get out of the company cleanly, usually with substantial rewards, based on just one event: either an IPO — an initial public offering (when the stock is first publicly traded) — or the sale of the company.

These two strategies however, often result in the top management, including the founder(s), either having to leave or have far less control over the company. This may be an acceptable option given the nature of the financial rewards involved.

Novice entrepreneurs often imagine being able to buy out their investors, but this is not usually a realistic option. In companies that are very successful, the investor has little motivation to sell and the amount of money needed to purchase their stock could be prohibitive. In less successful companies, the investors may want to get out, but the entrepreneur is unlikely to have the extra cash necessary to buy them out.

Exit plan options are briefly outlined near the end of this chapter, describing the major exit strategies and their advantages and disadvantages. The disadvantages assume the current management would like to have a continuing role in the company, which may or may not be true in your situation.

Preparing the Development, Milestones & Exit Strategy Section of Your Plan

In preparing a business plan for outside investors, the two most important aspects of your Development section are your milestones lists and the description of your exit plan. Through these, investors get a clear idea of how the company has grown, will continue to grow, and how they will realize their financial rewards.

> *"We want to know how this company gets to be larger than a small business. For us, most companies must be able to show that they could grow to the size of being an IPO (Initial Public Offering) in a realistic period."*
>
> **Ann Winblad**
> **Venture Capitalist**

For a plan to be used for internal purposes, more details can be included about the specific priorities for expenditures of resources, making your plan a useful tool that you can refer to frequently when making major expenditure decisions.

A Plan Preparation Form is provided for you to outline the Development section of your business plan.

Chapter Summary

The Development section of your business plan shows that you have given careful consideration to how your company will grow over time. By including a Future Milestones chart, you provide a clear timetable of your company's development and allow yourself to be judged by objective measurements. By describing the potential risks your company faces, you display confidence in your ability to overcome such risks. Investors will be interested in how they can recoup the money they have devoted to your company, and they will appreciate that you have considered a realistic exit plan.

"It's easy to get into an investment, but investors want to know, how do we get out? It's not good enough to just say that there will be a public offering, because selling to the public may not be realistic at times. Instead, you have to show you have an attractive business that other businesses will want to own, either because it complements an existing product line or on its own."

Eugene Kleiner
Venture Capitalist

Exit Plan Options

Option	Description	Advantages	Disadvantages
Go Public	Sell shares in the company to the public, traded on a stock exchange or "over the counter."	Stock easily convertible to cash, liquidity; current management stays.	Must be large company: approx. $25 to $50 million; highly regulated; management can be replaced by stockholders.
Acquisition	Bought by another existing company.	Receive cash and/or stock; current management may have continuing role.	Must be appropriate fit for existing co.; management leaves or has new boss.
Sale	Bought by individuals.	Receive cash.	Must find willing buyer; management goes.
Merger	Join with existing company.	Combined resources; current management may stay; may receive stock or some cash.	New partners or bosses; usually little or no cash; less control.
Buy-Out	One or more stockholders buy out the interests of another.	Seller gets cash; others stay in control of company.	Must have sufficient cash; seller must be willing.
Franchise	Sell concept to others to replicate.	Receive cash; current management stays; future potential.	Concept must be appropriate; legally complicated.
Hand Down	Give company to next generation.	Stays in family; current management may continue.	Family tensions; no cash; tax implications.
Close	End operations.	Relatively easy; feeling of being finished.	No financial reward; feeling of loss.

Development Plan Preparation Form

Describe your company's goals for the next five to ten years, in terms of position in the market, sales, number of employees, etc.: _____

_____

_____

_____

_____

_____

_____

_____

_____

_____

Describe the basic strategy you will use to reach those goals, and the priority for the expenditure of funds:

_____

_____

_____

_____

_____

_____

_____

_____

_____

Describe the major risks facing your company: _____

_____

_____

_____

_____

_____

_____

_____

Describe the exit plan for your investors: _____

_____

_____

_____

_____

_____

SAMPLE PLAN: Development

Development

Long-Term Goals

States vision of company.

ComputerEase plans to grow steadily over the next 5 years, becoming the premier provider of software training to businesses in the greater Vespucci area. By 2008, the company plans to have a market share of at least 50% of all corporate software training in the Vespucci area. Within 10 years, the company plans to have expanded throughout the Midwest, capturing at least one-third of the share of the corporate software training market in the region.

Strategy for Achieving Goals

Gives priority for expenditure of funds.

To accomplish this, the company plans expansion activities every year, adding both staff and training classrooms. This expansion will be financed primarily from income. As such, the officers of the company have a priority of committing funds from income to growth rather than to the distribution of profits.

The first priority for expansion is the addition of an in-house training staff and a second training classroom, most likely at the current location in downtown Vespucci. The second priority is to enlarge the marketing staff. Third, an additional location within the greater Vespucci area will be established. This is the growth plan for the first three years.

After that, however, to remain competitive, ComputerEase must have a presence and connection beyond the Vespucci area. As the company anticipates that corporate software training increasingly will be marketed on a nationwide basis, ComputerEase must have national connections. To do so, in the immediate future, plans call for becoming a member of a national software training association. However, more formal expansion is also needed.

By year three, the officers of the company will have assessed the nature of that formal expansion. Two options are foremost: to open additional ComputerEase company-run branches in other metropolitan areas or to franchise.

Greater Expansion Plans

The first route — additional company-run locations — will center on the Midwest as the area of expansion. ComputerEase will choose major metropolitan areas based on an assessment of sales potential and the intensity of the competition in each market at the time of expansion. It is estimated that at least one metropolitan area would be added each year. To fund such expansion, the company will require additional capital, which would ideally be secured from bank financing. In the event that conventional financing is not secured, funds will be sought from investors.

The ComputerEase concept also lends itself well to franchising. Since corporations with offices throughout the United States often prefer to have all their computer training provided by the same company, a franchise operation gives the company greater marketing clout. Moreover, the franchising concept produces additional revenue streams to the company from the franchisees, both from franchise fees and through the purchase of materials and staff training. If the decision is made to franchise, venture capital investment will be sought. Current investors could choose to liquidate their holdings in ComputerEase at that time or convert their holdings to stock in the franchise operation.

Describes potential exit opportunity for investor.

Risks Associated with Expansion

The biggest risk facing the expansion of ComputerEase is timing. Existing software training firms in other parts of the country are well-positioned to establish themselves as nationally-known providers. If they are able to market themselves on a national level, they represent not only potential competition on a national or regional level, but they could possibly enter the local market in direct competition.

To prepare for this eventuality, company management is closely following developments, and the company is prepared to enter into agreements with other software training companies. Such agreements include the possibility of merger, acquisition, or the provision of services under the name of the larger company, if necessary.

Recognizes and acknowledges potential risks.

## Chapter 16

The Financials

Numbers are merely the reflection of decisions you make.

How to Painlessly Deal with Numbers and Financial Forms

People in business usually fall into one of two categories: those who are fascinated with numbers, or those who are frightened by them. If you're in the first category, you are probably delighted to finally reach this section. You may have even skipped previous sections to do this one. If you are one of those in the second category, however, you're probably intimidated by the very prospect of having to fill in the forms encountered in this chapter.

Numbers Represent Your Decisions

Take heart: Numbers are neither magical, mysterious, nor menacing. They merely reflect other decisions you have made previously in your business planning. If you decided to advertise each week in your local newspaper, there's a number attached to that decision. If you projected sales at a certain level, there's a number attached to that decision as well.

Every business decision leads to a number, and taken together, these numbers form the basis of your financial forms. But numbers themselves are not decisions. You cannot pull a number out of thin air because the financial forms you are completing call for a specific figure on a specific line. Rather, your numbers should always be the result of careful planning.

"Anticipate that costs will go up; interest rates will go up; it will take longer than planned for construction. Everything costs more and takes longer than planned. Things go wrong. You can't have wishful thinking in your planning. Assume you've underestimated all costs and build in a cushion. Use a good accountant or bookkeeper, and a good lawyer, and listen to their advice. Get help in those areas in which you aren't familiar."

Martha Johnson
Restauranteur

Getting Control of Your Finances

Even if you are not responsible for preparing ongoing financial reports, you should have a working understanding of financial statements so that you can better control your company.

Financial statements provide you with the information you need to make decisions. Many managers mistakenly believe that they are in charge of the big picture, while bookkeepers and bean counters get caught up with mere details. Numbers are not just details: They are the vital signs of any business; you must understand your company's numbers to realistically assess the condition of your business.

Read Your Financial Statements

Get in the habit of reading your financial statements at least monthly, and make sure you understand what you read. Track items such as sales receipts on a daily or weekly basis. Don't wait for reports to come back from the accountants before knowing your cash position. You will find you have more confidence in your decisions if you comprehend the financial implications of each of your choices.

Try to view your financial statements in a relatively dispassionate manner. It is difficult, especially when you own your own business, to keep emotions from clouding your ability to properly examine your financial reports. If you know it has been a bad month, you may be tempted just to ignore that month's cash-flow or income statements. Don't.

Set Policies and Stick with Them

Set financial policies in place and stick with them, in good times and bad. Many businesses, even big companies, get in trouble through inadequate billing and collection procedures. Stay on top of your finances.

If you are establishing accounts for the first time, get professional assistance from an accountant or bookkeeper. A professional can set up your initial books, assist you in understanding financial terms, and give you valuable advice on billing, payment, and payroll procedures.

Cash-Basis Accounting

One aspect of your business an accountant will help you decide is whether to set up your books on an accrual basis or a cash basis. Most smaller businesses are generally advised to conduct business on a cash basis, meaning that income and expenses are entered in the books at the time money actually changes hands.

Thus, if you receive a $5,000 order in January, but you don't receive payment until March, the $5,000 credit appears as income only on your March statements. This gives a truer picture of a company's ability to meet its financial obligations than does accrual accounting.

Accrual-Basis Accounting

With accrual-basis accounting, income and expenses are counted at the time they are originally transacted; thus, the $5,000 order would show as

> "To help in forecasting sales, we conduct periodic trend checking. During the holiday period, this occurs formally every five days. We analyze the sales trend we're currently in, check the inventory spread, and try to anticipate what sales are likely to do in the immediate future."
>
> **Charles Huggins**
> **President, See's Candies**

income in January. If payment is never made, additional accounting entries would later be made to write off the loss. Larger businesses choose this accounting form to have a better sense of overall profitability.

Using the Abrams Method of Flow-Through Financials

One of the most difficult questions, especially for new businesses, is "Where do I get the figures for my financial forms?"

If you have been filling out the Flow-Through Financial worksheets throughout the previous chapters, you have already compiled many of the figures you need to complete the worksheets in this chapter. For instance, you have already computed your marketing budget in Chapter 10. Likewise, on other worksheets, you have detailed costs of salaries, equipment, and other aspects of your business.

Now just transfer the figures from each of your Flow-Through Financial worksheets (marked with the dollar-sign logo) to their appropriate line(s) on the Financials forms that follow. Refer to the chart on pages 240–241 to see on which form and line each specific figure should be placed.

Electronic Financial Worksheets

To make this process even easier, an Excel-based Financial Worksheets package is available for purchase as a supplement to this book. The worksheets are identical to the financial worksheets found in the book and embrace the Flow-Through Financials methodology used here. In addition, the electronic worksheets perform all calculations for you, generate charts, and allow you to "tweak" your numbers to obtain the most accurate financial picture. Once you are satisfied with your numbers, you can print out all the financial forms necessary to include with your business plan. To purchase the Electronic Worksheets, visit www.planningshop.com.

Types of Financial Forms

For the financial portion of your business plan, the three most important forms are:

- **Income Statement.** Shows whether your company is making a profit.
- **Cash-Flow Projection.** Shows whether the company has the cash to pay its bills.
- **Balance Sheet.** Shows how much the company is worth overall.

Other forms include:

- **Sources and Use of Funds.** Shows where you will get financing for your business and how you will spend the money invested or lent. A potential investor or loan officer will want to see this.
- **Break-even Analysis.** Shows the point at which sales exceed costs and you begin to make a profit. Advisable for internal planning.

"In financials, we look for professionalism. Use standard formats. Hire an accountant, not so much as to come up with your numbers but for your forms. We want to see a cash flow analysis as well as everything else in a standard annual report (balance sheet, income statement). You or an accountant should compare your numbers with those of existing companies. If they are very different from those of well-managed companies, they may be unrealistic."

Eugene Kleiner
Venture Capitalist

Abrams Method of Flow-Through Financials

Worksheet	Chapter	Transfer to	Use on Lines
Seasonal Factors	6, page 79	Cash-Flow Projection	Sales, Collections, Cost of Goods, Operating Expenses
		Income Statement	Sales, Cost of Goods, Marketing
Financial Patterns	6, page 83	Income Statement	Sales, Returns, Cost of Goods, Commissions, Utilities, Salaries
		Cash-Flow Projection	Sales, Cost of Goods, Operating Expenses
		Break-Even Analysis	
Marketing Vehicles	10, page 138	Marketing Budget (Chapter 10, p. 148)	
		Income Statement	Marketing
		Cash-Flow Projection	Operating Expenses
Marketing Tactics	10, page 140	Marketing Budget (Chapter 10, p. 148)	
		Income Statement	Profit Margin, Marketing
		Cash-Flow Projection	Operating Expenses
Monthly Marketing Budget	10, page 148	Income Statement	Marketing, Travel/Entertainment, Professional Services
		Cash-Flow Projection	Operating Expenses
Monthly Sales	10, page 150	Income Statement	Sales, Commissions
Projections	10, page 150	Cash-Flow Projection	Operating Expenses
Facilities	11, page 158	Income Statement	Rent, Utilities, Maintenance
		Cash-Flow Projection	Operating Expenses, Other Expenses
		Balance Sheet	Fixed Assets, Depreciation
Production	11, page 162	Income Statement	Cost of Goods, Salaries, Employee Benefits, Payroll Taxes
		Cash-Flow Projection	Operating Expenses
Supply and Distribution	11, page 168	Income Statement	Cost of Goods, Commissions
		Cash-Flow Projection	Cost of Goods, Operating Expenses

Worksheet	Chapter	Transfer to	Use on Lines
Equipment Schedule	11, page 164	Income Statement	Depreciation, Equipment Rental, Furniture and Equipment
		Cash-Flow Projection	Operating Expenses, Equip. Purchase
		Balance Sheet	Fixed Assets, Depreciation
Order Fulfillment	11, page 170	Income Statement	Postage and Shipping, Returns and Allowances, Salaries (Customer Service Personnel)
		Cash-Flow Projection	Operating Expenses
Research and Development	11, page 171	Income Statement	Allot costs to appropriate lines (e.g., salaries, equipment) or create separate R & D line
		Cash-Flow Projection	Operating Expenses
Other Operational Issues	11, page 174	Income Statement	Insurance, Professional Services, Other (for permits, licenses)
		Cash-Flow Projection	Operating Expenses
Start-up Costs	11, page 176	Income Statement	First month's operating expenses on appropriate lines
		Cash-Flow Projection	First month's operating expenses (and months for term payments)
		Balance Sheet	Current and Fixed Assets, Current and Long-Term Liabilities (for loans secured to pay costs), or Equity
Technology Budget	12, page 185	Income Statement	Depreciation, Equipment Rental, Furniture and Equipment
		Cash-Flow Projection	Operating Expenses, Equip. Purchase
		Balance Sheet	Fixed Assets, Depreciation
Compensation & Incentives	13, page 195	Income Statement	Salaries, Employee Benefits, Payroll Taxes
		Cash-Flow Projection	Operating Expenses
Key Management Personnel to Be Added	13, page 200	Income Statement and Cash-Flow Projection	Salaries (projections for future months and years)
Staffing Budget	16, page 248	Income Statement	Salaries, Benefits, Payroll Taxes
Monthly Cash Income Projections	16, page 250	Income Statement	Gross Sales (unless your business is accrual based)

- **Startup Costs.** For a new business shows the initial investment necessary to begin operations. A Startup Cost form can be found in Chapter 11, on page 176 and should be included in your completed business plan.
- **Assumption Sheet.** Shows those reading your financial statements how you determined the figures used. A good adjunct to other forms.

Time Frames Your Forms Should Cover

Generally, investors want to see financial projections for three to five years in the future, and historical records of the past three to five years for currently operating businesses. If possible, find out what periods of time your lending institution or potential investor wants to see and prepare your forms accordingly. Otherwise, prepare forms to cover the time frames cited below.

- **Income Statements.** First year: monthly projections. Years two and three: quarterly projections. Years four and five: annual projections. Existing businesses: actual annual income statements for the last three years.
- **Cash Flow.** First year: monthly projections. Years two and three: quarterly projections.
- **Balance Sheet.** First year: quarterly projections. Years two to five: annual projections. Existing businesses: current balance sheet and actual balance sheets for last two years.

General Financial Terms

The terms that follow are frequently used in financial forms. If you are in business, you should have a working knowledge of these terms.

Even if you're familiar with financial statements, take a few minutes to update your understanding of these key words; and if you've never produced (or reviewed) a financial statement before, study these terms until you feel comfortable with them.

Accounts Payable. Obligations owed to others; list of outstanding bills.

Accounts Receivable. Obligations owed to your company by others; a list of outstanding invoices.

Accumulated Depreciation. The amount of depreciation a company has already taken in the form of tax deductions; such accumulated depreciation must be accounted for when selling fixed assets.

Assets. Anything the company owns having a positive monetary value.

Current Assets. Assets that can be converted quickly, with relative ease to cash; these assets are designed to be turned over in the normal course of doing business, such as bank deposits, inventory, and accounts receivable.

Fixed Assets (or Property, Plant, and Equipment). Assets that are the ongoing means of doing business; such assets are generally cumbersome to turn into cash; includes buildings, land, and equipment.

Cash. Immediately available money in the form of currency, checks, or bank deposits.

Cost of Goods. Expenses directly associated with producing and making a specific product. Companies differ as to which expenses they attribute to cost of goods, but generally items such as source materials, direct labor, and freight are included.

Cost of Sales. Expenses directly associated with selling a product or service. This typically includes items such as sales commissions, distributor's fees, etc., but does not generally include more indirect costs such as marketing.

Current Liabilities. Any bills, debts, or obligations occurring in the ongoing course of business; any debt due within the next year. Includes accounts payable, accrued payroll expenses, and loans and credit lines with less than one year's maturity date.

Debt. An ongoing obligation of the company, such as a bank loan.

Depreciation. The wear and tear on fixed assets — not a cash expenditure, but an ongoing expense of the business as equipment wears down. A tax deduction.

Equity. Ownership of a company, usually distributed by means of shares of stock. A person who owns part of a company is said to have an equity interest in the company.

Fixed Costs. Ongoing expenses or overhead of a business that occur regardless of the amount of sales. These expenses usually include items such as rent, utilities, and salaries.

Gross Profit. Percentage of income your company realizes on each sale before administrative expenses.

Liabilities. Any outstanding obligation or debt of the company.

Long-Term Liabilities. Loans and other debts that come due in more than a year's time. This year's interest payments on such loans, or debt service, are included in Current Liabilities.

Net Profit. Amount of income after deducting all costs of doing business, including administrative overhead and other fixed costs.

Net Worth. Value of a company after deducting liabilities from assets.

Other or Intangible Assets. Aspects of your company that have value not easily interpreted in specific monetary terms or directly convertible to cash; assets such as a popular trademarked name and the good-will a company has built up over time.

Profit. Amount a company earns after expenses.

Pro forma. Financial statements based on projected future performance rather than actual historical data.

Retained Earnings. Net worth amount the company keeps internally for ongoing development of the business rather than distributing to shareholders.

Financial Symbols

The symbols below commonly appear on financial forms:

( ) Numbers appearing in parentheses are negative numbers; they represent losses.

— Single lines represent subtotals.

= Double lines represent totals.

000's This indicates that numbers are expressed in thousands.

Guidelines for Preparing Your Financial Forms

In preparing your financial forms, you will almost certainly have questions as to how to attribute certain expenses for your business. You might wonder whether you should ascribe sales commissions to cost of goods sold or to operating expenses. Accounting practices differ, so follow these guidelines:

When preparing your financial forms, keep these imperatives in mind:

1. **Be conservative.** Avoid the tendency to paint the rosiest picture possible; doing so reduces your credibility.
2. **Be honest.** Experienced financing sources will sense dishonest or manipulated figures; expect to be asked to justify your numbers.
3. **Don't be creative.** Use standard formats and financial terms; otherwise you look inexperienced to financing sources.
4. **Get your accountant's advice.**
5. **Follow the practices used in your industry.**
6. **Choose the appropriate accounting method.**
7. **Be consistent.** Make a decision and stick with it for all your accounts, otherwise you can't compare one year's figures to another.

Staffing Budget

In many companies, the costs associated with employees are often the largest expenses of the business. In any company, labor costs are a critical issue. When planning a business, it's easy to underestimate or overlook labor costs.

Number and Timing

You must first figure out how many employees you will need and exactly when you will need them. It is easy to underestimate this number, anticipating that you will only hire outstanding employees, all of whom will work to maximum capacity. But remember, employees will probably not work as hard or as long as you do, so don't plan your expenses based solely on your own level of productivity.

Some industries, such as those in the service sector, are particularly labor intensive. And in a small business, customers often expect very high levels of personal service, which can mean higher staffing levels. Even if yours is a sole proprietorship, you may occasionally need to hire some assistance, and you should plan accordingly.

If yours is a new business, you may want to talk with entrepreneurs in existing businesses about the level and timing of their personnel to help you devise your own projections. If you are changing the direction of an existing business, how will your new needs effect your staffing levels and deployment? Will current employees be able to be trained for new tasks, or will new staff need to be hired?

Not all employees will be hired at once, and not all employees will be permanent. The staffing budget allows you to change the number of workers in each category depending on the actual month(s) they work. You may have seasonal work which requires additional staff for some portions of the year. Timing your hiring can be very important in making certain you are adequately prepared for your workloads. Most people, even those who have been in business for a long time, underestimate the time it will take to hire and train new staff. Allow yourself realistic lead-time for staff recruitment, and don't forget to account for the costs of any temporary help you may need until permanent staff is in place.

Also, it's almost inevitable that you will at some point hire people who do not perform well. There will be costs associated with dismissing employees. These costs may include temporary help to fill their slots while you seek replacement and any severance pay that is required by their contract.

Benefits and Taxes

One of the first things you will need to do is to figure out the benefits that you will need and want to attract and retain qualified staff. These benefits may include health, life, dental, or disability insurance, pension benefits, and paid vacation.

Some employee costs are required by law. Check with your state's department of labor to find out about mandatory benefits, such as workmen's compensation. There will also be payroll taxes, which can add a substantial amount to your total employee costs. You may want to talk with an accountant or lawyer to learn what costs to anticipate with regard to benefits and taxes.

The upcoming Staffing Budget worksheet will help you plot out all the labor costs associated with your business. The worksheet is presented in a monthly format to allow you to reflect the changes in your staffing depending on when you hire new employees, add new divisions, or when you use seasonal or variable labor.

The information in the Staffing Budget transfers to the Salary/Wages, Employee Benefits and Payroll Taxes lines on your Income Statement, page 254. The supplemental Electronic Worksheets package available from www.PlanningShop.com includes the Staffing Budget and will automatically handle these calculations and transfers for you.

Cash Projections

An important fact to remember when preparing your financial projections is that you will often not receive full payment at the time of an actual sale or transaction. Projecting cash flow solely on the sales made, rather than cash actually received, will leave you seriously short on money.

Some industries have particularly long lag times between orders and payment. This can be especially true in manufacturing companies. A clothing manufacturer, for instance, may make sales many months before payment is due. Even in retail, you may find that you establish some credit accounts for very large or repeat customers and these customers take longer to pay.

Your business may allow payment terms over a number of months, or the type of work you do may make payment over time a necessity. In almost any company, some customers will be slow payers. While most customers may pay within 30 days, some may take as much as 120 days, and some will never pay at all. For instance, if you make a $10,000 sale in the month of February, you may only receive a deposit of $2500 in February, with the rest paid as partial payments through June. Of course, you can try to reduce the amount of slow or non-payers by requiring larger percentages of payment at the time of sale or delivery or by charging interest on unpaid balances, but it is still necessary to anticipate actual payment patterns in your cash flow projections.

It's also a good idea to differentiate between the income of each product or service line. While it may seem like a bit more work to keep track of each product or service line's income separately, this information will help you make decisions about the long-term direction of your company and better understand exactly where your profits come from.

Complete the upcoming Worksheet: "Monthly Cash Income Projections." The information from this worksheet can then be transferred to your "Cash Flow Projection" forms and to your "Income Statement" forms if you operate your business on a cash, rather than accrual, accounting method. If yours is an existing business, review your past records to determine the average payment pattern to use in this form. If you are new to business, check with others in your industry to see what are typical payment patterns. Be conservative in your projections. It's always better to find out that you have more cash than you anticipated rather than less.

Income Statements

The Income Statement is also frequently called either a Profit and Loss statement — P & L — or Income and Expense statement. This form shows how profitable your company is — how much money it will make after all expenses are accounted for. It does not give a total picture of what your company is worth overall, or its cash position.

> *"Projections are actually far less important than the assumptions to projections. Generally, poor financials tend to be negative indicators rather than good financials being positive indicators. Are you assuming you'll get an 80% market share when there's no way you'll get 10%? Do you think that way?"*
>
> **Andrew Anker**
> ***Venture Capitalist***

A company can be losing money but still be worth a great deal because it owns valuable property, or it can be profitable but still not have enough cash to pay its bills due to cash-flow problems. An income statement does not reveal either of these "hidden" situations.

You read an income statement from top to bottom. The first line accounts for sales. Each subsequent line represents deductions from income. The result is the company's profit (or, possibly, loss).

To prepare an income statement, accumulate detailed information about your sales and expenses. Specific lines on the form should mirror the categories by which you maintain your ongoing accounts. When completing the income statement, refer to the previous list of financial terms. Additionally, note these references:

Gross Sales. Total sales from all product line categories.

Employee Benefits. Items such as health and dental insurance; any other benefits with specific costs associated.

Depreciation and Amortization. The value of either fixed assets (depreciation) or intangible assets (amortization) that is allocated as a yearly expense or deemed to be lost each year through use or obsolescence.

Office Supplies. Usual office or business supplies, rather than the materials necessary to produce the item for sale.

Marketing. Advertising and marketing expenses other than Travel, Entertainment/Meals, which may have different tax treatments; transfer this figure from your Marketing Budget worksheet in Chapter 10.

Travel. Costs of necessary business travel, including airfare, hotels, taxis, etc.; auto expenses (which may have different tax treatment) can go here or on a separate line.

Entertainment/Meals. Costs of entertaining customers, potential customers, employees; including events, parties, meals, etc. These expenses typically are only partially tax deductible.

Insurance. Insurance premiums such as those for liability, malpractice, auto, or equipment insurance. Excludes insurance included in Employee Benefits line.

Professional Services. Attorney's, accountant's, designers, technology specialists, and consultant's fees.

Maintenance. Janitorial or cleaning services, regular maintenance programs or service contracts, and repairs.

Telephone/Telecommunications. Costs of telephone and telecommunications services. Costs of Internet access can go in this line or in Utilities.

Complete the historical (if applicable to your business) and pro forma income statements on the next few pages. Document income on a monthly (first year), quarterly (first two to three years), and annual basis

"What kind of numbers do we like to see? The more mature a business is, the more we rely on numbers. For a newer business, the numbers matter less and the words matter more."
Robert Mahoney
Corporate Banker

Staffing Budget

For Year: _____	January	February	March	April	May
Management					
# Employees					
Salary / wages					
Benefits					
Payroll taxes					
Total Costs					
Administrative / Support					
# Employees					
Salary / wages					
Benefits					
Payroll taxes					
Total Costs					
Sales / Marketing					
# Employees					
Salary / wages					
Benefits					
Payroll taxes					
Total Costs					
Operations / Production					
# Employees					
Salary / wages					
Benefits					
Payroll taxes					
Total Costs					
Other					
# Employees					
Salary / wages					
Benefits					
Payroll taxes					
Total Costs					
TOTAL					
# Employees					
Salary / wages					
Benefits					
Payroll taxes					
TOTAL COSTS					

NOTE: *A computerized version of this worksheet is available as part of The Planning Shop's* **Electronic Financial** **Worksheets** *package, available from www.PlanningShop.com.*

							$ ➤ $$ ➤ $$$
June	July	August	September	October	November	December	TOTAL

Monthly Cash Income Projections

For Year: _____	January	February	March	April	May
PRODUCT LINE #1 SALES **Cash Received**					
Current month sales					
30 days prior sales					
60 days prior sales					
90 days prior sales					
120 days prior sales					
Total Product #2 Cash Income					
PRODUCT LINE #2 SALES **Cash Received**					
Current month sales					
30 days prior sales					
60 days prior sales					
90 days prior sales					
120 days prior sales					
Total Product #2 Cash Income					
PRODUCT LINE #3 SALES **Cash Received**					
Current month sales					
30 days prior sales					
60 days prior sales					
90 days prior sales					
120 days prior sales					
Total Product #3 Cash Income					
PRODUCT LINE #4 SALES **Cash Received**					
Current month sales					
30 days prior sales					
60 days prior sales					
90 days prior sales					
120 days prior sales					
Total Product #4 Cash Income					
TOTAL CASH INCOME					

	June	July	August	September	October	November	December	TOTAL
$ ➤ $$ ➤ $$$								

Income Statement: Historical

For Year: _____	January	February	March	April	May
INCOME **Gross Sales**					
(Commissions)					
(Returns and allowances)					
Net Sales					
(Cost of Goods)					
GROSS PROFIT					
EXPENSES - General and Administrative Salaries and wages					
Employee benefits					
Payroll taxes					
Professional services					
Rent					
Maintenance					
Equipment rental					
Furniture and equipment purchase					
Depreciation and amortization					
Insurance					
Interest expenses					
Utilities					
Telephone service					
Office supplies					
Postage and shipping					
Marketing and advertising					
Travel					
Entertainment					
Technology					
Other:					
Other:					
TOTAL EXPENSES					
Net income before taxes					
Provision for taxes on income					
NET INCOME AFTER TAXES (NET PROFIT)					

	June	July	August	September	October	November	December	TOTAL
$ ➤ $$ ➤ $$$								

Income Statement: Annual by Month

For Year: _____	January	February	March	April	May
INCOME					
Gross Sales					
(Commissions)					
(Returns and allowances)					
Net Sales					
(Cost of Goods)					
GROSS PROFIT					
EXPENSES - General and Administrative					
Salaries and wages					
Employee benefits					
Payroll taxes					
Professional services					
Rent					
Maintenance					
Equipment rental					
Furniture and equipment purchase					
Depreciation and amortization					
Insurance					
Interest expenses					
Utilities					
Telephone service					
Office supplies					
Postage and shipping					
Marketing and advertising					
Travel					
Entertainment					
Technology					
Other:					
Other:					
TOTAL EXPENSES					
Net income before taxes					
Provision for taxes on income					
NET INCOME AFTER TAXES (NET PROFIT)					

NOTE: *A computerized version of this worksheet is available as part of The Planning Shop's* **Electronic Financial Worksheets** *package, available from www.PlanningShop.com.*

							$ ➤ $$ ➤ $$$
June	July	August	September	October	November	December	TOTAL

Income Statement: Annual by Quarter					$ ➤ $$ ➤ $$$
For Year: _____	1st Quarter	2nd Quarter	3rd Quarter	4th Quarter	TOTAL
INCOME **Gross Sales**					
(Commissions)					
(Returns and allowances)					
Net Sales					
(Cost of Goods)					
GROSS PROFIT					
EXPENSES - General and Administrative Salaries and wages					
Employee benefits					
Payroll taxes					
Professional services					
Rent					
Maintenance					
Equipment rental					
Furniture and equipment purchase					
Depreciation and amortization					
Insurance					
Interest expenses					
Utilities					
Telephone service					
Office supplies					
Postage and shipping					
Marketing and advertising					
Travel					
Entertainment					
Technology					
Other:					
Other:					
TOTAL EXPENSES					
Net income before taxes					
Provision for taxes on income					
NET INCOME AFTER TAXES (NET PROFIT)					

Income Statement: Annual for Five Years	Yr: _____	Yr: _____	Yr: _____	Yr: _____	Yr: _____
INCOME **Gross Sales**					
(Commissions)					
(Returns and allowances)					
Net Sales					
(Cost of Goods)					
GROSS PROFIT					
EXPENSES - General and Administrative Salaries and wages					
Employee benefits					
Payroll taxes					
Professional services					
Rent					
Maintenance					
Equipment rental					
Furniture and equipment purchase					
Depreciation and amortization					
Insurance					
Interest expenses					
Utilities					
Telephone service					
Office supplies					
Postage and shipping					
Marketing and advertising					
Travel					
Entertainment					
Technology					
Other:					
Other:					
TOTAL EXPENSES					
Net income before taxes					
Provision for taxes on income					
NET INCOME AFTER TAXES (NET PROFIT)					

$ ➤ $$ ➤ $$$

(years four and five). If necessary, adjust the form to meet the needs of your company.

The supplemental Electronic Worksheets package available from www.PlanningShop.com includes the Income Statement worksheets and will automatically handle calculations and transfers from other worksheets for you.

Cash-Flow Projections

For almost every business, cash-flow analysis is the single most important financial assessment. After all, if you can't pay your employees, your bills, or yourself, you're not going to stay in business long, and you're certainly not going to sleep very well at night.

The cash-flow projection is not about profit — it's about how much money you have in the bank. It doesn't tell you whether your company will show an overall profit at the end of the year or how many orders you are placing, but instead gives a real-life picture of the money going in and out of your business on a monthly basis.

Cash-flow analysis is particularly important for seasonal businesses, those with large inventories, or those that sell much of their merchandise on credit. You must plan for the slow months and for the long time lag between paying for materials and actually realizing cash receipts.

Maintaining historical cash-flow records gives you an idea of what to expect in certain months of the year and helps you plan future cash management. Get in the habit of keeping monthly cash-flow accounts. Complete the upcoming Cash Flow History worksheet if yours is an existing business.

In preparing these forms, separate out cash you receive from doing business (sales) and the cash you get from taking out loans or receiving investments (financing). This will give you a better sense of where your money is coming from and how much you are relying on credit. Note these items used in your cash-flow analysis:

Cash Sales. Sales made for immediate payment or prepayments.

Collections. Income collected from sales made in a previous period.

Interest Income. Income paid from bank and other interest-bearing accounts.

Loan Proceeds. Income from bank loans and other credit lines.

Cost of Goods. Actual payments made on items in this category. Cash and accrual accounting methods treat this line differently; consult your accountant.

Operating Expenses. Actual payments made on items in this category, minus depreciation (as depreciation is not an actual cash payment). Since cash and accrual accounting methods treat this line differently; consult your accountant.

Reserve. Money put into accounts for future, unanticipated expenses.

Owner's Draw. Money paid to owner in lieu of salary in a proprietorship, or money otherwise distributed to owners (except for expense reimbursement). In a corporation it is called a dividend and paid from after-tax income. Since this income to the owner is subject to federal and state taxes, your accountant may suggest that you add a provision for taxes to the income tax line on the cash-flow form.

Net Cash Flow. Money left over after all disbursements have been deducted from all cash received.

Opening Cash Balance. Amount of money in the bank at the beginning of the month being evaluated; should be the same as the previous month's ending cash balance.

Complete the following cash-flow analysis, on a monthly basis for the first year (or two) and quarterly for the next year. The supplemental Electronic Worksheets package available from www.PlanningShop.com includes the Cash Flow worksheet and will automatically handle calculations and transfers from other worksheets for you.

Balance Sheet

For those who are new to business, the balance sheet is probably the least understood of the financial forms. In essence, the balance sheet gives a snapshot of the overall financial worth of the company — the value of all its various components and the extent of all its obligations.

The balance sheet accounts for all the company's assets minus all the company's liabilities. The remaining amount (if any) is figured to be the net worth of the company. The net worth is then distributed as either belonging to the owners of the company — equity — or as retained earnings for the company to use. These allotments are listed in the Liabilities category. Once you do this, the amounts in the Assets and Liabilities categories are equal: they balance.

While entrepreneurs rarely view the balance sheet as a planning tool, bankers and investors rely on the balance sheet to give them a fuller picture of the company's value. Only on the balance sheet can one see the worth of existing property and equipment. Some companies own valuable land or buildings that far exceed the income of the actual business; other businesses own expensive machinery. Other companies may be profitable but heavily in debt.

Refer to the General Financial Terms section at the beginning of this chapter for an explanation of the items listed on the balance sheet. Additionally, note that the balance sheet uses the terms:

Inventory. The value of the stock you have on hand; this could include both raw materials and finished products.

> *"Cash flow is the only thing you worry about for the first four years anyway. Do cash projections! It was six months before I did profit and loss statements. The only number that matters is whether you can pay the bills."*
>
> ***Larry Leigon***
> ***Founder, Ariel Vineyards***

Cash Flow History

For Year: _____	January	February	March	April	May
CASH RECEIPTS **Income from Sales**					
Cash sales					
Collections					
Total Cash from Sales					
Income from Financing					
Interest income					
Loan proceeds					
Total Cash from Financing					
Other cash receipts					
TOTAL CASH RECEIPTS					
CASH DISBURSEMENTS **Expenses**					
Cost of goods					
Operating expenses					
Commissions / returns & allowances					
Loan payments					
Income tax payments					
Other expenses / equipment purchase					
Reserve					
Owner's draw					
TOTAL CASH DISBURSEMENTS					
NET CASH FLOW					
Opening cash balance					
Cash receipts					
Cash disbursements					
ENDING CASH BALANCE					

June	July	August	September	October	November	December	TOTAL
						$ ➤ $$ ➤ $$$	

Cash Flow Projection: Annual by Month

For Year: _____	January	February	March	April	May
CASH RECEIPTS					
Income from Sales					
Cash sales					
Collections					
Total Cash from Sales					
Income from Financing					
Interest income					
Loan proceeds					
Total Cash from Financing					
Other cash receipts					
TOTAL CASH RECEIPTS					
CASH DISBURSEMENTS					
Expenses					
Cost of goods					
Operating expenses					
Commissions / returns & allowances					
Loan payments					
Income tax payments					
Other expenses / equipment purchase					
Reserve					
Owner's draw					
TOTAL CASH DISBURSEMENTS					
NET CASH FLOW					
Opening cash balance					
Cash receipts					
Cash disbursements					
ENDING CASH BALANCE					

NOTE: *A computerized version of this worksheet is available as part of The Planning Shop's* **Electronic Financial Worksheets** *package, available from www.PlanningShop.com.*

	June	July	August	September	October	November	December	TOTAL
$ ➤ $$ ➤ $$$								

Cash-Flow Projection: Annual by Quarter

$\$ \blacktriangleright \$\$ \blacktriangleright \$\$\$$

For Year: _____	1st Quarter	2nd Quarter	3rd Quarter	4th Quarter	TOTAL
CASH RECEIPTS **Income from Sales**					
Cash sales					
Collections					
Total Cash from Sales					
Income from Financing					
Interest income					
Loan proceeds					
Total Cash from Financing					
Other cash receipts					
TOTAL CASH RECEIPTS					
CASH DISBURSEMENTS **Expenses**					
Cost of goods					
Operating expenses					
Commissions / returns & allowances					
Loan payments					
Income tax payments					
Other expenses / equipment purchase					
Reserve					
Owner's draw					
TOTAL CASH DISBURSEMENTS					
NET CASH FLOW					
Opening cash balance					
Cash receipts					
Cash disbursements					
ENDING CASH BALANCE					

Balance Sheet

$ ➤ $$ ➤ $$$

Balance Sheet

For Company: _____

For Period: _____ Ending: _____ , 20_____

ASSETS

Current Assets

Cash _____

Accounts receivable _____

Inventory _____

Prepaid expenses _____

Total Current Assets _____

Fixed Assets

Land _____

Buildings _____

Furniture / equipment _____

Fixtures _____

(Less accumulated depreciation) _____

Total Fixed Assets _____

Other Assets _____

TOTAL ASSETS _____

LIABILITIES

Current Liabilities

Accounts payable _____

Accrued payroll _____

Taxes payable _____

Short-Term notes payable _____

Total Current Liabilities _____

Long-Term Liabilities

Long-term notes payable _____

Total Long-Term Liabilities _____

Net Worth

Shareholders' equity _____

Retained earnings _____

Total Net Worth _____

TOTAL LIABILITIES AND NET WORTH _____

Include in the Financial section of your business plan.

NOTE: *A computerized version of this worksheet is available as part of The Planning Shop's* **Electronic Financial Worksheets** *package, available from www.PlanningShop.com.*

Fixtures. The property improvements owned by the business, such as lights, display cases, shelving units.

Accrued Payroll. The amount of money owed personnel for time expended by the date of the balance sheet.

Prepaid Expenses. Payments made for goods or services not yet received.

When completing the balance sheet, you may find you need more help with this form than with any other, especially when trying to figure accumulated depreciation or the worth of inventory. Get help from your accountant or have your accountant prepare the form. But you must still understand it.

Since much of the information on balance sheets does not change very quickly, you can prepare balance sheets primarily on a quarterly or annual basis (unless, of course, your potential funding sources wants monthly projections).

The supplemental Electronic Worksheets package available from www.PlanningShop.com includes the Balance Sheet worksheets and will automatically handle calculations and transfers from other worksheets for you.

Sources and Use of Funds

If you are seeking outside financing, either through loans or investors, those contemplating giving you money will naturally want to know what you're going to do with the money you raise. They will also want to see what other sources of money you have, if any, and whether you have contributed any of your own funds.

To provide such information, devise a one-page description of the sources and use of funds. This can go in the business plan itself or can be sent with the cover letter to potential financing sources. It should tell a potential investor that you have specific plans for the money you raise, that you are not taking on debts or giving up equity thoughtlessly, and that you will use funds to make your business grow.

Your "Sources and Use of Funds" statement is particularly helpful to you with investors or lenders if you show you are using your funds to start or expand a business rather than to offset existing debts (a use which investors notoriously dislike), if you already have some commitment of financing already from respected sources (which shows other people believe in your company); or are committing significant personal funds (which shows you believe in the project enough to take substantial personal risk).

In "Sources of Funds," you should include both funds you have received to date and the amounts you are now seeking, clearly delineating each.

In preparing the "Sources and Use of Funds" statement, consider the following issues and terms:

> *"A sure killer for a proposal is a plan that shows improper use of funds. If all the funds aren't going to build the business, we're not interested in financing it."*
>
> **Ann Winblad**
> **Venture Capitalist**

Sources and Use of Funds

Complete the following form to describe how much money you are seeking and how you will use the funds raised. Be as specific as possible: If you know what equipment you are going to buy, list it; if you have a loan from the First State Bank, state the name of the lending institution, amount and terms.

Number of funding rounds expected for full financing: _____

Total dollar amount being sought in this round: _____

Sources of Funds

Equity Financing:

Preferred Stock: _____

Common Stock: _____

Debt Financing:

Mortgage Loans: _____

Other Long-Term Loans: _____

Short-Term Loans: _____

Convertible Debt: _____

Investment from Principals: _____

Uses of Funds

Capital Expenditures:

Purchase of Property: _____

Leasehold Improvements: _____

Purchase of Equipment/Furniture: _____

Other: _____

Working Capital:

Purchase of Inventory: _____

Staff Expansion: _____

New Product Line Introduction: _____

Additional Marketing Activities: _____

Other Business Expansion Activities: _____

Other: _____

Debt Retirement: _____

Cash Reserve: _____

Submit this with the Financial section of your business plan.

Funding Rounds. The number of development stages at which you will seek financing from the investment community.

Total Amount. Amount of money sought in this round of financing, from all funding sources.

Equity Financing. Amount you will raise by selling ownership interest in the company.

Preferred Stock. Outstanding stock for which dividends will be paid. before other dividends can be paid for common stock or before other obligations of the company are paid; investors often want preferred stock.

Common Stock. Stock for which dividends are paid when company is profitable and has paid preferred stock dividends and other obligations.

Debt Financing. Amount of money you will raise by taking out loans.

Long-Term Loans. Loans to be paid back in more than a year's time.

Mortgage Loans. Loans taken out with property as collateral.

Short-Term Loans. Bridge loans, credit lines, and other loans to be paid back in less than a year.

Convertible Debt. Loans that are later convertible to stock at the funder's option, giving both the security of a loan and the potential of stock.

Investment from Principals. Amount of money that you or other key employees are contributing to the company, this can be in the form of cash or property.

Capital Expenditures. Purchase of necessary equipment or property.

Working Capital. Funds to be used for the ongoing operating expenses of the business.

Debt Retirement. Funds used to pay off existing loans or obligations.

Assumption Sheet

Financial forms are merely meaningless numbers unless they are based on decisions and facts. Your potential financing sources want to see how you arrived at your numbers and must be convinced that your assumptions are reasonably accurate. If, for instance, you have indicated your sales at a certain amount, investors want to see what size you are assuming the market to be and what percentage of the market you are assuming you are going to be able to secure. If those figures seem realistic, you increase your credibility; if those assumptions seem based on inaccurate numbers or overly optimistic projections, investors are going to look at the rest of your plan with greater skepticism.

It is good discipline for you, as well, to learn to develop an assumption sheet whenever you do financial projections. Otherwise, you can be too easily tempted to write down figures that look good on paper but have little to do with reality.

"In the financials, I look for a well-prepared, well-annotated balance sheet. And I like an Assumption Sheet with the Income Statement, so I know exactly how those figures got there."

Ann Winblad
Venture Capitalist

If you have worked through the business planning process, putting together an assumption sheet should be a relatively easy task. You have already asked yourself most of the questions called for on this form and have the answers available to you.

An assumption sheet should list purely straightforward information; it does not require substantial detail or explanation. You do not even need to use sentences, just provide the data in each category. (You can use the first sentence, as written on the worksheet, on your own assumption sheet.) Be familiar with these assumptions so that you are ready to defend your assumptions when meeting with investors.

Complete the upcoming Assumption Sheet and include a finished Assumption Sheet at the conclusion of your financial forms in your business plan.

Break-Even Analysis

Finally, you want to determine how much income you must earn to pay your expenses — at what point you break even. At the break-even point you are neither making a profit nor losing money; you have just covered the cost of staying in business and making your sales. Most people new to business assume their break-even point is when sales equal the amount of fixed expenses: rent, telephone, insurance, etc. Fixed expenses are easy to determine, since they are in place from the time you first open your doors, and they remain relatively stable regardless of the amount of sales.

But because almost all sales have some costs associated with them, you must also figure the variable cost of sales into your break-even analysis; otherwise you do not have a true picture of your cost of doing business.

For instance, if you are a florist and your fixed expenses (rent, utilities, salaries, etc.) are $20,000 a month, it's not just enough to make $20,000 in sales: You would still be losing money. You must pay for flowers, vases, delivery, commissions to floral wire services, etc., before you earn income on a sale. If these costs amount to an average of 30% of the cost of each sale, at $20,000 in income, you're still $6,000 in the hole ($20,000 in fixed expenses plus $6,000 in costs of goods).

The total cost of goods keeps rising as your sales rise; unlike your fixed costs, the figure keeps changing and is harder to pin down. But your gross profit margin — the average percentage you earn on each sale after direct costs are deducted —stays basically the same. (As you sell greater amounts, you may be able to increase your profit margin by receiving volume discounts; for the purpose of this exercise; however, you can assume a stable gross profit margin.)

To determine an actual break-even point, you must know your:

- Fixed expenses
- Gross profit margin (average percentage of gross income realized after cost of goods).

> *"The best business plans are a combination of a PowerPoint presentation and a succinct and well thought out operating model, showing how the business would be run on the revenue and expense side. The most important thing is that it's based on the formula: revenue equals price times quantity. It should be a 'bottom up' financial model rather than 'I'm going to get 10% of the market.'"*
>
> **Mark Gorenberg**
> **Venture Capitalist**

Then, to figure the amount of total sales needed to break even, you work the equation:

Fixed Expenses = Total Sales × Gross Profit Margin (GPM)

or, saying the same thing:

$$\frac{\text{Fixed Expenses}}{\text{GPM}} = \text{Total Sales to Break Even}$$

In the above example of the florist, we know:

- Fixed Expenses = $20,000
- Gross Profit Margin (GPM) = 70% (since cost of goods is 30%)

So, the numbers would look like:

$$\frac{20,000}{.70} = \text{Total Sales to Break Even}$$

Doing the arithmetic, we see that this florist must make $28,571 to reach the break-even point.

A break-even analysis is an important tool for your internal planning. However, it is not necessary for you to include a break-even analysis in a business plan submitted to outside funding sources. (Of course, there is nothing wrong with including it if you wish.)

Break-Even Analysis

Monthly Total Fixed Expenses (FE): $ _____

Gross Profit Margin, in percentage terms (GPM): _____ %

Divide: $\dfrac{\text{FE: \$ _____}}{\text{GPM: _____ \%}}$ = $ _____
(Sales to Break Even)

Complete the worksheet above to figure your own break-even point. The supplemental Electronic Worksheets package available from www.PlanningShop.com will perform a break-even analysis for you.

Chapter Summary

The financial portion of your business plan will consist mostly of the actual financial projections. You should include the following forms:

- Income Statement
- Cash-Flow Analysis
- Balance sheet

- Sources and use of funds
- Assumption sheet
- Startup Costs (for a new business)

Additionally, you will want to do a break-even analysis for your internal planning.

It is advisable to get professional help in putting together your financial forms and setting up accounts. Set good financial procedures in place from the beginning of your business and stick to them. If yours is an existing business, review your procedures to make sure you have adequate control of billing and payments.

Get in the habit of reviewing your financial statements regularly and understanding what you read. Don't leave the finances entirely up to others and don't be intimidated by numbers.

Assumption Sheet

The figures on the previous financial forms are based on the following assumptions:

Sales							Annual Growth
Product Line	Year $	Units	Year $	Units	Year $	Units	Rate %
Total							

Describe the projected increase / decrease in selling price of each product line / service. _____

_____

_____

Personnel / Management

Describe the number of employees and assumptions regarding total payroll projected in the financial forms.

_____

_____

Describe key management positions to be added and timing. _____

_____

_____

Gross Profit Margin

List the projected gross profit margin for each product line or service.

_____

_____

_____

Describe any major changes in cost of goods that are projected to affect gross profit margin.

_____

_____

_____

Key Expenses

Describe the timing and costs of key projected expenses.

Plant Expansion or New Branches _____

_____

Major Capital Purchases _____

_____

Major Marketing Expenses _____

_____

Research and Development _____

_____

Other Key Expenses _____

_____

Financing

Describe any financing debt (loans) that are projected to be added or retired.

_____

_____

_____

Describe the interest rates assumed to be in effect for these financial projections.

_____

_____

Other

Describe any other major developments that are assumed in creating your financial projections (such as strategic partnerships, competitive situation, etc.).

_____

_____

_____

_____

_____

Notes

SAMPLE PLAN: Income Statement Three-Year Projection

Income Statement

	2003	2004	2005
INCOME			
Gross Sales	**$233,000**	**$493,875**	**$818,615**
(Commissions)	9,610	61,360	82,920
(Returns and allowances)	0	0	0
Net Sales	**223,390**	**432,515**	**735,695**
(Cost of goods)	38,870	62,133	86,610
GROSS PROFIT	**184,520**	**370,382**	**649,085**
OPERATING EXPENSES			
General & Administrative Expenses			
Salaries and wages	89,000	176,800	226,600
Employee benefits	6,600	15,000	21,600
Payroll taxes	6,095	15,000	20,000
Professional services	7,550	5,000	6,000
Rent	10,500	39,000	39,000
Maintenance	600	2,400	4,500
Equipment rental	11,750	38,000	48,000
Furniture and equipment purchase	410	500	0
Depreciation and amortization	2,000	4,000	4,000
Insurance	3,400	4,200	5,500
Interest expenses	1,375	1,500	0
Utilities	2,200	5,000	5,500
Telephone service	1,750	1,200	2,000
Office supplies	3,395	5,000	6,000
Postage and shipping	2,505	3,600	5,000
Marketing and advertising	20,050	30,000	45,000
Travel	1,180	2,595	4,570
Entertainment	1,185	1,805	3,430
Technology	6,000	10,000	14,000
TOTAL OPERATING EXPENSES	**177,545**	**361,200**	**460,700**
Net Income before taxes	6,975	9,182	188,385
Provision for taxes on income	1,046	1,377	56,720
NET INCOME AFTER TAXES	**5,929**	**7,805**	**131,665**

Shows increasing profit margin.

Includes sales personnel salaries in General & Administrative expenses.

SAMPLE PLAN: Income Statement Annual

Income Statement
Year: 2003 (Actual through 8/31/03)

	Jan	Feb	Mar	Apr	May
INCOME					
Gross Sales	$0	$2,000	$2,000	$5,000	$12,000
(Sales commissions)	0	0	0	0	350
(Returns and allowances)	0	0	0	0	0
Net Sales	0	2,000	2,000	5,000	11,650
(Cost of Goods)	0	324	324	812	1,946
GROSS PROFIT	0	1,676	1,676	4,188	9,704
OPERATING EXPENSES					
General & Administrative Expenses					
Salaries and wages	2,500	3,700	5,700	6,200	7,700
Employee benefits	275	275	510	510	510
Payroll taxes	210	310	505	505	505
Professional services	2,500	250	2,000	200	200
Rent	0	0	0	0	0
Maintenance	0	0	0	0	0
Equipment rental	250	250	250	250	250
Furniture and equipment purchase	0	0	0	410	0
Depreciation and amortization	2,000	0	0	0	0
Insurance	400	0	0	200	0
Interest expenses	0	125	125	125	125
Utilities	250	60	125	210	160
Telephone service	100	50	100	100	120
Office supplies	450	125	215	185	125
Postage and shipping	210	80	310	65	450
Marketing and advertising	3,200	1,800	4,000	1,500	1,500
Travel	55	150	100	150	0
Entertainment	0	0	110	320	195
Technology	3,000	0	0	0	0
TOTAL OPERATING EXPENSES	15,400	7,175	14,050	10,930	11,840
Net Income before taxes	(15,400)	(5,499)	(12,374)	(6,742)	(2,136)
Taxes on income	0	0	0	0	0
NET INCOME AFTER TAXES	**(15,400)**	**(5,499)**	**(12,374)**	**(6,742)**	**(2,136)**

Includes materials and freight in Cost of Goods.

Includes variable labor in Salaries & Wages.

Purchased $10,000 in Furniture and Equipment and depreciated it over five years; entered on Depreciation line.

June	July	Aug	Sep	Oct	Nov	Dec	TOTAL
$16,000	$20,500	$28,000	$34,200	$41,800	$50,000	$21,500	$233,000
750	775	1,235	1,500	1,850	2,200	950	$9,610
0	0	0	0	0	0	0	$0
15,250	19,725	26,765	32,700	39,950	47,800	20,550	$223,390
2,595	3,449	4,741	5,691	6,926	8,400	3,662	$38,870
12,655	16,276	22,024	27,009	33,024	39,400	16,888	$184,520
8,400	6,300	9,900	9,100	10,100	11,100	8,300	$89,000
510	510	700	700	700	700	700	$6,600
505	505	610	610	610	610	610	$6,095
200	200	1,200	200	200	200	200	$7,550
0	0	2,100	2,100	2,100	2,100	2,100	$10,500
0	0	120	120	120	120	120	$600
250	250	2,000	2,000	2,000	2,000	2,000	$11,750
0	0	0	0	0	0	0	$410
0	0	0	0	0	0	0	$2,000
0	200	1,000	350	550	350	350	$3,400
125	125	125	125	125	125	125	$1,375
200	175	260	220	210	180	150	$2,200
130	100	250	200	200	200	200	$1,750
85	110	1,100	250	250	250	250	$3,395
85	260	60	410	75	300	200	$2,505
300	1,500	1,750	2,000	250	2,000	250	$20,050
25	100	0	150	150	150	150	$1,180
200	75	85	50	50	50	50	$1,185
3,000	0	0	0	0	0	0	$6,000
14,015	10,410	21,260	18,585	17,690	20,435	15,755	$177,545
(1,360)	5,866	764	8,424	15,334	18,965	1,133	$6,975
0	0	0	0	0	0	1,046	$1,046
(1,360)	5,866	764	8,424	15,334	18,965	87	$5,929

SAMPLE PLAN: Cash-Flow Projection

Cash-Flow Projection

Year: 2003

	Jan	Feb	Mar	Apr	May
CASH RECEIPTS					
Income from Sales					
Cash sales	$0	$2,000	$2,000	$5,000	$12,000
Collections	0	0	0	0	0
Total Cash from Sales	**0**	**2,000**	**2,000**	**5,000**	**12,000**
Income from Financing					
Interest income	0	0	0	0	0
Loan proceeds	15,000	0	0	6,000	10,000
Total Cash from Financing	**15,000**	**0**	**0**	**6,000**	**10,000**
Other cash receipts	20,000	0	10,000	0	0
Total Cash Receipts	**35,000**	**2,000**	**12,000**	**11,000**	**22,000**
CASH DISBURSEMENTS					
Expenses					
Cost of goods	0	324	324	812	1,946
Operating expenses	15,400	7,175	14,050	10,930	11,840
Commissions/returns & allowances	0	0	0	0	350
Loan payments	0	125	125	125	125
Income tax payments	0	0	0	0	0
Other expenses/equip purchase	10,000	0	0	0	0
Reserve	0	0	0	0	0
Owners draw	0	0	0	0	0
Total Cash Disbursements	**25,400**	**7,624**	**14,499**	**11,867**	**14,261**
Net Cash Flow	**9,600**	**(5,624)**	**(2,499)**	**(867)**	**7,739**
Opening cash balance	0	9,600	3,976	1,477	610
Cash receipts	35,000	2,000	12,000	11,000	22,000
Cash disbursements	(25,400)	(7,624)	(14,499)	(11,867)	(14,261)
Ending Cash Balance	**9,600**	**3,976**	**1,477**	**610**	**8,349**

Enters investment from S. Connors as Other Cash Receipts.

Operating Expenses is total of G & A and Sales Expenses minus depreciation.

Shows $10,000 Equipment and Furniture payment as January cash disbursement.

Cash disbursements deducted from opening cash balance and cash receipts.

June	July	Aug	Sep	Oct	Nov	Dec	TOTAL
$12,000	15,500	19,800	20,000	30,800	35,000	15,500	**$169,600**
4,000	5,000	8,200	14,200	11,000	15,000	6,000	**$63,400**
16,000	**20,500**	**28,000**	**34,200**	**41,800**	**50,000**	**21,500**	**$233,000**
0	0	0	0	0	0	0	**$0**
0	0	4,000	0	0	0	0	**$35,000**
0	**0**	**4,000**	**0**	**0**	**0**	**0**	**$35,000**
0	0	0	0	0	0	0	**$30,000**
16,000	**20,500**	**32,000**	**34,200**	**41,800**	**50,000**	**21,500**	**$298,000**
2,595	3,449	4,741	5,691	6,926	8,400	3,662	**$38,870**
14,015	10,410	21,260	18,585	17,690	20,435	15,755	**$177,545**
750	775	1,235	1,500	1,850	2,200	950	**$9,610**
125	125	125	125	125	5,125	10,125	**$16,375**
0	0	0	0	0	0	0	**$0**
0	0	0	0	0	0	0	**$10,000**
0	0	0	0	0	5,000	5,000	**$10,000**
0	0	0	0	0	0	0	**$0**
17,485	**14,759**	**27,361**	**25,901**	**26,591**	**41,160**	**35,492**	**$262,400**
(1,485)	**5,741**	**4,639**	**8,299**	**15,209**	**8,840**	**(13,992)**	**$35,600**
8,349	6,864	12,605	17,244	25,543	40,752	49,592	$0
16,000	20,500	32,000	34,200	41,800	50,000	21,500	**$298,000**
(17,485)	(14,759)	(27,361)	(25,901)	(26,591)	(41,160)	(35,492)	**($262,400)**
6,864	**12,605**	**17,244**	**25,543**	**40,752**	**49,592**	**35,600**	

SAMPLE PLAN: Balance Sheet

Balance Sheet

For ComputerEase, Inc.

For Year Ending: December 31, 2003

ASSETS

Current Assets

Cash	$35,600	
Accounts receivable	17,200	
Inventory	2,100	
Prepaid expenses	780	
Total Current Assets		**$55,680**

Fixed Assets

$10,000 in Furniture and Equipment shows as company asset minus depreciation taken as expenses.

Land	0	
Buildings	0	
Furniture / equipment	10,000	
Fixtures	0	
Less accumulated depreciation	(2,000)	
Total Fixed Assets		**$8,000**

Other Assets		0
TOTAL ASSETS		**$63,680**

LIABILITIES

Current Liabilities

Short-term loan from S. Connors due in less than one year.

Accounts payable	8,675	
Accrued payroll	3,050	
Taxes payable	295	
Short-term notes payable	5,000	
Total Current Liabilities		**$17,020**

Long-Term Liabilities

Long-term loan from L. Silver due in more than one year.

Long-term notes payable	15,000	
Total Long-Term Liabilities		**$15,000**

Net Worth

Owners' interest in company is valued at $31,660 at end of year.

Shareholders' equity	31,660	
Retained earnings	0	
Total Net Worth		**$31,660**

TOTAL LIABILITIES AND NET WORTH		**$63,680**

SAMPLE PLAN: Sources and Use of Funds

Sources and Use of Funds

Total Dollar Amount Being Sought: $80,000 in equity financing. The company prefers that this entire amount be secured from only one investor.

Funding Rounds: ComputerEase expects only one funding round for full financing. If the company were to later become a franchise, another funding round would be considered at that time.

USE OF FUNDS

Capital Expenditures

Leasehold Improvements	$5,000
Purchase of Equipment and Furniture	15,000
Total Capital Expenditures	**20,000**

Working Capital

Purchase of Inventory	5,000
Staff Expansion	25,000
Additional Marketing Activities	15,000
Other Business Expansion Activities	15,000
Total Working Capital	**60,000**

TOTAL USE OF FUNDS	**$80,000**

SAMPLE PLAN: Assumptions

Assumptions

The figures on the previous financial forms are based on these assumptions:

Sales by line ($ expressed in 000's)	2003	2004	2005	Growth Rate
	$ / Units	$ / Units	$ / Units	2004–05
Training Center classes (Corporate)	45.5 / 11	171 / 38	333.2 / 68	80%
On-Site (Corporate)	166.7 / 38	232.9 / 45	330.2 / 58	30%
Center classes (Saturday)	20.8 / 17	90 / 60	155.3 / 90	50%

These sales figures reflect price increases of 10% annually for corporate training center classes; 15% in 2004 and 10% in 2005 for corporate on-site training classes, and 10% in 2004 and 15% in 2005 for Saturday classes.

Personnel

The staff size of the company (two FT professionals and one PT support) will stay constant for the remainder of 2003. In 2004, the payroll increases to four FT professionals, one FT support, one PT support. In 2005, the payroll is projected at four FT professionals, one PT professional, and two FT support.

Expansion

Figures in these projections assume opening a second Training Center classroom 1/1/04. Direct costs associated with expansion include leasehold improvements, equipment/furniture, and marketing. Additional operating costs include equipment rental and addition of a staff trainer. This expansion increases capacity in corporate training classes by 100%.

Financing

To date, ComputerEase has been financed by a $30,000 investment from Scott E. Connors; a $15,000, 10% interest-only loan from L. Silver (Mr. Connors' sister-in-law), due 12/31/03; and a $20,000 no-interest loan from Mr. Connors, principal due on or before 3/31/04. Projections call for the retirement of $15,000 of the Connors loan in 2003, with the remainder by 3/31/04, and the remainder of the Silver loan when due. The 2004-05 financial projections assume securing an additional $80,000 of investment income by 1/1/04.

## Chapter 17

The Plan's Appendix

It's not over till it's over,
and even then it's not over.

Use an Appendix to Reinforce Your Plan's Content

One of the frustrations of developing a business plan is that you are limited in how much information you can include. You may be excited about your product's new packaging, a contract from a large customer, or positive market research results, but you should not go into great detail about these items in the business plan itself. Such details make the document too long.

Instead, your plan's Appendix is the proper place to provide information that supports, confirms, and reinforces conclusions you reach in the plan. An Appendix is where you give greater details about particular aspects covered in the plan, and you can include very specific details regarding market research, technology, location, etc. An Appendix is not the place, however, for any data that is essential to understanding your business. Essential information goes in the plan itself.

"If you have a lot of appendices, put them in a separate binder, so the plan itself stays small."

Ann Winblad
Venture Capitalist

Guidelines

If you choose to include an Appendix, follow these guidelines:

1. Your plan must stand on its own; many people do not read appendices, especially on the first examination of a business plan.

2. You don't have to include an Appendix at all; add one only if you believe the additional information is compelling (in the case of a plan for outside financing) or can be used for reference (in the case of internal plans).

3. Do not put totally unrelated information in the Appendix; the material in the Appendix should be directly related to or supportive of information in the plan itself.

4. Keep it short. The Appendix should be no longer than the plan itself. If your plan and Appendix are both fairly long, consider putting the Appendix in a separate binder.

Remember, your plan must not seem overly long or intimidating to the reader, so give the same careful consideration to what you put in your Appendix as you give to what you put in the plan.

Appendix Content Options

The kinds of information described below are appropriate for inclusion in an Appendix. Notice that this material all supports information already in your plan.

Letters of Intent/Key Contracts

One of the very best items that can be included in an Appendix is a copy of a letter of intent to purchase or a contract from a key customer, especially for a new business. This immediately shows that the business has a source of income and that customers are interested in the product or service.

Endorsements

Letters, articles, or other information from credible sources, particularly customers, reinforce the sense that the company is capable and the product or service desirable. Laudatory newspaper or magazine articles about the company are appropriate and convey the message that the company is well-established or able to generate publicity.

Photos

Photos generally do not belong in the body of the business plan; so if photos of your product, location, display cases, etc., are useful, include them in the Appendix. In most cases, avoid photos of management personnel.

List of Locations

If your company has numerous locations — stores, branch offices, plants — a complete list can go in the Appendix rather than in the plan.

Market Research Results

If you conducted extensive market research as part of your business planning process, you may want to include descriptions of your findings in the Appendix. You can also include information from city or county planning departments or other government agencies that give additional details about the nature of your market.

Resumes of Key Managers

If the resumes of your key managers are particularly impressive, consider including them in your Appendix; otherwise, the description in your Management section should suffice.

Technical Information

If your company is using or developing new technology, and the readers of your plan are knowledgeable in those areas, more detailed descriptions of your technology can be placed in the Appendix rather than in the business plan. You may also want to include technical drawings.

Manufacturing Information

If yours is a manufacturing business, you may want to include a detailed description of the manufacturing process or a flow chart describing the process.

Marketing Material

You can include nonbulky marketing material, such as a brochure or leaflet. For cumbersome marketing materials, such as packaging, use a photograph.

Work Schedule

You can include a work schedule describing how you utilize employees; such a schedule is useful when the company has more than one shift.

Floor Plan

Especially if yours is a retail or manufacturing business, you may want to include a floor plan showing the layout and use of space.

Other Information

You can also include other information derived from the business planning process, such as:

- Competitive Analysis (see Chapter 8).
- Marketing Budget (see Chapter 10).
- Equipment Schedule (see Chapter 11).

Any other information that you believe supports and reinforces information in your plan can be included in the Appendix.

"The only kind of market research that impresses me is to see what you've learned from testing your product in the real world and to get a list of those companies already using the product."

Ann Winblad
Venture Capitalist

Chapter Summary

Use an Appendix to provide information that is too extensive to be included in your business plan itself. Remember, if you are submitting your business plan to outside financing sources, the Appendix is likely to be reviewed only by those who have already read the plan and decided that it warrants further examination. If readers lose interest in your plan itself, the Appendix will go untouched. If after reviewing your plan, however, they are still interested in your business, the Appendix becomes a subtle marketing tool. So be certain to use it only for information that reinforces the sense that yours is a well-conceived, well-run business.

Section III

Putting the Plan to Work

## Chapter 18

Preparing, Presenting, & Sending Out Your Plan

It's not just what you've got;
it's what you do with what you've got.

Now that your plan is complete, or almost complete, it's time to put it to use. Ideally, this book has helped you work through the process of developing your plan and improved your understanding of the forces that affect your business success. If you now do nothing more than put the written document on the shelf and never look at it again, you will still have already reaped major benefits.

But a business plan is a working document, and you probably have a specific idea of how you intend to use it. Most likely, you want to utilize your business plan as 1) a tool for raising funds (either investments or loans); 2) an internal reference document to guide your company's development; or 3) a recruitment tool for key personnel; or all of the above. If you're using it for a class or a business plan competition, be certain to look at Chapter 20 for more insight.

Whether intended for internal or external use, your business plan must be made presentable for others. You must consider how you can best distribute the plan for maximum impact and how to make the finished plan an effective instrument for achieving your aims.

A Word About Confidentiality – Non-Disclosure Agreements

Once you begin to circulate your business plan, you inevitably begin to worry about the confidentiality of your information. Obviously, you don't

"Who you know is important. It makes a lot of sense to have first class consultants. Find out who are the good small business attorneys and accountants in town and hook up with them. Then you can believably say, 'I've found the best law firm, the best accountant, and now I'm looking for the best bank to complete my team.'"

Robert Mahoney
Corporate Banker

want your competitors, or potential competitors, to know your strategy or technology.

Most new entrepreneurs are probably overly concerned about issues of confidentiality. Very few business ideas, after all, are truly new — it's the execution rather than the concept that makes a business a success. Generally, bankers and sophisticated investors respect the confidentiality of plans they receive; they're financiers, not entrepreneurs, and aren't interested in running businesses. Nevertheless, it pays to be careful.

To help ensure confidentiality, you may want to draw up a "nondisclosure agreement," or NDA, for the recipient to sign before receiving your plan. You can use NDAs with less sophisticated investors, potential employees, suppliers, etc.

However, many professional investors — particularly venture capitalists — do not sign NDAs. This is standard policy with venture capitalists, and asking a venture capitalist to sign an NDA is viewed as a sign of inexperience. They see so many plans in so many related industries that they would inevitably have the possibility of a conflict. It is part of their business to respect the confidentiality of entrepreneurs, and they have their reputation at stake.

The best way to protect your information is to be selective about to whom you send your plan. Research your recipients and make certain they are not already funding a competitor. Check their reputations for honesty and discretion. Deal only with reputable people. On top of that, limit the number of copies of your plan in circulation and omit from your plan highly technical, sensitive information. You can provide that information later to only the most serious sources of potential funding.

An attorney can help you draft a nondisclosure agreement, and an example is provided on the opposite page.

Preparing Your Plan for Distribution

Your plan should look as good as the business really is. It is a shame to have an outstanding business overlooked or turned down by investors because the plan doesn't represent the company well.

Before you prepare your plan for either internal or external distribution, refer back to Chapter 3, "Making Your Plan Compelling." Now is the time to edit and proofread your plan; see how you can make the language more concise and clear. Have someone else edit and proofread the plan as well. You may want to use the services of a professional writer to help make your language clearer or a graphic designer to help you lay out your plan or create graphs and charts to enhance its impact.

Whether you prepare the plan yourself or with professional assistance, make certain it is a good representation of you and your company and is visually appealing. Pay attention to details of lay-out and graphics to make it easier to be read or scanned quickly. Once you are confident that

"If you need complete confidentiality, you should most likely not pursue venture capital as a source of funds. While venture capitalists are experienced in maintaining confidentiality, for a number of justifiable reasons, in general they will not sign confidentiality agreements. Also, if you do not need a lot of money at this stage, don't seek venture capital. You will be able to demand a better price and increase the likelihood of getting funding if the company is further developed."

Eugene Kleiner
Venture Capitalist

Nondisclosure Agreement

Nondisclosure Agreement

Re: (Company Name)

I agree that any information disclosed to me by _____ Company in connection with my review of the company will be considered proprietary and confidential, including all such information relating to the Company's past, present, or future business activities, research, product design or development, personnel, and business opportunities.

Confidential information shall not include information previously known to me, the general public, or previously recognized as standard practice in the field.

I agree that for a period of five years, I will hold all confidential and proprietary information in confidence and will not use such information except as may be authorized by the Company and will prevent its unauthorized dissemination. I acknowledge that unauthorized disclosure could cause irreparable harm and significant injury to the Company. I agree that upon request, I will return all written or descriptive matter, including the business plan and supporting documents to the Company.

Accepted and Agreed to:

_____
Signature

_____
Printed Name

_____
Company/Title

_____
Date

your plan is easy to read and visually stimulating, you can apply the final touches to prepare it for distribution.

Cover Sheet

The very first page in your plan should be a simple cover sheet (different from the cover letter). When binding your plan with a clear front cover (which is recommended), your cover sheet then becomes, in effect, your plan's cover. As such, it should make a positive first impression. It must be uncluttered and businesslike. On your cover sheet, include this information:

- The words "Business Plan."
- The name of your company.
- The date.
- A copy number.
- A disclaimer or confidentiality statement.
- The name, address, phone number, and email address of the contact person (for external distribution).
- The name of the division or department and contact person (for in-house corporate plans).
- The company logo, if desired.

This sounds like a lot, but it's not. You should be able to put all this information on a cover sheet and still leave attractive white space on the page.

If you are using a cover other than a clear front cover with the cover sheet visible, make certain that the name of your company is printed on the cover. Funders often have stacks of business plans on their desks; you want them to be able to easily locate your plan without having to open the cover.

Both you and your readers will find that page numbers make it easy to refer to specific information when discussing your plan. Rather than numbering the pages consecutively from start to finish (page 1, 2, 3, etc.), a better method is to number pages by section and page. Thus your Executive Summary would be 1-1, 1-2, 1-3, etc.; the next section 2-1, 2-2, 2-3, etc.; the next section 3-1, 3-2, 3-3, etc.; and so on. This pagination method enables you to update or make changes in one section without having to reprint the entire plan. Of course, if you change the order of sections to tailor your plan for specific readers, you have to re-number the plan.

Table of Contents

Any plan more than 10 pages long benefits from a Table of Contents. Place it at the beginning of your plan, immediately after your cover sheet and before the Executive Summary. Title your Table of Contents "Contents," and simply list the sections and page numbers on which each section starts. If you want to draw attention to particular portions of certain sections, do so by using subheadings for those sections in the Table of

Contents, but don't get carried away. After all, a business plan is relatively short, and your readers can find their way around fairly easily.

Date

Because securing financing can take a long while, be careful about distributing a plan that appears outdated. A reader who in November receives a plan dated March can easily assume that you have met with nothing but rejections for many months. Thus, it may be advisable to use only the year on the cover sheet: "Business Plan, 2004." You can also choose to generate a new cover sheet for each recipient including the month and year: "Business Plan, August, 2004." You needn't cite anything more specific than the month.

Copy Number

Number each copy of your business plan before distribution, and keep a list of which individual has received which copy. This way you can keep track of how many copies are in circulation, and, if necessary, can ask to have a copy returned. Most important, if a copy is circulated without your permission, it's easier to trace the responsible party.

Further, since you may revise your business plan as your business develops, you may produce different versions of your plan. To keep track of which version a recipient has, you may want to devise a code number or letter along with the copy number. Refrain from writing "Version 16" on your plan; it makes a poor impression. A code could look like "Copy C.4," which might indicate to you that it's the third version, fourth copy. "Copy 3.4" could indicate it's the third version, copy four, or it could be "Copy 7.4" to mean the version you completed in July, fourth copy.

Disclaimer

When circulating your business plan to outside funding sources, you want to make certain you don't find yourself in legal hot water. Difficulties can arise when you offer ownership in your company in return for an investment; in actuality, you are selling stock in your company, and federal law regulates the sale of stock.

The best way to protect yourself is to consult an attorney. You can also include a disclaimer on the front cover that indicates your plan is not an offering for sale but rather a document for information purposes only. The same disclaimer can also be used to help protect the confidentiality of your business plan, especially when you are not adding a nondisclosure agreement. Your attorney can provide you with the best language, but a typical disclaimer might look like this:

> This document is for information only and is not an offering for sale of any securities of the Company. Information disclosed herein should be considered proprietary and confidential. The document is the property of _____ Company and may not be disclosed, distributed, or reproduced without the express written permission of _____ Company."

Layout, Design, and Presentation

Because you must limit the total number of pages in your business plan, you may be tempted to fill each page from top to bottom. Resist this urge. A page crammed with too much information intimidates and may even annoy the reader.

People make up their minds about how difficult a page is to read before they actually start reading it. Therefore, leave sufficient " white space" (unused, blank space) on the pages of your plan to make the text appear inviting to the reader.

"Frame" your text by leaving a border around it. Generally, leave about a 1" margin on the top and right side, with a little more (such as 11/4") on the bottom and left side (to allow for binding).

Single-space your text, but leave double spaces between paragraphs. Keep your paragraphs short. Use either underlined or bold-print headers (such as the one directly below this paragraph) to begin each section or show a change of topic.

Choosing a Typeface

Software programs provide many choices of serif and sans-serif typefaces. A serif typeface is a more traditional style having small fine lines or "feet" which make words and lines of type easier to read; this is especially effective when a document has a lot of text, as in the case of a business plan.

More modern looking, sans-serif type has no fine lines. Use it for headings, lists, and other places where there is a limited amount to read.

Shown below, in their actual form, are a few of the more commonly used serif typefaces:

Garamond (used in the main text of this book)

Times or Times Roman

Bembo

Palatino

Here are some examples of sans-serif typefaces:

Univers Condensed (used in worksheets in this book)

Univers Bold (used in Sample Plan subheads)

Helvetica Condensed

Helvetica Bold

Arial Black

When selecting type for your business plan, follow these guidelines:

- Choose type that is easy to read and businesslike in appearance.
- Use no more than two plain and one italic typeface in your plan.
- Use a serif for the text, and serif or sans-serif type for headlines.

"Automatic turnoffs for a business plan? Writing on both sides of the paper. Typing mistakes. Not knowing how to present financials. Always use straightforward financials; don't get imaginative. Avoid fancy covers; use black or clear binders. Get it professionally typed, or better, desktop published. Looks count a lot."

**Robert Mahoney
Corporate Banker**

Type size is measured in "points." For text, 10-point type is recommended; smaller than 9 points is a strain to read. (You are now reading 11-point type.) Section headings and titles generally can be set in 12- to 14-point type.

Binding and Report Covers

Binding your business plan gives it a more polished, complete look. Professional binding is provided at most copy centers for just a few dollars.

Choose quality report covers in a professional color such as black, deep blue, or burgundy. Use a clear cover, with a title page, or a label on the front. Make sure the reader can see the name of your business without having to open the plan.

The Final Step: Editing Your Plan

Once you finish your plan, go through it again thoroughly. Find ways to make your sentences shorter and easier to understand.

Eliminate unnecessary words. Change passive verbs and jargon to clear, active language. For example, instead of saying "Profitability will have been reached by Teddy's Dog Togs in its third year of operation," be more direct with a sentence like this: "Teddy's Dog Togs will show a profit by year three."

A business plan must inspire trust. Misspellings, typographical errors, and improper grammar undermine trust. Proofread your plan for such mistakes and have at least one other person proofread it as well.

Preparing a Computer/Slide Presentation

For most sophisticated investors, such as venture capitalists, you will want to — or need to — prepare a computer presentation, outlining the highlights of your business plan, especially if you are invited to meet with them. A computer slide presentation is an excellent way of conveying the most important aspects of your business in a short time. (A computer presentation may be referred to as a "slide" show since each frame of a computer presentation is called a "slide.")

Some venture capitalists and other investment groups now prefer to see computer presentations instead of written business plans. However, you will still need a written plan, either to be reviewed before you are granted a meeting or to leave behind after you meet with potential investors.

A computer presentation is an excellent opportunity to make certain investors learn the strongest reasons to invest in your business. Since you control the content of your presentation, you get to highlight those aspects of your business that will be most compelling to your financing prospect.

Of course, the computer presentation should contain all the major points of your business plan. You need not present them in the exact order of the written plan, but you may have to explain some elements before other points

"The value of a PowerPoint presentation is that you (the entrepreneur) get to control the agenda of the meeting. Otherwise we can have an open-ended discussion, but I'm going to control the meeting through my questions rather than you guiding it through your presentation. If you have a computer presentation, you can make sure you make all the points you want to make."

Mark Gorenberg
Venture Capitalist

will be understandable. When you make your presentation, the investors will interrupt you to ask questions, challenge your assumptions, etc., so make certain you get to your most important points early in your slides.

The key points an investor will want to learn from your presentation are likely to be:

- The business concept
- The size and nature of the market
- What's happening with the competition
- What kind of growth you project
- Who's on your team

The most common software used to prepare such presentations is Microsoft's PowerPoint.™ To produce a PowerPoint presentation, you need merely outline the content of your presentation and choose a standard slide template. Of course, if you are adept at PowerPoint, you can create custom slides or include special effects. But you do not need — in fact you do not want — fancy or elaborate designs or distracting special effects for your slides. You want to keep the investors' attention on your business.

Don't try to overwhelm an investor with too many slides. While there is no exact number that will be right for every business, you should be able to convey all the key details of your company in no more than 10–20 slides. If you have too many slides, you're going to feel as if you have to rush through your presentation to get to them all.

The text of each slide should be primarily in short, bulleted points. You rarely need whole sentences on a slide since you will be there in person to explain the points in more detail. Put no more than 3-5 bullet points on a slide. You can use an effect to have bullet points appear one-by-one; this gives you control over the flow of information during your presentation.

Practice your presentation before you appear before investors. Make certain you are comfortable working with the computer and the software so that you are not distracted during your meeting.

Putting Your Business Plan on the Internet

Some entrepreneurs, especially those involved in internet-related or technology businesses, may choose to put their business plan on a website. There are many advantages to having your plan on the Internet: it is easily available to you or potential investors, you can update it frequently, investors can access it anywhere they can get on the Internet.

Of course, there are also many disadvantages. The biggest one is security. NEVER put a business plan on the Internet without making it password-protected. Even if you think no one will find it because it is at some obscure site, search engines may turn up your pages when looking for key words. Moreover, investors will be skeptical of any business plan that is essentially out there for the entire world to see.

Other disadvantages of having your plan on the Internet is that many people find it difficult to read a long document on a computer screen (assuming they don't print it out), it is hard to "flip through" to get an overview of your business or to have a colorful graphic catch a readers' eye, and if your potential reader is away from access to the Internet, they have no way of bringing your plan along to read.

If you do put your business plan on the Internet, create a cover page with hyperlinks to each section and/or subsections of your plan. You want the reader to be able to easily get to the information that interests them without having to scroll through pages of text.

Keep in mind that financial forms can be particularly difficult to read on the Internet and the formatting may be lost or distorted when printed out. Graphics, however, often work extremely well.

For all these reasons, always have printed copies of your business plan as well. Don't let the Internet be your only method of presenting your business to the investment world.

Updating Your Plan

Your quest for financing may take many months, and your plans for your company may change during that time, especially if yours is a new enterprise. You want to make certain that your written plan is always reasonably current with your actual business strategy and position.

So, before sending out a plan to a new financing source, review its contents and update it. Bring your financial information up to the close of the last month or quarter, revise your financial projections to reflect recent developments, and add descriptions of any new members of management.

It's best not to print too many copies of your plan at one time — you'll be more tempted to send out an old version if a stack of them are already printed and ready to go.

Chapter Summary

Your business plan should look as good as its contents. It should be a good representation of you and your company. Prepare your business plan with care, including active language, graphs and charts, and attractive page lay-out and fonts. You may also need to prepare other ways to present your business plan, particularly a computer slide presentation.

"If you put your plan in a secure area on a website, then it's a convenient way to get the plan to potential people to read. It's easy to read it, to print it, but it's much more accessible than paper. It's a lot less for me to carry if I want to read it at home or on the road. I can download it to my hard drive and read it on a plane. I could print it and throw it away, knowing it's always there for me to read."

Mark Gorenberg
Venture Capitalist

## Chapter 19

Looking for Money

Money buys you time:
when you run out of money,
your business runs out of time.

Not all money is equal. When you first start to look for financing, you imagine that you'll take any money you can find, but you should exercise care. The various sources of money require different types of return on their investments, have varying levels of sophistication and comfort with risk, and provide you with significantly different auxiliary benefits and disadvantages.

Whose money do you want? As you begin your search for financing, first stop and ask yourself these questions:

- Are you willing to give up some amount of ownership of your company?
- Are you willing to have debt that you have to repay?
- Are you willing to risk property or other assets?
- How much control of the direction and operation of your company are you willing to relinquish?
- What other help do you want from a funder besides money?
- How fast do you want to grow?
- How big do you want your company to be?
- What do you see as the long-term relationship between you and your funding source?

Keep in mind that you are going to have an ongoing relationship with your money source; make sure it is someone you can live with.

"Getting an investor is like getting married. But it's harder to divorce your investors than it is to divorce your spouse."

Mark Gorenberg
Venture Capitalist

Debt Versus Equity

Everybody who gives you money for your business wants something in return. Funders either want their money paid back with interest or they want to participate in the profits your company eventually makes. There are two basic formulations for financing your business: taking on debt or giving up equity (ownership interest) in return for investment income.

Debt Financing

> "We funded the initial two rounds of financing ourselves from our four partners. Later we took in limited partners, then our overseas distributor as an investor. Now we're looking for an investment partner capable of competing with the largest wineries in California so we can defend ourselves at the higher levels of sales. We know we will have to give up a significant stake in the company, but we're willing to do it on the theory that a small piece of a big pie is better than a big piece of a small pie."
>
> *Larry Leigon*
> *Founder, Ariel Vineyards*

Debt financing gives you the advantage of keeping complete ownership of your business. You keep control, and you keep all the eventual profits. You borrow a specific amount, and you have to repay only that amount plus interest, regardless of how profitable your company becomes. The lender does not share in the profits.

Because lenders do not reap the benefits of substantial profits, they have to reduce risk as much as possible. To do so, they may ask you to secure the loan with collateral of your assets (including your home). Using debt financing may jeopardize these assets if your business income is unable to pay back the loan, and if the business fails, you may still have the debt. This is a major risk, especially for a new entrepreneur. You should be extremely cautious before risking your home, your children's college education, or any other funds on which your lifestyle depends.

Loans from banks and other lending institutions (often referred to as conventional financing) are difficult to secure for new enterprises. Many banks will only finance businesses in operation more than three years, and very small businesses may have difficulty at any time. Credit unions may be somewhat more lenient than banks. And for very short-term financing, some small companies have even used cash advances on credit cards.

Be especially careful of shady lending companies that prey on small business startups; these companies make easy loans, requiring significant personal collateral, knowing most of the businesses they fund will fail and the assets will be seized. Or they charge hefty up-front fees to supposedly help find financing they can never truly secure.

Well-established businesses are far better candidates for conventional financing than startups. A healthy ongoing business needing funds for modest expansion activities should certainly consider bank financing. If the business is incorporated, the company itself can take on the loan debt and shield the owners from personal liability in most cases.

Equity Financing

Equity financing, on the other hand, allows you to avoid the personal risk of taking on debt. Instead of committing to repay a specific amount of money, you instead give the investor a piece of the eventual profits. This takes the form of stock in the company or a percentage ownership. If your company is very successful, an equity investor may end up receiving many times the amount originally invested. However, if the company fails to produce sufficient profits, these investors may never get their money back.

Thus, equity investors often want to participate in decision-making to ensure that the company operates in a manner that will produce profits. They may take seats on your board of directors or even play an active role in management.

In some cases, you may have to give up so much equity that others actually have controlling interest in your company. In this case, the investors might even be able to remove you from management altogether. Still, a capable investor can bring you sound business advice, useful business contacts, and may be able to provide you with additional future financing.

Equity financing is a usual and practical method of funding start-up companies. Most of the best-known entrepreneurial high-technology firms are financed through equity investors. The popularity of investing in start-ups — and thus the availability of money — goes through cycles. It is far easier to get a new venture funded at a time when the marketplace is rewarding new entrepreneurial endeavors, particularly through growth or increase in the valuation of the company and its stock.

Because it has proved so successful, equity investing has become institutionalized through venture capital firms, angel investors, and other entities, such as small business investment companies. But equity financing need not be sought only from these professional funding sources. Your accountant or attorney may put you in touch with someone who is looking for an investment, or your brother-in-law or college roommate may be willing to underwrite your business.

Sources of Money

Where do you go to find the money you need? And what are the obligations and benefits you receive from each source? Two charts near the end of this chapter outline the various sources of debt and equity financing available for businesses.

When choosing a financing source (and you do choose them, just as they choose you), pay particular attention to the personal qualities of the individual and the reputation of the venture financing company you use. Just as not all banks are alike, certainly not all investors are alike.

You want to choose a financing source that:

- Stands by you during difficult times and works to overcome setbacks.
- Deals with you in a professional and businesslike manner.
- Values your contribution to the company.
- Maintains open and clear communication with you.
- Is fair, ethical, and honest.

Ideally, your financing source also brings you sound business advice, excellent business connections, and the ability to help secure future financial support. These qualities are particularly important when looking for an angel investor or venture capitalist. Such an investor is likely to play a

"If you start from scratch and you want steep growth, you have to have the ability to finance internally due to very large margins, or you'll have to reconcile yourself to either selling out or accepting financing from outside sources and giving up equity."

Larry Leigon
Founder, Ariel Vineyards

very active part in your company; make certain that it is someone who offers your enterprise other benefits in addition to money.

Venture Capitalists

As you search for money, you probably will hear the term "venture capitalist" quite often, but those who use the term may be referring to different entities. True venture capital firms are among the most sophisticated investors available, typically providing an entrepreneur with more than money. Their knowledge, experience, and connections may prove to be as important to your company as the dollars they bring.

Venture capital firms invest large sums of money pooled from various sources such as pension funds and institutional investors. These private firms are established expressly for the purpose of investing in developing companies. Their partners and associates generally have a background in business management and/or the industries in which they invest.

Venture capital firms typically invest only in companies they believe can grow to be very large: often in the hundreds of millions or billions of dollars in eventual value. As such, they generally invest large amounts of money at one time to help these companies grow quickly. They are not appropriate vehicles for companies with more modest goals or financial needs.

Venture capital firms specialize in particular industries or stages of a company's development. If your company is just in formation, you need to look for a venture capital firm that invests in "seed" or "early stage" companies.

Expect venture capitalists to take a very active role in the growth and development of your company, sitting on your Board of Directors, selecting key executives, perhaps even determining the nature of your role in the business. Because they will have such influence, if not control, over the fate of you and your company, choose your venture capitalist wisely.

Private or "Angel" Investors

A frequent source of capital for new or smaller entrepreneurial companies is the private, or "angel," investor. Private investors are usually well-to-do individuals, seeking investments that provide more personal satisfaction and the potential of greater financial reward than are offered by conventional investments such as stocks and bonds. Private investors can be an excellent source of financing.

Being an "angel" investor has become more popular over the years, and there are now organizations or groups of angel investors. These groups help facilitate meetings between entrepreneurs and potential investors. Often, "angel" investors who are part of an angel network can provide a broader range of assistance (in addition to money) than a single private investor. Other methods of finding "angel" investors is through professional financial advisors, accountants, attorneys, etc., who often know of wealthy individuals seeking investment opportunities.

Of course, the quality and nature of private investors varies widely. Some are entrepreneurs who were successful in business and now want to use their money and expertise to invest in companies related to their area of expertise. These "angels" may bring outstanding assets to your company.

Other private investors may have little to offer besides money. Less sophisticated investors often have unrealistic expectations regarding the amount and timing of profits. Frequently, they are unfamiliar and uncomfortable with risk, and they may apply pressure for producing profits far earlier than a business can reasonably manage or than is healthy. If you do pursue private investors, make certain that the investor understands the nature of your business and be particularly conservative in your projections of how much profit you will produce and when.

Small Business Investment Companies

Small Business Investment Companies (SBICs) and Specialized Small Business Investment Companies (SSBICs) are private firms which exist to provide both investment financing and long-term loans to small businesses. Some SBICs provide only equity; others rely on debt, and some provide either. Each SBIC has its own policy.

SBICs are licensed by the U.S. Small Business Administration (SBA) and may receive funds from the government for the purpose of investing in small businesses. SBICs are willing to consider any small business. SSBICs restrict their investments to companies operated by minority or economically disadvantaged entrepreneurs.

SBICs are good vehicles for financing a small business. However, most of them maintain rigorous evaluation procedures, and you will have to meet some of the same criteria required when applying for conventional financing or funding from venture capitalists. Many of the SBICs now only make loans, and they will seek the same type of collateral and evidence of credit worthiness as banks.

U.S. Small Business Administration

The SBA guarantees loans from other institutions; it does not make loans directly (except for Vietnam-era veterans and disabled persons). If you are seeking financing, the SBA can provide you with a list of lending institutions active in giving loans to small businesses. Remember, these banks and institutions must approve your application, so you must meet bank criteria to qualify. Typically, new businesses do not qualify for SBA-guaranteed loans. The SBA guarantee, however, sets interest limits and may make a difference if the lending institution is "on the fence" about your loan. Expect to provide a personal guarantee for any loan you are granted.

The SBA has created some other loan programs that may be more accessible for new businesses. The "micro-loan" program offers very small amounts of money to companies. These are administered through non-profit and community organizations.

> "For a bank, it's more important to have our fallback positions covered than our upside measured. A bank is different than a venture capitalist; we don't get larger profits if the company is very successful. So we spend most of our time assessing the fallbacks in a plan in case of error. The fallbacks we look to are receivables, guarantees (collateral), inventory, and fixed assets."
>
> **Robert Mahoney**
> **Corporate Banker**

Friends and Family Members

Be careful when financing your business through family or friends, either with loans or investments. This money may be the easiest to secure, but may cause you to risk personal relationships; by mixing your personal and business affairs, you may find you make both your business and personal life more difficult. Unsophisticated investors are nervous about money — they don't understand that it takes time before profits are realized. They view every natural delay or setback with alarm.

"The best and most exciting way to start a business is when you're financially strapped. Then, you have to be creative to keep things going. You have to shop carefully and creatively if you don't have much money. I managed to get a lot out of a little money. The goal was to make enough product to produce at least a small income stream, enough to keep making more."

Deborah Mullis
Entrepreneur

If you do take a loan from a personal source, later repay it with the required interest, and subsequently become very successful, the friend or relative may not understand why he or she does not participate in the profits. And, if you are unable to pay back the loan, the relative may never forget and may remind you of your failure at every family occasion for the next 20 years.

Customers – Raising Money Through Revenue

Never forget the power of making sales. The very best money comes from customers. You neither have to give up a piece of your company (as with investors) nor do you (necessarily) have to take on debt (as with a loan). In the process of looking for money, don't overlook the potential of finding money through actual sales.

Customers bring you more than money. They show potential investors that you have a company that is meeting real market needs. Having orders, of course, may cost money. If you are fortunate enough to land a big order when your company is still young, you may not have the resources to fill those orders. But this is a better time to approach financing sources. You may find a bank or other lender much more receptive when you have a contract in hand. Some banks are particularly aimed at entrepreneurs. You may also find investors are much more willing to meet with you when you have customers, especially if any of your customers are companies that demonstrate to them your ability to land important deals.

The fund raising process can take a long time, so consider the possibility of building your business through income while you look for the capital you need. Sales are good.

Improving Your Chances of Getting Funded

When using your plan to raise money, you can increase your chances of getting funded by researching potential funders, their interests and areas of expertise. You can further enhance the possibility of success by understanding how the funding process works, how long it takes, and how to stay in touch with potential funders.

Researching Your Recipients

It pays to do a little homework on potential funders so that you understand the nature of the investments or loans they make. It's a waste of everyone's time to send a business plan for your service business to a venture capital firm that funds only manufacturing companies, or to submit a loan for your new business to a bank that only funds companies established for more than three years. You'll end up waiting weeks or months just to hear an inevitable "No."

Instead, a little research can save you a lot of time. Often, this can be accomplished with just a few phone calls, especially if your potential funding targets are established venture capital firms or banks. These institutions are used to answering questions about their funding patterns and have definite procedures and guidelines. Start by visiting their websites. Many venture capital firms outline exactly what types of companies they fund, the criteria for their investments, and include a list of companies they have already funded – their "portfolio" companies. If you can't find what you need on the Internet, don't hesitate to contact these professional financing sources for information; they'd much rather answer your questions now than waste their time having to process a business plan in which they have no interest.

With other sources, such as private or angel investors, it may be somewhat harder to get information. If they are a member of an angel investing network, they may list the types of companies they are interested in. They are far less likely to offer specific criteria than venture capitalists. Nevertheless, it is quite businesslike to send a letter of inquiry to ascertain the kinds of investments they are willing to consider before submitting your plan to them.

When researching potential funding sources, these are the questions you want answered:

- Do they fund businesses in your industry?
- Do they fund businesses in your sector?
- At what stage of business development do they provide funding?
- What are the minimum and maximum amounts of funding they consider?
- What are the minimum and maximum potential sizes of the businesses they fund?
- What other criteria do they use to make their funding decisions?
- On what basis do they generally provide funding: equity or debt?
- What other companies in your industry have they funded previously?
- What kinds of information do they require you to submit with your plan? For instance, how many years of financial projections do they want to see?

Once you have this information, you can better determine whether a funding source is appropriate for your business. Make sure your type of business and financial scope fall within the interest areas of your potential recipient. Don't send a plan requesting an investment of $50,000 to a venture capital firm that only funds companies seeking a minimum of a million dollars. (Many do.)

"There are lots of reasons not to go to venture capitalists. First, it takes a long time to get an answer, from one to eight months. Second, very few businesses get funded by venture capital. We accept only one out of 200 plans. You may not want to become a very large business; venture capitalists are interested in businesses that will become large. Finally, you may not be willing to make a commitment to go public or be acquired. Venture capitalists need a way to get their money out."

Ann Winblad
Venture Capitalist

If possible, you also want to find out less tangible information about your funding sources. What is the potential funder really like? When deciding on funding, does the funder tend to place more emphasis on the experience of management, the product or service, or the market potential? Does the funder take a very long time making decisions, or do they respond quickly? Once they've financed a company, how does the funder perform as an ongoing partner? What's the funder's reputation in the industry?

Some of these questions you can ask in a phone call to an associate or member of the funding institution; better yet, you can request an informational interview with the funder (see below).

You can also get a great deal of information about funders by joining entrepreneurs' groups in your community or industry. Many larger cities have organizations in which entrepreneurs help one another get started, and members often have first-hand experience with funding sources.

If the funder is prominent, you may find information about them on the Internet or through sources such as magazine and newspaper articles. Next, see if you can talk to any others already funded by the same source, particularly those funded in the last few years. They can supply a wealth of information, and if you hit it off with them, perhaps they will even arrange an introduction to the funder for you.

Informational Interview

If you intend to send your plan to a large or well-established funding source, such as a bank or major venture capital firm, consider asking for an informational interview to get a feel for the institution and to better determine exactly what it is looking for in a business.

Request this only after you have finished researching your funding source and your plan is complete. The interview need not be long; ten to fifteen minutes may be sufficient. Your meeting doesn't have to be with a partner or decision maker: An associate may be more willing to meet with you. Even an administrative assistant can be a source of a great deal of information.

It won't be easy to get such an interview, so treat any interview you are able to secure as an excellent opportunity, even if it's with a secretary. This is the beginning of your relationship with the funder, and you want to make a positive impression. Moreover, you then know a person inside the company, and when you send your plan, you can send it directly to that person.

Don't choose your prime funding target for the first interview you schedule. Get some experience with your second or third choice. You'll be less nervous, and you'll learn how to make a better impression when you finally meet with your first choice.

Finding an Intermediary

The best way to distinguish your plan from the many others received by a funding source is to find someone known to the funder to act as an

---

"If you already have one or two successful stores, you have a much better chance of receiving funding from a venture capitalist. Venture capitalists in the retail field are looking for a proven concept with experienced management. They are looking for 'cookie cutter' concepts, businesses that can be repeated almost identically from location to location."

Nancy Glaser
Business Strategies
Consultant

"If I get a phone call from somebody I respect about a plan, then that plan gets more of my attention. Who refers a plan to me can be quite important, but in the end the plan has to stand on its own."

Eugene Kleiner
Venture Capitalist

intermediary. Intermediaries can either send or deliver the plan personally or can allow you to use their name when you send or deliver the plan yourself.

The best intermediary is:

- Someone in a related business to the funder.
- Someone who received financing (and whose business was successful) from the funder.
- A friend or relative of the funder.
- Someone highly regarded in the industry or community, even if not known personally by the funder.

Having an intermediary does not guarantee you'll receive funding, but it improves your chances of getting a fair and careful review.

If you are fortunate enough to secure intermediaries, be sure to send them a copy of any cover letters you have sent using their name (and perhaps a copy of your business plan as well). Potential funding sources may very well call an intermediary about your business, and when this happens, you want the intermediary to remember who you are.

Do not use a funder as your intermediary to send your plan to another funder unless there is a specific reason, otherwise it raises the question of why your contact isn't providing the funding. If, for instance, you are trying to raise money for a new retail concept and you know someone who funds companies only in the software industry, then it makes sense for her to send your plan to a friend who funds retail companies.

Tailoring the Plan for Your Recipients

Once you have researched your potential funders, you should organize your cover letter and Executive Summary to highlight those aspects of your business most likely to fit the needs and interests of each funder. Is the venture capital firm particularly interested in patentable new technology? Will the bank fund only those companies established for more than three years? Does the division president want to see new market opportunities? If so, discuss these areas in the first paragraph of your cover letter or place more emphasis on them in your Summary.

Be certain to target your Executive Summary to address the concerns of the company rather than just an individual's preferences. Remember, your plan is most likely to end up in the hands of someone other than the person to whom it was sent originally.

Cover Letter

You must include a cover letter with any plan you send or deliver to a potential funding source. The cover letter will probably be read before the plan, so make certain it entices the reader to give careful consideration to your business.

"The best way to get introduced to a bank is through someone who already has a relationship with that bank. Come through a friend who's a customer or a lawyer or accountant. Open an account yourself. References are important in getting an introduction to a bank, but they are irrelevant in the decision to loan itself. Except, of course, if you have references from major customers who show their intention to buy from you."

Robert Mahoney
Corporate Banker

"In a cover letter, I want to know how you knew who I was. How did you get to me? Who are the other people pulling for you? The first plans I read are those that come to me from a credible source."

Ann Winblad
Venture Capitalist

The best way to start a cover letter is with this sentence:

"_____ (name of intermediary) suggested that I contact you regarding my business, _____ (name of business), a _____ (type of business)."

For example, the first sentence might read:

"Aaron Schneider suggested that I contact you regarding my business, AAA, Inc., a food products and service company."

This immediately draws attention to the person connecting you to the funding source and gives you a measure of credibility (assuming, of course, that your intermediary is credible.)

Next, indicate why you (or the intermediary) feel that the recipient is an appropriate funding source. Continuing with the above example, the next sentence might read:

"He knows of your experience in funding food product companies and believes you might find AAA, Inc. of interest."

If you don't have an intermediary, your first sentence should state the name and nature of your company and why you have chosen to send your plan to the recipient. It should read something like:

"Knowing of your interest in funding food product companies, I am enclosing a copy of the business plan for AAA, Inc, an established food products and service company now seeking financing to enable us to expand operations."

Generally, your cover letter should state:

- Why you've chosen the particular funder to receive your plan.
- The nature of your business.
- The developmental stage of your business.
- The amount of funds sought.
- Whether you are looking for an investment or a loan.
- The terms of the deal, if appropriate.

Keep your cover letter brief. It should motivate the recipient to read your plan, not replace the plan itself. A sample cover letter is provided for your review at the end of this chapter.

Following Up

Your job is not done once you have sent out your business plan; you must follow up on its progress to ensure receiving an answer from your funding source. Some investors or banks tell you exactly when you can expect to hear from them. Others are far less diligent in their communication with fund seekers. You must take the initiative.

Don't become a pest, however. Keep your inquiries brief and professional, and don't call or email too frequently. You might call for the first time about a week after sending your plan, just to inquire whether the plan has been received by the funder. During this first phone call it is appropriate to ask when you can expect to hear from the funding source or when you may call back. It's perfectly acceptable to request an appropriate time to follow up again: "May I call back in two weeks to check on my plan's progress?"

Generally, refrain from calling any funding source more frequently than every two weeks. And if they ask you not to call, DON'T.

Email and Voice Mail

Much of your interaction with potential funding sources will be through email and voice mail messages. As such, you want to take some time preparing what you want to say before you pick up the phone or hit the "Send" button.

Email can be an excellent way of reaching people who are too busy to meet with you or to speak with you on the phone. It is also a particularly appropriate way to follow up on business plans that you have already sent. But be careful: most funding sources are inundated with emails and phone calls — yours can easily be viewed as another intrusion.

Keep all your initial or uninvited emails and voice mails short. You have a better chance of having your message read or listened to if it is not too long. If you've worked on your "elevator pitch" (below), you should be able to quickly explain the nature of your business.

If you have the name of an intermediary who suggested you contact the funding source, use that name right away, whether in a voice mail or email. In an email message, you might put the intermediary's name in the "Subject" line to make it more likely the recipient will open your message.

For a voice mail message, state the nature of your call and your business up front and then clearly and slowly leave how you can be reached. Describe your company in "big picture" terms: do not go into too many details; they may misunderstand the nature of your business. Always indicate that you will also phone back — that gives you an opening to call again without seeming too pushy.

Your voice mail message might be something like, "Aaron Schneider suggested I call you about my new food products and service company, AAA, Inc. Aaron thought our approach to growth and our established customer base would interest you. I'd appreciate the chance to speak with you. I can be reached at 650-555-1000 or you can email me at arnie at aaa.com. I will also try you again in a couple of days. Thank you."

Your email message can be very similar to your voice mail. It should be short and direct, and you should provide a way for them to contact you by phone. You can include the address of your website, if you have one up

"Emailing a summary is now the most common and the best way to convey a plan. Email a summary with the idea of trying to set up a meeting to present a full presentation."

Mark Gorenberg
Venture Capitalist

and running, and you are willing to have the potential funder see it before they've talked to you. Refrain from using any attachments, especially in your first contact. Be careful not to be too vague in your "Subject" line, such as "Great Business Opportunity" or "New Business Venture." You don't want your recipient to think your message is spam and delete it without even opening it.

"The Elevator Pitch"

When considering a prospective investment, venture capitalists and other investors often want to hear what they call the "elevator pitch." This is the concise description of a company — its product or service, market, competitive advantages — that an entrepreneur could give in the time it would take to ride up an elevator (and not an elevator in a skyscraper!) An "elevator pitch" shows you understand your business. (If you're unclear on your strategic position, you'd still be mumbling as you pass the fifteenth floor.)

Your "elevator pitch" doesn't have to be made in an actual elevator to be useful. You'll find you'll use it often: in emails to prospective financing sources, to introduce yourself and your company at networking events, to describe your business to potential customers. Take a few moments to concisely describe your strategic position below:

Your "Elevator Pitch"

My Company...

Named: _____

Does: _____

_____

_____

Serves Which Market: _____

_____

Makes Money By: _____

_____

Is Like What Other Companies: _____

_____

Will Succeed Because It: _____

_____

_____

Aims to Achieve: _____

_____

Chapter Summary

If you are raising money for your company, you can increase the chances of raising the capital you need through preparation, research, and cultivating contacts. Research your recipients and tailor the presentation of your plan to the recipient's interests and concerns. Choose your potential funding sources wisely; remember that your funding source will become an ongoing participant in your business. And be realistic. You must always give something in return for the money you receive.

Sources of Debt Financing

	What They Look For	Advantages	Disadvantages
Banks and Lending Institutions	Ability to repay, collateral, steady current income from business.	No profit-sharing; no obligation for ongoing relationship after repayment; definite preset amount to repay. **Best For:** Established companies needing funding for specific activities; short-term cash-flow problems.	Difficult to secure for new businesses; must often risk personal assets; same financial obligation regardless of business' income. **Worst for:** Ongoing operational expenses; new companies with relatively inexperienced management.
Loans from Family or Friends	Likelihood of repayment; your personal character; other personal considerations.	Easier to secure than institutional loans; specific amount to repay; no profit-sharing. **Best For:** Companies with no other option; companies with secure future.	Can jeopardize personal relationships; unsophisticated lender often nervous about money; probably no professional expertise; often get unsolicited advice and frequent queries. **Worst For:** Very risky enterprises; entrepreneurs with difficult family circumstances.
Cash Advance on Personal Credit Cards	Ability to repay.	Relatively easy to secure. **Best For:** Businesses requiring small amounts of money for a limited time; short-term cash-flow problems.	High interest rates; limited amount of money; ties up and risks personal credit. **Worst For:** Ongoing, long-term financing.

Sources of Equity Financing

	What They Look For	Advantages	Disadvantages
Venture Capitalists	Businesses in their area of interest; companies that can grow to significant size; experienced management; new technology.	Large sums available; sophisticated investor familiar with industry; can bring expertise, connections, and future funding; understand business setbacks and capital risk. **Best For:** Potentially large companies; sophisticated entrepreneur or industry wizard.	Difficult to secure; must have exit possibilities in three to seven years; take substantial, perhaps controlling, equity in company. **Worst For:** Small and medium-sized businesses; inexperienced entrepreneurs.
Private Investors	Good business opportunities with better potential rewards than conventional investments such as the stock market; appealing concept.	May fund small and medium-size businesses; easier to secure than professional venture capital or bank loans. **Best For:** Smaller companies; those able to locate relatively sophisticated or capable investor; those with appealing business concept.	Often unsophisticated, nervous investor; take equity in company; may want involvement in decisions without having necessary expertise; long-term relationship; expects profits soon. **Worst For:** Companies requiring long development time before profitability; companies needing additional business expertise.
Investment from Family and Friends	Interest in you and your business concept; chance to make money.	Easier to secure than other investors; no set amount to repay. **Best For:** Companies with no other options; entrepreneurs having friends or relatives with significant business or industry expertise.	Jeopardizes personal relationships; long-term involvement; unsophisticated nervous investor; makes friend or relative a decision maker in your business; doesn't understand risk. **Worst For:** Very risky enterprises; companies requiring long development time before profitability.

SAMPLE PLAN: Cover Letter

Ms. Tamara Pinto
617 North Compton Boulevard
Vespucci, Indiana 98999

Dear Ms. Pinto:

Opens with reference to intermediary.

My attorney, Mr. Kenneth Pollock, suggested I write to you regarding my business, ComputerEase. I am currently seeking an investor, and I believe that the company would coincide with your interest in technology-related service businesses.

ComputerEase is positioned to take advantage of the market opportunities presented in the corporate software training field. This is a relatively new field, and no companies yet dominate the market. ComputerEase, through a professional approach to marketing, experienced management, and an emphasis on outstanding customer support and service, can become the premier provider of software training in the greater Vespucci area. From that base, the company will be able to expand to become a regional force.

Specifies amount of funds sought.

We are seeking $80,000. We anticipate this will be the sole round of funding. The funds will be utilized to add one training center location, expand staff, and increase marketing activities.

I appreciate your consideration of the business plan for ComputerEase. I will telephone in approximately 10 days to see if you have any questions or how we may proceed.

Thank you.

Sincerely,

Scott E. Connors
President

## Chapter 20

Using Your Plan for Classes & Competitions

*Once in a while, what you learn in school
you can actually use in real life.*

Since this book was first published, it has been adopted for use in hundreds of universities and business schools throughout the United States as a standard text. (It's even used by Culinary Academies to help future chefs plan restaurants!) It is also regularly employed as a guidebook for teams preparing business plans for competitions, often sponsored by business schools. While the fundamental issues covered in this book are as applicable for entrepreneurs, corporate in-house teams, or students, this section is designed to help address the special needs of those who are preparing a business plan as part of a class project or to enter it in a business plan competition.

"Entrepreneurship"

People are starting new businesses in record numbers. Entrepreneurs get more respect and understanding from the business community at large than they did in years past, and more and more people hope to one day start and run their own company. In a 1999 study by the research firm Yankelovich Partners, over one-third of Americans predicted they would own their own business within a decade.

Increasingly, people are not just going out and starting a company, they're preparing for it. There's been an explosion of interest in classes on starting and running new companies, and a new field of study and research has developed. Business schools around the United States and throughout the world have responded by developing classes, even majors, in "entrepreneurship."

Do Class or Competition Plans Differ from the "Real World?"

One major difference in preparing a business plan for a class or competition is you're much more likely to be working with a team — as equals — rather than having one entrepreneur with a vision driving the process. In the "real world," it's often clear who the leader and final decision maker is.

This places more importance on managing the process of developing your plan and the process of decision making. One of your first tasks will be to figure out how you will make decisions, assign tasks, stay on top of due dates. In fact, in some classes, part of your grade may be determined by how well you manage team dynamics. While this makes the business planning process more complicated than in the "real world," it helps you develop the very much needed "real world" skills of working with a group to build a business.

Another major difference from the "real world," is the way your plan will be "judged," whether by a professor or a competition judge. When you're out there actually raising money, potential funders have their own set of criteria by which they're going to review your plan that may be very different from the criteria in a competition or class. The most important difference is that classes and competitions typically place more emphasis on the quality of the written plan itself. In the "real world," a company with a genuine likelihood of being very successful might get funded even if their plan was somewhat sloppy. Additionally, potential funders base much of their decision on their opinion of the capabilities of the key founders, often more than on the content of the plan or the business concept. You might have a terrific plan — one that would get you an "A" in a course or an award in a competition — that potential funders don't believe you're capable of executing.

Perhaps the biggest difference, however, may be the passion you bring to the process. When you develop a business plan in the real world for your own business, you have a vision of the company you want to create; you're driven by a desire to create something new or a lifelong dream of owning your own business. The downside to this passion, however, is that the visionary entrepreneur may not bring as much objectivity to evaluating the business concept and assessing the likelihood of success since their dreams are at stake. If you can, bring a bit of passion, without losing objectivity, to your class or competition business plan process.

The Team Process

As was said above, one of the major challenges of developing a business plan for a class or competition is working with a team. Mastering the dynamics of working together in a group — how to reach decisions, allocate tasks, communicate, etc. — will help prepare you for the very real situations you'll be in when developing an actual business.

The key steps in managing your process include:

"When we're looking at an entrepreneur in the real world, we definitely judge an entrepreneur at how realistic they are in understanding their financial growth, their business models. In college competitions, we tend to look more at the concepts and the products that they're building and don't put very much weight on the financial sections where they really don't have much experience."

Mark Gorenberg
Venture Capitalist and
Competition Judge

- Choosing Your Team
- Devising a Decision-Making Process
- Selecting The Business
- Identifying Key Issues
- Assigning Tasks
- Re-evaluating Assumptions
- Integrating The Work: Preparing and Presenting the Plan

Choosing Your Team

Perhaps no decision you make will be as important as who you choose to be part of your team. Your people determine your success. The same is true when you start an actual business — with one difference. If you start a business and your Vice President of Marketing isn't working out, you can fire them. You don't always have the option of jettisoning members of your class or competition team. So choose carefully. (In some class situations, team members are assigned, and you don't have a choice.)

When choosing team members, you may be tempted to just put together a group of your buddies. Resist this temptation! While it is absolutely an advantage to have a group of people who work together well, you want to put together the best team possible. Your buddies may not have the range of knowledge or skills to help you form a well-balanced team, and, if you're honest, some of them may not be as responsible as you need them to be.

When putting together your team, look for a balance among the functional areas you'll address in your plan. Think of this as putting together the founding group for your new business: having three great marketers may be overkill, leaving you without sufficient depth in operations, technology, or finance. If you're planning a technology company, definitely try to balance your technology strength with management capability. It's certainly possible to form a business solely around the work of one technology genius, but you'll need capable managers to actually make the business work.

The traits to look for when choosing members of your team are:

- Capability, even excellence, in a functional area;
- Responsibility in carrying out assigned tasks, follow-through;
- Intelligence, ability to evaluate data and think creatively;
- Communication and interpersonal skills;
- Ability to work together in and with a group; and
- Willingness to work hard and long to get the job done.

Before finalizing your team, you may want to interview potential team members to see what skills and capabilities they have as individuals and whether you'd work well together as a group.

Making Decisions

The first decision any group must make is to decide how they're going to make decisions. Devising a clear and fair decision-making process makes

"The best teams in university competitions tend to be well rounded. Engineers have reached out to people in the business sector, and business school people have reached out to those in other disciplines. The most successful plans are those that cross-pollinate people between different departments. The teams that are almost all from one discipline tend to have group think."

Mark Gorenberg
Venture Capitalist and
Competition Judge

"I strongly suggest teams choose people from different functional areas. Look for people who can work together, who are responsible, who will follow through. Seek cross-functional balance."

Bill Leban, Ph.D.,
Business School
Professor

every other decision easier and the group interaction more pleasant. The important thing in devising a decision-making process is that all team members "buy in" to the process. This doesn't necessarily mean you have to make all decisions by consensus or by a vote — the team may be willing to have one person always have the final say — it just means all members of the team must agree to the process. If you get too far along in the process without determining how you make decisions, you may find yourself at the end of the project still fighting over issues.

One basic area of concern is which decisions members of the group can make individually — will team members have complete say-so over their areas of responsibility — and which decisions have to be made by the whole team. You may want to operate by consensus, by taking a vote, or by requiring unanimous decisions. If you choose to make decisions by consensus — by having the group discuss an issue until a decision emerges — you need a sense of whether the group is capable of doing so in a reasonable amount of time, whether all members of the team will participate in discussions, and whether team members each respect the opinions of other group members. You may also want to discuss what happens if you can't reach consensus. If you require unanimous decisions, you are, in effect, giving each member of the team a veto.

If you have a strong team leader — perhaps the person who has pulled others in to work on their "vision" — that person may expect to make most of the decisions. Discuss how well this will work with the other team members.

Choosing Your Project

How do you decide which business you're going to plan? Some classes or competitions may limit the kinds of businesses you can select as a project, but more often, you have a universe of options from which to choose. Since the quality of your business plan necessarily rests on the nature of the business you're planning, choose carefully.

You may have a team member with a very clear vision of the business they want to plan. Perhaps they've even formed the team around their business concept. If so, you're ahead of the game, but it's still useful to submit their idea to the same kind of scrutiny you would give to all other suggestions. This will help you identify possible obstacles and challenges to their business idea.

If you don't have a particular business idea chosen, you'll probably start your selection process with a brainstorming session of team members to come up with a list of possibilities. In fact, some professors require you to submit a number of potential business plan projects. Refer back to the section and worksheet on the Business Concept in Chapter 1 to help you focus your selection process.

You'll probably narrow down your choices to a few that innately seem reasonable to you and your team members. To start to choose between them, ask these additional questions:

"How do you decide what business you're going to plan? Ask yourself, What is of interest? What could work? What do people in the group have backgrounds in? How much do you know about your area? What is the likelihood of this being successful? Where can we get the Research? How are we going to do the research? Where can we get information? What about the competition?"

**Bill Leban, Ph.D.,
Business School
Professor**

- How do team members' backgrounds, skills, and knowledge relate to each business; do we have sufficient expertise to understand each business?
- What is of interest to the members of the group?
- Do members of the team have unique talents or knowledge that could give us a clear competitive advantage in a particular business?
- How possible is it for us to gather the information we need about each business in the time allotted?
- How do these businesses fit the values and social concerns of team members?
- What other factors affect our ability to prepare a plan for each of these businesses? And most importantly,
- What business do we believe has the best chance of success?

Identifying Key Issues

Once you've decided which business you're going to plan, you need to identify the key issues you'll have to address in developing that plan.

This is the time to discuss the business concept in greater detail. Get the group together to go over the Business Concept worksheet in Chapter 1. Be critical: don't be afraid to tear your business idea apart. Ask yourself all the tough questions that a reader — whether a professor, judge, or potential funder — is inevitably going to ask. The best method to identify key issues is by asking yourself questions (see Chapter 2), so have a brainstorming session to come up with those questions.

Once you have a list of questions, you then have a list of issues to examine. Use the worksheet Research Questions in Chapter 2 to organize and clarify those issues.

Assigning Tasks

In assigning tasks, the first decision you'll probably want to make is to choose a group leader. It's often far easier to work in a group if there is one person designated as the "leader." The group can decide the nature and extent of the responsibilities of the leader, but it's generally helpful to have one key person act as the focal point for reporting in, setting meetings, etc.

You can choose to divide up tasks based either along functional areas or share all tasks among team members. Some teachers may require you to rotate tasks among team members so that each member gets experience in all the areas.

Functional Division: This more resembles the "real world," where each person would prepare the portion of the plan related to their job responsibilities. For example, the V.P. of Marketing would do the marketing section, the C.O.O. would prepare the operations section, etc. The advantage to dividing tasks along functional lines is that it makes the best use of the skills and talents of the team members and the best use of time. The dis-

"The team brings their expertise from a number of different areas. The group members not only establish the plan, they buy into the plan, and as they implement the plan, they have a better understanding of what their focus is, their strategy, their goals. The discussions themselves are important. They are better able to make decisions because they have a better understanding of what they're trying to do."

Bill Leban, Ph.D., Business School Professor

advantage is that team members may end up with little or no understanding of areas other than their own, the quality and content of information may be inconsistent, and if one member doesn't perform well, that entire area of the plan suffers.

Shared Tasks: In this division of responsibilities, each member of the team works on every, or most every, issue. You may assign tasks then by time: this week everyone works on marketing, next week everyone works on operations, etc. The advantage is that members of the team get a better understanding of all the issues facing the business, the topics may be covered more thoroughly since more people are working on them, and you may spark cross-functional creativity. The disadvantage is that it is very duplicative, takes more time, and may leave you with too little time to explore each area.

You can also work on some combination of this division: giving one person prime responsibility for a particular area over the course of the project but having the entire group work on each area for a short period of time.

Once you have figured out how you are going to divide tasks, you need to develop an assignment sheet, making clear who each task is assigned to and due dates. The worksheet Assignment Sheet follows on page 325.

Re-evaluating Assumptions

Towards the end of the planning process, prior to putting the written plan and presentation together, you'll want to revisit your original assumptions and assess what aspects of your business need to change. As a result of your research and data — and as you've become more familiar with the industry, market, and competition — you'll have a much better idea of what might actually succeed. This is the time to come together, as a group, to re-evaluate your original assumptions and re-adjust your business concept or strategy.

Give yourself time in your planning process to have such an assessment meeting; it's easy to find yourself running up to your due date with only time to put the plan together. In some classes, the professor may require you to do a reassessment as part of the assignment.

Be willing to change. It may be difficult — once you've got sections of your business plan written and you just want to turn it in and be done with it — to go back and re-think or re-write part of your plan and your business strategy, but it's worth it. You'll find you not only plan a more realistic business, but you've got a better chance of getting a good grade or winning a competition.

Integrating the Work: Preparing and Presenting the Plan

Once all the assignments have been finished, and the individual sections of the plan developed by individual team members, you'll need to prepare the actual written business plan and/or computer presentation. Even though each member of the team may be required to write their section of the plan, you're far from finished when they turn their sections in.

"Assumptions are critical. Establish your assumptions, look at your assumptions, reevaluate them."

Bill Leban, Ph.D., Business School Professor

You'll likely find that you have a very uneven document: some sections more thorough than others, some more clearly written than others, etc.

You'll first have to determine how the group will handle those sections that are deemed to be insufficient. Typically your future is tied together with your teammates, whether for a grade or a competition prize, so you probably won't want to let one section be noticeably weaker than the others. Put one, or at most two, team members in charge of completing the written plan. It's difficult to write a very good document by committee. Others can be in charge of the graphics, computer slide presentation, etc.

Finally, decide who will be giving the presentation of the plan, if an oral presentation is required or an option (take it!), and then practice that presentation. You don't want to be caught fumbling at the last minute, figuring out who is going to stand up.

More details on preparing and presenting your plan are provided in Chapter 18, and you may also want to prepare your "Elevator Pitch" as described in Chapter 19.

Special Considerations for Classes

Many business, finance, or entrepreneurship classes require you to develop a business plan, often as part of the "capstone" or concluding course of your entire curriculum. The process of putting together a compelling business plan is designed to demonstrate that you can integrate the knowledge you've gained from your various courses and can relate them to one another and to a real world situation.

Generally, the issues for preparing a successful business plan for a class — and getting a good grade — are the same for preparing any business plan. There are a few areas where plans for classes differ. Professors and teachers are likely to place more emphasis on the following:

- How well integrated the different sections of the plan are.
- How well documented the sources of information are.
- How realistic it is; how well it reflects an accurate assessment of the real world situation.
- Whether you've included a clear statement of assumptions, and whether those assumptions are realistic.
- Whether the assessment of risk is adequate, reflecting real world constraints.

In a class, you're also likely to be judged by how well the team has worked together — how well you've managed the process of putting together the plan, so pay particular attention to your group dynamics.

Finally, in a class, the quality of your written plan is always critical. Don't be sloppy. Pay attention not only to the content of the plan — making certain you've covered all sections thoroughly — but also to the look and quality of the written document itself. Refer back to Chapters 3 and 18 on how to make your plan compelling.

"In giving grades or awards what we look for: How well they integrate what they're doing. Is the plan weaker in one area than another, is it balanced? Does the plan have sufficient information? Enough support for assumptions? Is it logical? Could it work? Is there a high probability it can be accomplished? Is your management team able to implement? Could it be presented to a funder for financing? Some instructors use peer review as part of the grading; they ask members of the team to rate how well the team members worked together."

Bill Leban, Ph.D.,
Business School
Professor

Special Considerations for Business Plan Competitions

There are dozens, if not hundreds, of business plan competitions sponsored throughout the country. Many are conducted by leading universities and business schools, such as the Massachusetts Institute of Technology (M.I.T.), Stanford University, the University of Texas, and the University of California, Berkeley to name just a few. Some are sponsored by private industry or consulting firms, others are conducted by Small Business Development Centers, business associations, even business magazines.

Most of these competitions give cash prizes to the winning entries. The stakes in some competitions can be substantial sums of money. But perhaps even more important than the prize money, leading business plan competitions attract the attention of venture capitalists and corporations on the look-out for promising new enterprises in which to invest. Success in a business plan competition may lead directly to success in getting your company funded.

Each business plan competition has its own rules and requirements. Most business school competitions require either some or all of the company's team members to be students (or perhaps former students). Some competitions may be limited only to new businesses; others may allow plans from entrepreneurs who are already running their businesses but wish to expand.

Tricks for Improving Your Chances in Business Plan Competitions

- **Understand the nature of the competition.** A competition sponsored for business plans by M.I.T. will have a different emphasis (and group of judges) than a competition sponsored to help small businesses get started.

- **Put together a cross-functional team.** Find team members with complementary backgrounds and skills. Judges often look to see if you have the depth of expertise needed. If your background is in marketing, balance your team with team-members who are skilled in other functions, such as technology, operations, finance.

- **For an annual competition, talk to past winners or entrants, if possible.** They can give you insight into how the competition really works and what the judges look for. If the competition sponsor shares examples of previous years' winning plans, look at a number of entries — not just the first prize winner; you'll get a better feel for how they distinguish among entries.

- **Research the judges.** What areas of interest and expertise do they have? If they are investors themselves (e.g., venture capitalists), what types of businesses do they invest in? Such information gives you a sense of the level of industry and technology knowledge they'll bring to their judging.

- **For university competitions, call on alumni members for advice or information.** In fact, this may be the perfect opportunity to get a personal meeting with a potential funder (or employer) who happens to be an alumnus of your university or business school.

"Secrets to winning? Showing a propensity that you're writing the plan to start a real business rather than just writing it as an exercise. Having a well-rounded initial team. Really doing your homework counts even more in a competition because financials aren't typically well thought-out; having a realistic set of financials that mirrors a real business tends to be much more novel in a competition and shows a level of sophistication. Having a plan that looks at the market first rather than the products — that's extremely positive and tends to characterize most of the winning plans. Businesses that have unique technology tend to be viewed more highly than in the real world where market size is typically viewed as more critical than uniqueness of product."

Mark Gorenberg
Venture Capitalist and
Competition Judge

- **Be real.** Unless the competition is specifically seeking plans for visionary businesses, judges are much more likely to be impressed with a concept that has a good chance of succeeding in the real world, even if it is on a smaller scale than a totally ground-breaking concept.

Chapter Summary

Preparing a business plan for a class or competition is very much like preparing a plan in the "real world." However, you are more likely to be working with a team, and so you face the challenges of group decision making and managing the team process. The quality of your written document is particularly important in classes, even more than in the real world. Be as realistic as possible; you'll improve your chances for getting a good grade —or winning a competition — if your business plan reflects the real world situation. Good luck!

"Plan to do your plan. This is an exercise in project management."

Bill Leban, Ph.D., Business School Professor

Team Process Checklist

In the space below, describe specifics and set dates for accomplishing each step in the team process. This is much like setting milestones for your business — except that you are setting milestones for your team to assure a great outcome in the class or competition!

Task	Specifics	Date Completed
Choose Team Members:		
Devise a Decision-Making Process		
Select the Business		
Identify Key Issues		
Assign Tasks (see assignment sheet on opposite page)		
Re-evaluate Assumptions		
Integrate The Work & Prepare and Present the Plan		

Assignment Sheet

Use this worksheet to indicate assignements to team members and due dates for each task.

Task	Assigned To	Due Date	Completed
Industry			
Market			
Competition			
Strategy			
Marketing			
Operations			
Technology			
Management			
Social Responsibility			
Development			
Financials			

## Chapter 21

Internal Planning for Existing Businesses & Corporations

*Planning isn't just what you do to go into business;
it's what you have to do to stay in business.*

If You Have an Existing Business

While the entire business planning process described in this book is aimed at both new and existing businesses, companies already in operation have the ability, and need, to examine key marketing, operating and financial activities more closely. This in-depth analysis particularly benefits those companies undertaking the business planning process for internal planning purposes rather than as a method of securing outside funding.

Ongoing internal planning is a must for any business; it enables you to stay competitive. A thorough planning process forces you to look closely at the dynamics of the current market situation rather than rely on old assumptions. Regular, ongoing planning enables a company to more quickly adapt to new market forces and incorporate new technological advances.

Internal planning provides you with the opportunity to examine ways to keep costs down and increase your profitability. In the constant press of day-to-day business, taking time out to think about what you do and in which direction your company is headed gives you more control over your company's future and better information on which to base crucial business decisions.

The Purpose of Internal Planning

When undertaking your internal planning process, you must first assess the goals and purpose of the process for your company.

Generally, internal planning can take one of three forms:

- **Evaluating.** To provide information on company performance.
- **Goal Setting.** To establish annual or periodic objectives.
- **Problem Solving.** To address a particular issue or concern.

These types of plans differ only in their objectives and scope; the process in each case is relatively similar. All three require that you assemble or develop sufficient information to enable you to evaluate and assess current company conditions; obtain necessary personnel to be involved in the evaluation of the data compiled; and have the ability to bring an honest and critical eye to the examination of your company's situation.

The Evaluational Plan

An evaluational plan provides management with the information needed to make decisions. Data gathering and assessment, rather than the recommendation of specific actions or the setting of specific performance objectives, are emphasized in this type of plan.

Such a plan particularly benefits a company that has not made a close examination of its operations or the market conditions for some time, or it may be used annually by a company that wants to do an in-depth analysis of these factors on a regular basis. An evaluational plan might be the most appropriate type for a company in which all decisions are made at upper levels of management only, and the input of middle management and staff is given relatively little weight.

The Goal-Setting Plan

Probably the most widely used type of corporate business plan is that with the purpose of annual or periodic goal setting.

The function of this plan is not only to evaluate current and past conditions within the company and its environment, but to establish the specific, measurable objectives which departments and/or individuals are expected to achieve.

Some of the areas in which specific objectives may be set include:

- Total Revenues
- Sales per Employee
- Revenues per Customer
- Profit Margin
- Inventory Levels
- Production Time
- Collection Activity

Many companies set performance objectives in these and other areas annually, based on past performance and projections of future conditions. Performance objectives should be:

- **Measurable.** With specific numbers or dollar figures attached rather than merely subjective qualities or quantities.

- **Reasonable.** Based on a fair assessment of current and past activity and a temperate projection of future conditions rather than on an unreachable ideal.
- **Time Specific.** Delineating a clear time frame in which the objectives are to be achieved.
- **Motivational.** Neither impossible to reach nor too easily accomplished, either of which will reduce employee motivation.

The Problem-Solving Plan

Another option for internal planning is to narrow the planning process to a few key issues to be addressed. This type of problem-solving process focuses on the top priorities for operational improvement rather than on an overall evaluation of company performance. Planning for problem solving, however, should not take the place of more comprehensive planning; you still need to look at your complete operations. But it offers you a method of focusing resources and creativity on one or two areas in order to make significant gains in performance.

A problem to be solved can be assigned to a department or division, but often it is advisable instead to assemble a task force to tackle the issue. Such a task force allows management to bring together staff across divisional or departmental lines.

Keep in mind that to a large extent whom you choose to participate in the task force will determine the outcome. If the task force is composed only of staff members who have been with the company for 20 or more years, it is unlikely you will come up with fresh approaches to the problem. If the members are too inexperienced, on the other hand, they will neither have the necessary knowledge of the realities of the business nor will their recommendations be viewed with much authority.

The problem-solving process consists of:

- **Defining the Problem.** Either management or staff may delineate the areas of concern or challenges.
- **Assembling the Team.** Limit the number of people involved and bring together only those whose contribution will move the process forward; choose team members more for their intelligence, attitude, and knowledge than for job title or data access.
- **Considering Solutions.** Persistent problems often require creative solutions; be willing to make changes to achieve results.
- **Recommending Specific Activities.** Suggest the changes or enhancements necessary to solve the problem.

Large Corporations

Many, if not most, larger corporations now develop business plans annually on either a company-wide, divisional, departmental or team level. *The Successful Business Plan: Secrets and Strategies* serves as a guidebook for developing a plan at any of these levels, whether corporate-wide or for an

"Each major marketing division and each staff department must come up with a strategic plan and an annual plan. The strategic plan focuses on the critical issues for the next three years: issues such as declining demographics, product substitutions, discount competition, increased supply prices. It addresses the business environment, the customers, the competitors, the suppliers, and other key issues. There are very few financial schedules. The annual plan starts from the bottom up, and it is very specific. It must make sure all the strategic objectives are being addressed and includes: profit/loss statement; cash-flow analysis; capital spending; inventory analysis, including turnover by product line and mark-downs; and lead time analysis for reaching particular objectives. Both the strategic plan and the annual plan are done every year, but not at the same time."

George James
Former Sr. V.P. & CFO
Levi Strauss & Co.

individual team. For departmental or team planning, some sections may require modification to accommodate specific circumstances or may not be applicable at all.

As you work through the book, utilize the described process and worksheets but adapt the material to your specific situation and needs. While the term "you" is used throughout the book, particular actions might be carried out by a subordinate, research department, or other members of the planning team. Nevertheless, the person making the final decisions should be sufficiently informed about the planning process and have access to raw data enabling him or her to competently evaluate the action plans recommended by others.

If yours is a particularly large or complex business, you may want to separate your business plan into two sections, one containing the specific financial performance objectives and the other examining more strategic and long-term issues facing the company.

Bottom-Up/Top-Down

The business planning process in large corporations is most successful when conducted as a cooperative effort between those on the top of the decision-making ladder and those who actually carry out the decisions. A one-way planning process without the involvement of both management and staff leads to a company-wide lack of commitment to the plan and inevitably undermines its effectiveness.

In establishing and participating in the business planning process, management has these responsibilities:

- Clearly communicating the specific goals and importance of the planning process.
- Establishing the time frame for completion and execution.
- Assembling the appropriate personnel and making time available for them to participate.
- Bringing in additional outside expertise if necessary.
- Making available the necessary resources for the planning process.
- Being open and responsive to results and recommendations of the plan.

Likewise, staff has certain responsibilities in the process:

- Identifying areas of concern and specific problems.
- Defining the resources and outside expertise required for the planning process.
- Providing the necessary data and information.
- Honestly and diligently evaluating the data gathered.
- Viewing the planning process as necessary and beneficial.
- Realizing the limitations of their roles in decision making.

"We have a business research department that conducts research for all divisions to assist in their planning process. It analyzes overall economic trends and conditions and is also available for specific concerns of divisions. Each division can initiate research activities from this department."

George James
Former Sr. V.P. & CFO
Levi Strauss & Co.

Ratio Analysis

You may be surprised by how much you can learn about your company and its profitability from a few relatively simple calculations. Even if you think "number crunching" is only for bleary-eyed accountants, you will discover that figures are vital business tools. Particularly useful are the key ratios indicating how one activity or figure relates to another.

For instance, the key ratio of return on equity compares total net profit after taxes to the total amount of money invested in the company. Dividing profit by the amount of equity allows you to see exactly how much each invested dollar earned. This is a vital number for your business as it shows how effectively you used the money you had to spend. The return-on-equity ratio is particularly important for investors who want to know how efficiently the money they invested is being used to create profits.

When evaluating these ratios and using them as a planning tool, you want to look for ways to increase productivity by decreasing the amount of assets necessary to generate sales, reducing your debt, and increasing the amount of profitability made on each sale.

The principal value of computing ratios for your company is in comparing them from one time period to another. In this way, you can assess the progress your company is making in controlling costs and increasing profitability and the trends you see developing in these areas.

Another important way to utilize this information is to compare these key ratios in your company with the ratios of other similar companies in your industry. These figures are available in financial publications such as the annual review by Dun & Bradstreet, the *Almanac of Business and Industrial Financial Ratios,* published by Prentice-Hall, and from industry trade associations. A comparison of your ratios with those of other leading companies will give you a better sense of your company's performance and competitive position.

The Key Ratio Analysis worksheet on pages 334–335 shows how to calculate many of the most important measurements of your business. The ratios included on this worksheet help you better understand the profitability of your company and specific operations, how well your company manages the assets it has at its disposal, and your cash-flow situation. A brief discussion of the four ratios you will find on the Key Ratios Analysis worksheet is provided below.

Liquidity Ratios

Liquidity ratios show the extent of the readily available assets, indicating your company's ability to meet short-term debts. Generally, you want to try and increase liquidity and decrease amounts tied up in inventory. Specific types of liquidity ratios include:

- **Current.** How capable the company is to cover short-term debts with short-term assets. (Be certain to use current rather than total assets and liabilities from balance sheets.)

"Each division is given a great deal of latitude in what their plans are like. We have just a few ground rules: The plan has to reach a minimum stated rate of return. We have no imperative for growth, just for profitability. If growth threatens the rate of return, then don't grow; and we need to understand the cash flow implications, and we need to see how working capital and fixed assets are affected."

George James
Former Sr. V.P. & CFO
Levi Strauss & Co.

- **Quick or "Acid Test."** How well the company could cover short-term debts without selling inventory; this ratio should always be greater than one.
- **Inventory to Net Working Capital.** How much of the company's cash is tied up in inventory.

Profitability Ratios

Profitability ratios show how much the company has earned and the profits made on sales. Your goal is to have the percentages as high as possible. Profitability ratios include:

- **Profit to Sales.** Relationship of total sales to actual profitability after all expenses.
- **Return on Equity.** Profitability in comparison to the investment of stockholders.
- **Return on Assets.** Profitability in comparison to both investment and loans; how productive the company's total assets are in producing profit.
- **Gross Profit Margin.** Income after the direct costs of sales are deducted.
- **Net Profit Margin.** Income after all expenses are deducted.
- **Earnings per Share.** Amount of income expressed in terms of each share of common stock held.

Debt Ratios

Debt ratios show the extent of the company's debt and its capacity for engaging in additional borrowing; generally, the lower the percentages, the stronger the company's financial position. Debt ratios include:

- **Debt to Assets.** How much the company has relied on borrowing to finance its operations.
- **Debt to Equity.** How much the company owes creditors in comparison to the value owned by stockholders.

Activity Ratios

Activity ratios show how productively the company uses its assets, and how much value the company gets for the inventory or other assets it maintains. The greater the ratio value, the further each dollar goes (except with the Average Collection Period, which ideally is a low figure). Activity ratios include:

- **Inventory Turnover.** Dollar value of the inventory it takes the company to generate sales.
- **Inventory Utilization.** Average amount of money the company has invested in inventory.
- **Inventory Units Turnover.** How much inventory the company has on hand in relation to inventory sold.
- **Fixed Asset Utilization.** Amount of plant and equipment used to generate sales.
- **Total Asset Utilization.** Amount of all assets required to generate the company's sales.

- **Average Collection Period.** Length of time that the company's income is tied up in accounts receivable.

Key Customers

In most businesses, the "80-20 rule" applies to revenues. This rule states that 80% of your income comes from 20% of your customers. This means that a relatively small number of customers are often crucial in determining your success.

In most cases, this 20% is composed of actual individual customers. However, in some cases, it may be a specific type of customer who makes up the bulk of your business.

If indeed your business is dominated by a few key customers (or types of customers), you should take a careful look at their buying patterns and motivation. These customers are vital to your ongoing financial well-being; you want to gain as much insight into their purchasing behavior as possible.

Additionally, you can gain a much better understanding of your customers by examining the significant customers you have recently gained and the important customers you have recently lost. This type of examination of trends in your customer base gives you a sense of how the market views your company and the future direction of your company's sales.

The Key Customer Analysis worksheet, which follows the Key Ratio Analysis worksheet, assists you in evaluating the activity of your key customers.

Touching Base with Your Plan

In corporate business planning, a natural tendency exists to spend a great deal of time and energy putting together a business or annual plan, and then once the planning process is finished, forget the conclusions reached and go back to business as usual. This not only wastes a great deal of resources, it creates a high level of cynicism about the importance and value of the planning process.

To make your business plan a meaningful working document, schedule periodic evaluation meetings to get back in touch with the plan. Perhaps once a month at a staff meeting, the plan can be reviewed and progress assessed. At the very least, the plan should be reviewed quarterly with both management and staff participating in the evaluation. Don't let your business plan gather dust; use it.

Chapter Summary

Existing businesses require business planning as much as start-up enterprises. Planning is a necessity for any company aiming to improve its operations, increase its profitability, or maintain or enlarge its market share. Planning is a regular part of your business, not a once-in-a-business or once-in-a-decade undertaking. Long-term success depends on proper planning: it's the only way to keep up with the competition.

Key Ratio Analysis

Liquidity Ratios

$$\text{Current} = \frac{\text{Current Assets}}{\text{Current Liabilities}}$$

$$\text{Quick or ``Acid Test''} = \frac{\text{Current Assets} - \text{Inventory}}{\text{Current Liabilities}}$$

$$\text{Inventory to Net Working Capital} = \frac{\text{Inventory}}{\text{Current Assets} - \text{Current Liabilities}}$$

Profitability Ratios

$$\text{Profit to Sales} = \frac{\text{Net Income after Taxes}}{\text{Sales}}$$

$$\text{Return on Equity} = \frac{\text{Net Income after Taxes}}{\text{Equity}}$$

$$\text{Return on Assets} = \frac{\text{Net Income after Taxes}}{\text{Average Total Assets}}$$

$$\text{Gross Profit Margin} = \frac{\text{Sales} - \text{Cost of Sales}}{\text{Sales}}$$

$$\text{Net Profit Margin} = \frac{\text{Net Income after Taxes}}{\text{Sales}}$$

$$\text{Earnings Per Share} = \frac{\text{Net Income after Taxes}}{\text{Number of Common Shares Outstanding}}$$

Debt Ratios

$$\text{Debt to Assets} = \frac{\text{Total Debt}}{\text{Total Assets}}$$

$$\text{Debt to Equity} = \frac{\text{Total Debt}}{\text{Total Equity}}$$

Activity Ratios

$$\text{Inventory Turnover} = \frac{\text{Cost of Sales}}{\text{Ending Inventory}}$$

$$\text{Inventory Utilization} = \frac{\text{Cost of Goods Sold}}{\text{Average Inventory at Cost}}$$

$$\text{Inventory Turnover in Units} = \frac{\text{Total Number of Units Sold}}{\text{Average Number of Units in Inventory}}$$

$$\text{Fixed Asset Utilization} = \frac{\text{Sales}}{\text{Average Net Fixed Assets}}$$

$$\text{Total Asset Utilization} = \frac{\text{Sales}}{\text{Average Total Assets}}$$

$$\text{Average Collection Period} = \frac{\text{Accounts Receivable Annual Sales}}{360}$$

Key Customer Analysis

Describe purchasing patterns and motivations of past, current, and new customers.

Key Current Customers

Customer	Products/Services Purchased	Number of Units Purchased	Sales $ This Year	Sales $ Last Year	Sales $ Prior Year
1.					
2.					
3.					
4.					
5.					
6.					

Major New Customers

Customer	Reason for Purchase	How Was Sale Secured	Sales $ This Year	Sales $ Last Year	Sales $ Potential
1.					
2.					
3.					
4.					
5.					
6.					

Major Lost Customers

Customer	Products/Services Purchased	Reason for Loss	Potential for Regain	Last Annual Purchase $	Previous $ High Annual
1.					
2.					
3.					
4.					
5.					
6.					

## Chapter 22

Time-Saving Tips

*"I've been on a calendar,
but I've never been on time."*
—Marilyn Monroe

Speeding the Process

Developing a business plan takes time. It's not unusual for the entire process, from business concept to finished plan, to consume many months, especially for a new business. A plan for a new business takes considerably longer than a plan for expansion or growth of an existing company.

Nevertheless, there are a number of short cuts that can save you time and get your plan finished faster. Remember, you don't want to rush the process, but you don't want to spend so much time preparing a plan that you never get your business going.

Sometimes you have to have a business plan fast, and you may only have time to put together an abbreviated overview of your business. While that is not an ideal way to present your business plan, there are occasions when you have no other choice. The section "When You're Really, Really in A Hurry" (below) outlines how to prepare your business plan very quickly.

General Time Saving Tips

Here are ways to make your business planning process quicker and easier:

- **Prioritize the most important areas.** Not all sections of your plan are equally important. Make certain you have enough time to spend on those aspects of your business that most effect your long-term success or your chances of getting funded (if that's what you're using your business plan for.) Don't squander time on areas you already understand well or are relatively less crucial to your goals. At the beginning of your plan preparation, identify which topics are the most important and address those first.

- **Develop a research plan.** During the course of your plan preparation, you need to gather a lot of information. While you may start on the Internet, you'll soon have to make many excursions away from your office or home, such as to industry meetings, interviews with other entrepreneurs, or visits with potential suppliers. You can avoid having to repeat these tasks over and over again if you outline all the information you're likely to need at the beginning of your business planning process. For instance, a vendor may be able to tell you not only about the kind and costs of goods, but they may know a lot about your potential competition and also about customer preferences. You'll want to ask about all of those in one meeting, rather than going back.

  So start your research plan by making a list of all the information you want and potential sources of that information. Then put them in a logical order. As you go along, you'll find you need additional information, of course, but a research plan will reduce the amount of times you'll have to go back to the same source and will keep you moving forward.

- **Organize all that paper!** You will amass an amazing amount of paper during the process of developing a business plan and searching for information through stacks of reports, notes, and brochures will consume a great amount of time. So right from the start, organize your material so you can refer back to it quickly and easily. Set aside a separate file drawer or file box for your planning materials. Create individual files that correspond to the sections of your business plan, such as target market, competition, and operations, and sections for miscellaneous material and possible appendices. One trick is to use a notebook binder or binders with tabs separating the sections of your plan. If you're finding important information on the Internet, either print out the relevant pages and put them in your file, or save the pages to the appropriate file on your computer (see below). Keep all your material together in one place, and start filing papers in their appropriate sections right away.

- **Keep track of the most important information as you go along.** As you research your business, you're going to come across important data that you will want to use in your plan. Some of these will just be tidbits, e.g., U.S. Census Bureau figures on target market size, industry growth statistics, etc. Avoid having to go back and read through entire papers or research reports by setting up a tracking system to file important items of information as you come across them. The best way to do this is by creating a separate computer file in your word processing program for each section of your business plan (plus miscellaneous information) and enter important data into the applicable file as you come across it. These can just be notes; they don't have to be whole sentences or blocks of information. But be absolutely certain to indicate where the information came from, so you can give the necessary attribution without having to go back and look up the source. When not using a computer, use a colored highlighter to indicate the important information in each document, transfer that data to its appropriate computer file as soon as possible, and then file the material in the related file of your file drawer. You may have to photocopy some items because many documents will relate to more than one section of your plan. This method will really save you time. When you start to write your plan, you'll have almost all the information you need at your fingertips, in exactly the right place. And you'll be able to see which sections are missing sufficient detail.

- **Use a spreadsheet.** If you don't have a computer and have never even used one, this doesn't mean you should go out and buy one and learn to use it and the accompanying software. That won't save either time or money. But if you have a computer and fairly good computer skills, using a computerized spreadsheet (e.g., Microsoft's Excel™) will make it easier and quicker to make the constant, necessary changes in your financial projections. If working with a spreadsheet is impractical, using even some simple bookkeeping software (e.g., Quicken™) will make re-figuring your financials faster.

- **Get help.** It's not necessary to do every part of your business plan yourself. You can save a lot of time by spending a little money to hire a consultant to help. Many professional services can move your business planning process forward faster and improve the quality of the finished product. You may want to use the assistance of a professional business plan consultant and/or research services (see Chapter 2). Although it may be somewhat costly, if you don't understand financial forms, are seeking funds from very sophisticated investors, or are an existing business, consider using an accounting firm to prepare your financials. This often saves time, but more importantly, it increases investor confidence in your numbers.

When You're Really, Really in a Hurry

Sometimes you just don't have much time at all, and the thoroughness of the plan isn't as important as the speed with which it is prepared. What if a potential investor asks to see your business plan before she leaves town next week? What if a planning department needs your business plan before they can approve your building permit?

It's never a good idea to overly rush putting a business plan together, and you should try to avoid it if at all possible. (Can you ask the potential investor if you can give her your plan when she returns?) But sometimes you have no choice. In those instances, you can use the steps below to streamline the process:

1. Figure out which information is most important. If you're looking for an investor, generally the most critical issues are:
   - The business concept
   - The size and nature of the market
   - What's happening with the competition
   - What kind of growth you project
   - Who's on your team

   Concentrate on addressing those issues first.

2. Go to the plan preparation forms at the end of each chapter and complete them. These forms act as an outline for the text of your plan.

3. Go to the financial forms in Chapter 16. The three essential financial forms are the income statement, cash flow, and balance sheet. Concentrate on those. If you're stumped on where to get figures, refer back to the Flow-Through Financial forms. A list of these is in Chapter 16. These forms will give you a structure for figuring out the information you need to complete all your financial forms.

4. Go back to Chapter 18. You'll find tips on how to lay out the plan for the best presentation and how to prepare a computer presentation (which you may also need to do in a hurry).

5. If you're looking for funding, prepare your "Elevator Pitch" (Chapter 19). That will help you know how to explain your business quickly and confidently.

These steps will enable you to prepare a plan quickly — possibly even in a weekend! But remember, you don't want to rush the process so much that the plan is not a good reflection of you and your business – you never get a second chance to make a first impression.

What to Avoid

One of the worst ways to save time on a business plan is by purchasing a computer program with standardized text or boilerplates, where you just add your company's name, industry, and financials. This can be tempting, because it seems as if most of the work has been done for you. But this "cookie-cutter" approach can be counter-productive, especially if you're using your business plan to raise money. Potential funders may ask you some tough questions, and they'll want to see that you understand what's behind the information you've put on paper.

Remember, the most important part of developing a business plan is the planning. You have to ask yourself the questions and work through the issues so that you understand which factors are most important to your success.

Chapter Summary

It's natural to be intimidated by the prospect of preparing a business plan if you've never created one before. But that intimidation can easily lead to procrastination, which wastes a lot of time. Try to let go of your fear and take the process one step at a time. On the other hand, you don't want to rush through the business plan process just to produce a written document. You need to know what's behind the words you put on paper.

Remember: A business plan doesn't have to be perfect; no plan is. You just have to make an honest, best effort. You don't have to anticipate every possible situation, and it's not necessary to make revision after revision until you get it absolutely right. No plan written has ever been truly finished. Every plan could be improved, and every plan continues to change even after it's supposedly completed. So don't let the process overwhelm you. As the ad says, " Just do it!"

Section IV

Special Considerations

## Chapter 23

Considerations for Internet, "e-Businesses"

*Business doesn't change
just because you're using a computer.*

The Internet is now a part of every business. At the very least, every company needs to put up a simple website. But if the Internet is an integral part of your company's strategy and operation, you face additional issues as you develop your business plan. When you begin to think about your company's Internet activities, you are likely to think first of the many concerns you have about technology. Yes, the technology is critical — you can't run an Internet business if your technology doesn't work and work well — but there are other, more basic aspects of running a business on the Internet that are at least as important to your success.

This chapter is designed to help you better address the business and strategic aspects of your Internet business activities, as well as giving you a structure to outline your technology needs, whether you are:

- Starting an "e-business," one that primarily exists and operates on the Internet;
- Planning the Internet aspects of your new business;
- Adding or expanding an Internet component to your existing company's operations; or
- Transitioning your company from a "real world" business to an Internet business.

This Chapter does not address issues of using the Internet as an internal company tool, nor does it discuss "intranets," private company networks.

While this chapter is aimed at issues specific to the Internet, keep in mind that as dramatic a change as the Internet has made to business life, business fundamentals still apply. They're just more complicated on the Internet. For instance, you have to find and retain customers whether in the real or virtual world — it's the same issue — but the techniques for acquiring those customers may be less familiar on the Internet.

The Four Main Purposes of an Internet Site

All websites are not alike, and not all Internet sites have to make money — at least not directly. While some companies may launch websites to conduct transactions — buying and selling merchandise or information — the web can be a powerful tool for furthering all types of business goals. The four main purposes of Internet sites can be described as:

- Transactional
- Content
- Promotional
- Relational

Transactional

These are the type of sites referred to as being engaged in "e-commerce" and are probably what you think of as "doing business on the Internet." On transactional sites, sales are actually made on the site. Perhaps the best known example is the company that showed the world that e-commerce was viable: amazon.com. But a transactional site doesn't have to be limited to selling merchandise — you could sell data or downloadable music or subscriptions to your online magazine. You could also be a broker, where others buy and sell on your site, such as the auction site, eBay. The key to transactional sites is that sales take place on the site. Operating a transactional site is actually running a business on the Internet. As such, you must deal with issues such as collecting payment, keeping track of customers, fulfillment of orders, etc. A transactional site can be a company's only method of selling to customers, or it may be an expansion of an existing "land-based" company, enabling them to sell to customers via the Internet.

Content

Some sites are designed primarily around the content they provide users. This content can be general, such as a site run by a newspaper or magazine; based on a particular topic, such as sports or finance; or provide detailed information aimed at a specific audience, like legal research. Search engines are also content sites. Content sites can be free or the user can be charged for accessing the content, or a mix of both free and fee-based content. The key to content sites is that users come to the site because of the information they find there and choose whether or not to return to the site based on the quality of that information. Most content sites get some or all of their income from advertising and sponsorships. Running a content site is running a "media" business, and you must know how to create or compile content of continuing interest.

"Content tends to be an important aspect of what people look at in an e-commerce site because it gives them a side not only of buying and selling goods but having expertise on that site to help in that process. One model that's emerging is contextual commerce which is having a buyer going to a site initially for its content and then having that content help drive a buyer to buy."

Mark Gorenberg
Venture Capitalist

Promotional

The Internet offers the potential of reaching customers from all over the world, and many businesses use an Internet site primarily to attract new customers to their land-based offerings. In essence, their website is an advertisement or extended brochure, and the site is designed as a sales tool. This can be effective in certain industries, such as travel, where customers are willing to spend time doing online research. It's also good for "niche" businesses which offer hard-to-find or specialty items or services. If you're hoping to find new customers with a promotional site, ask yourself: "Will people be willing to spend some time online looking for a business like mine?" You can also use a promotional site to give in-depth information about your company to those who hear about you "off-line," making it convenient for them to learn more about you.

Relational

A website can also be a cost-effective method of providing customer service and maintaining relationships with current customers (or employees.) You can post specials, provide ways for customers to track their orders, provide technical support or upgrades, etc. Such relational sites can be very powerful and extensive (for example, Federal Express' site in which customers can get detailed information on the status of their shipment) or can be very simple. A relational site can also be used to allow customers or users to build a relationship with each other, through online bulletin boards, chat rooms, etc.

These purposes are not mutually exclusive, and the lines between them can be blurry. In fact, transactional sites often do best when accompanied by interesting content, and well-visited content sites typically add transactional components.

What Is Your Business Model?

When starting or running an Internet business, you will be faced with an unusual question: "What is your business model?" In other words, how will you make money? This is an unusual question because in "land-based" businesses, the answer is usually simple: we will sell something to customers at a profit.

But the Internet is a relatively new venue for commercial activities, and the business models are still in formation, changing, and evolving. Some companies, "e-commerce" companies, intend to make money the traditional way: by selling something to customers at a profit. Other companies behave more like "land-based" media companies, making money through advertising. Other models have also emerged on the Internet, and new business models may yet develop.

Some of the business models for companies on the Internet include:

- Sales of merchandise
- Sales of data or information

"The thing people need to focus on is adding value. We have not done any straight e-commerce deals because if you separate out all the noise, there's no value added, they've just aggregated a lot of commodity products. Whether you own a customer or not, that customer is not loyal to you because you have not added any value to them. If you don't add any value, you don't own the customer. You may have them now but you don't ultimately have them."

Andrew Anker
Venture Capitalist

- "Brokering," bringing others together for commerce and taking a commission on their activities, such as through online auctions
- Download of products, such as software or audio
- Per use model: audio or video on demand
- "Application services provider," software used from main server on a leased or purchased basis
- Advertising
- Sponsorship/strategic partnerships: receiving payment for special ad placement or access to users, etc.
- Subscriptions to allow continuing access to site or data
- Nonprofit: donations and other public support
- Timed use (basically extinct; old model for AOL and other proprietary services)

Understanding your business model is critical for planning your Internet activities. Everything about your Internet presence depends on what business model you choose. You have to know how you intend to make money to determine what your site will look like, what kinds of technical functionalities you need, what kind of users you want to attract, what kind (if any) customer service to provide, etc.

It is very likely that you will employ more than one of these business models. For instance, if you have a successful e-commerce, transaction-based, website — one that attracts a lot of users — you may also want to sell advertising on that site. It is also probable that your business model will change over time. However, you should have a clear sense of which business models will be primary at the time you launch your company or Internet presence.

If you are submitting your business plan for an Internet business to a potential investor, include a clear statement of your business model, specifying what percentage of your income will come from which business models. Practice describing your business model verbally, as well, because you can be certain you will be asked about it. To help you prepare that statement, use the worksheet 'e-Business' Business Model on the next page.

What is Your Strategic Position?

Just as in the real world, to succeed on the Internet, you have to have a compelling strategic position that enables you to compete successfully against others. The meteoric rise of some early Internet companies led some to believe that success on the Internet was primarily a matter of raising enough venture capital to blanket the media with advertising. The attitude was that if you threw enough money at making a site's name well-known, you'd have a brand name. It's not so easy.

The Internet offers many incredible opportunities, both for new businesses and for existing companies, but just being on the Internet and having a war chest of marketing dollars are not enough. Customers still need

'e-Business' Business Model

Check each of the following ways in which your e-business intends to make money and what portion of your total revenue will come from each model.

Business Model	Specifics	% of Revenue
Sales of merchandise		
Sales of data or information		
Brokering		
Download of products		
Per use model		
Application services provider		
Advertising		
Sponsorship/strategic partnerships		
Subscriptions		
Nonprofit		
Timed use		

a compelling reason to come to you, and once there, they need a compelling reason to buy and to return. On the Internet you have even more potential competitors — many of them as well funded, or better funded, than you. Thus, to succeed you need a meaningful competitive advantage, a defensible strategic position.

Keep in mind, also, that since the Internet makes comparing prices relatively easy for customers, there's a tendency for products to be turned into commodities — items purchased primarily on the basis of price. Therefore, when determining your strategic position for the Internet, be wary of basing it solely or primarily on price: you will be facing constant downward pricing pressure, and it will be hard for you to survive. Instead, look for ways to add "value" for the customer, so that purchasing from you is a distinctly different experience than purchasing from a competitor.

For more information on strategic positioning, see Chapter 9.

Building Customer Relationships

If yours is a business that exists solely or primarily on the Internet, you have a unique challenge: how do you create a bond with your customers when they do not interact with you in any physical way? There is no human salesperson, no physical building, no voice on the phone. How do you create a welcoming environment for your customers when there is no environment? Moreover, in a situation where relatively little can be discerned about you by the customer — they can't see your offices, your store, your employees — building a relationship of trust is even more important than in the 'real' world.

Some of the factors that enhance the quality of the user's experience and increase their trust in you (and therefore, their willingness to do business with you) include:

- **Brand name/Strategic Partners.** Customers still seek name brands; it gives them confidence in the quality and consistency of the company's products, services, and reliability. If your company already has a brand name "off-line," you want to leverage that name to your Internet presence. If you have not yet developed a brand name, you can attempt to become a brand name on the Internet (which takes a great deal of money, as well as time and luck), or you can enter into an alliance with another company or companies with recognizable brand names as a means of increasing a customer's confidence in you.

- **Quality of the site.** Just as a customer judges a retail store by the location, decor, furnishings, etc., a visitor to an Internet site determines how they feel about you by the quality of their experience. Are the graphics pleasing, the site well-designed and easy-to-use? Does the technology work? Is the content clear, interesting, and well-written?

- **Quality of order fulfillment and customer service.** Perhaps the most important factor of all in building customer trust is whether their orders are processed correctly, in a timely fashion, and that complaints or problems are handled well. Since receiving an order may be the customer's

"You have to show that you have a propensity to get strategic partners and that key partners aren't locked up with other players. More than other categories, the e-business world is like playing musical chairs with other companies. If it looks like other companies have already claimed all the chairs, investors fear there may not be a chair for you."

Mark Gorenberg
Venture Capitalist

only physical contact with the company, one bad experience may end a relationship with a customer forever.

- **Ability for other customers to "rate" products/services.** Providing a method or areas for customers to participate in reviewing or rating some of your online offerings not only gives them more information before they make their purchases but is also reassuring, since you're willing to point out the bad as well as the good.

- **Ability for customers to reach someone.** When all else fails, people want to talk to people. Providing a way for customers to reach a real human being, whether to solve any problems, ask questions, make a complaint, etc., is extremely reassuring.

- **Getting "certified."** Some organizations and businesses now provide screening procedures by which they will "certify" your site based on their criteria. Such criteria may relate to the physical existence of your company, your legal and financial status, your privacy policies, etc. One such certification program is run by the Better Business Bureau at www.bbb.org.

Never forget that your company exists primarily on a customer's computer screen. You have a continuing need to make yourself more real to your users.

Developing Your Internet Site

Every Internet site has two main aspects:

- The Front-end — what the user experiences and interacts with
- The Back-end — the technology and fulfillment that makes everything happen

These two are directly related to your strategic position: you'll need to design both a user experience and a back-end execution that sustain and support your strategy. For instance, if you are positioning your company as the most complete source of a particular type of product, you will need a powerful database and excellent search mechanism to help your users navigate through their myriad of choices and a careful front-end design to keep them from being overwhelmed or confused.

Front-end and back-end issues are inter-related; your technology will depend on what you want your user to experience, and your user's experience will be determined and limited by the technology.

Front-End Issues

Front-end issues include:

- **The design of the site:** the "look and feel," the "user interface"
- **Usability:** how easy it is for the user to understand and interact with the design
- **The site map:** how the site is laid out, how users 'navigate' or move through the site

- **The features and functionality:** what the user will be able to do on the site
- **"Sticky-ness:"** how well it keeps users on the site rather than clicking away
- **Personalization:** how much the user will be able to customize the site for their own preferences
- **Merchandising:** how you feature and promote the items or information you are selling

Graphic Design and Usability

Graphic design considerations for an Internet site go far beyond issues of how a site looks. A graphic designer who creates outstanding designs for print may not be able to create a very effective Internet site. Design and usability are closely related and should be considered together. While you may want a site that looks exciting, you primarily want to make certain users can easily interact with the design elements easily. On the other hand, some sites choose extremely functional designs that are not very attractive, with the result that the user gets a less satisfying experience. Great design should be very useable.

As part of your design process, you need to know how most of your users will be connecting to the Internet. If you're designing a business-to-business site where most users will be connected with a very fast Internet connection, your design can be more graphic-intense and you can use more animation, "java script," audio or video, etc. If yours is a business-to-consumer site and most users have a slow connection, keep the graphics light.

Design elements should be determined by asking yourself "What does my target customer need?" A person buying furniture on the web may need an opportunity to see fairly detailed photos, possibly from different angles. On the other hand, a user buying paper clips may just want a description and prices. Don't give customers more than they need, it only takes time and can get customers frustrated. You can, however, give them the option to get more information (bigger pictures, more details, audio/video). Allow your users choice.

Test your site. First, test your site design on different Internet browsers to see how the design changes. Test it with different speed connections and on different computers. Before you launch your site, conduct some user testing of the design and usability. This doesn't mean you have to hire a focus group, but ask a number of people with about the same level of experience as your target market to use the site and see how easy or difficult it is for them. Keep in mind, that one of the great advantages of the Internet is that you can make changes relatively easily.

Site Map

Before you can begin to build your Internet site, you have to design a "map" of the site. Websites are, by the nature of the Internet, non-linear, but you have to have an architecture of the site to make it understandable. Devising a site map gives you (and your users) a structure from which to move around and helps you plan your technology. It is probably easiest to sketch out a site map on paper first.

Once again, your site design, like your graphic design, is dependent on the nature of your users. If you are designing a site for technically-proficient users, you can afford to have a more complex site design, with more layers, but if you're designing for a consumer site, you want to stay relatively simple. Generally, you want to minimize the number of clicks it takes for the user to find what they need. Make it easy for users to get to what they're looking for; with each extra click, you lose a percentage of your users.

Merchandising Your Site

Remember, if you are running an e-commerce business, you are a merchant doing business on the web, and like any merchant, you have to know how to present your merchandise in ways that make customers want to buy, buy now, and ideally, buy more. This is true whether you're selling tangible merchandise like books, or intangible merchandise like data.

Supermarkets learned long ago that part of their merchandising strategy was to put milk and bread at the back of the store so that customers had to come in and walk past many other items before they got to the thing that brought them to the store in the first place. That way the customer would remember, "Oh, yeah, I need cereal," or be tempted by and purchase a bag of Oreos. You won't want to make customers go to the "back" of your Internet site: they'll be frustrated if they can't find what they want right away. But you need to consider how you place and present your "merchandise" in ways that encourage customers to buy and to, ideally, buy more than they originally came for.

On the Internet, merchandising is still a developing art. Many future Internet companies will beat the competition because they devise more effective ways to merchandise. Some of the ways you can merchandise on the Internet are a function of the technology you employ, and you need to understand how your technology enables or restricts your ability to merchandise your products or services. A few ways to merchandise on the Internet include:

- Providing interesting and informative content that enhances user interest;
- Personalizing the information so that customers are presented with items they are likely to want;
- Enhanced search or suggestion capabilities so customers are given choices they might not have considered;
- Interesting or unusual bundling of items;
- Cross-selling, by suggesting related items when a customer buys.

Features and Functionality

For you to make your site effective, your users have to be able to "do" the things they want to do and that you need them do. You may also gain an advantage over competing sites by making your site more functional or with more convenient features. A critical part of the planning of your site is determining exactly what functions and features you need to include, and then making certain your technology supports those. If, for instance, you are conducting transactions on your site, you will need security for taking customers' credit card numbers, a "shopping cart" for customers to select their orders, a way to have customers complete their orders easily, confirmation of orders, etc. However, you might want to add some "bells and whistles" to these basic functions, such as enabling customers to file their shopping preferences or credit card numbers for future orders, ways to track the status of previous orders, methods to "store" their choices until a future time. Perhaps you want to be able to alert customers by e-mail when a new product arrives that is likely to interest them.

Your functions and features should be determined before you select your back-end technology. As you learn about your choices in technology, you'll find there are other features that you can incorporate or that some functions you'd like can't be done without adding a great deal of expense. It's critical to keep in mind your essential functions as you design and choose your technology.

Use the Front-End Issues worksheet on the following pages to determine which issues are most important to your business and your users.

Back-End Issues

An Internet site is much like an iceberg: there's far more to it than meets the eye. This is particularly true for e-commerce sites. While your users see the front-end, the quality of their experience and the effectiveness of your company depend on your back-end structure.

The first thing you need when designing your back-end is technical expertise. If you don't possess this yourself, you need to get a good technology person to help you. The range of issues you must deal with can be daunting, yet your decisions are critically important to your business. You will face questions such as: Which platform you'll use: Unix, WindowsNT, Linux? What software will you use? Will you buy an off-the-shelf software package or build from scratch? Will you hire your own staff or out-source technology functions?

If you are not a technical person, it can be a challenge finding the right kind of person to help you make decisions. Begin by talking to a number of people who are involved with Internet companies to find out what kind of person you need before you look for a specific individual. If your back-end needs are modest, you may be able to rely on your Internet Service Provider to assist you. There are also a number of companies that provide e-business packages with many of the basic functions included.

If yours is an Internet-centric business, you should get a technology person as part of your own company's team. You'll be continually faced with technology questions, and you need someone who is part of the company to help you make those decisions.

A few back-end issues are considered below.

Front-End Issues

Describe the key features that will distinguish your e-business' front-end.

Quality of User Experience

What features do you want and/or need to have? _____

_____

_____

_____

What makes your design pleasing and easy to understand? _____

_____

_____

_____

How many clicks does it take for users to find what they need? _____

What is the speed of the Internet connection of your target market? _____

Have you laid out a site map? ☐ Yes ☐ No   If so, how easy is it to use? _____

_____

What have you done to increase "stickiness"? _____

_____

_____

What have you done to make it more likely customers will buy? _____

_____

_____

_____

What have you done to prompt additional purchases? _____

_____

_____

_____

How consistent is the design with different browsers and at different Internet connection speeds? _____

_____

_____

How have users reacted when you tested the design and functions with them? _____

_____

_____

_____

Front-End Issues (continued)

Features

Indicate the specifics of each site feature and mark whether it is: A — Absolutely Necessary, D — Desirable, or N — Not Necessary

Feature	Specifics	How Necessary
Ability to Reach Live Service Rep		
Advanced Search Capabilities		
Personalization		
Registration		
Shopping Cart		
Security		
Storing Customer Preferences		
Storing Customer Payment Info		
Real-time Inventory Information		
Prompts of Related Items		
Customers Review & Rate Products		
Other:		
Other:		
Other:		

Choosing a Platform

This is perhaps the most critical technology question because the platform is the basic operating system you will use to run your company. Some platforms are more complicated and/or expensive than others, and some platforms are more "scaleable" — they have more ability to expand as your company grows. You want to make certain your platform is a good fit with your company's current capabilities and future needs.

Some of the issues to consider when choosing a platform include:

- How scaleable is it: can it grow with you?
- What does it cost?
- What does the hardware it runs on cost?
- How much time does it take to get up-and-running?
- What kinds of people does it require; how difficult is it to use?
- How hard is it to maintain?
- How well does it integrate into the software I want to use?
- Can it handle bursts of increased use — traffic?

Customer Service, Inventory Management, and Order Fulfillment

Customer retention is perhaps the most critical factor to consider when setting up an e-business. It took a lot to get the customer to come to you. How will you keep the customer coming back? Some studies show the number one factor in whether a customer will return to an e-commerce site is customer service. Did they get their order on time? Was their order correct? If there was a problem, could they easily return the merchandise? Speak to a company representative?

Customer service and order fulfillment is the heart of your business. It often seems the least exciting issue to deal with — because it's the nuts-and-bolts of your operations, not the snazzy design or the "gee whiz" technology — but it's the most important. Everything in your company depends on your customer having a positive experience when they buy from you. Your software and hardware choices should be made based on what your need to fulfill orders accurately, on time, and to be responsive to your customers.

Customer service, inventory management, and order fulfillment are interrelated. Ideally, your database is designed so that customers know whether a product is in stock before they order, each customer order then gets reflected in inventory and begins the fulfillment process.

If you are dealing with a tangible product, your order fulfillment process will involve third parties. At the very least, you'll work with delivery services, such as UPS, FedEx, the U.S. Postal Service. It's likely you'll also have suppliers of finished goods, warehouse operators to store goods before shipping, or fulfillment houses (companies that warehouse and ship orders for you). Part of your planning process for an e-commerce business entails identifying the necessary third parties and negotiating arrangements with them.

The worksheet Back-End Issues on the following pages help you outline your third party needs.

Inventory Management

If you are planning to sell tangible products on your e-commerce site, the first question you must answer is "Where will you get your inventory from?" If you plan to sell only products that you currently manufacture, that answer will be easy: you'll provide your own inventory. But many e-commerce sites are actually "e-tailers;" they sell others' products just as retailers do in land-based companies.

How you handle inventory is critical to your success and is a part of your strategic positioning. One of the reasons amazon.com was able to succeed so quickly in the early days of e-commerce was that they had a supplier who was able to fulfill "one-off" orders of books. In most industries, it is much harder to find wholesale companies who can fill small orders and ship directly to customers.

If you sell products supplied by others, decide how you will handle inventory: will you take possession of that inventory? If so, how will you warehouse it and ship it to customers? If not, what is the nature of your relationship with the supplier, how will you integrate your ordering process with them, and who 'owns' the customer? These issues all directly impact your financial performance. A company that holds inventory will have more capital tied up in that inventory, the costs of warehousing, and losses on unsold goods. A company that doesn't take possession of goods may lose control over the quality of the order fulfillment process, may pay more for fulfillment by the supplier, and faces the possibility of losing the customer to the supplier.

One area to be particularly careful with is the issue of who "owns" the customer. If you are acting as a "broker" bringing together customers with other suppliers, or if you are relying on suppliers to fulfill your orders, you want to make certain that the customer's primary relationship remains with you. It is very expensive to acquire customers, and you don't want them spirited away by suppliers, who can then sell to them directly. Choose your suppliers carefully, negotiate your contracts with an eye to customer retention, and design your order taking and fulfillment process so you always own the relationship to the customer.

Software

Your software choices are dependent on what you are trying to do and what you need to do. In most cases, the centerpiece of your software is your database. Your database contains the information you need to run your business: your inventory, your customers, your visitor data, etc. Since your database is the core of your site's functionality, many of your other software choices will be limited based on whether or not they can easily work with your database. And since your database contains all your most important information, it may not be easy to change databases later, without great effort or cost.

Back-End Issues

Hardware

What platform will you use? _____

What database will you use? _____

Where will your technology staff come from?

In-house? Specify: _____

Out-source? Specify: _____

Software

Will you develop software in-house, buy off-the-shelf, or customize off-the-shelf products? Specify:

_____

How will Internet purchases/activities integrate with your current database/inventory systems/software?

_____

_____

List your key software needs. _____

_____

For each major software program, including operating system and database, determine:

Name of Software:				
Compatibility				
Expandibility/Scaleability				
Cost				
Hardware Cost				
Installation Time				
Support Staff Required				
Maintenance				
Ability to Handle Traffic Surges				
Overall Reliability				

Website Hosting

How much website traffic do anticipate in the first two years? In subsequent years?

_____

Which hosting companies will provide the best service, expertise, quality, and price for your traffic needs?

_____

_____

Back-End Issues (continued)

Inventory

Where will your inventory come from? _____
_____
_____

Where will your inventory be warehoused? _____
_____
_____
_____

Who will do order fulfillment: packing, shipping, etc? _____
_____
_____
_____

Will you provide real time inventory information? ☐ Yes ☐ No If so, how will the customer know at time of purchase if product is available and how will you manage that service? _____
_____
_____
_____

Indicate third party arrangements you'll need, have lined up, and specifics:

☐ Suppliers: _____
_____

☐ Warehouse: _____
_____

☐ Order fulfillment _____
_____

☐ Delivery services: _____
_____

☐ Customer service/Tech support outsource: _____
_____

☐ Other: _____
_____
_____

In general, when selecting software programs, look for those that:

- Are compatible with your other programs, particularly your database
- Your staff members have used previously
- Are widely in use, so you can find future employees or consultants who know how to use them
- Provide you with the most flexibility if you later change
- Are less expensive, both to purchase or to change, so if you make a mistake it's less costly.

Compatibility is generally far more important than cost. The cost of transferring your data later is likely to be higher than the difference in cost when purchasing.

When considering your software needs, you will also be faced with the question of whether to develop the software specifically for your company or to buy "off-the-shelf" software. The advantage of having your own software is that it can be designed specifically for your particular needs and may provide you a competitive advantage if you're able to devise advanced proprietary functions. The disadvantage is that it is more costly, more time-consuming, less compatible with other programs, and it may be harder to find people to work on in the future.

Keep in mind that the single most important factor in your software choice is that it works — and works well and works reliably. Unreliable software ruins your user's experience, and they won't return to your site. Reliability is critical.

If You Build It, Will They Come?

Putting a business on the Internet can be relatively easy. The hard part, as the history of the Internet has shown, is making money.

To run a financially viable e-business, you not only have to attract a sufficient number of visitors to your website, but then you have to find a way to convert those visitors into buyers — or earn income from them in some other way. And you have to attract and convert them in a manner and a timeframe that allows you to stay in business and make a profit.

As with any business, you'll need a marketing plan for your Internet-based company. The marketing plan should outline the steps you'll take to let potential customers know about you. But while a land-based business may only compete with other stores in its neighborhood — on the Internet, it competes with the entire world.

Companies that serve a niche market or provide unique or hard-to-find products often have greater success than more general e-businesses, with lower marketing costs. In effect, they've limited their online world to a small "neighborhood."

When developing the marketing plan for your Internet-based business, here are marketing vehicles to consider:

"The ideal team: ability to move real fast, understand customer acquisition and retention, understand product merchandising, understand back-end logistics, have an understanding of how to build a computer system that's scaleable and has high performance. But first and foremost it's someone who understands the value of customer service."

Mark Gorenberg
Venture Capitalist

Search Engines

Most people use search engines to locate websites of interest. Search engines (such as Google) work by using software to "crawl" through millions of sites, looking for certain words, phrases, links, and other indicators of what users can find on a site.

Each search engine company uses its own algorithms to determine how websites get ranked in results. They continually revise these algorithms, with the intent not only of improving the quality of the results, but to defeat the efforts of those who try to outwit the system to get their sites ranked higher.

Trying to improve your search engine ranking can easily be a full-time job. If being listed high in search engines is critical for your company's success, you may need to hire (and budget for) at least one full-time search engine specialist.

The important thing to remember is that search engines rank sites based on searches through a site's web pages. So, by doing a few simple things, you can improve your rankings:

- Use phrases that searchers are likely to use. Use straight-forward terms instead of (or in addition to) marketing language. For instance, if you're a mortgage broker, make sure you use the phrase "mortgage broker" in addition to using sentences such as, "I'll help you find the best mortgage rate."
- Refer to your geographic location. Many searchers will add a location to their search terms (e.g., "mortgage broker in Phoenix"), so be certain to mention your city, county, state or province, and country.
- List your products or services individually. The more specific you are, the more likely your website will show up in relevant searches. The mortgage broker's website might list "30-year fixed rate," "15-year fixed rate," "adjustable rate mortgages" and so on.

Directories

Directories take a slightly different approach to helping users find sites of interest. Directories (such as Yahoo) are organized by topic areas. Directories, unlike search engines, are compiled by humans, not software. You can increase the speed by which your site shows up in directories by submitting them for inclusion.

Purchased Advertising

Another way to increase the likelihood of attracting visitors to your site is through online advertising or purchased links. Of course, these expenses should be considered as part of your overall marketing budget. A couple of options include:

- **Keywords:** Search engines sell "premium listings" based on keywords. In other words, if your company makes bicycle parts, you can pay to be listed at the top or side of search engine results for the words "bicycle parts," "bicycle gears," or "bicycle brakes," etc. Often, this can be a very effective and affordable method of advertisement, especially for those in narrow niche areas.

- **Advertisements:** Just as in the real world, you can pay for ads to get your name known on the Internet. Advertising seems to work best on sites that are closely related to your product or service.

Partnerships and Relationships

Make it easy for potential customers to find you from other sites they're visiting. For instance, if you are serving a specific geographic community, make certain you are listed on local directory websites, often run by local newspapers, Chambers of Commerce, or tourist bureaus. Get listed on sites related to your industry and ask the businesses you do business with to link to you: a mortgage broker might ask to be listed by real estate agents she works with and offer to list them on her website in return.

Your Own Online Marketing

There are a number of ways that you can use the Internet to promote your business and drive customers to your site that do not require third-party participation. Two options include:

- Include your website address in a tagline on all your emails.
- Create an electronic newsletter. A periodic newsletter sent by email to your customers (clearly allowing them to unsubscribe, of course) may be appreciated, especially if it contains information useful to them or pricing specials.

Offline Marketing

Most of your customers will find you from the "real" world rather than from the virtual one. To increase that likelihood, you can take some of the following steps:

- **Make your web address visible:** Include your website address on everything — your packaging, your stationery, your mailing labels, your invoices, etc.
- **Public relations:** If appropriate, attempt to get press coverage for timely activities, with information provided on your website.
- **Advertising:** Use real-world ads to promote your website.

General e-business Principles

When running your e-business, keep in mind some general principles:

- **Organize your site logically:** A well-organized site increases the likelihood that users will click through to many more pages of your site, rather than clicking away to another site. Poorly organized websites create user frustration because they can't easily and quickly find the information or products they want.
- **Make sure your technology works:** This may seem obvious, but for an e-business, fully functioning technology is part of its essential business operations.

- **Keep your site fresh:** As in any merchandising situation, you must rotate your online "stock." Even if the merchandise you are offering is old (for example, antiques), the presentation on the website should be up-to-date and changed regularly. Customers will not return to see the same stagnant site over and over.

- **Display your website's address on every page of your website:** Users may find your site by clicking from another site. With some technologies (i.e., "frames") your website address will not be particularly visible to the user and will not be stored as a favorite bookmark. Make it easy for users to remember your online address.

- **Keep costs low:** While this is true for every business, it is especially true for Internet-based companies. The Internet is still a relatively new and changing medium. The best protection for unexpected developments is to keep your overhead low, making it easier to adapt.

Chapter Summary

The Internet offers many exciting possibilities both for new and existing companies. However, business fundamentals still apply on the Internet as in land-based businesses. You need a strategic position that differentiates you from competitors and gives customers a compelling reason to visit your site, buy, and return. With an Internet-based business, you have to plan both what the customer sees (the front-end) as well as what they don't see (the back-end) and make certain everything works consistently. Pay attention to the basics, such as customer service and order fulfillment. And don't forget to develop an ongoing marketing plan to drive traffic to you.

## Chapter 24

Considerations for Retailers

Customers expect the best.

What You Need to Know if You're a Retailer

Retailers are on the front line of business. As such, they are perhaps the most vulnerable type of business enterprise. In retail businesses, consumers, rather than other businesses, make up the bulk of purchases and income. Consumers are more immediately affected by economic fluctuations than are business customers, and retail operations are often the first to feel the strength or weakness of consumer confidence. It's never easy putting your fate in the hands of consumers.

Consumers are often fickle customers — you may find that the merchandise they bought in great quantities last month (and for which you have placed a large reorder) suddenly doesn't sell at all. But when you don't have what customers want on hand, they can easily turn to your competitors. It's easy to find yourself with too much inventory — or too little.

Retailing in the "real" world has become even more competitive as the Internet has made it possible for consumers to have literally a world of retailers from which to shop, right at their fingertips. This presents downward pricing pressure on your business while making it even more critical that you create a memorable shopping experience for your customers. For real-world retailers, winning customer loyalty — and keeping it — may be the biggest challenge of all.

Retail Trends

Retail shopping has changed dramatically over the last decades. Shoppers once preferred large metropolitan or suburban department stores offering a broad range of both apparel and household merchandise, appealing to middle-class shoppers. These consumers tolerated mid-range prices and house brands. Stores such as Sears, Montgomery Ward, and J.C. Penney were the dominant examples of this type of retail operation. Consumers supplemented their department store shopping with purchases from local merchants who were able to provide greater convenience at prices only slightly higher than department stores charged.

Over time, shoppers became more demanding. Seeking greater selection and/or more competitive prices than this general department store/neighborhood merchant model provided, retailers began to polarize at both ends of the cost spectrum. The general retailer model is now more that of the discount superstore, exemplified by Wal-Mart or Target, or the warehouse store with deeply discounted prices, such as Costco, at one end of the spectrum; or the premium upscale department store, e.g., Nordstrom, at the other end.

As part of controlling costs, discount retailers must limit their selection of merchandising. That leaves an opening in the marketplace for "category-buster," "big box" superstores specializing in specific types of merchandise, such as electronics, sporting goods, home repair, office supplies, even books. These "superstores" typically offer far greater variety in their particular category than either the large general retailer or the independent retailer can offer.

Another prominent trend in retail has been the increasing domination of franchise and large-chain operations in areas of retail that used to be the exclusive domain of the neighborhood merchant. Local pharmacies are a vanishing species, having been replaced by larger drugstore chains. The corner bakery is now most likely a La Petite Boulangerie or Mrs. Fields. The chain stores and franchises moved to Main Street as well as to the mall.

But nothing requires major changes in retail strategy as much as the Internet. The Internet creates new powerful retailers. Names such as amazon.com become brand names, as recognizable as long-established retailers, such as Barnes & Noble. Along with these new "e-tailers," many manufacturers also use the Internet to sell directly to customers, cutting out the "middle-man" – you. With the Internet, customers have more options, more information, and often lower prices available. The whole world is your competitor.

Options for Retailers

With such a situation, how can you survive? How does the entrepreneur compete in this retail environment? Three options exist:

"Successful stores today tend to fall into one of two formats: superstore or microspecialist. Characteristics of the superstore include: 1) broad and deep merchandise assortment in a major business segment: Stores tend to be large, carry commodity products satisfying functional needs and offer national brands; 2) no frills — self-service format in lowest cost distribution channel; 3) low margin, lowest prices; 4) business-to-business component or consumable products, or both; and 5) convenience with one-stop shopping with broad assortments. Characteristics of the microspecialist include: 1) carefully edited, broad assortment within a narrow product segment: stores tend to be small, carry lifestyle merchandise which satisfies emotional needs, and the consumer perceives the assortment as unique; 2) quality service and upscale ambiance; 3) high-margin, full-priced oriented; and 4) convenience with a carefully edited assortment."

Nancy Glaser
Business Strategies
Consultant

First, you can think big: You can position your company and seek the necessary financing to become a major market leader, either a superstore, chain store, franchise operation, or major Internet retailer.

Second, you can buy a franchise outlet, building your business by associating with a national name, recognizing the trend toward chain and franchise stores.

Third, you can develop a "boutique" orientation for your independent operation, offering customers something uniquely different from what they can get from a superstore, franchise, or Internet site, creating a special connection between you and your customer.

Making a Difference in Retail

Today, more than ever, the keys to successful retailing are buying, merchandising, salesmanship, and customer service.

Buying

Perhaps no aspect of retail operations is as crucial as the careful and selective buying of merchandise. Retail buying is a critical skill, virtually an art form. Many first-time retail operators fail to understand the complexities of buying, imagining that buying will be the most enjoyable part of their operations. If you have no experience in buying for retail, either find a partner or key employee who has such experience or delay opening your own business until you have developed sufficient knowledge.

Buying is usually accomplished by:

- Sales representatives calling upon buyers;
- Buyers attending trade shows;
- Buyers purchasing through catalogs or websites; or
- Buyers purchasing directly from the manufacturer.

When you purchase directly from the manufacturer, without going through a sales representative, you may be able to get lower prices. However, a good sales representative can help you choose the right merchandise and give you advice on selecting inventory.

When buying, pay particular attention to these factors:

- Nature and quality of merchandise (as it relates to your store)
- Price
- Minimum quantities required
- Reorder availability
- Delivery times
- Seasonality
- Payment and return policies
- Exclusivity

"Retail is an intensely personal business, and service is the key to retail success. You must have the right pricing and product mix for your market. But what keeps people coming into your establishment is service and the consistency of quality."

Nancy Glaser
Business Strategies
Consultant

Small operations often find themselves in a bind, having to pay more for the smaller quantities they need and being offered the most limited credit options. Try to negotiate discounts based on other factors, such as delivery times or methods, early payment, or total purchase from vendor rather than purchase in one product line. Be sure to look at industry sources on the Internet; you may be able to find a buying cooperative that enables you to purchase as part of a group, lowering prices to you.

If part of your retail strategy is to offer unique products to your customers, you may want to choose items that customers aren't likely to find at superstores or chains. Buy quantities carefully. Most products have limited shelf lives: Summer sportswear must be marked down in autumn, and this year's fax machine will soon be replaced with a less expensive model having more features. On the other hand, the shopper who wants a bathing suit today will probably not wait to buy from you in two weeks, which is when you expect your next delivery. You're stuck with merchandise if you buy too much; you lose sales if you buy too little. That's why buying is an art.

Merchandising

Once customers enter your store, how much will they buy? You can increase both the likelihood of a purchase and the average amount of purchases by carefully merchandising your products. Merchandising includes all aspects of the company's presentation to the customer — from product displays, to store decor and fixtures, to the music playing in the background, to the way the salespeople are dressed. You want to send a message about your products even before the customer talks to a salesperson or looks at a price tag.

A tried-and-true method of merchandising is to bring people as far back into the store as possible. As you shop, notice that sale items and staple commodities are located in the back of each store. Management knows that many customers come in looking for these products, and the goal is to make the customer walk past the non-sale or rotating merchandise first. The longer customers stay in the store, the more likely they are to buy.

Capture Customers' Attention

If your store is in a mall or shopping street with casual foot traffic, your window displays and merchandise displays located at the front of the store must entice customers to come in and shop. Once customers enter your store, your displays and decor must create an atmosphere which makes them feel comfortable, encourages them to stay, and motivates them to buy.

Customers want to feel excited about their purchases, particularly when buying impulse or non-staple items. Shopping is a recreational activity as much as a necessity, so make shopping in your store a pleasurable, even entertaining, experience. No matter what, keep your retail space CLEAN. Nothing discourages sales more than a dirty store, with the possible exception of a surly salesperson.

Here are some helpful merchandising hints:

- Rotate and restock your merchandise frequently.
- Keep your store visually interesting.
- Have the appropriate merchandise displayed for the current season.
- Keep your merchandise fresh; remain aware of current styles.
- Provide discounts for quantity purchases (e.g., 10% off 3 or more).
- Place small impulse items at the check-out point.

Salesmanship

In retail operations, sales personnel are the pivotal force in increasing sales, yet all too often they are hired thoughtlessly, with far more emphasis given to the employee's willingness to work for low hourly wages than to the individual's sales ability. But every interaction a salesperson has with a customer is an opportunity to increase sales; if you are using untrained or incapable salespeople, you're undoubtedly losing revenue.

The components of an outstanding sales force include:

- Wise hiring and prudent firing.
- Regular, meaningful training.
- Recognition and financial incentives for success.
- Employees who know and appreciate the merchandise.
- Management that respects the sales force.

Sales techniques that successful retail salespeople utilize include:

- Greeting customers and making them feel welcome.
- Asking specific rather than general questions to help customers find what they are looking for.
- Suggesting add-on or accessory items to go along with a customer's intended purchase.
- Suggesting specials or promotional items.
- Offering alternative suggestions if customers can't find what they want.

Customer Service

Customer service is an increasingly important aspect of retail sales. Certain levels of customer service are required for any store: Even in large discount stores, customers expect to have the ability to return items, to have questions answered politely, and to have employees treat them with respect. But in some stores, particularly independent stores, a high level of customer service can actually be an important element of your strategic position, distinguishing you from lower cost competitors.

Since creating a bond between you and your customers is critical for retail success, make certain you are offering a complete range of customer service, from having polite and knowledgeable salespeople, the attitude you show to customers when they are in your shop or on the phone, to the support you give them after purchase.

"We strive for consistency and quality in the way a customer is treated when they walk in a store. We constantly remind salespeople that their job is to enable the customer to have an experience that will make them satisfied and happy, so the customer will want to come back. It's easy to give the customer a happy experience. The rules are simple: smile; know the product; take care of even whimsical requests; make sales suggestions; offer samples; if there's a problem, make it right; make the customer feel as if they're coming to your home."

Charles Huggins
President, See's Candies

Shrinkage

A major problem in retail operations is theft, both from shoplifters and from employees. Establish security procedures that reduce the amount of shrinkage you experience. Sometimes this means that small, expensive merchandise is kept in locked display cases; overall, some kind of technological security system may be put in place.

Choose a security system carefully; you don't want your customers to feel they are in a police state, but you want to discourage the army of professional thieves from targeting your store. Make sure your security system is appropriate for your type of shop, merchandise, and clientele: An electronics store in an urban setting can post a uniformed guard at the door, check every customer's purchase, and few people will be offended. That same system in a suburban boutique would discourage customers from returning.

Chapter Summary

These are the issues most likely to be foremost on the minds of potential funders of retail businesses:

- Has the entrepreneur chosen the right location? In retail, location is almost always an essential ingredient for success. The location must be appropriate for the retail concept and provide a market sufficient to sustain the business' profitability.

- Is the retail concept clear? Retail operations now must have distinct personalities. Customers want to know what they can expect immediately when they walk in a store. The entrepreneur must be able to articulate a clear definition of the nature of the merchandise, price points, and customer base.

- Are the profit margins sufficient? Has the company priced its merchandise high enough to account for all expenses and overhead? Will the market support this pricing level?

- Is the management experienced? Retail attracts many novice entrepreneurs, and investors are properly wary of inexperienced management. What expertise specifically related to retail does the management bring?

- Can the operation be expanded by becoming a chain or a franchise? Is the retail experience able to be duplicated or dependent on particular factors that could limit growth? What potential exists for the company to become a much larger operation?

When finalizing a business plan for your retail business, place particular emphasis on those areas above.

## Chapter 25

Considerations for Manufacturers

It's not only what you make;
It's what you do with what you make.

All Manufacturers Face Similar Challenges

Whether your company is a large automobile maker with thousands of employees or a small operation producing handmade jewelry, you have to deal with similar manufacturing concerns. When you take raw materials and fabricate them into a finished product, regardless of the size or the amount of that product, you face some of the same challenges in improving your production process so that it increases your productivity and profitability while still maintaining quality.

Manufacturing can be conducted on either a continuous or intermittent production basis. The continuous method produces goods in a veritable constant stream: The production equipment is operated without interruption for long periods of time, producing the same product over and over. With intermittent production, on the other hand, the production line may be stopped frequently or interrupted to make changes in the production process. Merchandise is produced in smaller quantities, with more product variation, and the production equipment or layout may have to be adapted to accommodate different product manufacturing requirements.

Generally, continuous production reduces the cost of each unit produced since there is less un-utilized down-time due to the production change-overs. Intermittent production is used for merchandise made to order, unique products, and smaller quantities. Products made through an

"We use the Andon system, a series of cords or buttons that allow employees to shut down the production line when they see a problem. Each team member is responsible for quality all through the process. Our inspection system exists to validate our system of producing quality throughout the process rather than to find problems at the end of the production line."

Michael Damer
New United Motor
Manufacturing Inc.

"Jidoka is one of our basic philosophies. It is the principle of guaranteeing quality in the process itself. Don't allow defective parts to go from one manufacturing process to the next; don't wait for the end product to be manufactured and only then find the defect. Each team on the production line must think of the next stop as its customer, and they are the customers for the previous stop. Therefore, it's their job to make sure they are both receiving and producing quality."

Michael Damer
New United Motor
Manufacturing Inc.

intermittent process cost more to produce and must be priced higher than mass-produced products to cover the nonproductive time of the equipment and staff.

Trends in Manufacturing

Technological changes and foreign competition are revolutionizing manufacturing. Today it takes far fewer workers to make the same product as years ago. The products themselves have changed, often utilizing new materials and new technology. Competition has become far more intense, with foreign competition at all levels of the marketplace. A manufacturer, even a small manufacturer, must be positioned to respond to a constantly changing economic environment.

Quantum Technological Changes

It used to be that manufacturing changed slowly and incrementally, with products and equipment evolving through sequential, small improvements. Now, however, changes tend to be revolutionary as much as evolutionary, and manufacturers are faced with an explosion of new technology and materials developed through chemical processes.

These changes often substantially reduce production costs and create intense competitive pressures. Thus, the DVD player you manufacture today to sell at $300, tomorrow will likely be faced with a competing product offering more features at a lower price. With such a scenario, your product becomes almost impossible to sell profitably.

Improved Information Systems

Bar coding and optical scanning now allow manufacturers to track inventory and sales on a constant basis. Companies such as Levi Strauss & Co. now get electronic data instantaneously and directly from retailers, providing immediate information on inventory. This allows the company to know exactly how many units must be produced to replace those units sold, facilitating faster production time and reducing excess inventory.

Changing Organization of the Production System

Influenced by foreign management techniques, U.S. production systems are changing to give production workers more input into designing the production process. Those who actually work on the front line of production increasingly shape the methods they use to manufacture goods. This trend is profoundly affecting the nature of management-labor relations.

Demand for Quality

Consumers no longer tolerate inadequate goods. They place great importance on quality when making their purchasing decisions, forcing manufacturers to maintain higher standards. Thus, quality control must become an integral part of the production process, and companies must take steps to ensure that very little of their merchandise falls below their high standards of quality.

Strategies in Manufacturing

Production Planning

You can substantially increase your manufacturing productivity and maximize your profit margin through careful production process planning. Many companies, especially smaller enterprises, give relatively little thought to the production process. They pay attention to the specific tasks that need to be accomplished and neglect the overall production system. As a result, they often experience short or excess inventories, underutilized plant capacity, or delays in shipping product.

Every manufacturer, no matter how small, should have a production manual. This manual should indicate the lead time necessary for the purchase and delivery of inventory, the maximum and minimum inventories of both raw material and finished goods to be maintained at various times of the year, and the labor requirements and labor deployment schedules. It should also indicate the planned utilization of equipment.

Careful Inventory Control – "Just-in-Time" Manufacturing

Inventory represents money sitting around. Every piece of raw material or finished good waiting in a warehouse ties up capital, making it unavailable for more productive uses. You must minimize your inventory levels. At the same time, there are also costs associated with having too little inventory. Without materials, you may have employees unable to do their jobs; without finished products, you may not be able to fill orders.

The goal is to keep inventories as low as possible while still being able to maintain production and meet demand. Inventory management is a crucial aspect of manufacturing. Work closely with your suppliers to reduce the amount of time necessary for delivery of goods and to lower the minimum quantity for orders while maintaining quantity discounts. Ask vendors to warehouse your purchased materials for you, thus reducing your overhead costs.

Examine how you move materials around your production plant. Many companies never address this issue adequately and find themselves faced with virtual chaos on the plant floor. Improper materials handling results in loss of goods, longer production time, and increased safety hazards. Examine the locations where materials are stored. Observe how they move from one part of the production system to another and how finished goods are prepared for shipping. Even large companies find themselves with bottlenecks of goods unable to be finished or shipped due to inadequate attention to the manner in which materials are distributed internally.

Subcontracting

Subcontracting can be an attractive option for manufacturers as a means of reducing costs and increasing capacity utilization. You can use subcontracting both ways: to have subcontractors work for you to fabricate components of your finished product, or for you to act as a subcontractor for

"Just-in-time inventory management aims not at producing a steady stream of products to sell, but at replenishing those products which have already been sold. At each job station, we have only 11/2 hour of inventory; our safety stock of inventory is only 3 days. Inventory from California suppliers is only 1 day. This helps insure quality, because if we see a problem with a part, it can be caught quickly and without huge quantities involved. It improves safety, since each work station is less cluttered. It reduces costs since we have less money in inventory and less rework is required. Parts aren't replenished until they are used. This is a 'just-in-time' rather than a 'just-in-case' system of inventory management. This system requires: 1) employees managing the information system right; 2) good relationships with suppliers, so we know we can get parts on time; and 3) good quality from suppliers, because we cannot have many rejects."

Michael Damer
New United Motor
Manufacturing Inc.

other manufacturers. Using subcontractors yourself reduces the cost of maintaining equipment, inventory, and labor. Subcontracting out to others is an attractive way to use the equipment and labor you already have in place to produce more product than you are able to currently sell, and it gives you access to additional distribution outlets.

Companies of any size can take on subcontracting work. Even large automobile manufacturers produce components, such as windows, for other manufacturers. Consider the alternative uses to which you can put your production plant. Can you utilize your excess capacity to produce something for another company?

Joint Venturing

Manufacturers are in a good position to create partnerships with other companies for the production and sale of products. Since manufacturers have links to both ends of the production system — raw materials at one side and distributors or retailers at the other — they have numerous opportunities for developing strategic relationships to help finance expansion activities.

Thus, a vendor of raw materials may be willing to help underwrite the costs of research and development of a new product incorporating those materials. Or a major retailer may see the value of a new product and work with the manufacturer to create it. Consider entering into joint ventures with suppliers, customers, distributors, and retailers to finance new products or the marketing of existing products in new ways.

Adding Perceived Value

The same products from two different manufacturers may be very similar in terms of purpose, functions, and production costs, and yet differ widely in price. One company may be able to command higher prices for its products by adding perceived rather than intrinsic value to its merchandise.

A "brand name" is perhaps the most widely used method of adding perceived value. Customers are more comfortable buying products from companies they know, relying on the fact that the product is likely to be of good quality and the company more willing to stand behind its merchandise. The costs of developing a brand-name product are substantial, however, as it usually requires large advertising and promotion budgets. You must also insure consistency in quality and similarity in design. (See also the section on Branding in Chapter 9.)

A less expensive way of adding perceived value is through improved product design. Two telephones may work identically, but the one with the sleeker, more modern appearance may be more appealing to customers and leave them with the impression that the internal technology is superior. A specialist in product design can increase the perceived value of your merchandise, and you may only have to pay a one-time charge for these services, which makes each unit you produce more valuable. Finally, attractive packaging may convey added value. Consider the ways that you can increase the perceived value and thus, the price of your products, especially via those methods that require relatively little investment.

Chapter Summary

When assembling a complete business plan for your manufacturing business, place special emphasis on areas having the greatest impact on the success of such businesses. These questions are likely to be foremost on the minds of potential funders of manufacturing businesses:

- How substantial are the barriers to entry for new competition? Since manufacturing companies usually require large amounts of initial investment, funders want to ensure that your company is sufficiently protected from competition so it will be able to gain an adequate market share to be profitable. Some barriers to entry you can stress in your business plan to reassure investors include patents, special expertise required to produce your product, engineering difficulties, large initial capital outlay, and lack of access to distribution systems.

- Does your company depend on key production personnel for its success? If so, what contractual or other arrangements has the company made to ensure that these key employees will stay with the business and will not go to work for competitors or compete themselves? What contingency plans has the company made if these employees become unavailable?

- What steps has the company taken to reduce production costs? How has your company organized its inventory, equipment, and labor utilization to maximize profitability? Have you brought in experts on production design and scheduling to assist in the development of a well-organized production process?

- Does your management understand production? Many entrepreneurs who establish manufacturing companies understand the product but not how to produce it on a mass, profitable basis.

- How will your company remain competitive in the coming years? What emphasis do you place on research and development? Are the research and development budget and staff adequate? What new products does the company have under development? How often do you plan to introduce new products? What other steps is your company taking to enhance its product line in the future?

Tailor your business plan to respond to these questions. Make certain they are answered thoroughly, because they represent the issues having the greatest impact on the future success of any manufacturing enterprise. Addressing these concerns increases the positive impact of your completed business plan with potential funding sources and helps ensure the viability of your company for the long term.

## Chapter 26

Considerations for Service Businesses

*When you sell a service,
you sell yourself.*

Many Types of Service Businesses

Service businesses comprise the most diverse sector of the economy. Neither retail nor manufacturing can match the service sector in the breadth of companies that fall under its rubric.

Accountants, aerobics studios, and airlines all are considered service businesses. A physician and a pipefitter may appear to have little in common, but they are both service providers.

This diverse sector includes many unrelated industries. Some service industries are aimed primarily at the corporate market, providing essential business services; others focus on personal services and home and auto maintenance. These distinctions are referred to as either:

- Business-to-business, or
- Business-to-consumer.

A wide variety of additional industries come under the service category, such as transportation, entertainment, insurance, and construction.

Common Factors of Service Businesses

While service industries may vary greatly in the nature of the particular service provided, these industries are characterized by a number of features that define "service." If yours is a service business, notice how the following factors apply to your company.

Intangible Product

Unlike manufacturers or retailers, service businesses sell an essentially nonmaterial product. Customers buy a process, advice, or result, rather than a tangible item.

Consider what customers actually receive in tangible terms when they hire an attorney, go to a film, or pay for an exercise class, and you realize that very little of the worth of the service is conveyed in tangible form. With an attorney, it is not the piece of paper on which a contract is written that has value, but the knowledge the attorney brings to the task of drawing up the contract. At the movies, it is not the screen or the seats that interest the customers but the images and story projected on the screen, which disappear completely after two hours. And at the exercise class, it is the customers who actually do the work; they are paying for motivation, encouragement, and instruction.

Subjective Judgment of Quality

Because services sell only intangible products, few objective criteria exist by which to judge quality. Most judgments about the quality of services are subjective, based on the opinion of the service receiver. Which exercise teacher is best: the one who makes you work the hardest or the one who lets you go at your own pace? Which movie is better, the action-packed police drama or the romantic love story? These are completely subjective evaluations.

The few objective measures that can be used to judge service quality are usually not known by the consumer. For example, with an attorney, even though other lawyers might be able to tell if key provisions were included or omitted in a contract, most clients using legal services are not sufficiently knowledgeable to be able to judge the quality of the attorney's work. They only know whether or not their lawyer has inspired their trust.

Relatively Few Barriers to Entry

Generally, it is relatively easy to start a service business rather than a retail or manufacturing company, because physical inventory and equipment may play a small part in the value of the product. It costs far less to start a bookkeeping service than to open a production plant. While specific expertise may be needed by the bookkeeper, this expertise is widely available and non-patentable. While this is good news to you when you are first contemplating starting a service business, it means little or no protection is offered to keep you from facing new competition in the future.

Perishable "Product"

Most service providers sell their time, and time is the most perishable commodity of all. A hairdresser has only so many hours during the day to sell; if that time is not booked with clients, then the hairdresser loses money that can never be regained. An airline offers a seat on a plane; if the plane takes off half full, the income from the other seats is lost forever. In your service business, note the ways in which your "product" has a limited time during which it can be sold.

"The first thing about service is that it is imperative that the CEO of the company really believes in it. If the CEO only gives lip service to the concept of outstanding service, that attitude is reflected all the way down the line."

Andre Tatibouet
President, Aston Hotels

Significant Time Lapse Between Use

Some services are used on a continuing or regularly recurring basis, such as janitorial, child care, barbers, or bookkeeping. But most service businesses are used by customers intermittently, in response to particular needs. Thus, a small business may use an attorney only a few times over twenty years; a customer may hire an interior decorator once every five-to-ten years; and vacation travelers may use an airline only once a year.

Quality Depends on the Actual Service Provider

When you buy a laser printer from a computer store, you depend more on the manufacturer than on the retailer for quality. But when you go to an accounting firm, the individual accountant who actually does your work is as important, or more important, than the reputation of the overall accounting firm itself. The person performing the service generally determines the quality of the service provided.

Trends in Service Businesses

The nature of service businesses is changing in response to economic, sociological, and technological developments. As customers spend a higher percentage of their disposable income on services, they become more demanding about the quality of those services. As the economy becomes more service industry-intensive, competition becomes keener. In recent years, the trends described below have characterized the service sector.

Speed

Customers demand increasingly faster delivery of services. The customer used to getting eyeglasses within an hour, photo processing in thirty-seven minutes, and letters instantaneously by fax, is frustrated having to waiting three weeks for a doctor's appointment and then spending an hour in the waiting room. Smart service providers look for ways to accommodate consumers' faster pace of life.

Franchising

Making "brand names" out of service providers through franchise operations is a rapidly increasing trend. Franchises have developed in service industries such as real estate sales and hair salons. They have even developed in professional service fields, such as medical, legal, and dental services. This trend will continue, bringing national or regional advertising budgets into the competition for services.

Increased Integration

Service providers are learning that their customers prefer the convenience of "one-stop shopping" and are including a broader range of related services under one roof. Moreover, they are adding products to augment their service line. Some service businesses actually find that the retail products produce greater profits than the services themselves.

Strategies for Improving Your Service Business

You can take a number of steps to make your service business more competitive in light of the factors and trends affecting the service sector. These steps are equally applicable whether yours is a small, one-person operation or a company with hundreds of employees.

Make Your Product More Tangible

Since services are inevitably intangible, customers have a hard time understanding what they are buying. By making your services seem more concrete, you increase the comfort level of the consumer. Consider selling "packages" of services.

For instance, an attorney might offer a "small business startup" package, that covers incorporation, a trademark search, lease review, and writing a standard personnel contract. In this way, clients know exactly what they get for their money; with an hourly fee, clients are more likely to be nervous about using a lawyer.

Develop a Distinct Image

Take steps to distinguish yourself from the competition. Identify the qualities that are unique or central to your company and emphasize those in your marketing and sales activities. In particular, show how your people make your company. Don't scrimp on your marketing budget.

Cultivate Referral Sources

Since consumers usually are unable to distinguish among competitors themselves, they often rely on recommendations from others. Identify those individuals or firms that are likely to be good sources of on-going customer referrals and develop a program to cultivate and communicate with them.

Stay in Touch with Your Customers

Because your customers may not deal with you for long periods at a time, they may forget about you. This means they are less likely to refer other customers to you and may not return to you even if they were pleased with the service they received. Customer-based marketing is an essential part of a service business. Send newsletters, email, direct mail, business greeting cards, or use other methods to stay in touch with your customers.

Encourage Timely Purchases

Since you are selling a perishable commodity — your time — you need to encourage customers to purchase your services in a timely fashion. Special promotions, limited time offers, and discounts during slow periods should be considered.

Stress Quality Control and Employee Training

Unlike a retail or manufacturing operation where the customer's primary interest is in the product, in your service business the employee who provides the service is key. Thus, it is crucial that you establish standards of performance that every employee is expected to maintain and quality-control checks to make certain that the standards are being met. Hire the best employees you can; train them well, and pay and reward them fairly.

Find Ways to Use Excess Capacity

How will you deploy your staff during slow periods? If you are paying for an employee, and the employee has nothing to do, you are wasting the excess capacity of your service company. Use your service employees for marketing or other business activities in slow times, and consider ways of subcontracting work from other service providers if appropriate.

Chapter Summary

When putting together a completed business plan for your service business, emphasize the areas that most determine success in service industries. These are the questions most likely to be foremost in the minds of potential service business funders:

- Is there really a strong enough market for this service at the prices necessary to be profitable?

- Does the staff possess the technical expertise or skill necessary to provide this service effectively? Will new staff require significantly high levels of expertise?

- Since labor is a proportionately higher percentage of the cost of a service business (rather than inventory or raw materials), what steps has management taken to control labor costs?

- Have sufficient funds been budgeted for an effective marketing plan and is the plan well conceived?

- Has management taken steps to ensure adequate quality control to maintain a high level of service?

- Does the service business have the potential to become a franchise operation or to open more locations? How does it get to be bigger than just a small business?

As you work through your business plan, be certain to provide the details necessary to answer the questions listed above. Expand the marketing and employee training and utilization sections of your plan; other sections of operations may be less important.

## Chapter 27

Business Planning in a Weak (or Strong) Economy

In times of boom or of bust, entrepreneurs follow their dreams and seize opportunities

How much does the economy matter to your business plan? Is it possible to start a good business in a bad economy? If your industry is in a slump, can you succeed? If your region is booming, does that mean your new business will be a sure thing?

Whether the economy is strong or weak, some people start new businesses and others expand their existing companies. In times of boom or of bust, entrepreneurs follow their dreams and seize opportunities. But every business is affected by outside economic factors. No matter how solid a business concept or well-organized its operations, economic conditions play a significant role in the ultimate success of an enterprise.

First, it is important to understand just how major a role outside economic conditions can have on your own business planning. Here are some of the many ways those outside economic influences will affect you:

- Your ability to raise money from investors and the terms you will be offered
- The availability and interest rates of conventional financing, such as bank loans or equipment leases
- The spending habits and financial strength of your potential customers
- The cost and availability of labor
- The cost and availability of business resources, such as office space or production facilities, raw materials or inventory, equipment, and furniture

- The terms you are able to secure from suppliers
- The availability and responsiveness of professional and other service providers, such as attorneys, accountants, and consultants

As you think about these factors, however, don't just look at the overall or national economy — you must look at the specific economic conditions your own business will encounter. After all, while the overall economy may be contracting, your own industry or geographic area may be experiencing growth, or vice versa.

This section explores some of the considerations for you to keep in mind when developing your business plan, whether you are facing weak or strong economic conditions — whether in the overall economy, your industry, or your geographic location.

Starting or Expanding a Business in a Slow Economy

Surprisingly, a weak overall economy often leads to the creation of many healthy new businesses.

Over the last three decades, there has been a pattern during economic slowdowns: New business formation has held relatively steady, and the jobs and innovations created by new businesses have led the eventual overall economic recovery. Indeed, some of the great, large companies that are now household names were founded during recessions or economic downturns, including companies such as Microsoft, Kinkos, Hewlett Packard, and FedEx.

This is not just a coincidence. Weak economies give new businesses many advantages and offer substantial opportunities.

Here's what happens: In weak or uncertain economic conditions, existing companies are typically cautious, even scared. Some are financially damaged. As such, they eliminate new initiatives and put their primary emphasis on cost-cutting. They cut back on marketing, research and development, new product launches, customer service, and so on. They reduce capital expenditures and stop expanding and innovating. In some cases, they eliminate product lines or complete divisions, even those that have been relatively profitable.

This leaves a lot of customers unserved or unhappy. Entire target markets are neglected. That creates the perfect environment for new, more innovative, businesses to thrive.

New companies are thus able to come in and grab market share from existing companies — a situation that would have been much more difficult, if not impossible, if these older companies had been focused on growth, quality, or service, instead of reducing costs.

In fact, the management consulting firm, Mercer Management, studied 116 companies that aggressively cut costs in the recession of 1990-91. Their findings showed that of these companies, only 29 percent of them were able to grow profitably in the latter half of the decade when the economy was booming. Cost-cutting is not a healthy, long-term strategy.

But the timidity of other companies can be your gain. The key to developing a business plan in a slow economy is to understand how to exploit the positive factors and mitigate the negative factors.

Positive Factors:

- **Market opportunities:** As stated above, a weak economy creates many openings in the market. The competition is often weaker and stodgier. If you offer an innovative solution to customers, your competition is likely to be slower to respond.

- **Lower fixed costs:** One significant advantage of starting or expanding a business in a weak economy is that costs are typically much lower. With less demand for space and facilities, you'll find expenses such as rent far lower than in a strong market. Other fixed expenses, such as furniture, equipment, computers, etc. are also likely to be lower.

- **Higher quality of labor available:** Good help is always hard to find, but it's particularly difficult in a strong employment market. But in weak economic times, some of the best workers become available, as big companies lay off large numbers of workers without regard to their individual capability. Some of the most talented workers take early retirement or don't choose to stay in a job with shrinking resources. This makes a much larger pool of highly qualified workers available to new companies than in strong economies.

- **Lower labor costs:** Likewise, the greater availability of labor means that labor costs will be lower. Since you have a larger pool of potential employees to choose from, you have more leverage in setting salaries and benefits, and job applicants have fewer demands and lower expectations.

- **Opportunity cost:** The cost of starting a new business entails more than just the startup costs of the business. You also have to consider the loss of the opportunity — your job — that you are leaving. A good paycheck, benefits, advancement opportunities — are all difficult to give up for a relatively risky venture such as a new business. But in a poor economy, you may have already lost your job or have been offered an early retirement package. Workplace morale may be bad and advancement opportunities non-existent. It's much easier to start a new business if you have to sacrifice fewer current opportunities.

Negative factors:

- **Less investor money available:** In a poor economy, investors get cautious. Private investors, such as angel investors, often have less money to invest as their prior investments (for instance, stock portfolios) lose value. They are less willing to take chances with their money and less eager to fund new ventures. Corporations reduce or eliminate strategic venture investment funds and venture capital firms are more cautious. It's tougher to find financing.

Lipstick sales have proved to be a reliable signal of economic downturns. The "Leading Lipstick Indicator" is based on the idea that when consumers feel less confident about the future, they turn to less expensive indulgences. "When things get tough, women buy lipstick. Lipsticks have always done well in stressful times. During past recessions…lipstick sales climbed…"

Leonard Lauder, Chairman of the Estee Lauder Company

- **Less favorable terms:** In these tougher conditions, even when you *are* able to find financing, you're almost certainly going to be offered much less favorable terms. You may have to give up a greater percentage of equity or company control in return for fewer investment dollars.

- **Risk-averse customers:** In tough times, customers become more cautious. They are more hesitant about their expenditures; often less eager to try untested suppliers unless offered significant benefits. It may be harder to get in the door.

- **Customers expect bargains:** A poor economy usually means a buyer's market. That's good when your company is doing the buying (for equipment, rent, etc., as above) but it's not so good when you're the one doing the selling. Customers will expect lower prices and more favorable payment terms.

- **Bargain-offering competitors:** New competitors often offer customers excellent prices as a means of securing market share. Just as this is likely to be part of your strategy, you may find others entering the market, fiercely competing with you on price.

As you develop your company's strategic position, here are some strategies that take advantage of conditions in a slow or down economy:

- **Raise money through sales or conventional financing:** Since it will be both more difficult and more costly (in terms of equity) to secure funding from investors, look for other options. The best strategy is ALWAYS to try and raise money through sales. Go out and get customers and then, if necessary, get conventional financing (such as bank loans or equipment leases) to manage cash flow. During a slow economy, it is possible that interest rates will be lower and the cost of such conventional financing less.

- **Choose "counter-cyclical" industries:** Some industries have historically performed particularly well during economic downturns. These include personal care (such as beauty salons), repair services, bill collection, inexpensive entertainment, and small personal indulgences. Look for those industries that are either counter-cyclical or minimally affected by the economy.

- **Offer customers innovative ways to reduce risks and costs:** Often, customers are under financial pressure, and are seeking cheaper, more value-driven alternatives than they get from current product or service providers. Keep in mind that customers are looking for immediate benefits, not just higher overall return on investment.

- **Look for customers that bring you immediate income:** Just as customers are looking for immediate benefits, you should target customers who bring you immediate income, rather than just long-term benefits, name recognition, and so on. Cash is critical and should be your first priority when choosing a target market.

- **Keep your costs down:** This is always good advice, but it is particularly true at times of economic weakness. Money is tough to get — whether from investors, bankers, or customers. Make certain you get the most from every dollar.

- **Seek "outsourcing" opportunities:** As big companies reduce their permanent, in-house workforce, they look for outside contractors to pick up the slack. Hiring outside contractors is not only cheaper for them, but easier to justify to their management. Look for opportunities to be an outside contractor to bigger companies.

- **Lock in lower costs and favorable terms:** A weak economy is a good time to secure low rates and favorable terms on items such as rent, equipment leases, raw materials, and inventory. Having lower fixed costs — and flexible terms — will enable you to be more competitive when the economy recovers.

Starting or Expanding a Business in a Strong Economy

Of course, opportunities don't just exist in bad economic times — good economies often mean great prospects.

The benefits of starting or expanding a business in a strong economy seem obvious — customers are more willing to spend, investors are more willing to invest, lenders are more willing to lend. New ideas seem possible in an atmosphere of overall optimism.

But that doesn't mean that a good economy guarantees success. Indeed, the history of the boom times of the late 1990's is all too familiar. Thousands of new ventures were launched with an unprecedented amount of venture money invested, and yet a large percent of those new enterprises are no longer in existence.

However, those boom times provided many lessons on what not to do in a strong economy: spend money wildly, expand too quickly, expect customers to adopt new technologies overnight, and be overly confident of success.

When developing your business plan for a new or expanding business in a strong economy, keep in mind the positive and negative factors.

Positive factors:

- **Greater amount of investor money available:** In a strong economy, more investors are eager to open their wallets. Both private investors (angel investors) and institutional investors (corporations, venture capital firms) have money to invest and are willing to take chances. As the value of the rest of their financial portfolio (for instance, stocks and bonds) increases, these investors feel capable of taking greater risks by investing in new enterprises. That means a wider variety of new businesses can secure funding.

- **Better terms for investments:** Because there is more investment money available, the terms you are offered will likely be fairly favorable to you. In a strong economy, you will most likely have more leverage on issues such as the percent of equity or management control you will have to give investors in return for their cash.

- **Customers have more money:** In a flush market, customers have more money to spend and are quicker to make purchasing decisions. You'll be able to charge higher prices and demand better payment terms.
- **Customers are more willing to take risks:** With more money available, customers feel more confident about taking some risks. This makes a strong economy a good time to introduce new ideas or new products.

Negative factors:

- **Labor is hard to find and expensive:** In a strong economy, workers keep their jobs. This reduces the available labor pool for new enterprises and makes employees more expensive.
- **Competition is tough:** Your competitors have more money to spend on marketing, innovation, service, and so on. It's tougher for you to enter a market with strong competitors.
- **Customers are less price sensitive:** While this makes it possible to charge higher prices, it makes it more difficult to enter a market by merely offering lower cost solutions. Customers are less willing to try a new, untested supplier merely to save money.
- **Costs are higher:** In a strong economy, all costs are likely to be greater — rent, equipment, furniture, inventory, materials, and so on. Your fixed costs will be a greater percentage of your overall budget.
- **Space is harder to find:** It is not only a higher cost of rent that you will have to contend with in a strong economy. You may find it difficult, if not impossible, to find space in the location you want at any price.

Some strategies to pursue when starting or expanding a business in a strong economy:

- **Raise money from investors:** As there is more investment money available, you are likely to have greater success at raising venture funds, with better terms, in a strong economy than in a weak one. Of course, there are always drawbacks with giving up equity, but finding investors is a reasonable option if outside financing is necessary.
- **Offer to pick up excess demand:** As the economy recovers from a downturn, businesses are hesitant to rush to add permanent employees or add additional production capacity. They want to make certain any recovery is long-lasting before taking on these additional, fixed expenses. As a result, large companies often face excess demand at the early days of an economic recovery. They may be interested in subcontracting some of their excess demand to you – as a way of retaining the customer without committing to a fixed, ongoing expense.
- **Stay flexible:** Especially if you are offering a new or untried product or service, build in the ability to respond to changing demand or customer needs. Even if demand is high at first, this may be more a reflection of customers' willingness to experiment, rather than reflecting a real market need.
- **Spend money wisely:** One of the most important lessons of the 1990's

was that businesses — no matter how well-funded — need to carefully manage their funds. Hundreds of millions of dollars were wasted on elaborate marketing plans, rather than building better products or customer relationships. Watch your money, no matter how strong the economy or customer demand.

- **Put money away:** Build up a cash reserve. Neither the good times nor the bad times last forever.

Chapter Summary

A business started in a weak economy is like an animal born in a drought — there are less resources available, so it has to learn to be tough and creative to survive. But its competition is weakened; older animals are less able to effectively compete against an agile, hungry newcomer. A business started in a strong economy is like an animal born in a time of plenty — there are plenty of resources, making it easier for a larger number of animals to survive. But the competition is also strong; older animals are better able to fend off the advances of younger newcomers.

Every business is affected by outside economic conditions, but that doesn't mean that the external economy necessarily determines a company's chance of success.

Section V

Reference

Outline of a Business Plan

Business Terms Glossary

Funding Sources

Research Sources

Entrepreneurs' Sources

Index

Outline of a Business Plan

I. Executive Summary

II. Company Description

A. Legal Name and Form of Business

B. Mission Statement/Objectives

C. Names of Top Management

D. Location and Geographical Information

E. Company's Development Stage

F. Trademarks, Copyrights & Other Legal Issues

G. Company Products or Services

H. Specialty Business Information

I. Financial Status

J. Milestones Achieved to Date

III. Industry Analysis and Trends

A. Size and Growth

B. Maturity of Industry

C. Vulnerability to Economic Factors

D. Seasonal Factors

E. Technological Factors

F. Regulatory Issues

G. Supply and Distribution

H. Financial Considerations

I. Anticipated Changes & Trends in Industry

IV. The Target Market
A. Demographics/Geographics

B. Lifestyle and Psychographics

C. Purchasing Patterns

D. Buying Sensitivities

E. Size and Trends of Market

V. The Competition
A. Competitive Position

B. Market Share Distribution

C. Barriers to Entry

D. Future Competition

VI. Strategic Position & Risk Assessment
A. Company Strengths

B. Market/Industry Opportunities

C. Risks Assessment

D. Definition of Strategic Position

VII. Marketing Plan and Sales Strategy
A. Company's Message

B. Marketing Vehicles

C. Strategic Partnerships

D. Other Marketing Tactics

E. Sales Force and Structure

F. Sales Assumptions

VIII. Operations
A. Plant and Facilities

B. Manufacturing/Production Plan

C. Equipment and Technology

D. Variable Labor Requirements

E. Inventory Management

F. Supply and Distribution

G. Order Fulfillment and Customer Service

H. Research and Development

I. Capacity Utilization

J. Quality Control

K. Safety, Health, and Environmental Concerns

L. Shrinkage

M. Management Information Systems

N. Other Operational Concerns

IX. Technology Plan
   A. Technology Goals and Position
   B. Internet Goals and Plan
   C. Hardware Needs
   D. Software Needs
   E. Telecommunications Needs
   F. Technology Personnel Needs

X. Management and Organization
   A. Principals/Key Employees
   B. Board of Directors
   C. Consultants/Specialists
   D. Management to Be Added
   E. Organizational Chart
   F. Management Style/Corporate Culture

XI. Community Involvement & Social Responsibility
   A. Social Responsibility Goals
   B. Company Policies
   C. Community Activities

XII. Development, Milestones & Exit Plan
   A. Long-Term Company Goals
   B. Growth Strategy
   C. Milestones
   D. Risk Evaluation
   E. Exit Plan

XIII. The Financials
   A. Income Statement
   B. Cash Flow
   C. Balance Sheet
   D. Break-Even Analysis (if desired)
   E. Plan Assumptions
   F. Uses of Funds

XIV. Appendix

Business Terms Glossary

See also Chapter 16, Financials, for definitions of financial terms.

24/7. Twenty-four hours a day, seven days a week. A term used to describe a service, Internet site, or other activity that is continually available.

Accrual Based Accounting. An accounting method whereby income and expenses are entered on the books at the time of contract or agreement rather than at the time of payment or receipt of funds.

Advisory Board. A non-official group of advisors; has no legal authority or obligation.

Angel. A private individual who invests their own money in new enterprises.

Barriers to Entry. Those conditions that make it difficult or impossible for new competitors to enter the market: two barriers to entry are patents and high start-up costs.

Board of Directors. The members of the governing body of an incorporated company. They have legal responsibility for the company.

Capacity. The amount of goods or work that can be produced by a company given its level of equipment, labor, and facilities.

Capital. The funds necessary to establish or operate a business.

Cash Based Accounting. An accounting method whereby income and expenses are entered on the books at the time of actual payment or receipt of funds.

Cash Flow. The movement of money into and out of a company; actual income received and actual payments made out.

Collateral. Assets pledged in return for loans.

Conventional Financing. Financing from established lenders, such as banks, rather than from investors; debt financing.

Convertible Debt. Loans made to a company that can be repaid with stock ownership (or a combination of stock and cash), usually at the lender's option.

dba. "Doing business as. . ." a company's trade name rather than the name by which it is legally incorporated; a company may be incorporated under the name XYZ Corporation but do business as " The Dew Drop Inn."

Debt Financing. Raising funds for a business by borrowing, often in the form of bank loans.

Debt Service. Money being paid on a loan; the amount necessary to keep a loan from going into default.

Deferred Compensation. Salary delayed until a future date; often taken by principal employees as a method of reducing expenditures in early years of operation.

Disbursements. Money paid out.

Distributor. Company or individual that arranges for the sale of products from manufacturer to retail outlets; the proverbial "middle man."

Downside Risk. The maximum amount that can be lost in an investment.

Due Diligence. The process undertaken by venture capitalists, investment bankers or others to thoroughly investigate a company before financing; required by law before offering securities for sale.

e-Business. A company that operates and exists primarily on the Internet.

e-Commerce. Conducting sales and transactions on the Internet.

Equity. Shares of stock in company; ownership interest in a company.

Event. Investors or others may speak of an "event" taking place, usually a time at which value can be liquidated from the company. Commonly a funding round, acquisition, or an IPO.

Exit Plan. The strategy for leaving an investment and realizing the profits of such investment.

Funding Rounds. The number of times a company goes to the investment community to seek financing; each funding round is used to reach new stages of company development.

"Going Public." To issue an IPO (see below).

Initial Public Offering (IPO). The first time the company's stock is sold to the general public (other than by a limited offering) through stock market or over-the-counter sales.

ISP: Internet Service Provider. A company that provides access to the Internet and/or hosts a company's Internet site.

Lead Investor. The individual or investment firm taking primary responsibility for the financing of a company; usually brings other investors or venture capital firms into the deal and monitors the investment for all.

Leasehold Improvements. The changes made to a rented store, office, or plant, to suit the tenant and make the location more appropriate for the conduct of the tenant's business.

Letter-of-Intent. A letter or other document by a customer indicating the customer's intention to buy from a company.

Licensing. The granting of permission by one company to another to use its products, trademark, or name in a limited, particular manner.

Limited Partnership. An investment method whereby investors have limited liability and exercise no control over a company or enterprise; the general partner(s) maintain control and liability.

Liquidity. The ability to turn assets into cash quickly and easily; widely-traded stocks are usually a liquid asset.

Manufacturing Companies. Businesses which make products from raw or unfinished materials generally to be sold to intermediaries (such as stores and dealers) rather than the end-user.

Market Share. The percentage of the total available customer base captured by a company.

Milestone. A particular business achievement by which a company can be judged.

Mind Share. A relative sense of the awareness level a company has achieved in its target market versus the recognition and awareness of its competition.

Net Worth. The total ownership interest in a company, represented by the excess of the total amount of assets minus the total amount of liabilities.

Options. The right to buy stock in a company at a later date, usually at a pre-set price; if the stock rises higher than the original price, an option holder is likely to exercise these options.

Outsource. To have certain tasks, jobs, manufacturing, etc. produced by another company on a contract basis rather than having the work done by one's own company "in-house."

Partnership. A legal relationship of two or more individuals to run a company.

Profit Margin. The amount of money earned after the cost of goods (gross profit margin) or all operating expenses (net profit margin) are deducted; usually expressed in percentage terms.

Proprietary Technology or Information. Technology or information belonging to a company; private information not to be disseminated to others.

Receipts. Funds coming in to the company; the actual money paid to the company for its products or services; not necessarily the same as a company's actual revenues.

Sole Proprietorship. Company owned and managed by one person.

Strategic Partnerships. An agreement with another company to undertake business endeavors together or on each other's behalf; can be for financing, sales, marketing, distribution, or other activities.

Term Sheet. A proposal by an investor of the terms on which they will make an investment in a company.

Traffic. When used for an Internet site, describes the amount of use, the number of visitors the site receives.

Venture Capitalist. Individual or firm who invests money in new enterprises; typically this is money invested in the venture capital firm by others, particularly institutional investors.

Working Capital. The cash available to the company for the on-going operations of the business.

Funding Sources

Private Investors

The Angels' Forum LLC
P.O. Box 1605
Los Altos, CA 94023-1605
(650) 857-0700
fax: (650) 857-0773
email: inquiries@AngelsForum.com
www.angelsforum.com

ACE-Net
Whittemore School of Business and Economics
University of New Hampshire
http://ace-net.sr.unh.edu/pub

ACE-Net was originated by the U.S. Small Business Administration to build a nationwide network to link angel investors with entrepreneurs seeking funding. The website links to local network members.

International Sources

British Venture Capital Association
3 Clements Inn
London, WC2A 2AZ
phone: 020-7025 2950

fax: 020-7025 2951
email: bvca@bvca.co.uk
www.bvca.co.uk

European Venture Capital Association
Minervastraat 4
B-1930 Zaventem (Brussels)
Belgium
phone: +32 2 715 00 20
fax: +32 2 725 07 04
email: evca@evca.com
www.evca.com

International Angel Investors Institute
960 North San Antonio Road
Los Altos, CA 94022
www.angelinvestors.org

A non-profit organization, instituted by angel investors, to facilitate angel investing internationally as well as in the U.S., and to bring angel investors and entrepreneurs together. Open for membership to entrepreneurs.

Business Plan Competitions

Global Network of Business Plan Competitions
http://50K.mit.edu/global/globalnetwork.php

The MIT $50K Entrepreneurship Competition maintains this list of business plan competitions worldwide.

MIT Entrepreneurship Competition
http://50k.mit.edu

Stanford University
http://bases.stanford.edu

Stanford conducts both an entrepreneur's business plan competition and a social entrepreneur's business plan competition for socially-conscious for-profit and not-for-profit companies.

Loans and Venture Capital Sources

The Capital Network
3925 West Braker Lane, Suite 406
Austin, TX 78759
(512) 305-0826
fax: (512) 305-0836
www.thecapitalnetwork.com

The Capital Network provides matching services to bring entrepreneurs together with funders. Particularly strong for the Texas area.

The Garage
3300 Hillview Avenue
Suite 150
Palo Alto, CA 94304
phone: 650-354-1800
fax:650-354-1801
www.garage.com

The Garage is a for-profit company intended to help startup companies interact with and secure funding from potential investors.

Greater Philadelphia Venture Group
www.gpvg.com

Investors' Circle
320 Washington Street
Brookline, MA 02445
(617) 566-2600
fax: (617) 739-3550
inbox@investorscircle.net
www.investorscircle.net

The Investors' Circle is a network of investors making private investments to socially responsible companies. They circulate proposals (for a fee) to their members and twice a year hold venture fairs where socially-responsible businesses can present for funding.

Mid-Atlantic Venture Association
2345 York Road
Timonium, MD 21093
(410) 560-5855
fax: (410) 561-2238
www.mava.org

The National Association of Government Guaranteed Lenders
P.O.Box 332
Stillwater, OK 74076
(405) 377-4022
fax: (405) 377-3931
email: naggl@aol.com
www.naggl.org

NAGGL is the association of banks and lending institutions that are active in offering SBA loans.

National Association of Small Business Investment Companies
666 11th Street, N.W. Suite 750
Washington, DC 20001
(202) 628-5055
fax: (202) 628-5080
www.nasbic.org

Small Business Investment Companies (SBICs) and Specialized Small Business Investment Companies (SSBICs) invest in small businesses. These are private companies licensed by the SBA.

National Venture Capital Association
1655 North Ft. Myer Drive, Suite 850
Arlington, VA 22209
(703) 524-2549
fax: (703) 524-3940
www.nvca.org

The National Venture Capital Association is a leading organization composed of venture capitalists and private equity investors. A list of association members is available for a fee. The list includes names of venture capital firms, addresses, phone numbers, and contact persons, as well as geographic and industry preferences and stages of companies funded. Excellent.

Silicon Valley Capital Network
(408) 541-7627

State or City Offices of Business or Economic Development

Many states and cities maintain offices to encourage business expansion and increased employment opportunities. Generally, these offices only offer advice and perhaps some lists of resources. However, in some cases, actual loans or grants may be available, particularly for job creation in economically stressed areas.

U.S. Small Business Administration (SBA)
409 3rd Street, S.W.
Washington, DC 20416
www.sba.gov

The SBA maintains lists of banks and other lending institutions most active in making loans to small businesses in each geographical area. It also provides a loan guarantee program (not actual loans) to existing businesses and direct loans limited to special categories such as Vietnam-era veterans and the disabled.

Venture Capital Institute
www.vcinstitute.org

Conducts seminars for professional venture capitalists and entrepreneurs.

Venture Investing Conference
(212) 279-2525

VentureOne — VentureSource
www.ventureone.com

Western Association of Venture Capitalists
3000 Sand Hill Road, Building One, Suite 190
Menlo Park, California 94025
(650) 854-1322
www.wavc.net

This association of more than 140 members represents virtually all of the professionally-managed venture capital firms in the Western United States. A membership roster is available free by mail.

Publications

Galante's Venture Capital and Private Equity Directory
published by Alternative Investor
Alternative Investor
170 Linden St.
Wellesley, MA 02482-7919

Published by the VentureOne group, this directory lists over 2,000 American and international venture capital and angel investors. It is very expensive to purchase, so check for availability at a good library.

Pratt's Guide to Venture Capital Sources
published by Thomson Financial/Venture Economics
195 Broadway, 10th Floor
New York, NY 10007   To order:
(646) 822-2000   (212) 830-9368
fax: (646) 822-3230   fax: (212) 956-9634
www.ventureeconomics.com

This long-standing annual directory lists more than 1400 venture capital sources in the United States and Canada. It lists contact information, recent investments, capital under management, and is cross-referenced by investment preferences, investment stage and other key information. It is very expensive to purchase — either in print or through web access — so check for availability at a good library.

The Red Herring
www.redherring.com

Magazine that tracks venture investing. Good insight and background on the venture capital community and recent deals.

Research Sources

U.S. and U.S. State Government Resources

Bureau of the Census, U.S. Government
www.census.gov

Information on population and projections, housing, income, etc. The Economic Census profiles the U.S. economy every 5 years, from national to the local level. Detailed resource city by city, industry by industry. Great source of averages on sales, size and number of companies in your area.

www.census.gov — Click on "Economic Census"

www.census.gov/main/www/stat_fed.html — Index to other sites with government statistics.

www.census.gov/sdc/www/ — Guide to all the states' Internet sites with statistics on individual states. Many state sites then list related sites with additional information for that state.

Government Printing Office
www.gpo.gov

Information from the U.S. Government on federal laws, governmental departments, etc.

Consumer Information Center of the U.S. Government Services Agency
www.pueblo.gsa.gov/smbuss.htm

Small business publications include topics such as trademark, copyright, health care, and federal programs for the Americans with Disabilities Act.

Louisiana State University
www.lib.lsu.edu/gov/fedgov.html

List of the internet sites of all government agencies and bureaus. Maintained by Louisiana State University Library.

International Resources

Guide to Canadian Government Statistics
www.statcan.ca

Very clear and easy to use. (English and French both available)

Canadian Census
http://www12.statcan.ca/english/census01/release/index.cfm

Guide to International Statistics
www.census.gov/main/www/stat_int.html

Country by country and international organizations. For the latest information on business and population of countries throughout the world.

Export.gov
www.export.gov

A rich resource of information, designed primarily for American countries engaged in international trade, Export.gov provides substantial, in-depth information about markets and industries throughout the world.

The World Bank
www.worldbank.org

This international organization compiles data world-wide. It offers free data by topic or country, links to online databases, as well as publishing its own economic reports.

General Business & Industry Resources

American Management Association
1601 Broadway
New York, NY 10019
(800) 262-9699
fax: (212) 903-8168
www.amanet.org

Offers reports and studies on general business and industry specific issues, including best practices in selected industries.

American Society of Association Executives
1575 I Street, N.W.
Washington, D.C. 20005-1168
(202) 626-2723
TDD (202) 626-2803
fax: (202) 842-1109
www.asaenet.org

To locate a trade association for your industry, most of which offer research, information, suppliers, trade shows, etc.

Gale Research's Encyclopedia of Business Information Sources
Lists trade associations, sources of information, and major trade publications. Available in most major libraries.

Columbia Books National Trade and Professional Associations of the United States
Available in most major libraries.

Dialog
U.S. Headquarters
11000 Regency Parkway, Suite 10
Cary, NC 27511
(919) 462-8600
fax: (919) 468-9890
(800) 334-2564
email: customer@dialog.com
www.dialog.com

Paid database and research service. Highly used in business.

LexisNexis
(800) 227-4908
www.lexisnexis.com

Paid database and research service. Highly used in business and legal professions.

Risk Management Association
One Liberty Place
1650 Market St., Suite 2300
Philadelphia, PA 19103
(800) 677-7621
fax: 215-446-4101
www.rmahq.org/Online_Prods/onlineprods.html

This association that serves the banking industry produces the most-relied on study of financial performance and ratios of over 600 industries. Their Annual Studies are available online on a per-industry basis for a small fee.

Standard & Poor's Industry Surveys
www.standardandpoors.com

Provides information both on industry trends, issues, and terms and reports on revenues and earnings of leading companies in the industry. Some information available online; publications available in most major libraries.

SRDS or Standard Rate and Data
1700 Higgins Road
Des Plaines, IL 60018-5605
Phone: (800) 851-7737
(847) 375-5000
Fax: (847) 375-5001
www.srds.com

Reliable source of information on all publications and media outlets, including business publications, consumer magazines, online advertising, direct marketing lists, radio, cable and television. You have to subscribe to get information online, but copies of their books are in larger public libraries.

The Advertising RedBooks
121 Chanlon Road
New Providence, NJ 07974
(800) 340-3244
www.redbooks.com

This directory contains detailed profiles of nearly 13,500 U.S. and international advertising agencies, including accounts and brand names represented, fields of specialization, gross billings, and contact information on agency personnel.

Credit & Other Information on Specific Companies

Dun & Bradstreet
103 JFK Parkway
Short Hills, NJ 07078
(973) 921-5500
www.dnb.com

The grand-daddy of corporate credit reporting. "Running a D&B" is common language for checking out a company's standing and credit. Has over 10 million businesses in its database. For a modest cost, D&B can give you — and interpret — information on specific companies including amount of sales, number of employees, types of customers, ownership, loans, liens and judgments. You can get this information about potential customers, competitors, even vendors.

Hoover's Online
(800) 486-8666 or (512) 374-4500
fax: (512) 374-4505
www.hoovers.com

Background information on individual companies. Basic information (officers, industry, company background, etc.) free; additional information for a fee. Also links to other sources of specific information on companies.

Human Resources/Personnel Issues

Society for Human Resource Management
www.shrm.com

Leading organization of HR directors and staff. Excellent, deep site on human resource topics.

Advanced HR
www.advanced-hr.com

Provides salaries and stock options for pre IPO companies. Fee based. But offers free limited access for startups.

Manufacturing

American Society for Quality
P.O. Box 3005
Milwaukee, WI 53201-3005
(800) 248-1946
www.asqc.org

ISO 9001 International Quality Standards
ISO Easy
PO Box 21
Middletown, NJ 07748
(732) 671-7130
email: info@isoeasy.org
www.isoeasy.org

National Association of Manufacturers
1331 Pennsylvania Avenue, NW
Washington, DC
(202) 637-3000
fax: (202) 637-3182
email: manufacturing@nam.org
www.nam.org

Marketing

American Marketing Association
311 S. Wacker Dr., Suite 5800
Chicago, IL 60606
(800) AMA-1150
fax: (312) 542-9001
www.marketingpower.com

American Demographics Magazine
www.demographics.com

Technology and Internet Issues

Forrester Research
400 Technology Square
Cambridge, MA 02139
(617) 613-6000
fax: (617) 613-5000
www.forrester.com

Gartner Group/Dataquest
56 Top Gallant Road
P.O. Box 10212
Stamford, CT 06904-2212
(203) 964-0096
fax: (203) 316-6300
www.gartner.com

Jupiter Communications
Jupiter Research
23 Old Kings Highway South
Darien, CT 06820
(203) 662-2800
fax (203) 655-4686
www.jupiterresearch.com

Social Responsibility Resources

Business for Social Responsibility
609 Mission Street, 2nd Floor
San Francisco, CA 94105-3506
(415) 537-0890
fax (415) 537-0889
www.bsr.org

A national association of over 1,400 companies interested in implementing responsible corporate policies and practices. BSR provides information on corporate leadership practices, conducts research and education workshops, develops practical business tools and provides consulting services and technical assistance to its member companies.

Computer Professionals for Corporate Responsibility
P.O. Box 717
Palo Alto, CA 94302
(650) 322-3778
fax: (650) 322-4748
www.cpsr.org

Impact Online
www.impactonline.org

A nonprofit organization dedicated to increasing volunteerism through the Internet.

Social Venture Network (SVN)
www.svn.org
www.svneurope.com — Social Venture Europe

A membership organization of successful business and social entrepreneurs dedicated to changing the way the world does business. Provides opportunities to exchange ideas, share problems and solutions and collaborate on an ad hoc basis with their peers.

Social Venture Partners
www.svpintl.org

An organization uniting and encouraging the establishment of local social venture partner organizations (SVP) in the U.S. and internationally. SVPs enable entrepreneurs and other professionals to use their entrepreneurial skills to assist non-profit causes.

Entrepreneurs' Sources

The Planning Shop
555 Bryant Street, #180
Palo Alto, CA 94301
(650) 289-9120
fax: (650) 289-9125
www.PlanningShop.com

The Planning Shop, the publisher of this book, is the central resource for business planning information and advice. At the site, you can find a downloadable template of Excel spreadsheets to match the financial worksheets in *The Successful Business Plan*. In addition to information and tools for developing a business plan, The Planning Shop's website provides information on starting, growing, and running a business, including links to the columns by Rhonda Abrams.

Other Resources

Association of Small Business Development Centers
8990 Burke Lake Road
Burke, VA 22015
phone: (703) 764-9850
fax: (703) 764-1234
www.asbdc-us.org

Over 1,000 Small Business Development Centers exist around the United States, many located at community colleges. SBDCs are a partnership of private enterprise, the Government, higher education, and industry. SBDCs offer individual counseling and assistance, seminars, technical help, libraries, etc. Services are generally free. An outstanding, often overlooked, source of information for entrepreneurs.

Better Business Bureaus/Better Business Bureau Online
4200 Wilson Blvd
Arlington, VA 22203
(703) 276-0100
fax: (703) 525-8277
www.bbb.org
www.bbbonline.org

A long-respected organization of businesses that agree to adhere to certain standards. BBBOnline offers a certification program for Internet sites to increase users' confidence in sites' reliability or privacy policies.

Entrepreneurial Edge
58220 Decatur Road
P.O. Box 8
Cassopolis, MI 49031-0008
(800) 232-LOWE (5693) or (616) 445-4200
http://edge.lowe.org

Run by the Lowe Foundation, a non-profit organization dedicated to assisting entrepreneurs. Extensive website of resources and articles.

Entreworld
Kauffman Center for Entrepreneurial Leadership
4801 Rockhill Road
Kansas City, MO 64110
(816) 932-1000
www.entreworld.org

Run by the Ewing Marion Kauffman Foundation, a non-profit organization dedicated to assisting entrepreneurs. Extensive website of resources.

FWE — Forum for Women Entrepreneurs
1825 South Grant Street, Suite 310
San Mateo, CA 94402
phone: (650) 350-1090
fax: (650) 350-1093
www.fwe.org

Founded in 1993, the Forum for Women Entrepreneurs (FWE) serves entrepreneurial women who are building or leading high-growth technology and life science companies. Started and headquartered in the San Francisco Bay Area, FWE has chapters in Seattle, San Diego/Orange County, Los Angeles, and Paris.

Inc. Magazine and Website
www.inc.com

Leading magazine for growing businesses. Website offers substantial archive of articles on business issues.

Quicken Small Business
www.quicken.com/small_business

Website maintained by the company that makes Quicken financial software. Contains background information on many topics; particular strength is taxes and financial.

NASE — National Association for the Self-Employed
P.O. Box 612067
DFW Airport
Dallas, TX 75261-2067
(800) 232-6273
www.nase.org

Membership organization providing a number of services to self-employed and small businesses, including insurance, discounts, etc.

NAWBO: National Association of Women Business Owners
8405 Greensboro Drive, Suite 800
McLean, VA 22102
phone: (703) 506-3268
fax: (703) 506-3266
www.nawbo.org

Membership group of women-owned businesses, with many local chapters around the country. NAWBO's research arm, Foundation for Women Business Owners, researches information on women entrepreneurs.

SCORE — Service Corps of Retired Executives
409 3rd Street, SW, 6th Floor
Washington, DC 20024
(800) 634-0245
fax: (202) 205-7636
www.score.org

Provides retired business owners as counselors for individual assistance and conducts workshops on business skill topics.

SBA — Small Business Administration of the U.S. Government
409 3rd Street, S.W.
Washington, DC 20416
(800) 827-5722
www.sba.gov

U.S. government agency dedicated to assisting and advocating for small businesses. Primary responsibility is administering guaranteed loan program. Offers resources or links to resources on various entrepreneurial issues. Maintains offices in larger cities throughout the country. Website is an excellent link to government sources to assist businesses.

Software Developers' Forum
111 W. St. John St., #200
San Jose, CA 95113
(408) 494-8378
fax: (408) 494-8383
email: info@sdforum.org
www.sdforum.org

Long-standing, well-regarded Silicon Valley group of entrepreneurs, primarily in high tech. Sponsors or co-sponsors many seminars and programs on general entrepreneurship and start-up issues. Conducts one-on-one meetings with venture capitalists. Maintains resource center for software developers. Not limited to high tech businesses.

Women in Technology International
www.witi.com

An organization devoted to increasing the number of women in executive roles in technology and technology-based companies. More oriented to employees than to entrepreneurs, but still a good source of information and excellent conferences. Regional chapters.

Index

GET YOUR PLAN *FINISHED FASTER* WITH
Electronic Financial Worksheets

Designed from the ground up to work hand-in-hand with *The Successful Business Plan: Secrets & Strategies!*

Worksheets are identical to those found in the book—no new formats to wrestle with!

All the math and calculations are done for you!

"Help Balloons" provide convenient information and advice, and refer you to the relevant pages in the book for further information.

Built on Microsoft Excel, the powerful industry standard for generating compelling financial reports.

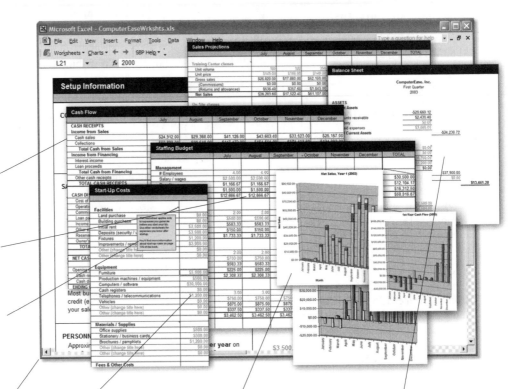

Fill out the information in one worksheet and it automatically transfers to other appropriate worksheets.

Charts and graphs are automatically generated for you!

When you're finished, just print out your Income Statement, Cash Flow Projections, and Balance Sheets and add them to your plan!

Designed for readers of this book!

Now you can easily complete the financial worksheets for your business plan on your computer! The Planning Shop has developed this Excel-based package of worksheets and financial statements to work hand-in-hand with your copy of this book.

True "Flow-Through Financials"

Taking the flow-through technique Rhonda uses in this book one-step further, now you can enter your financial figures just once, and they'll automatically flow-through to all the other relevant statements, performing necessary calculations along the way!

Download your copy today at our lowest price:
www.PlanningShop.com/worksheets